P9-CNC-439

3 1006 02449 1224

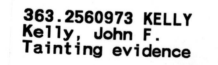

363.2560973 KELLY
Kelly, John F.
Tainting evidence

East Regional   SEP 2 5 1998

EAST REGIONAL

*f***P**

ALSO BY PHILLIP K. WEARNE

Return of the Indian

TAINTING EVIDENCE

INSIDE THE SCANDALS AT THE FBI CRIME LAB

JOHN F. KELLY

PHILLIP K. WEARNE

THE FREE PRESS

New York   London   Toronto   Sydney   Singapore

THE FREE PRESS
A Division of Simon & Schuster Inc.
1230 Avenue of the Americas
New York, NY 10020

Copyright © 1998 by John Kelly and Phillip Wearne
All rights reserved,
including the right of reproduction
in whole or in part in any form.

THE FREE PRESS and colophon are trademarks
of Simon & Schuster Inc.

Designed by Carla Bolte

Manufactured in the United States of America

10   9   8   7   6   5   4   3   2   1

Library of Congress Cataloging-in-Publication Data

Kelly, John F.
    Tainting evidence: inside the scandals at the FBI crime lab/
John F. Kelly, Phillip K. Wearne.
        p.   cm.
    Includes bibliographical references and index.
    1. FBI Laboratory.   2. Crime laboratories—United States.
3. Criminal investigation—United States.   4. Criminal
investigation—United States—Case studies.   I. Wearne, Phillip.
II. Title.
HV8141.K47   1998
363.25'6'0973—dc21   98-17910
                                                              CIP

ISBN 0-684-84646-2

For Fred Whitehurst, Cheryl, and Jharna
who have all lived the consequences of doing the right thing.

CONTENTS

ACKNOWLEDGMENTS

Many people made this book possible, the first and most important being Fred Whitehurst, who had the courage to speak up and refused to be deflected. The FBI has broken many a lesser man, including some of its own. As neither lawyers nor forensic scientists, we relied heavily on outside expertise and guidance. Stephen Kohn and David Colapinto of Kohn, Kohn and Colapinto and the National Whistleblower Center were exceptionally generous with their time and expertise as was Professor James Starrs of George Washington University in Washington, D.C. Professor Bill Thompson and Dr. Benjamin Grunbaum were unstinting in their guidance through the minefield of DNA typing. Jack King, in charge of public affairs at the National Association of Criminal Defense Lawyers, and the staff in Senator Charles Grassley's office, in particular Kris Kolesnik, were unfailingly helpful. Thanks also to Alex, Andrea, and Ananda for forbearance during the writing of this book—for putting up with the long periods away from home, the piles of documents on the floor, and the incessant interruption of telephone calls. And to Alan Francovitch who set us off on this trail but did not live to see the results, we trust this would meet with your approval. Like many others, we miss you.

PROLOGUE:

EXAMINING THE EXAMINERS

The tall, graying legislator strode past the American flag onto the platform of Committee Room 226. With a quick adjustment of his black-and-white spotted tie, he seated himself at the center of a semicircular dais under the carved eagle on the hardwood-paneled wall. As the lights of six television cameras were switched on and photographers and cameramen began to jostle for position, Senator Charles Grassley of Iowa began to read slowly from three sheets of paper. It was his opening statement as chairman of the Senate Subcommittee on Administrative Oversight into the Courts at hearings entitled, "A Review of the FBI Laboratory: Beyond the Inspector General's Report."

His purpose, he explained, was to help restore public confidence in federal law enforcement in general and the Federal Bureau of Investigation in particular. But the facts the senator went on to outline hardly seemed likely to do that. The hearings had had to be postponed twice, he stated, because of the FBI's refusal to cooperate by supplying requested documentation and by making FBI employees available to testify without the bureau's lawyers present. This, Senator Grassley said, was despite FBI director Louis Freeh's appeal for more oversight to another congressional subcommittee just four months earlier, when he had stated that the FBI could be the most dangerous agency in the country if "not scrutinized carefully."

Senator Grassley said the FBI was being hypocritical. "It is not the message that rings true. It's the actions. The Bureau's actions contradict the director's assertion that it is inviting oversight. And until the actions match the words, the ghosts of FBI past are still very much in the present." He went on to say that he expected the requested documentation to arrive the moment the hearings finished. In fact, within an hour, Senator Grassley had to apologize to the packed committee room for being "so cynical." The documents had arrived but were so heavily redacted as to be virtually useless, he said, holding up page after page of blacked-out FBI memos.

Senator Grassley's hearings took place in the wake of the release five months earlier of a damning 517-page report by the Inspector General's Office of the Department of Justice, the result of an eighteen-month investigation into the FBI laboratory. The investigators had included a panel of five internationally renowned forensic scientists, the first time in its sixty-five-year history that the FBI lab, considered by many—not least, by itself—the best in the world, had been subject to any form of external scientific scrutiny. The findings were alarming. FBI examiners had given scientifically flawed, inaccurate, and overstated testimony under oath in court; had altered the lab reports of examiners to give them a pro-prosecutorial slant, and had failed to document tests and examinations from which they drew incriminating conclusions, thus ensuring that their work could never be properly checked.

FBI lab management, meanwhile, had failed to check examinations and lab reports; had overseen a woefully inadequate record retention system; and had not only failed to investigate serious and credible allegations of incompetence but had covered them up. Management had also resisted any form of external scrutiny of the lab and had failed to establish and enforce its own validated scientific procedures and protocols—the same ones that had been issued by managers themselves in an effort to combat the lab's known shortcomings in the first place.

But the IG's report, shocking as its conclusions were, was severely limited. It had looked at just three of seven units in the FBI lab's Scientific

Analysis Section, a fraction of the lab's total of twenty-seven units.* The IG had been mandated to look into the specific allegations of just one man, Dr. Frederic Whitehurst, a Ph.D. chemist and FBI supervisory special agent who for eight years, until 1994, had worked solely on explosives-residue analysis—trace detection, and identification of the residue left behind by explosions in the lab's Materials Analysis Unit.

For nearly ten years, until he was suspended and put on "administrative leave" just weeks before the IG's report was published in April 1997, Whitehurst had reported his own observations and what others had told him. Underpinning his complaints and their persistence were three things: the unscientific nature of so much of what was being passed off as science in the FBI lab; the culture of pro-prosecution bias rather than scientific truth that pervaded the lab, including the possibly illegal withholding of exculpatory information; and the complete inability of the FBI lab or its management to investigate itself and correct these problems.

Not only had the IG report confined itself to Whitehurst's admittedly limited sphere of knowledge within the FBI lab, it had no mandate to look into the evidentiary matters raised, to ask how particular cases might have been affected, or to look at the possibility of charges against FBI lab employees heavily criticized by the report. Given the plentiful evidence of pro prosecution bias, false testimony, and inadequate forensic work, it was only logical to assume that cases had been affected. How many people might be in jail unjustly? How many might be on Death Row by mistake? If innocent people were in jail for crimes they did not commit, how many guilty ones were walking the streets?

Senator Grassley and others in Congress quickly realized that the inspector general's report had to be the beginning, not the end. The issues Whitehurst had raised, the inspector general had investigated, and now the hearings were examining further, went to the heart of the credibility of justice and the courts in the United States. In the end, the IG's report had raised more questions than it had answered, not least perhaps the

---

* Even a recent history of the FBI lab, as this book is, presents one accounting dilemma. The number of units and sections, and even their names, have changed continuously over the years. A case in point is the Hairs and Fibers Unit, later called the Microscopic Analysis Unit, now named the Trace Evidence Unit. Ultimately, the problems described here remain, regardless of the name.

most important of all: How had this happened in the first place and how might it be avoided in the future?

The task of assessing what exculpatory evidence had been withheld, how many cases had been affected, and who in the FBI lab, if anyone, should face charges for what had been uncovered had now fallen to a task force in the Criminal Division of the Justice Department. The task force had to identify the prosecutors in each case, then release forensic documentation to them in order to allow them to decide if anything crucial had been withheld. The floodgates, in other words, were controlled by the nation's prosecutors, whose records had been built on legal victories they were now supposed to question. "Is it cynical to question whether these prosecutors are virtually the worst officials to objectively evaluate tainted evidence in their own cases? Clearly the fox is guarding the henhouse," noted Congressman Robert Wexler at the hearings.

The Justice Department refuses to provide updates as to the progress of the task force or even to name its members. However, the scale of the potential fallout is clear: Just one of the numerous examiners heavily criticized by the IG's report handled more than six hundred cases in a decade of work at the FBI lab. Defense lawyers believe that thousands of cases will be affected. "The IG's report was a starting, not a finishing point," says one attorney. "I think we will be living with the ramifications of this for years, and not just in terms of the number of appeals you can expect. No defense lawyer in the country is going to take what the FBI lab says at face value any more. For years they were trusted on the basis of glossy advertising. Now the real product turns out to be a dud."

As Fred Whitehurst, a mustached Vietnam veteran sat, arms crossed, at the back of the room, Senator Grassley went on to recount that it was "the FBI's say-one-thing-do-another habit" that made him hesitant to simply accept assurances that everything was now in order at the FBI lab. "The subcommittee's investigation has revealed that systemic problems remain at the lab. . . . The problems exist and flourish because of a cultural disease within the FBI," Grassley continued. "The question is, how will these changes ensure the integrity of the scientific process within the lab, which seeks to discover the truth, when a culture exists within the FBI to apparently cut corners and slant lab reports in favor of the prosecution, which seeks to convict. The IG report did not reconcile this dilemma. The FBI will not admit the problem exists. That is why we are here today."

During the hearings, senators would hear Congressman Robert Wexler call for legislation to ensure the FBI's "future integrity" and express outrage that Whitehurst, "the courageous whistle-blower, was out . . . while dozens of FBI agents who suppressed evidence, altered evidence, or testified falsely were still there." Clearly angered by what he had heard at the previous hearings four months earlier, Wexler would now accuse the IG of failing to draw logical conclusions from its own findings. How could obvious lying on the witness stand not be considered perjury? How could the systematic alteration of lab reports to make them more incriminating not be considered intentional?

The committee would hear four past and current FBI lab employees all express support for Whitehurst and the general charges he had made. They would hear Dr. Drew Campbell Richardson, an adviser to the FBI lab's deputy assistant director and a highly qualified scientist, say that the FBI lab ignored scientific evidence that did not suit its purposes. They would hear how Bill Tobin, the FBI's metallurgist, and Jim Corby, Whitehurst's former boss, had made repeated complaints about the same examiners Whitehurst had accused, only to have them ignored. And they would hear how one of those heavily criticized in the report had been promoted to head the FBI lab's Explosives Unit, despite being under investigation at the time, passing over Ed Kelso, a widely respected firearms instructor and bomb expert with twenty-five years experience.

———

This book seeks to explore how all this happened. It seeks to go beyond the inspector general's informative but restricted investigation of the FBI lab and tell the story that the report did not. It seeks to go beyond Fred Whitehurst's serious but limited allegations and show how what he charged applies to other parts of the FBI lab that were never investigated. We have done this with the help of hundreds of hours of interviews of current and former FBI lab staff and thousands of pages of documents, memos, lab reports, interviews, and audits, many of them only released under the Freedom of Information Act after months of stonewalling by the FBI and the IG's office. Some of these documents were the raw material of the IG's report, a number of them indicating problems with lab units and cases never investigated by the investigators.

There was, of course, no cooperation from the FBI in the writing of this book, although we were allowed to talk to Fred Whitehurst on the same terms as the rest of the media—essentially, without reference to specific cases. In August 1997, the authors submitted a request to interview twenty past and present lab staff; in September we were told our request had been lost; in October it was still pending. In November the authors received a letter thanking us for our interest in the FBI but turning down our request. One of the themes of this book is the FBI's obsession with how it appears rather than what it actually is. This book and its subject did not fit the Bureau's agenda.

In the Introduction and Chapter 1 we look at the state of forensic science in this country and the FBI lab in particular. We show that while claiming to have investigated Whitehurst's allegations and found no problems, management was fully aware that there were massive problems with the FBI lab, its science, its supervision, and its safety. We show that management knew that if it ever agreed to real external scrutiny, if it was ever forced to publish the research data on which its forensic tests were based, if it ever had to make public the results of its internal proficiency tests, the image of the FBI lab as the best forensic laboratory in the world would rapidly dissolve. For this, as Senator Grassley remarked at the Senate hearings, is a culture that rewards "public image-building over discovering the truth."

The extent of the lab's dysfunction becomes clear in Chapters 2 through 8, where we look at major cases the FBI lab has handled. In particular, we detail the failings of four key FBI staff members—Terry Rudolph, Tom Thurman, Roger Martz, and David Williams—whose practices in several high-profile cases demonstrate the dangers of the lab's modus operandi. Some of these are cases the IG looked at—the World Trade Center bombing, the Unabomber investigation, the VANPAC case, the O. J. Simpson trial. Others are cases the IG did not investigate or examined only partially—the lab's role in the Ruby Ridge investigation, the Jeffrey MacDonald case, the Oklahoma City bombing.

All of these are celebrated cases involving massive forensic and other investigative resources. The FBI lab's role in all of them raises a huge and still unanswered question: If this is what happens in these high-profile, well-scrutinized cases, what is happening in thousands of less publicized ones?

In talking to dozens of forensic scientists and FBI lab personnel, one thing has become clear to us. Few were surprised at the revelations of the IG report. Many people, inside and out, have known for many years that there were serious problems at the FBI lab. Very few, however, inside or out, have chosen to speak out. With a few honorable exceptions, forensic scientists outside the FBI lab have been reluctant to take on the Bureau, which now wields enormous power throughout the profession, through training programs, research grants, and consultancy work. Many of those working inside the FBI lab seem to have been intimidated by the climate of fear that is a constant theme of Fred Whitehurst's 237 written complaints. In failing to come forward, or in some cases even to support Fred Whitehurst when he did, they have only themselves to blame for the broad-brush condemnation with which all at the FBI lab, good or bad, have now been tainted. They are in essence living testimony to what Senator Grassley describes as the FBI's "cultural problem."

INTRODUCTION

FORENSIC SCIENCE
THE PROMISE AND THE PRODUCT

Scientific crime-solving, or sci-crime—it is an image upon which much of the FBI's awesome reputation is based. Humans are fallible, are inclined to lie, and are often motivated by anything but the truth. The history of crime fighting in the United States is littered with eyewitnesses who misidentified a suspect, defense lawyers who persuaded juries to find reasonable doubt, and suspects who had credible alibis. The physical evidence, on the other hand, is the silent, definitive witness. The traces of explosives on Timothy McVeigh's clothes in Oklahoma City, the bloody shoe-prints left by the killer of Nicole Brown Simpson and Ron Goldman in Los Angeles, the saliva traces recovered from the sealed envelope of a letter claiming responsibility for the bombing of the World Trade Center . . . all these offer certainty. And certainty equals proof.

The means of making physical evidence proof is forensic science, the application of science to legal processes, the application of science to crime fighting. Together or apart, the words "forensic" and "scientific" are today commonly used as everyday adjectives that imply definitive, detailed, and comprehensively argued. It is an image burnished by popular television detective series such as *Quincy* and the coverage of big cases by Court TV, an image epitomized by the source of the country's most famous forensic science: the FBI's crime lab.

Each year half a million people hear and see the case for forensic science when they take the public tour of the FBI headquarters in downtown Washington, D.C. The J. Edgar Hoover Building is a monstrous, sandy-brown structure that somehow exudes the brooding presence of the man whose name it bears. With an overhanging, slanting top floor—the seventh at the front, the eleventh at the back—the FBI's HQ looks as though it might topple onto the traffic in Washington's Pennsylvania Avenue at any moment. Passing the black-and-white photographic portraits of FBI directors and the rogues gallery of the Bureau's "Ten Most Wanted" fugitives, visitors take a narrow escalator to the only working part of the FBI they will see on their visit—the laboratory. 61 YEARS OF FORENSIC SCIENCE SERVICE, DNA: THE SILENT WITNESS proclaims the sign that greets them. It's the sort of public relations exercise of which J. Edgar Hoover, the FBI's former director—"The Boss" as he was known to agents for nearly fifty years—would wholeheartedly approve. To Hoover, image was everything, a legacy that thrives at the FBI to this day.

"The examiners you see are working on real cases," says the guide, as children press their faces to the panes of glass that are all that separate the watchers from the watched. "The FBI is the only place in the United States with a full forensic lab," she adds, spinning through DNA, Firearms-Toolmarks, Hairs and Fibers, Materials Analysis, Chemistry and Toxicology, and Questioned Documents—some of the visible components of the lab's seven-unit Scientific Analysis Section. Here the victims of serious crime—rape, murder, violent assault—are reduced to a piece of bloodstained clothing, a hair from the carpet, an invisible explosives residue on a nondescript piece of debris. Only if photos, tapes, or handwritten notes come in as part of the evidence do such people have the faces, voices, or hands that make them real.

What the tourists see is actually just a fraction of what makes up the FBI's Laboratory Division. The Scientific Analysis Section is one of just four lab sections located at FBI headquarters, all with a bewildering range of state-of-the-art expertise, technology, and capacity. Today's Investigative Operations and Support Section grew out of the Questioned Documents Unit, where examiners detected crime by chasing paper records. They look at everything from receipts to handwriting comparisons, targeting everyone from drug smugglers to kidnappers. Documents also handles all types of impressions—tire treads, shoe-prints, handwriting, or typing imprints. Today this section includes the specialist polygraph, or "lie detector," unit, a computer analysis unit, a special photographic unit, and specialists in analyzing racketeering records—illegal gambling, prostitution, loan-sharking, and money-laundering records.

The Special Projects Section is even more diverse, with seven units that handle film, video, and photographs of suspects or victims; the famous artists "impressions" of witnesses' descriptions of suspects; crime scene plans; and now computer art and design. The aging or reconstruction of faces of suspects or victims and the reconstruction of crime scenes are a specialty. This section also prepares all forms of graphics or film used as exhibits at trial and the false credentials or documentation needed by FBI agents or informants for undercover work. Here too is the Evidence Control Center, responsible for the receipt, assignment, and tracking of the thousands of lab samples that are subjected to hundreds of thousands of examinations every year.

Finally, practicing one of the oldest and best-known disciplines of forensic science, there is the FBI lab's Latent Fingerprint Section. Here the main task is developing and comparing fingerprints, palm prints, footprints, and even lip prints with some of the estimated 200 million imprint records stored at the FBI's National Crime Information Center in West Virginia. Under an automated fingerprint identification system now being developed, law enforcement officials anywhere in the country will soon be able to instantly match sample prints with those in the database by means of portable computer images.

Much of the work in all lab departments is clinical, routine, and tedious, even though the samples, which can range from soil to bullet casings, are often anything but. Yet this is by far America's biggest, most important, best equipped, and most famous crime lab. As an examiner here you never know what you are going to get—it could be a rape one day, an explosion the next, and a product-tampering case the day after that. "Here you might start work on the case of a lifetime any day, anytime," says one employee. And it could come from anywhere. As well as its own cases—federal crime or crime that involves more than one state—the FBI lab takes work from state, county, and municipal law enforcement agencies across the nation. As a result, its 694 staff handled 136,629 pieces of evidence and performed nearly 700,000 examinations in 1996.[1]

In the past twenty-five years forensic science has been transformed, "growing up so fast that even the most sophisticated researchers cannot keep up," according to *Time* magazine.[2] Nowhere more so than in the heart of the FBI lab, the Scientific Analysis Section. Here the traditional scientific paraphernalia, the test tubes, gas tanks, and microscopes that recall school chemistry classes rub shoulders with infrared spectroscopes, Apple and Compaq computers, and mass spectrometers. Forensic science is now genetics and microbiology in DNA typing, nuclear physics in neutron activation analysis, analytical chemistry in infrared, ultraviolet, or X-ray spectrometry, and statistics in computerized number crunching.

These new technologies have in many cases been grafted onto a profession that in many of its traditional subfields, such as fingerprints, questioned documents, ballistics, hairs and fibers, and explosives, is not actually based on science at all but on subjective comparisons by individual examiners. Yet either way, whether the "soft" science of the traditional visual comparisons of two hairs, bullets, or fingerprints or the "hard" science of neutron activation analysis or DNA typing, forensic science ultimately cannot avoid the human factor. The examiners who do the tests, run the machines, and make the comparisons are people. At the FBI lab and the nearly four hundred other crime labs in the United States, those people have turned out to be as flawed as the eyewitnesses, juries, or lawyers who make up the rest of the judicial process.

But if scientific crime-fighting is fallible and flawed, those problems rarely come to light. One exception was in July 1994, when *USA Today* and the Gannett News Service published a survey. Believing that the claim that the bloody glove found on O. J. Simpson's estate had been planted was far-fetched, the newspaper trawled legal and media databases for comparative cases. They found eighty-five instances since 1974 in which prosecutors had knowingly or unknowingly used tainted evidence that had convicted the innocent or freed the guilty. In the same period, forty-eight people sentenced to death were freed after convictions were found to be based on fabricated evidence or because exonerating or exculpatory evidence was withheld.[3] And these were just the known cases, cases which for one reason or another had come to light or made the news. "In the United States we take science as gospel," said Ray Taylor, a San Antonio, Texas, lawyer and forensic pathology expert, commenting on the survey. "The public perception is that faking science is rare. The truth is it happens all the time."[4]

The tip of this iceberg has been some shocking individual examples. Fred Salem Zain was a police forensic expert in West Virginia and Texas for nearly fifteen years. Hired as a chemist by West Virginia's police crime lab in 1979, he testified as an expert in dozens of rape and murder cases about tests he had never done and results he had never obtained. Despite complaints, nothing was done. Colleagues taped a magician's wand to one of Zain's lab machines in frustration. In 1989, Zain became head of serology at the Bexar County Medical Examiner's office in San Antonio, Texas. When asked to review Zain's work, a Dallas forensic specialist found rampant fraud and falsification. In one case, Zain had testified about blood evidence when no blood had even been found; in other cases he reported performing tests his lab was incapable of doing. Zain was fired. At the last count, five men jailed for rape and murder had had their convictions overturned as a result.

West Texas pathologist Ralph Erdmann, who worked as a contract medical examiner in forty counties, faked more than one hundred autopsies on unexamined bodies and falsified dozens of toxicology and blood reports. Dozens of other autopsies were botched. In one case, he lost a head. Then there was Louise Robbins, a college anthropology professor who claimed the ability to match a footprint on any surface to the person who made it. Robbins appeared as an expert witness for over a decade in more than twenty criminal cases throughout North America before her claims were seriously undermined. Her testimony helped put more than a dozen people behind bars, including an Ohio man who spent six years on Death Row before his conviction was overturned on appeal.

Michael West was a forensic dentist from Hattiesburg, Mississippi, who appeared as a scientific expert more than sixty times in ten states until 1996. At least twenty of these were capital murder cases. West became famous for his controversial use of long-wave ultraviolet light and yellow-lensed goggles to study wound patterns on a body. The equipment is standard: Ultraviolet light can enhance features on the skin. What West claimed he could see was not standard: No other forensic expert could pick up the lines and marks he claimed to see. Robert Kirschner, a former deputy chief medical examiner who testified against West, says what he did was closer to voodoo or alchemy than science. "History is full of people who claimed they could see things, from ghosts to UFOs," says Kirschner. "But claiming it and proving it are two different things."[5]

The biggest and self-proclaimed best forensic lab in the world has not been immune to such rogues. In February 1975, an internal FBI investigation into the activities of Special Agent Thomas Curran, an examiner in the FBI lab's serology unit, revealed a record of perjury, incompetence, and falsification. At the trial of Thomas Doepel for rape and murder in Washington, D.C., in 1974, Curran testified under oath that he had a bachelor's and a master's degree in science; that both Doepel and the victim were blood type O; and that the defendant's shorts bore a single blood stain. In reality, Curran had no degree in anything; Doepel, on retesting, turned out to be blood type B; and the shorts evidenced two, not one, bloodstains.[6]

After further complaints, FBI special agent Jay Cochran was instructed to do a full review of Curran's work. Curran's aberrations, like Zain's, were common. Curran had issued reports of blood analyses when "no laboratory tests were done"; had relied on presumptive tests to draw up confirmatory results; and had written up inadequate and deceptive lab reports, ignoring or distorting test results. "The real issue is that he chose to ignore the virtue of integrity and to lie when asked if specific tests were conducted," Cochran's report to the then head of the FBI laboratory, Dr. Briggs White stated.[7] It was an early warning of what could happen at the FBI lab. Tom Curran turned out to have lied repeatedly under oath about his credentials, and his reports were persistently deceptive, yet no one—FBI lab management, defense lawyers, judges—had noticed. When they did, there was no prosecution for perjury.

Of course, every profession has its rotten apples. Forensic science is no different from the law, medicine, academia, law enforcement, or anything else. The issue is not the Zains or Currans per se, but the questions their conduct raises. How did they get into the profession? How did they get away with it for so long? Why are they not stopped and punished? Why do juries, judges, prosecutors, and even defense attorneys believe them?

Take a close look at forensic science and answers are not hard to come by. The first shock is that most forensic scientists are not in fact independent experts. About 80 percent of forensic scientists in North America are affiliated with police or prosecution agencies. Most of these work in police laboratories; many are themselves law enforcement officers, as are most of their superiors. Fred Zain was a state trooper, promoted to lieutenant; Tom Curran was an FBI special agent. The potential conflicts of loyalties and interests is obvious. Scientists are expected to retain a critical sense, to follow nothing but reason, to maintain an open mind. We expect the results, the science, to bear witness in court unencumbered by any other considerations. Complete impartiality may be an aspirational ideal, but what chance is there of coming anywhere near this ideal if the police or FBI pay your wages?

"It is quite common to find laboratory facilities and personnel who are, for all intents and purposes, an arm of the prosecution," notes James Starrs, a professor of law and forensic science at George Washington University in Washington, D.C. "They analyze material submitted, on all but rare occasions, solely by the prosecution. They testify almost exclusively on behalf of the prosecution. . . . As a result, their impartiality is replaced by a viewpoint colored brightly with prosecutorial bias."[8] William Thompson, a professor of criminalistics at the University of California, Irvine, agrees: "The culture of such places, run by police or agents, for police or agents, is often just inimical to good scientific practice. The reward system, promotion, incentives . . . in the end your pay check is based on successful prosecutions, not good science."[9]

Nowhere is this truer than at the FBI laboratory in Washington, the pinnacle of the forensic science mountain in the United States. Institutional bias here is enshrined in the limitation of the availability of the lab and its services to state and federal law enforcement agencies. The FBI lab works for the prosecution and no one else. It is reinforced by the FBI lab's reluctance to give or take second opinions. Generally, evidence submitted to the FBI laboratory cannot be taken elsewhere, or vice versa, even though that might be considered the peer review deemed essential by scientists. The FBI lab is happy to clear suspects and frequently does. However, defense teams need to get a court order and be prepared to share any findings with the prosecution if they want to use the government-funded facility. Indeed, the lab is even off-limits to defense experts who want to observe testing.

The prosecutorial attitude was made clear by one lab veteran now working privately: "People say we're tainted for the prosecution. Hell, that's what we do! We get our evidence and present it for the prosecution." [10] In the FBI laboratory "getting results," the declared aim of FBI director Louis Freeh, means securing prosecutions. But that is only part of the story. Those on the public tour staring through the viewing windows of the Scientific Analysis Section of the FBI laboratory might be surprised to learn that many of the white-coated figures hunched over microscopes or spectrometers are FBI agents. Some have science degrees, but many, particularly, ironically, those in the most senior positions, do not. They are FBI men and women working for an FBI laboratory.

For more than twenty years the FBI resisted replacing its special agents who work in the laboratory with civilian scientists. Even now, after several years of replacing agents with such personnel, FBI agents continue to run the lab, occupying virtually all the senior management and examiner positions. FBI special agents bring an "extra dimension" to the analysis of physical evidence, the FBI insists. The ideal lab specialist "stands in the shoes of the investigator in the field, whom he is serving," as John McDermott, a senior FBI official, put it to a congressional subcommittee in 1981.

Serving the investigator or serving justice? Close liaison between examining agent and investigator, the core of the FBI's argument, can easily create bias that is often so subtle as to be unconscious. In the first place, there is simply the method of working. "Sometimes they're [the investigators are] pretty confused about what they want, so we'll call them up to find out what they're trying to prove," the then FBI Firearms-Toolmarks Unit (FTU) chief Jack Dillon told one author. "Often we can suggest some better ways of doing it." [11] By "doing it," of course, Dillon means trying to build a case for prosecution. "That is what I have come to call putting the cart before the horsing around," says Professor Starrs. "They're effectively running the investigation backward, starting with a hypothesis of guilt, then going out to try and prove it. That is not science. These people aren't scientists." [12]

Second, there is suggestive incrimination. Numerous studies have shown that advance warning of the results anticipated, even something as simple as looking for a match or positive identification, is significantly more likely to produce those results. In just one example, experiments in 1975 demonstrated that a witness told by police that a suspect was in an identification lineup was seven times more likely to pick out a suspect than those advised only that a suspect might be present. Expectations can be unconsciously passed on, verbally and nonverbally.

One good example of suggestive incrimination comes from Evan Hodge, a former FTU chief at the FBI laboratory. In an article entitled "Guarding Against Error" he tells the story of a police inspector who took a 1911A1 model .45-caliber pistol to a lab for confirmation that it was a murder weapon. "We know this guy shot the victim and this is the gun he used," the examiner was told. "All we want you to do is confirm what we already know so we can get the scumbag off the street. We will wait. How quick can you do it?" The examiner gave them their instant identification. The suspect confessed and led the police to a second pistol, also a .45, also a 1911A1 model, which lab tests demonstrated was the real murder weapon. "We all do this [give in to investigative pressure] to one extent or another," Evan Hodge admitted, arguing that the only solution is to remove the sources of it from the laboratory completely.[13]

Investigators in the field, and the close contact the FBI lab advocates with them, are one source of pressure. There are many more. Prosecutors are one. Politicians, another. The public, yet another. Few criminal cases today do not lean on forensic science, and as the search for the means to combat crime has intensified, so have the expectations. At the FBI, major cases like TRADBOM (the bomb attack on the World Trade Center in New York City) and OKBOM (the Oklahoma City bombing) get the sort of priority, as well as the public and political attention, that is, in itself, a source of pressure. These cases are too big to leave unsolved in the lab, too big to lose in court. The government will throw infinite investigative and legal resources at them. Lower down the crime lab chain, the stakes may be just as big locally. Careers may depend on results. "Don't expect to get re-elected as a district attorney in this country if a particularly heinous crime goes unsolved on your patch," notes one southern lawyer.[14]

Fred Whitehurst's complaints stemmed from such pressures, in particular the culture clash between the needs of science and the needs of law enforcement that are accentuated by the dominance of a law enforcement ethos rather than that of science in the FBI lab. Many accused him of being unable to make the distinction between pure and practical science. Yet Whitehurst is actually quick to acknowledge the uniqueness of the forensic process within science. The forensic scientist seeks to link a sample to an individual, to a substance, to distinguish it from other specimens in a way no other scientist would even attempt. The forensic scientist's standard fare is the sort of degraded, soiled sample that a research scientist would trash if it ever came near his or her laboratory. The forensic scientist's goal is not pure knowledge but practical supposition.

Whitehurst's contention is simply that such ends have to be underpinned by scientific method, proven protocols, and validated procedures or they yield no proven truth, the ultimate aim of both law and science. Forensic science has to use procedures and processes that have withstood traditional scientific scrutiny—i.e., been subjected to publication and peer review, the sort of "institutional skepticism" that is the cornerstone of the scientific process. Forensic science examinations should be fully documented, subject to cross examination, and the results and process available to the defense. The reality is somewhat different. The openness, democratic debate, public dissemination, and protracted research that are the hallmarks of proper science contrast sharply with the secrecy, haste, and authoritarian hierarchy of the crime lab.

For years, some lawyers and many scientists have argued that forensic science is hardly a branch of science at all in its refusal and institutional inability to accept or conform to scientific norms. With relatively little research done in forensic science itself, there has been a propensity to adopt or adapt half-baked research done elsewhere. The result: Time after time definitive research in the field of forensic science has only been done after questions have been raised about the accuracy and reliability of its procedures, usually in court. The FBI lab, with the biggest forensic science research facility in the country—the Forensic Science Research and Training Center at Quantico, Virginia—has been at the center of many of the resulting disputes.

The forensic history of voiceprints—the claim that a spectrograph could be used to produce a unique pattern for any single individual's speech—is particularly instructive. With limited research concluded, a number of courts ruled voiceprints admissible. Only when scientists from other fields challenged the spectrograph research and a major scientific controversy erupted did the FBI ask the National Academy of Sciences (NAS) to review voiceprint technology. An NAS evaluation committee quickly concluded that the theory had not been validated.[15] Yet, incredibly, many courts continued to allow the admissibility of voiceprints long after the NAS study had been published.

Those that present science to the public at public expense are surely obliged to understand its basic precepts. Yet many in the FBI lab do not, as Chapters 2 through 8 of this book amply illustrate. Court records throughout the country are littered with examples. In a recent aggravated assault and burglary trial in Montana, FBI fingerprint expert Michael Wieners asserted that a fingerprint experiment he had done was "scientific" but not "completely scientific." It was not surprising he could not tell the difference. Challenged about his familiarity with peer-reviewed literature on fingerprints, Weiners replied: "Peer reviewed? Could you explain that?"[16]

Complaints about such ignorance preceded Fred Whitehurst's arrival at the FBI lab in 1986. In 1981, three prominent independent forensic scientists criticized FBI science and testimony, citing three cases in a paper delivered at the annual meeting of the American Academy of Forensic Sciences (AAFS) in Los Angeles.[17] The first was a bank robbery case in which the FBI examiner seemed to have been unable to distinguish between a class characteristic and an individual characteristic in identifying a canvas bag, despite having a master's degree in forensic science. In the second case, a rape and murder with semen, blood, saliva, and hair samples, the paper criticized the FBI's typing procedure. The critics also pointed out that two FBI hair examiners who had studied the same hair specimens had disagreed on such fundamentals as how many samples there were, whether they had been bleached, and whether they had pulled roots. The third case involved gun residue on a shooting victim's hands that could have exculpated his wife, the defendant, yet had not been mentioned by the FBI examiner.

The authors of the paper stressed that they did not consider these cases aberrations. These case studies were, they claimed, typical of the problems that occurred repeatedly in crime labs and courts. They noted that FBI lab practice was considered standard by many courts, but emphasized that they were not singling out the FBI laboratory. The Bureau did not see it that way. Shortly after the presentation, a former head of the FBI lab, Thomas Kelleher, Jr., charged that the authors, Peter Barnett, Ed Blake, and Robert Ogle, Jr., had violated the code of ethics of the AAFS in making the presentation. They had, Kelleher claimed, misrepresented the role of the lab and the conclusions of FBI examiners. Thus, the actual leveling of the charges became the subject of an investigation by the AAFS's ethics committee.

Ultimately it was decided that there was not "sufficient evidence of misrepresentation of data" by the authors to support the FBI's allegation. "The FBI's allegations were preposterous. I think we made them look ridiculous," says Ed Blake, a longtime critic of the FBI's forensic science.[18] "We chose the FBI lab to show that crime labs could get it wrong because we thought they were big enough to take a little criticism," chuckles Robert Ogle, Jr. "Fortunately, there was someone with a scientific background on the ethics committee. They just said: 'Look, this is bullshit. You can't bring ethics charges against people for giving a scientific paper at a scientific meeting.'"[19]

Years later, Whitehurst's charges and his treatment would mirror those of these three, whose observations, along with Whitehurst's, would be vindicated by the inspector general's report. As the three critics pointed out in a letter to Professor Starrs's quarterly newsletter, *Scientific Sleuthing Review*, their paper cited "errors or insufficiencies on the part of the original examiner . . . management deficiency, . . . [and] a lack of knowledge." The IG report, sixteen years later, cited "failures by management" and "significant instances of testimonial errors, substandard analytical work and deficient practices."[20] The damage done to confidence in crime labs in general and the FBI lab in particular might have been avoided if the substance of their charges—not the fact that they had been made—had been addressed back in 1981, the three pointed out. But the FBI lab was incapable of addressing these issues or indeed of changing anything about the way it operated. Indeed, the very manner in which the FBI handled Whitehurst's complaints—dismissing them, burying them, then attacking the messenger rather than the message—illustrated how little the culture of the FBI lab had changed since 1981.

At the core of what the critical experts were alleging is the poor practice that riddles the FBI lab and much forensic science in the United States. Documentation is a case in point. Examiners have proven remarkably loath to write up their bench notes in any adequate scientific manner. No names, no chain of custody history, no testing chronology, no details of supervisory oversight, no confirmatory tests, no signatures—such omissions are quite normal in FBI lab reports. What the reports do contain is obfuscation and overstated conclusions written in an often incomprehensible style that some experts have termed "forensonics." Undefined terms such as "match" or "identical to" are common; chronicled scientific procedures and protocols to justify them are not.

The motive seems to be to say as little as possible as unintelligibly as possible with what passes for scientific jargon and process. Numerous conversations with former FBI lab personnel and attorneys have left no doubt why. Since lab reports are "discoverable" and have to be handed to the defense, the FBI lab believes that as little as possible should be given away. The approach to research is no different. The publication of findings or methodologies might be used to undermine the prosecution of cases, so the rule that has evolved is to avoid dissemination. In short, the FBI's interpretation of the adversarial approach on which the U.S. judicial system is based works to serve neither science nor truth.

As such, the FBI lab's reports have shocked those outside the U.S. forensic science community. "If these are the ones [reports] to be presented to court as evidence then I am appalled by the structure and information content. . . . [T]he structure of the reports seems to be designed to confuse," concluded Professor Brian Caddy, head of the forensic science unit at Strathclyde University in Scotland on being shown the FBI lab's forensic reports in the Oklahoma City bombing case.[21]

Much the same goes for protocols or established procedures. Traditionally, many FBI forensic scientists have not used protocols—the recipes for analyses and the touchstones of scientific procedure—despite the fact that all scientists accept that not using them produces only experimental, not proven, outcomes. Indeed, in some crime labs, established protocols do not even exist. "Basically what we've got is a kind of oral tradition, like medieval English, the Venerable Bede, instead of a regular scientific protocol manual," claimed Stephen Jones, Timothy McVeigh's first defense lawyer in the Oklahoma City bombing case, who has looked into FBI lab procedures in some depth. "The advantage of the oral tradition, of course, is that no one knows what it is."[22]

Such shortcomings are often accentuated in court. Here pressure from prosecutors is direct. All too often the important caveats that punctuate forensic science, phrases such as "including but not excluding," "possible but not certain," "compatible with but not incompatible with," are forgotten. All too often "could" becomes "did," an opinion becomes a fact, tests that only suggest are said to prove. Even if the forensic scientist is sufficiently guarded, prosecutors or even judges are often less so.

"The expert may say something quite guarded like 'was similar' and within minutes you'll hear the prosecutor reinterpret that as a definitive identification," complains Professor Starrs. "How many times do you hear the word 'match.' What the heck does it mean? It must be the most overused word in forensic science."[23] Indeed, surveys have demonstrated that there is no agreement on the definition of such key terms among forensic experts themselves.

In the cauldron of the courtroom, testifying beyond one's expertise becomes common, especially under the FBI's system, where auxiliary examiners, often civilian scientists, actually do the tests, but principal examiners, invariably FBI agents, have tended to do the testifying. All too often the fingerprint expert is invited to comment or even speculate on the bloodstains, the firearms expert on the nature of the bomb explosive, the documents examiner on the toolmarks. When only one expert is appearing in a multidiscipline case, it's tempting for prosecutors or defense lawyers to go for an opinion; it's also tempting for examiners to embellish, exaggerate, or even lie about their credentials. The case of the FBI's Tom Curran, who was variously a zoologist, a biologist, and a psychologist for different court appearances, is exceptional only in degree.[24]

Incredibly, forensic scientists do not have to establish competence by obtaining a license or certification—even from their peers. There are no federal requirements and, to date, no state has demanded them. There are, to be sure, professional bodies. The American Board of Criminalists conducts very general proficiency tests, the American College of Forensic Examiners holds ethics exams, and perhaps the most highly regarded, the American Academy of Forensic Sciences, is a professional body whose members elect and promote each other on merit. But membership in none of these is a prerequisite to work. There is no certification or minimum standards for a very simple reason—the profession as a whole has opposed it. As long ago as 1976 certification boards were established in five areas of forensic science in an effort to establish peer-based bodies that would review credentials, run qualifying exams, agree on ethical standards, and certify practitioners in their particular fields. Guidelines were put to the nation's crime lab personnel in a referendum. They rejected them by a 2–1 vote.[25]

Some such as Ed Blake see the forensic science profession as a sort of medieval guild, with crime lab directors, led by the FBI lab and its management, acting as the police chiefs, employing, as they do, four-fifths of the profession. Certainly the failure of the professional associations to assert themselves has left a vacuum crime lab directors seemed to have filled, in deciding who will practice and on what terms. As David Stoney has remarked, in the absence of certification and thus effective sanction, there is, in many ways, no forensic science profession as such: "What are the entry requirements? Employment and function. One joins the profession when one is hired by a crime laboratory and one begins to write reports and testify in court."[26]

In the 1970s, the FBI lab began to flex its muscles to organize the crime labs of the country to fill this vacuum. In 1973, Duayne Dillon, a criminalist from California, stunned an audience at an AAFS meeting by stating that the greatest impediment to the widespread adoption of criminalistics in the U.S. judicial system was the existence of the FBI laboratory.[27] He was actually well intentioned; Dillon was referring to what he saw as the isolation and exclusivity of the FBI lab and its belief that there was no need for other crime labs in the United States. It was also well aimed; Dr. Briggs White, then the director of the FBI lab, was sitting in the audience. Furthermore, it was brilliantly timed; J. Edgar Hoover had died the previous year and Clarence Kelley, keen to shed a little light in the Bureau, took over the FBI in July of that year.

It made sense for the FBI to encourage the development of local crime labs; it reduced the Bureau's workload. It also made sense to link new crime labs to Washington, where there was expertise, information, and resources. That year, the FBI lab started training courses for non-FBI crime lab personnel. The following year, in 1974, Dr. Briggs White was appointed chairman of what was named the American Society of Crime Laboratory Directors (ASCLD), an organization designed to improve cooperation and communication among crime lab directors in the pursuit of "common objectives." A quarterly magazine, Crime Lab Digest, began publication shortly afterward. In 1976, the FBI proposed setting up the

Forensic Science Research and Training Center (FSRTC) in Quantico, Virginia, on the grounds of its training academy. By 1978, the thirty-nine-thousand-square-foot facility was under construction.

By the early 1980s, the FBI was the overwhelmingly dominant force in servicing the rapid expansion of forensic science facilities, training everyone from managers to technicians; developing new forensic science techniques, ranging from toxicology to hair identification; and funding research in academia and private industry across the country. Duayne Dillon could not have imagined the consequences of his criticism. "ASCLD and FSRTC gave huge power to a federal agency that had not been active in forensic science organizations," he said years later. "Suddenly the FBI lab's clout increased enormously."[28]

The FBI's new power and the enhanced status the country's crime lab directors enjoyed as a result of being more closely associated with the bureau was a fatal blow to the possibility of any agreed-on, enforceable ethical code in forensic science. Every two or three months, Professor Starrs, best known for the spotlight he sheds on the profession in his quarterly newsletter, *Scientific Sleuthing Review*, gets a phone call from someone in a crime lab. "They say, 'I know the defense attorney isn't going to ask the right questions and they're going to convict this guy. What should I do?' Or: 'They said the guy's on the brink of a confession and they want me to fabricate a fingerprint report,'" he reports.[29] Starrs has become a sort of confessor figure because as long ago as 1971 he started arguing publicly for the adoption of an ethical code.[30] What he proposed nearly thirty years ago could be as useful today. On personal issues, Starrs suggested:

1. No consideration or person should dissuade the forensic scientist from a full and fair investigation of the facts on which opinion is formulated.
2. The forensic scientist should maintain an attitude of independence, impartiality, and calm objectivity to avoid personal or professional involvement in the proceedings.
3. A forensic scientist should not tender testimony that is not within his/her competence as an expert, or conclusions or opinions within the competence of the jury, acting as laymen.

On procedures, Starrs advocates:

4. Utmost care in the treatment of any samples or items of potential evidentiary value to avoid tampering, adulteration, loss, or other change of original state.
5. Full and complete disclosure of the entire case in a comprehensive and well-documented report, to include facts or opinions indicative of the accused's innocence and the shortcomings of his/her opinion that might invalidate it.
6. Forensic scientists should testify to the procedures undertaken and the results disclosed only when opinions can be stated in terms of reasonable scientific certainty.
7. That unless there are special circumstances of possible intimidation or falsification of evidence, a forensic scientist for the prosecution should permit the defense to interview him/her before the trial, an obligation that should not be contingent on the approval of the prosecutor.

Since they were first articulated in 1971 these principles have formed the core of other prospective ethical codes. In 1987, Dr. Joseph Peterson, from the Department of Criminal Justice at the University of Illinois, suggested a very similar six-point code to the American Academy of Forensic Sciences at their annual general meeting in San Diego. The American College of Forensic Examiners, incorporated under the motto "Science, Integrity, Justice," has, since 1993, based its ethics certification exam on the same principles.

Awareness and agreement is one thing, however, adherence another, and forensic science has none of these three. In court, the flaws resulting from the absence of an enforced set of ethical standards, qualifications, and certifying procedures tend to be magnified. The minimization of admissibility standards in recent years has made matters worse. For decades, courts applied a general acceptance standard for the admissibility of novel scientific evidence. Known as the *Frye* test, a ruling dating back to the prohibition of polygraph evidence in 1923, the criterion was simple: Evidence was acceptable in court if the technique or science it was based on had gained general acceptance in the scientific community. But in 1975, the *Federal Rules of Evidence* were adopted, with Rule 702 effectively supplanting *Frye*. After 1975, all a scientific or technical expert had to do was satisfy the judge that he or she could provide mere assistance to the jury beyond the latter's competence.

It is this basement threshold more than anything else that has given rise to the growing concern about what has been termed "junk science" in U.S. courtrooms. Its apogee seems to be one of many examples cited in Peter Huber's book *Galileo's Revenge: Junk Science in the Courtroom*: a "soothsayer" who, with the help of "expert" testimony from a doctor and several police officials, was awarded $1 million by a jury for the loss of her "psychic powers" following a medical scan. Although the emphasis was on civil cases, criminal cases were not immune to the contagion. Cases are now being settled on the type of evidence that the scientific community had rejected years before.

The inability of courts to tell the difference between real and junk science was partially responsible for what seems like downright laxity when faced with the shortcomings of forensic examiners. Ralph Erdmann, the medical examiner from Lubbock County, Texas, cited previously, pleaded no contest to seven specimen felonies involving faking autopsies, falsifying evidence, and brokering body parts, yet got only a ten-year probation order and community service. Fred Zain, the West Virginia and Texas serologist, was acquitted of a variety of criminal charges brought against him in West Virginia.

Part of the problem in Zain's case was illustrative—it was not even clear if he had broken the law. Zain just left the impression his tests showed more than they could, claims medical examiner Vincent DiMaio, Zain's former supervisor. "It's unethical, yes, but not illegal."[31] Even where there was clear illegality, as with FBI examiner Tom Curran's perjury, prosecutions were rare or nonexistent. And these were the prominent cases, the cases that were exposed. Most of the time the inadequacies in the way forensic science is practiced go far less noticed than in the Zain, Curran, or Erdmann cases.

There are several legal obstacles to rooting out bad forensic science. The first is lawyers themselves. Few are prepared to orchestrate a defense around a scientific subject or technology they know little about; even fewer are prepared to spend the hours or weeks it may take to prepare. The vast majority of law schools still offer no specific courses devoted to scientific opinion or expert witness testimony. "You can ignore high profile cases like O. J. Simpson. That is not typical. Forensics for lawyers has been a real blind spot," notes one defense lawyer.[32] The frequent failure to challenge forensic experts has preserved an often undeserved mystique. "You might as well be a high priest," says John Murdock, a crime lab director.[33]

Financing is another obstacle. Experts cost money, the vast majority of defendants do not have it, and the courts are often reluctant to spend it by authorizing the funds to pay for a defense expert. The result has been what some experts have termed "an economic presumption of guilt." Many courts have required defendants to cross near impossible thresholds of proof of need in order to secure the help of court-ordered experts. Ironically, proving an expert would make "a material difference" to the defense case or that doing without one would result in an unfair trial, as many courts demand, often in itself requires an expert.

The net result is obvious. The vast majority of defendants in criminal courts in the United States do not have access to forensic expertise, even though they will almost certainly face forensic evidence from the prosecution, according to Jack King, public affairs spokeman at the National Association of Criminal Defense Lawyers. The prosecution's access to crime laboratories, the latest technology, and an unlimited range of expertise in the most serious cases means that, of all the disparities between defense and prosecution in the criminal justice system in the United States, that in the forensic field may be the greatest. The impact on the outcome of a case, where a defendant's life or liberty is on the line, can be equally disproportionate.

Yet even having a defense expert may make little difference. Defendants have no right even to know if a forensic expert is going to testify against them in federal court, and they certainly have no right to confront the scientist who actually performed the tests that might incriminate them. These obstacles are only part of discovery and disclosure rules that are stacked against defendants. Rule 16 of the Federal Rules of Criminal Procedure makes all "results and reports" of scientific tests discoverable to the defense. But who says such a report has to be written? Even if a scientific test is performed, even if dozens of scientific tests are performed, no written report is required. And oral reports are not discoverable. That is a loophole the FBI and other crime labs have proven adept at exploiting.

Rule 16 says nothing about the bench notes, the findings, calculations, or records made during testing. There is no mention of the graphs or printouts that basic forensic tools such as chromatographs or spectrographs produce. Court after court has ruled that these are not discoverable, despite the fact that it is these, rather than the reports, which are often deliberately perfunctory and conclusory, that allow other experts to assess and check the scientific work carried out. "The crime lab controls everything—results, tests, samples," says Bill Thompson, a professor of criminology. "As a defense attorney you're lucky to get a two-page lab report saying it's your guy, he's guilty, thank you very much."[34]

One classic example came in the 1983 trial of Wayne Williams, charged with two of some thirty deaths of young African-Americans in and around Atlanta. Barry Gaudette, a hair and fiber expert working with the FBI's prosecution experts, testified about complex tests done over eleven days of examination, but solely from bench notes. They were ruled not subject to discovery, despite a defense appeal to the Georgia Supreme Court. Another expert testified about the graphs produced by a spectrophotometer, an instrument used to compare the color of fibers taken from the supposedly rare carpet in Williams's bedroom and from his car with those taken from clothes on the victims' bodies. The Georgia Supreme Court again denied discovery even though, paradoxically, it recognized that the interpretation of them formed the basis of the expert's testimony. Despite being highly relevant, even material, to a defense case, the graphs were not subject to discovery. As a result, the guilty verdict in the case stood.

This sort of tilting of the scales of justice has left some defendants obtaining more information, often enough to clear themselves or secure a new trial, under the Freedom of Information Act than under discovery provisions. In some cases what has subsequently been released seemed to be what lawyers call *Brady* material, after the landmark judgment in 1963 that determined that the suppression of evidence material to guilt or punishment, evidence that is favorable to an accused person, is a violation of due process.

An obligation to preserve evidence would seem to be at the heart of the *Brady* decision. If evidence, specimens, reports, or bench notes are destroyed or discarded, how can anyone determine what is exculpatory? But on two separate occasions the Supreme Court has declined to interpret the *Brady* ruling as including a duty to preserve evidence. Startling amounts of evidence—bullets, blood samples, hair—are routinely trashed at the FBI and other crime labs. Some of this, such as the ammonium nitrate crystals that implicated Timothy McVeigh in the Oklahoma City bombing (see Chapter 6), is absolutely crucial material. At the FBI lab, an even larger amount of paperwork—reports, bench notes, and charts—has been lost in a filing and record-retention system no one, including management, seems to be able to rely on (see Chapter 2).

With no duty to preserve evidence, the right of a defendant to test or retest evidence becomes even more crucial. Yet there is no such right written into Rule 16, and the FBI lab and most crime labs in the country grant no such right. Those seeking the right are routinely told they will have to get a court order. Photographing or otherwise chronicling testing procedures has been resisted for years by crime labs. All kinds of excuses, ranging from security to space, have been offered as to why the FBI lab cannot allow defense experts to witness tests on its publicly funded premises.

Under the circumstances, the necessity for regulation of crime laboratories is obvious. Yet they remain unregulated. What inspection and accreditation there is is voluntary and subjective. This makes crime labs an anomaly even within the laboratory field. In 1967, the Clinical Laboratory Improvement Act set minimum standards and regulations for some clinical laboratories after proficiency testing had revealed widespread deficiencies. Following further testing that showed a marked improvement in standards, in 1988 the law was strengthened and extended to cover all clinical labs.

The new legislation introduced mandatory standards for technical and supervisory staff, licensing requirements, and uniform quality assurance procedures. Forensic laboratories were excluded from the legislation in both 1967 and 1988. The result? "Clinical laboratories must meet higher standards to be allowed to diagnose strep throat than forensic laboratories must meet to put a defendant on death row," in the words of Eric Lander, a molecular biologist.[35]

Crime labs were considered too good to need regulation. In reality they were anything but, as the first and to date only national examination of forensic science labs revealed in a series of tests done between 1974 and 1977. More than two hundred forensic laboratories, all of which participated voluntarily, carried out all or some of twenty-one proficiency tests across a broad range of "evidence" types. The FBI joined the program late and dropped out early, performing eighteen of twenty-one tests and acting as the "referee" for other labs in five of these. Although the FBI claimed its examiners came to no "improper conclusions," the overall results were absolutely shocking. Seventy-one percent of those labs participating were found to have reported faulty results in a blood test, 51.4 percent made errors in matching paint samples, and nearly 68 percent failed a hair test. Some 35.5 percent of crime labs failed in soil examinations and 28.2 percent made mistakes in firearms identification—a mainstay of forensic science work.[36]

The errors stretched from handwriting comparisons to hair examination, and the causes were just as broad, according to the examiners. The Forensic Sciences Foundation, which carried out the study, blamed misinterpretation of the test results by careless or untrained examiners, mislabeled or contaminated samples, inadequate databases, and perhaps most serious of all, faulty testing procedures. They made a string of recommendations: more resources; better education and training; accreditation and certification programs; and ongoing proficiency and quality assurance systems.

The results alarmed Don Edwards, a former FBI agent who as a California congressman had some responsibility for oversight of the FBI in his capacity as chairman of the House of Representatives Subcommittee on Civil and Constitutional Rights. In 1979, he began raising questions about practices at the FBI lab, specifically the lack of accountability. Two years later, Don Edwards began trying to pressure the FBI into accepting outside proficiency testing, but got little support from his colleagues and outright opposition from the Bureau. "[He] tried to use the bully pulpit of his chairmanship to embarrass/cajole the FBI to do the right thing. . . . The Bureau consistently rejected his efforts," says longtime assistant counsel to the subcommittee James Dempsey.[37] Based on years of trying to oversee the FBI lab, Don Edwards himself has no doubts: "The FBI lab should be independent of the FBI. It has a basic conflict of interest in working for the prosecution."[38]

The pressure did force the FBI lab to adopt internal proficiency testing in 1981. The industry as a whole decided to react by establishing an accreditation arm of the American Society of Crime Laboratory Directors (ASCLD), known rather cumbersomely as the American Society of Crime Laboratory Directors/Laboratory Accreditation Board (ASCLD/LAB). Application for accreditation was voluntary, and the inspectors, who were other crime lab personnel, were trained by the FBI lab at its training facility at Quantico. As such, ASCLD/LAB's description of itself as "independent, impartial, and objective" was debatable. An offshoot of ASCLD, the system was voluntary and internal, secretive and anonymous, in effect a self-regulatory response to growing external criticism.

By December 1996, more than fifteen years after ASCLD/LAB's inception, only 138 of the nearly 400 crime labs in the United States had earned accreditation.[39] ASCLD/LAB refuses to say how many crime labs have tried and failed to get accredited, and no other information on their proficiency tests has been made public. Today, forensic scientists disagree on what form proficiency testing should take; whether it should be "blind," where the examiner does not know they are being tested, or "open," where it's known to be a test; whether it should be administered externally or internally, and whether the results should be made public or kept private. However, almost all forensic scientists agree on the importance of proficiency testing, most on the advantages of external scrutiny. "It's very easy to just get into a habit of doing things a certain way without seeing that there might be problems," says Richard Tanton, a crime lab director in Palm Beach and a former president of ASCLD. "It happened in our lab. ASCLD/LAB inspectors came in, made suggestions, and we made changes."[40]

The best indication of how crime labs have been performing since the 1970s comes from a fee-based voluntary proficiency testing program run by the Forensic Sciences Foundation and Collaborative Testing Services. Results of testing between 1978 and 1991 have now been published, and although direct comparisons with the previous testing are almost impossible, they remain alarming. Dr. Joseph Peterson, who categorized the results, concludes that "there were some areas of improvement and some areas that hadn't changed much."[41] Forensic identification of blood and drugs had improved but still showed errors. Comparative identifications of fibers, paint chips, glass, and body fluid mixtures such as semen all showed improper comparison rates of more than 10 percent, some substantially more. They were, in Dr. Peterson's words, "categories of serious concern." The new and growing area of explosives identification also seemed to be a problem.[42]

But improvement or not, was any error rate acceptable in a country that throughout the 1980s was resorting increasingly to capital punishment? And if the results of a lab's proficiency tests are not published, how can juries base their verdicts on results whose reliability is unverifiable? "It's one thing to argue about the acceptability of the science used, but what about the actual practice of that science? If they aren't doing it right —and all the evidence is that crime labs are not—what's the point of arguing about whether they should be doing it in the first place?" asks Professor Thompson. "If the lab results are wrong, they've no relevance to anyone's guilt or innocence."[43]

Occasionally, proficiency testing in one specialist area of forensic science exposes widespread incompetence. In 1995, Collaborative Testing Services tested 156 U.S. fingerprint examiners—the cornerstone of forensic science—in a proficiency test sponsored by their professional body, the International Association for Identification. Only 44 percent (68) of those tested identified all seven latent fingerprints correctly. Some 56 percent (88) got at least one wrong, 4 percent (6) of these failing to identify any.[44] In all, incorrect identifications made up 22 percent of the total attempted.

In other words, in more than one in five instances "damning evidence would have been presented against the wrong person," noted David Grieve, editor of the fingerprinters' magazine, the *Journal of Forensic Identification*. Worse still, examiners knew they were being tested and were thus presumably more careful and freer from law enforcement pressures. Calling for immediate action, Grieve concluded: "If one in five latent fingerprint examiners truly possesses knowledge, skill or ability at a level below an acceptable and understood baseline, then the entire profession is in jeopardy."[45] The same must be true of every suspect in the country, the vast majority of whom never get a fingerprint expert onto their defense team or any chance of a reexamination. Many crime laboratories routinely destroy fingerprint evidence.

It is clear that forensic science is massively error-ridden, while the flaws in the sole laboratory accreditation program designed to improve performance are obvious. ASCLD/LAB has no powers to regulate or inspect a crime lab or to stop a lab that has failed inspection from doing examinations in criminal justice cases. Many U.S. crime labs have never even risked inspection and the possibility of failing, most notable among them the one that bills itself the premier forensic science laboratory in the world—the FBI lab in Washington.

The FBI's reasoning for not applying for accreditation is much the same as that it gives for opting out of the national proficiency testing program after 1977: cost, pressure of work, and relevance. More recent variations on these themes have included casting aspersions on ASCLD/ LAB's ability to undertake an accreditation process for a forensic laboratory as large and diverse as the FBI's, or even insisting that since the FBI lab would secure accreditation easily there was no point in spending the time and money going through the process. In fact, as demonstrated in Chapter 1, internal memos have shown that managers at the FBI lab have known for years that the FBI lab could not meet ASCLD/LAB accreditation criteria. Practice, procedures, and even the plant at the world's premier forensic lab have been judged totally inadequate by the FBI itself.

The FBI lab could not publish its proficiency results for the same reason. Yet that has not stopped FBI lab managers from pretending otherwise, maintaining the image at the cost of the reality. In April 1981, the then head of the FBI lab, Thomas Kelleher, told a congressional subcommittee that the FBI's participation in the testing program of 1974– 75 had been "to see that we didn't appear to say, 'This is for everyone else but not for you.' "[46] He went on to imply that the tests were beneath the FBI's examiners. "The level of proficiency offered was far below that of the FBI examiners that were working in the particular areas of our laboratory."[47]

That was the official line. Most managers seemed to have known that the reality was rather different. More than sixteen years later and long since retired, Kelleher talked to the authors about the need for ASCLD/LAB accreditation or some other form of external oversight. "The FBI lab was always going to need the sobering influence of an impartial organization that says 'You might be big, but you're not great,' an organization that says, 'You'll only be big, if . . .' " He concludes, "After all, how do you challenge people to do better if everyone's always telling them they are the best?"[48]

It was a million-dollar question, not least because Tom Kelleher's successors at the FBI lab would spend years avoiding such external scrutiny. The FBI lab now does its own internal proficiency tests, the results and methods of which it has bitterly resisted releasing to the courts or the public, sometimes dropping cases rather than releasing data when ordered to do so by the courts. The following chapters illustrate why. A number of FBI lab examiners are incompetent and negligent and inclined to slant their results and testimony to ensure the most incriminating results, even if that means trampling the demands of natural justice. For years FBI lab examiners have worked in a lab highly vulnerable to contamination, and many have followed scientific protocols, if indeed they had them, only if they chose.

FBI lab managers have not only known all this for years but have also known the real significance of breaking some of the most fundamental rules of scientific practice. They have connived with both the incompetence of examiners, to prevent any possible embarrassment to the bureau, and with the bias in examination, because it ensured "results"— successful prosecutions that reflect well on themselves. A key part of this, maintaining the myth that this was the best forensic lab in the world, has always been blocking external scrutiny by ASCLD/LAB inspectors or anyone else who would expose that myth. For years, the emperor has indeed had no clothes. However, he could never be seen to be naked if the image of the FBI's crackerjack technosleuths, resolving every case presented, was to be upheld.

As the FBI lab came to dominate the crime lab profession and, by extension, forensic science in the United States during the 1980s and 1990s, the fatal flaw at the heart of the FBI would become more and more incongruous. As the FBI's research and training facility came to dominate forensic science research in this country during the 1980s, the laboratory division continued to employ and promote researchers and examiners who patently ignored the most basic scientific procedures and fixed results. As its own staff patently ignored ASCLD/LAB guidelines on documentation, record retention, and report writing, the FBI lab would exhort others to follow the guidelines in the pages of its periodical, *Crime Lab Digest*. Thousands of personnel from other crime labs would be trained by an institution that failed to train or supervise its own staff. Hundreds of crime lab managers from around the country would be trained by an FBI

Laboratory Division run by managers who failed to check examiner's work, ignored repeated complaints about sloppy or negligent work, and even promoted some of the worst offenders.

It was a scandal that kept on growing, affecting hundreds, maybe thousands, of lives. A scandal of atrocious forensic science that not only threatened to punish the innocent but to free the guilty. A scandal that demonstrated that J. Edgar Hoover lived on, that the FBI lab was unaccountable even to the rest of the FBI, let alone to Congress, the scientific community, or the general public. It was a scandal that when it finally broke would be all the more devastating as a result of years of pretense, denial, and face-saving, years of putting image before reality.

1

THE WHISTLEBLOWER VERSUS
THE FRIENDS OF LOUIE

"You must be Dr. Snyder. I'm Fred Whitehurst and this is my colleague, Terry Rudolph," said the brawny six-foot-two-inch FBI agent, stretching out a hand. "We're from the FBI lab in Washington. If we'd known we were going to be testifying against you we'd have brought a copy of your book for you to sign," Whitehurst joked. Dr. Lloyd Snyder, one of the country's leading experts on the identification of chemical substances and coauthor of a basic text on the uses of liquid chromatography, thought how unlike the normal FBI agent Fred Whitehurst, chemist and explosives-residues expert, seemed.

Indeed, the whole thing seemed a little bizarre. Here he was in May 1989 waiting to testify for the defense in the trial of Steve Psinakis, a man the U.S. government was accusing of plotting to ship explosives to the Philippines as part of efforts to topple the government of Ferdinand Marcos eight years before. Since the alleged offenses, Marcos had fallen, the opposition had become the government, and Psinakis, a Greek-born American citizen, had returned to Manila and been acclaimed as a Philippine Lafayette. However, on setting foot back in the United States, Psinakis had been arrested and indicted.

Now a subplot to this curious prosecution was about to emerge. For nearly three years, since shortly after being assigned to Terry Rudolph as a trainee in June 1986, Fred Whitehurst had been complaining with increasing bitterness to the FBI lab's management about Rudolph's sloppy work. Rudolph was the sole explosives-residue analyst at the FBI laboratory—examining the trace evidence left on debris after explosions. Yet Fred Whitehurst claimed Rudolph rarely did confirmatory tests, only occasionally ran standard tests for comparison purposes on the lab machinery, and never seemed to clean his workbench. Whitehurst was convinced that Rudolph drew conclusions that were not justified scientifically by the data from his examinations and seemed to relish having a work area that resembled a pigsty.

Rudolph's work in the Steve Psinakis case crystallized Whitehurst's worst fears. Although Rudolph had assured prosecutors that his explosives-residue examinations in the case were sufficient, and that his conclusions would stand up under cross-examination, Assistant U.S. Attorney Charles "Ben" Burch had doubts. Facing Lloyd Snyder as a defense expert, Burch tried to guard himself against potential disaster by retrieving the key evidence, including a knife and a pair of pliers, and asking Whitehurst, as the FBI lab's current explosives-residue examiner, to take another look.

Whitehurst found what he had come to expect from Rudolph. The lab report showed that a white powder recovered from the tools had been identified as pentaerythritol tetranitrate (PETN), a powerful, brisant explosive, by means of liquid chromatography. However, there was no mention of possible sources of PETN residue other than explosives, and no mass spectrometry or X-ray diffraction testing that would have confirmed the initial identification. Rudolph seemed to have reached a definite conclusion about the presence of PETN that was not scientifically justified by the tests conducted. He had also been incredibly vague about what he had done. His laboratory report dated February 18, 1982, stated that the tools had been "instrumentally examined." Whitehurst suspected the vagueness was deliberate. As Rudolph had told him while he was still a trainee: "The more cryptic the [lab] notes, the less chance the defense counsel has to question the results."[1]

Until you face a real defense challenge, that is. Although Whitehurst confirmed Rudolph's main result—tiny amounts of PETN had been
found, picograms, one millionth of one millionth of a gram—Whitehurst
was troubled. In Whitehurst's view, Rudolph was careless with evidence;
traces of explosives were probably everywhere in his work area. With no
background-contamination test against which to judge the result, such
tiny amounts could have come from anywhere. Despite Whitehurst's repeated complaints, there seemed to have been no check or monitoring
for background contamination since he arrived at the FBI laboratory
three years earlier.

Whitehurst had been pondering all this on the flight to San Francisco. If, under oath on the witness stand, he was asked about it, he knew
he would have to reveal his reservations. And briefed by Lloyd Snyder,
the defense lawyers were sure to ask the critical questions. But as he
mulled it all over, his dilemma deepened. Learning that the prosecutor
had called for Whitehurst's tests and now intended to introduce them
without consulting the court, Judge Robert Schnacke dismissed the jury
for the afternoon to determine the admissibility of the new evidence. He
was miffed and ruled against; Whitehurst would not testify.

Rudolph, meanwhile, was exposed at the evidentiary hearing, as
Whitehurst had imagined he would be. Asked why certain tests he was
describing were not in his notes, Rudolph replied: "When I examine a
case I put in my notes things that are important to me when I . . . give
testimony. I don't write my notes for the United States Attorney. I don't
write my notes for the defense. I write my notes for myself."[2] Questioned
further, Rudolph went on to say that he had done thousands of tests since
1982 and could not possibly remember them all. This prompted Judge
Schnacke to ask the obvious: "Isn't that one of the reasons you keep
notes?"[3]

The judge found some of Rudolph's assertions so absurd that he
seemed to hesitate about the admissibility of the testimony as a whole.
Rudolph insisted that he had relied on factors other than just his liquid
chromatography test in making his PETN identification. One of these
was his eyesight. The white powder from the knife and a known sample
of PETN "compared essentially identically" under a microscope. He implied that confirmatory testing took too long. Liquid chromatography
took a few minutes, whereas something like X-ray powder defraction, a

confirmatory test, would take forty-five minutes. In the end the judge allowed his testimony, insisting that if Rudolph persisted in being so positive about his confirmation he might have to intervene. "Even with the FBI, completion of all necessary processes in investigations is an awfully good idea," Judge Schnacke concluded.[4]

When the defense moved to exclude Rudolph's testimony because it offered an investigative rather than scientific opinion, Psinakis's lawyer raised a key issue: was Rudolph primarily an FBI agent or a scientist? Rudolph seemed to bolster his forensic certainty by citing his training as an FBI agent, a training that he implied gave him some special investigative insight, the defense claimed. It seemed to fall to the judge to make it clear. "He is entitled to tell the jury what he based his conclusion on," he announced dismissing the defense motion. "Some of these things may be a little strange for a scientist, but he will be testifying as a scientist, not an FBI agent."[5] Years later, following its own investigation, the inspector general's office was to agree. "Rudolph's approach represents a fundamental misunderstanding of the role of a forensic scientist," the report concluded. "At best, Rudolph's explanation for his opinion in *Psinakis* represents incompetence."[6]

Faced with all this, Whitehurst left the courthouse and went for a walk. It was a long one—nearly twelve hours. He had a lot to think about as he walked through Chinatown, down to the harbor, through the tourists thronging San Francisco's famous quays. An innocent man might get a long jail term on the basis of flawed science, faulty procedures, and possibly contaminated evidence. Should he, could he, would he, let it happen? Standing back was against Fred Whitehurst's nature. At seventeen years of age he had dived into a frozen lake to save the passenger of a car that had skidded off the road. In Vietnam, where he had distinguished himself by winning four Bronze Stars, he had once stopped a group of GIs raping a Vietnamese woman with a rifle muzzle. As he walked, he remembered the exhortation of John Burke, one his trainers at the FBI academy, back in 1982: "As an FBI agent you can't just stand there . . . you have to do something."[7]

Fred Whitehurst had always tried to do something, beginning a one-man effort to improve the FBI lab from the moment he arrived. Working weekends and evenings, he had set about calibrating machines, cleaning work areas, and even buying equipment essential to a modern forensic laboratory, often from government surplus. A gas chromatograph, hydrogen generators, a high-performance liquid chromatograph, fume hoods, Whitehurst installed them, repaired them, cleaned them.

The truth was that, starved of funds and scientists, isolated from the forensic science community, and convinced of its own infallibility, the FBI lab had fallen dangerously behind scientifically during the 1970s and 1980s. And not only in terms of machinery and manpower. As international protocols, policies, and standards emerged in both new and old fields of forensic science, the FBI found itself stranded on the sandbanks of its own presumption and arrogance. If you were the best, what could you learn from anyone else, even in a field moving so fast that the best could not keep up?

Pedantic, methodical, straight as an arrow, Whitehurst had quickly established himself at the FBI lab as a man who took the memos from the FBI's top brass exhorting employees to report all instances of "waste, fraud, and abuse" literally. But although he banged out complaints about racism, abuse of travel vouchers, and unauthorized leave on his desktop computer at home at night, his major grouse was always the science and state of the FBI lab. To him this was a black-and-white issue, not one of the dubious shades of gray law enforcement seemed to demand: "I just could not see why it was so hard to do it right, to bring the lab up to standard. Morally, it was just wrong not to try."[8]

A finicky scientist who took everything far too literally in the eyes of many of his colleagues, Fred Whitehurst was perhaps just the sort of man you would want handling your forensic tests if it was your life or liberty on the line. It was this conscience, this drive to do the right thing as he saw it, that drove Fred Whitehurst to seek out Lloyd Snyder again, the day after his long walk in San Francisco. Snyder was a chemist, a scientist, someone who would understand the significance of his reservations. Snyder, Whitehurst believed, would take action. He did—going straight to the defense team.

"I was really startled by what he said," Snyder recalls. "Your first thought really is, 'Why is someone in this position doing this? Is he some sort of weirdo?' "[9] In an adversarial judicial system, where opinions are formulated and positions adhered to sometimes in spite of the scientific evidence, most defense experts would have asked the same question. In the eyes of both the prosecution and the FBI, Whitehurst had committed the ultimate sin—disclosing what he viewed as exculpatory evidence to the defense without even consulting the bureau or the prosecution.

The government's case against Steve Psinakis quickly fell apart. To loud cheers from the crowded courtroom, he was cleared of all the charges. The prosecutors, Joseph Russoniello—himself a former FBI agent —and his colleague Charles Burch, felt let down. Within days, they had fired off an angry four-page letter to John Hicks, acting head of the lab. The acquittal raised "serious questions" about "the FBI laboratory's procedures," they complained.[10]

Building on Whitehurst's quite limited reservations, they pointed out that at both the scene of the crime and in the laboratory, agents had used the same set of cotton gloves to handle all the evidence seized at Psinakis's home, risking cross contamination. They pointed out that Terry Rudolph had relied on hearsay evidence from the case agent to help form an opinion as to what chemical residue was on the tools. "The FBI chemist is being asked to independently ascertain the existence of a substance, not just regurgitate information he has received from the field," they pointed out.[11] Burch and Russoniello noted that liquid chromatography was nothing more than a presumptive test that was scientifically inadequate to draw the definitive conclusions Rudolph had reported. Given this, why, they asked, had Rudolph's work not been reviewed by a peer or superior before it was deemed adequate to go to court? Why was there no protocol specifying what analytical-instrumental tests should have been performed to identify such trace elements?

The letter refused to criticize Whitehurst for drawing attention to the inadequacies of the laboratory's forensic science. Indeed, Burch praised Whitehurst: "He seemed to me to be a person who was sincerely concerned about the integrity of the judicial process and the FBI lab's role."[12] It was an extraordinary thing for prosecutors in this position to say. Whitehurst was an obvious scapegoat, yet Burch and Russoniello refused to shoot the messenger and deflect blame from themselves. Not so the FBI lab. If the prosecutors refused to blame Whitehurst, the Bureau did not.

Knowing that what he had done was a serious breach of FBI protocol, on returning to Washington Whitehurst made an immediate appointment with the head of the lab, Roger Castonguay, and told him what happened. An internal investigation by the Administrative Services Division into a self-confessed "improper engagement with members of the defense team" moved into gear. The ASD report acknowledged that Whitehurst's concerns were legitimate, but concluded that "the manner in which he articulated those concerns constituted an egregious display of poor judgment."[13] He should have raised his concerns with the case agent, the prosecutor, and laboratory management, not the defense, the ASD concluded, citing the FBI's rule book, the *Manual of Administrative Operations and Procedures*, specifically a section entitled the "Confidential Nature of the FBI's Operations."

Ignoring Rudolph's inadequacies and the lab's own management shortcomings, the issues Whitehurst had tried to focus on, James Greenleaf, the FBI's associate deputy director of administration, duly informed Whitehurst in October 1990 that he would be suspended from duty without pay for seven days and placed on probation for six months. Today Whitehurst displays the letter of censure as a sardonic badge of honor. Framed, it hangs alongside his Bronze Star citations from Vietnam in his modest wood-framed house in La Plata, Maryland.

An FBI gagging order still prevents Fred Whitehurst from discussing his actions in the *Psinakis* case. On the face of it, it was a strange case for which to break all the rules and risk his career. After all, Whitehurst had actually confirmed Rudolph's PETN results. His concern about possible contamination was just that, a concern. It was, in essence, speculation, something scientists are not supposed to engage in. Although he had helped highlight the other inadequacies of Rudolph's work in the case, in Lloyd Snyder the defense probably had the means to expose those inadequacies even without Whitehurst's help. Finally, Whitehurst had made similar complaints about Rudolph many times before, sometimes in cases in which he seemed to have much stronger evidence of wrongdoing.

But it was undoubtedly these previous complaints—and management's failure to address them—that were the key to Whitehurst's actions in the *Psinakis* case. By May 1989, when he testified, Terry Rudolph had left the lab, leaving what seemed to Whitehurst to be a ticking time bomb of inadequate casework—of which the *Psinakis* case was just one example. If nothing had been done while Rudolph was in harness, what chance was there that going through the proper channels—the lab, the prosecution, the case agents—would yield any results now?

Exposing what was going on in the FBI lab to real scrutiny was his aim, and Fred Whitehurst, over time, succeeded brilliantly as a result of his actions in the *Psinakis* case. First, in coming under a microscope in the San Francisco courtroom, Rudolph made some stunning admissions about his own work and, by extension, the whole culture of the FBI lab: laziness, broken machinery, working backward from the evidence as presented by case agents, unscientific conclusions, overstating results, failing to keep adequate notes, lack of protocols, inadequate supervision. Directly or indirectly, Rudolph admitted all these failings—all of which were now on the record. Worse, throughout his testimony Rudolph implied he was simply adhering to standard FBI lab policy in acting the way he had.

Second, in taking such dramatic action, Whitehurst set off a chain reaction of five audits over the next six years by FBI lab management of Rudolph's work. Each successive investigation being a reflection of the inadequacy of the last, the audits would ultimately not only vindicate Whitehurst's complaints but prove one of his main contentions—nothing would improve until the FBI lab was submitted to some form of external, independent scrutiny.

Convinced that it was the best, without any objective proof, certain that it made no mistakes, while refusing to publish the results of its own proficiency tests, the FBI lab was incapable of investigating itself. This was the Hooveresque world that allowed no room for errors or agent misconduct. Worse still, this was the Hooveresque world that had internal investigation systems dedicated to achieving precisely that—systems designed to ensure no significant wrongdoing was ever uncovered. That way no one, staff or management, was seen to commit the cardinal sin of embarrassing the Bureau.

By 1989, having watched the tour-guided visitors stream past his window for three years, having worked to the constant backdrop of the FBI's image building, Fred Whitehurst had begun to piece together this other picture, this other reality at the lab. In the contrast between the public face and the private reality, the lab was undoubtedly one of the last redoubts of undiluted Hooverism in the FBI. No accountability, no monitoring, managed by agents, not scientists—it was the sort of environment where abuses could thrive and no one told tales.

The lab always had been a secretive backwater, run like a "private club," according to Don Edwards, the former congressman and ex–FBI agent. From the moment Hoover had established the lab in 1932, housed in a converted lounge chosen because it had a sink, a succession of directors, including Hoover himself, had taken little personal interest, beyond the public relations value of the odd VIP tour. As a result, an all-powerful management had run its own show here for decades. Cloaked in the mystique of the science they practiced, buttressed by their steadily growing importance to crime fighters throughout America, the lab became unaccountable even within the FBI. "There was never a squeaky wheel at the lab. No one ever even came to me with a complaint, let alone an allegation of skewing results. Of the five FBI divisions I handled, the lab was the only one that never had problems," recalls Oliver "Buck" Revell, associate deputy director of the FBI from 1989 to 1991.[14]

This secrecy, unaccountability, and club atmosphere had long made the lab a perfect place for some of Hoover's personal operations and obsessions. It was in the FBI lab that Hoover had stored his obscene files, a mixture of pornography and intelligence or gossip concerning the sexual misconduct of public figures that would become the basis of his legendary ability to blackmail politicians and opponents.[15] It was here in the laboratory that technicians compiled and copied excerpts from the electronic surveillance tapes of Martin Luther King's hotel bedrooms before they were sent to King's wife, Coretta, with an anonymous threatening letter addressed to the civil rights leader himself.[16] It was here in the laboratory that Hoover stored the huge stonecutter he had ordered to help examine rock and shale samples, an anonymous source told the authors. The boss had wanted his vaunted scientists to tell him if he should make some speculative investments in companies tendering for oil prospecting rights out West.

But at some point it was inevitable that the gap between image and reality would start to close. Whitehurst's few words with Lloyd Snyder were a start; a snowball had started rolling. With Burch's letter in July 1989 it landed right on then acting FBI lab chief John Hicks's desk. "I share your concerns," Hicks replied to Burch. "And as a result of this matter, I have instituted an internal audit of the protocols used in the identification of explosives residues."[17] That did not actually happen, something that would come back to haunt the FBI lab in upcoming cases such as that of Roy Moody in the VANPAC investigation and the World Trade Center bombing. What actually did begin was a rather halfhearted audit, or rather, a series of halfhearted audits, of Rudolph's work that continued over the next six years.

In fact, the Terry Rudolph affair, Whitehurst's complaints, and Burch's letter were not the only indication that things were badly wrong at the FBI lab. Management knew it; their own inspectors were telling them so. Internal documents, memos, reports, and letters released under the Freedom of Information Act demonstrate that the kind of abuse Terry Rudolph was being exposed for at the *Psinakis* trial was quite common at the FBI lab. Much of what Rudolph was doing was, as he had implied on the witness stand, actually standard practice, not individual abuse.

About the time Whitehurst was suspended in November 1990, a study committee was set up to look at how practice in the FBI lab compared to that necessary for accreditation by ASCLD/LAB. It was part of the FBI's Total Quality Management program, a pet project of FBI director William Sessions, a private sector concept designed to eliminate wasted time and resources by getting employees to do things right the first time around. The committee looked at both the Laboratory Division as a whole and the individual units separately, and from March 1991 onward started to report back to lab director John Hicks. The findings did not make pleasant reading. On protocols, peer review, evidence handling, the checking of techniques or tests, the monitoring of expert testimony, error rectification, contamination prevention, safety, complaints procedure, proficiency testing, you name it, the FBI lab was woefully below par.

One memo, dated March 27, 1991, that was dispatched to John Hicks, his deputy, Matt Perez, and every unit chief summarizes the situation succinctly. The problem, it states, is twofold. In some units, policies and procedures have become "diluted, unofficially altered or ignored."[18] In others, policies and procedures were not even in place. Evidence handling was just one example. "If the Laboratory intends to improve its services and quality while truly insuring the integrity of the evidence submitted, it will be necessary to restate existing or implement new policies dealing with certain basic and critical procedures," stated the memo. "Believing that all Laboratory examiners were trained to follow the same standarized and court-accepted procedures, we were shocked to learn of the variety of ways in which evidence was logged, marked, or in some cases, not marked at all."[19]

The committee told John Hicks and the unit chiefs that some

examiners ignore "some of the basic tenets of handling evidence.... [M]ore often than not work space is left completely unattended and unlocked with evidence spread all over the tables and desk tops. Under the ASCLD guidelines, this practice is unacceptable." [20] The memo cited other issues of concern, such as access to the evidence, the trail of evidence through the lab, protection of evidence from loss, cross transfer and contamination, and proper storage. These were all issues that Fred Whitehurst had complained about for almost five years. The scale of the problem was reflected in the policies the committee had to propose to satisfy specific provisions of ASCLD/LAB standards, seven basic procedures on marking, sealing, and preventing contamination.

On technical procedures, the committee's basic findings were no better. In particular, the committee had problems with ASCLD provision 14211, which asked any lab seeking accreditation one of the most basic questions in forensic science: Whether new technical procedures were thoroughly tested to prove their efficacy in examining evidence before being implemented in casework? "The committee is of the opinion that this is not always accomplished in the Laboratory Division.... Frequently we believe that decisions are made to follow a procedure due to the lack of time and/or resources which might be required to properly evaluate the process. It is not until the examiner or the process comes under attack in the court that we recognize the problem created by our own failure to substantiate the work." [21]

The committee proposed that each lab section establish a peer review council, to which new ideas and methodologies should be subjected. They also addressed the basics by proposing that "every examiner and technician be made fully aware of their appropriate protocol manuals." [22] One trouble was, as a later memo, dated September 9, concluded, some units did not even have one. "After completion of the inspection phase of our internal study, it became clear that there was no consistency of manuals, from unit to unit. Some units have an 'administrative' manual, some have a 'protocol manual,' some have both as well as other manuals," the study group wrote, adding, "Manuals are a key element in establishing and maintaining quality control within the laboratory." [23] The committee proposed five manuals covering administration, protocol, safety, quality control, and training as a minimum for each unit. For those who did not even know what a protocol manual looked like they attached a helpful outline for the contents of protocol manuals prepared by the National Committee for Clinical Laboratory Standards.[24]

The committee also had problems with the FBI lab's blind proficiency-testing program, which it termed "weak and too infrequent." [25] Some units and specialties did no proficiency testing at all, it discovered. ASCLD/LAB rated its numbered provisions important, desirable, and essential, with labs having to score 50 percent, 70 percent and 100 percent in each category, respectively. With external proficiency testing anathema to the FBI lab, and likely soon to be upgraded from desirable to essential, the FBI lab had to address the issue, the committee warned.[26] Another problem was the monitoring of examiners' testimonies, already an "essential" item under ASCLD/LAB's accreditation terms. The memos make it clear that some FBI lab managers had proposed seeking a "waiver" of this provision, something the committee opposed.[27]

Despite these findings, the committee somehow concluded in September 1991 that the FBI lab as a whole could secure ASCLD/LAB accreditation if the issue of blind proficiency testing and the monitoring of testimony were resolved. Yet within days of stating this, the study committee sent John Hicks an apparently contradictory memo detailing how seven individual units had failed to implement protocol and evidence-handling policies the lab chief had approved as recently as May of that year.[28] Indeed, the whole process seemed flawed. The committee makes it clear that their assessment that the FBI could secure ASCLD/LAB accreditation was based on what unit chiefs had told them and the assumption that the policies, effectively corrective actions, approved by Hicks were in fact being implemented. "We did not attempt to . . . verify compliance," the committee noted.[29]

If that seemed like a whitewash, some in the FBI lab seemed to agree. In December 1991, James Mudd, an FBI ASCLD study committee member, observed an ASCLD/LAB inspection of another lab. He quickly realized it was far more thorough than anything the FBI had undergone. He told his boss, James Kearney, who memoed Hicks. What the study committee had done "lacked sufficient depth," he said. "A more thorough and in-depth self-evaluation, based on ASCLD/LAB criteria, should be undertaken by the Laboratory Division." [30]

The truth was that the lab was incapable of inspecting itself, not least because management did not appear to agree on the actual purpose of the inspection. Some seem to have seen it as a means of bringing the lab up to ASCLD/LAB standards and securing accreditation, while others seem to have seen it as a means of avoiding external scrutiny by being able to proclaim that the FBI lab now met those standards. Hicks told the IG that the lab had not sought accreditation during his tenure because of the costs and time required, that it was not essential, and because of "doubts by management whether the Laboratory needed to be formally accredited."[31]

Yet the main reason the FBI lab had done anything at all during this period was that external pressure was growing. Galvanized by the advent of DNA, the courts, Congress, and even a new quality assurance program, the FBI began to subject the FBI lab to increased scrutiny from 1989 on. The possibility of identifying individuals genetically heralded a revolution as significant as that brought about by fingerprinting a century earlier. Yet DNA typing was science—microbiology, genetics, and statistics—adapted from diagnostic and clinical laboratories, with their rigorous protocols, procedures, and research. When the forensic world started to use it without any such platforms or precautions, other scientists started to alert lawyers and legislators to the inadequacies of the crime labs' methods.

On June 26, 1989, Judge Douglas Keddie of the Yuma County Superior Court in Arizona ordered the FBI to release its open proficiency-test data, including all the raw material on which the results were based, for its DNA typing procedures. Judge Keddie decided that defense experts Drs. Simon Ford and Randall Libby needed them to prepare adequately for a *Frye* admissibility hearing.[32] On September 15, James Kearney, the laboratory division's section chief at the Forensic Science Research and Training Center, wrote to Ford to tell him the FBI was preparing to release the data as ordered, but six days later he had changed his mind.[33] Kearney furnished the results but none of the background material that would have allowed Ford and Libby to assess the subjective criteria on which the actual decisions had been made. The price was high: to avoid being held in contempt of court, the prosecution was obliged to withdraw all DNA evidence in the case.

This was not an isolated example. In several instances, when ordered to release the data underpinning its methodology the FBI refused. When it did release such data, particularly in the DNA sphere from 1989 onward, it was frequently found to be unscientific, flawed, and even downright false by a number of critical geneticists and microbiologists. Kearney himself seemed to know there were problems. In his letter to Simon Ford, he cited the self-critical analysis privilege, a provision of tort law that allows companies exemption from the legal threat of having to release potentially damaging information.[34] The theory is that the exemption will encourage companies or institutions to investigate safety problems or faults more thoroughly if exempt. The FBI seemed to be using it to protect rather than correct.

It was a fact Kearney seemed to admit when appearing personally before a court in Iowa in December 1989. In another effort to prevent the release of proficiency-test data he seemed to say that the defense might use the results of proficiency tests to "pistol-whip" laboratories.[35] One potential solution was simply to destroy proficiency-test records. On April 20, 1990, the FBI's legal counsel responded to an inquiry by John Hicks for "legal advice on the destruction of DNA proficiency-test records."[36] The nine-page memo recommended against this action on a variety of legal grounds: "Destruction at this point will forseeably invite speculation that the destroyed proficiency test data contained damaging information which discredits at least an examiner, or at worst, the process itself."[37]

In hearings beginning in 1989, Congress was being alerted to all this by a series of witnesses. One letter to Congressman Edwards cited the Arizona case and another in San Diego Superior Court, where the FBI had refused to turn over the raw data that formed the basis of the testimony of its testifying research chemist, Bruce Budowle.[38] The author, Jeff Brown, a public defender from California, contrasted this attitude to that propounded in a recent guest editorial by FBI director William Sessions in the *Journal of Forensic Sciences*.[39] Sessions had emphasized the need for scientific information to be carried from place to place, "passing it around at the speed of light," and had reminded his readers that science was a search for the truth.

"Judge Sessions might as well be heading up an entity different from the FBI, for the FBI's actual practices not only do not conform to its Director's principles, but are contrary to them," Brown wrote.[40] Why did the FBI have such problems submitting to external regulation or publishing its proficiency tests if it was adhering to its own quality assurance guidelines for DNA analysis, laid out earlier that year by James Mudd in the FBI's own *Crime Lab Digest*, Brown asked? Mudd had prescribed proficiency testing, independent external audits, and a strict adherence to federal, state, and local health and safety regulations as the means of quality control in crime labs, Brown noted.

In fact it was not until 1992, after years of advocating it for others, that the FBI lab even adopted a formal quality-assurance implementation program. Run by James Mudd, it was based primarily on the ASCLD/LAB standards for accreditation. Stuck down in Quantico at the FBI's research and training center, the program was for many a suitable distance away from the day-to-day activities it was supposed to monitor. Indeed, the whole thing was a ponderously slow business. It was 1993 before quality control coordinators for each unit in the FBI lab were appointed; it was November 1993 before they were all trained. Finally, as the program began to audit quality assurance in the lab by means of more internal inspections, it soon became clear that much of what had been recommended, endorsed, and dictated in 1991 had yet even to be implemented by the separate lab units.

In January 1994 John Hicks was forced to reissue a September 1991 memo to all unit chiefs ordering the establishment of the manuals covering protocols, safety, training, administration, and quality control.[41] By mid-1994, full implementation of a formal quality-assurance plan had been pushed back to December 1995—more than three years after Mudd had begun work on it. The truth was that management was either actively resistant or passively indifferent to any change at the lab, something that would become even more obvious under a new FBI director who seemed intent on an overhaul of the whole Bureau.

———

It was a dream come true. The U.S. flags rippled in the breeze, the band played good military marching music, and the crowd, mostly well-turned-out FBI agents, applauded on cue in the summer sunshine. It was September 1, 1993, and Louis Joseph Freeh, progressively FBI agent, prosecutor, and judge, the boy who had pretended to be J. Edgar Hoover when playing cops and gangsters in North Bergen, New Jersey, was taking the oath of office as director of the FBI. Now he could be the Boss for real; now he could be "J. Edgar Freeh," as his mother, Bernice, still kidded him.[42]

The insularity and abuses of power that had marked Hoover's reign were presumably what Freeh had in mind when he referred obliquely in his speech to "the failings of our past." In fact, the failings were hardly distant. In April that year the botched storming of the Branch Davidians' compound in Waco, Texas, by the Bureau of Alcohol, Tobacco, and Firearms (ATF) and the FBI had left eighty-three people, including seventeen children, dead. In July, an Idaho jury had acquitted the two men targeted by the FBI siege at Ruby Ridge, Idaho—"one of the worst law enforcement debacles of recent years" according to *The Washington Post*. Then, throughout the spring and summer of 1993, FBI director William Sessions had refused to resign, despite being found transgressing a number of ethical precepts by the Justice Department.

If Freeh wanted the job, President Bill Clinton and Attorney General Janet Reno wanted a white knight. Freeh had made his name as an FBI street agent infiltrating the mob in New York, fighting the organized crime Hoover had always denied existed. As a special prosecutor, handpicked by the attorney general, he had gone on to put away Walter Leroy Moody, a serial bomber whose victims had included a judge in Alabama in 1989. Freeh's reputation, track record, religious belief, and lifestyle all sounding, at times, too good to be true, brought instant credibility to the floundering Clinton White House.

But the assembled agents were no less delighted than their political masters. For the first time since the appointment of Clarence Kelley in 1973, a former agent was being trusted to run the Bureau. As a detached judge, an outsider, William Sessions, "the Director" as he had insisted on being addressed, had never really seemed to understand the Bureau. He had ended up a victim of what one FBI insider called a "palace puzzle coup." "Louie," as Freeh now insisted on being called, was, by contrast, coming home. "They [the agents] thought they had died and gone to heaven," recalled one congressional aide later. "They thought, 'Finally we've got one of our own. It'll be like the golden era when the Bureau ran the world.' "[43]

In his speech, Freeh emphasized the importance of going back to basics, catching crooks, putting more shoe leather on the streets. Mahogany row, the offices of the FBI's most senior officials on the seventh floor of headquarters, was the first to feel the impact. Most were called in to justify their jobs. Many did not manage it. Within weeks, the position of associate deputy director was abolished, top officials lost their special assistants, and the post of assistant section chief was liquidated. A major restructuring began with the ousting of Assistant Director G. Norman Christensen, the man who headed Sessions's Total Quality Management program, a scheme that had eventually included the new quality assurance program for the lab.

Within days, Freeh began to fulfill his pledge to slim the headquarters bureaucracy and beef up the field. One hundred and fifty agents were reassigned to local field offices in Baltimore and Washington in phase one; the same number in phase two. The shake-up did not ignore the laboratory. At least, it was not intended to. Louis Freeh's commitment to getting more agents back into the field dovetailed neatly with the GAO's thirteen-year-old recommendation to Congress that the FBI laboratory employ fewer of its expensive agents as examiners and more civilian scientists. At the end of 1993, Freeh proposed a radical plan to do just that. "He wanted to slash the number of agents in the lab from one hundred and twenty to fifty. Virtually all of them were senior people, the ones with responsibility for the examination of evidence or the supervision of the examination of evidence," recalls John Hicks.[44] "I proposed a plan to do it with one unit, Questioned Documents, as a sort of prototype. He wrote a note on the proposal asking why we didn't do it with all units and much faster."[45]

Having spent nearly twenty years fighting off external efforts to get agents out of the lab, management now found itself fighting one of its own. All the old arguments about the special qualities agents brought to forensic science were wheeled out, along with some of the Bureau's biggest guns. FBI staff had to act as both agents and examiners when they went out into the field; it took years to train new examiners and there was already a huge backlog of work at the lab; successive internal studies had proved the value of agent-examiners. "It was all so presumptuous. He moved far too fast and no one thought it through," insists Buck Revell, special agent in charge of the Dallas field office at the time and a former FBI associate deputy director with responsibility for the lab.[46]

With management objecting and dragging its feet, the program limped along. Some lab agents were happy to go, but others were not and could not be replaced overnight. But Freeh knew that successive directors' efforts at reform of the Bureau had been stymied by midlevel managers, career bureaucrats. Nowhere were they more entrenched than in the lab. Showing all his old streetwise wiles, Freeh did what he had begun to do on his endless trips to FBI field offices—appealed directly to the grunts over the heads of their officers. When he came to the lab, he eschewed much of the official tour to talk to some of the nearly six hundred employees directly, asking them to call him if they had any problems or suggestions. At least one agent did, wanting to discuss the reassignment program. Freeh asked for a memo on the issue, which was generally supportive of the new line. Freeh then called the agent at home to thank him.[47]

Ironically, management's forebodings proved justified. With recruitment to replace those reassigned slow and the average time served in some units, such as Questioned Documents, dropping from around fourteen years to three, the backlog of work at the lab, already considerable, soared. So did the complaints. In July 1994, in an effort to slow the ever-growing flow of casework, the FBI lab ceased to take evidence in property-crime cases from state and local law enforcement agencies. "Within months of Freeh's decision to reassign agents, things were just grinding to a halt," one former lab examiner says.

Replacing the old hierarchy was a new one, fourteen Freeh assistants, at least ten of whom were personal appointees. The new inner circle was headed by Chief of Staff Robert Bucknam, a former prosecutor with Freeh in the Southern District of New York. Bucknam's brother James came in to take responsibility for the sensitive issue of interagency relations. The new palace guard bypassed and replaced the "old boys network" as it had been known, earning a new epithet inside headquarters —"Friends of Louie." Lower down the hierarchy, Freeh followed the same principle, bypassing the normal channels and often ignoring the recommendations of the FBI's promotions board to bring in those he knew personally. Charges of cronyism were inevitable.

No one benefited more than two key players in the Moody case Freeh had prosecuted back in 1991. The first was Howard Shapiro, Freeh's number two in the Moody trial, who left Cornell University Law School to take up the newly created post of general counsel. Young, sharp, and ambitious, Shapiro became a sort of legal bodyguard and general sounding board on everything from the ongoing investigations of Fred Whitehurst's complaints to dealing with the Bureau's political bosses in the White

House and Justice Department. The second major beneficiary was Larry Potts, the FBI inspector in overall charge of the Moody investigation. Affable, direct, and very popular, Potts had been rewarded for his success against Moody with the position of assistant director, Criminal Investigation Division, in 1991. Despite coming under intense investigation for the Ruby Ridge debacle, Potts would become acting deputy director of the Bureau within fifteen months of Freeh's arrival.

Other Friends of Louie were entrenched lower down the hierarchy. Freeh's tour of the lab brought him back into contact with more than a few with whom he had worked closely in the past. Top of the list was Special Supervisory Agent James "Tom" Thurman, a bomb expert and principal examiner who within a year of Freeh's appointment as director would be promoted to head the fourteen-strong team that made up the Explosives Unit. Thurman's testimony on pipe bombs and explosions had been crucial to Freeh's successful prosecution of Roy Moody. A mustachioed, avuncular type, Tom Thurman looked the army officer he had been for most of the 1970s.

Thurman's interest in bombs—or improvised explosive devices, IEDs in military jargon—had begun as an officer commanding an ammunitions company in Korea. He had joined the FBI in 1977 and worked in the FBI lab since 1981, with the investigation of the downing of Pan Am Flight 103 over Lockerbie, Scotland, in December 1988 and the Moody case being the highlights of his career. His work on both incidents had brought him minor star status and not just in the quasi-military world of bomb buffs. In 1991, he had been profiled as the "Person of the Week" in the regular Friday night slot on ABC World News. "I love putting the bad guys away," he told the television crew, as he recounted in detail how he had traced the Lockerbie bomb back to two Libyan intelligence officers.

The "bombers," as the Explosives Unit staff were known, were a race apart even within the rarefied atmosphere of the FBI lab. In the first place, the Explosives Unit was relatively new, carved out of the Firearms-Toolmarks Unit in 1972, as terrorism and anti–Vietnam War bombings had increased. Second, the unit was small, seven agent-examiners and seven technicians. Third and most significant, the physical explosives examinations, crime scene investigations and bomb data identification that the "bombers" did were not scientific. The bomb unit made no pretense about this: "It's a dirty, sometimes dangerous job, and is based on learning from others," says Denny Kline, a former FBI explosives examiner.[48] Much of the job was based on test models, working out what damage any particular blast might do by reconstructing the bomb and the crime scene down at the range at Quantico, Virginia. "You learn by trial and error," says Chris Ronay, the unit chief Tom Thurman succeeded. "Although hopefully not too much error."[49]

The FBI's Explosives Unit handed all scientific analysis over to chemists, metallurgists, or technicians in the Materials Analysis and Chemistry and Toxicology units or even the Latent Fingerprint Section. However, it was the principal examiners among the "bombers" who made the decision as to what explosives evidence should go where and what the results meant in the context of the overall investigation. As such they would often interpret the results of others. It was a recipe for a culture clash—and more: The objective science of the chemist versus the subjective art of the bomb technician. The oral tradition of the "bombers" versus the written protocols of the scientist. The practical world of the explosives expert dealing with pounds of explosives and blast pressures in the debris of the crime scene versus the theoretical finesse of the trace analyst dealing with millionths of a gram of residue back in the clinical environment of the laboratory.

The nature of the job meant that pseudomilitary, nonscientific attitudes were entrenched in the Explosives Unit. Many were suffering from what one forensic scientist termed "testosterone poisoning." Dave Williams, the principal examiner for the World Trade Center bombing throughout 1993, the year Louis Freeh took over the reins at the FBI, was typical. A zoology graduate, he joined the Explosives Unit as a technician for five years before spending another five years in an FBI field office and returning to the lab in 1987. "I knew within two hours of entering the World Trade Center what type of bomb we had and how big it was," Williams asserted with the sort of arrogance and certainty that riled forensic science colleagues.[50]

The prominence and attention focused on the Explosives Unit and its staff was partially a reflection of the increased workload and importance of the cases they were handling. The World Trade Center bombing, Lockerbie, the ongoing Unabomber attacks—these were just the tip of a rapidly growing iceberg. Between 1985 and 1994 the number of bombings or attempted bombings in the United States nearly tripled to 3,163.[51] The crude efforts of white segregationists in the South in the 1960s and the anti–Vietnam War protesters of the 1970s had, it seemed, planted seeds in both the criminal underworld and the suburban mainstream. Bombs were easy to make, especially with instructions from readily available manuals such as the *Terrorists' Handbook* and the *Anarchists' Cookbook*. Power source, detonator, explosive—all these were everyday items in hardware stores, grocery shops, and farm supply outlets. Radio Shack was known as "the bombers' store" by the examiners in the FBI Explosives Unit. Everything you needed, bar the explosive, was on the shelf.

The Explosives Unit worked closely with the Chemistry and Toxicology Unit (CTU), the place where specimens were identified as one or some of the tens of millions of organic chemicals that literally make up the world. In some ways this was the core of the lab's Scientific Analysis Section. Virtually every piece of evidence involved chemical analysis, or what might be termed "molecular fingerprinting," at some point. Most of what CTU did was pure science, not just chemistry and toxicology, but biology, bacteriology, and even a bit of physics.

Drug analysis, poison identification, arson evidence, explosive composition—all such requests from the Evidence Control Center or other units found their way to CTU. As a result the unit had some of the lab's most sophisticated equipment—mass spectrometers, liquid chromatographs, gas spectrometers, electron microscopes. The escalating war on drugs and the proliferation of product-tampering cases in the 1980s had raised the profile of the CTU unit, bringing it national attention in celebrated cases.

The chemists and toxicologists had been led since 1989 by Roger Martz. Martz had spent virtually all his FBI career in the lab, having graduated from the University of Cincinnati in 1974 with a degree in biology. In the forensic science world, Martz was best known for his adaption of mass spectrometry to identify drug residues in human hair, a technique used in the prosecution of Washington, D.C., mayor Marion Barry for cocaine use. Energetic, trim, and ambitious, Martz was a confirmed, self-proclaimed Friend of Louie, displaying a photo of himself with the director in his lab office.

Their relationship went back to the Moody case, where Roger Martz, like Tom Thurman, had provided vital forensic evidence for one of Freeh's most celebrated prosecutions. "They both had access to Freeh, and he promoted that sort of personal association," says one former manager. "Once we were having some sort of anniversary celebration for Martz at the lab, and to our surprise Freeh just popped in." Indeed, early on, lab managers had high hopes for life under Louis Freeh, given his favorable experience of the lab in the Moody case. "We thought his relationship with Martz and Thurman would be a very positive thing for the lab," recalls John Hicks. "That's one of the reasons the pressure on rapid reassignment was such a surprise. It became a bit like working with a no-huddle offense. Things would happen and you just wouldn't know why."[52]

Roger Martz had testified as an expert in dozens of cases, some of which had made national headlines or even become books. One was the case of an elderly couple who disappeared at sea from their yacht, which was later found in the possession of a young couple. Analyzing a small amount of a white residue found inside a luggage trunk that had drifted onto a deserted beach, Martz managed to prove it had contained a body, enough evidence to prosecute the young couple for murder. Another case had been a pair of cyanide poisonings by means of adulterated Excedrin tablets in Washington State in 1986. Examining the contents of five bottles of the tablets, Martz quickly confirmed not only the presence of potassium cyanide, the poison, but some little green specks. They turned out to be particles of a rare algicide, a product Stella Nickell, the wife of one of the victims, had bought for her fish tanks and then crushed with the same mortar and pestle as the poison. Nickell was convicted of a double murder.

But old friends and recalcitrant management were not the only reasons the FBI lab came to Louis Freeh's immediate attention as he settled into the director's chair in room 7176. By 1993, Fred Whitehurst's complaints about the lab had reached the very highest level. In February 1993, just months before he was ousted, FBI director William Sessions had met twice with Whitehurst, on one occasion in the presence of David Binney, the deputy director, who stayed on under Freeh. It was decided at these meetings that his complaints should be referred to the FBI's Office of Professional Responsibility. But by 1993 Fred Whitehurst had begun to despair of the bureau's ability to investigate itself and was looking around for external help.

That same year Whitehurst approached Stephen Kohn and David

Colapinto, lawyers from the National Whistleblower Center, a nonprofit agency representing employees who blow the whistle on waste, fraud, corruption, or law breaking and are guaranteed protection under the Whistleblower Protection Act of 1989. In February 1994, Stephen Kohn would write to the FBI demanding a proper examination of Whitehurst's complaints by a special counsel or some other form of independent prosecutor to avoid any further conflict of interest. At about the same time, Whitehurst had started taking some of his complaints to the Office of the Inspector General (IG) in the Department of Justice, which had limited oversight responsibilities for the FBI. As a result, in October and December 1993, Whitehurst was approached and interviewed about his complaints by personnel from the IG when they were doing a routine audit of the FBI lab.

All this meant that Frederic Whitehurst and his complaints were one of Howard Shapiro's first big problems in his new job in the J. Edgar Hoover Building. Replying to Kohn, Shapiro stated that the FBI's new Office of General Counsel (OGC) would conduct an investigation itself. Two lawyers from OGC, Steven Robinson and John Sylvester, carried out the investigation, reporting back to Shapiro in May after interviewing Whitehurst and other lab staff and reviewing documentation from previous investigations. The authors have obtained a copy of this memo, albeit redacted. The OGC lawyers generally concluded that the lab had investigated each of Whitehurst's allegations fully and had taken appropriate action. The one exception was Whitehurst's complaints about Terry Rudolph. Robinson and Sylvester concluded that Rudolph's work would not withstand significant legal and scientific scrutiny and recommended that Material Analysis Unit chief James Corby do a complete review of Rudolph's casework—a review Corby actually had been advocating for years.[53]

The fact that the OGC investigation revealed nothing of Whitehurst's complaints about the alteration of reports or testimony by unqualified examiners and found no suggestion "that any Laboratory Division or other FBI components have covered up any past problems"— all activities later confirmed by the IG's investigation—was in itself an indication of what Whitehurst was complaining about. Yet there are interesting asides in the memo to Shapiro. One comment ran: "The QA/QC [quality assurance/quality control] Officer advised that the FBI would not meet miminal accreditation standards until changes are made in several areas of the LD [Laboratory Division]. . . . [I]t does appear incredulous [sic] that the premier forensic laboratory in the world is not accredited." [54]

Within days of the memo, a formal audit report from the IG at the Department of Justice was published. It was not a scientific audit, and its main informants were the lab's users, FBI field offices, and state and local law enforcement authorities. As such it could be expected to give the lab a clean bill of health. Yet even this sort of inquiry turned up major problems, confirming how little had changed in the three years since the ASCLD study committee had reported its findings to John Hicks. Once again, the IG audit made it clear that the problem in the lab was less the procedures and protocols, more the people and management. "It appears that the LD has acceptable QA/QC guidelines, but they have not been fully followed or enforced in some LD units," it concluded. [55]

Evidence control was, the audit admitted, a nightmare. The auditors examined 96 requests from a universe of 22,321, submitted in an eighteen-month period between 1991 and 1993. In eight instances, case-file documentation did not explain how and when requests, specimens, and results were routed among lab units. On this basis the auditors estimated that the case-file documentation for 1,861 requests, or 8.5 percent of the total, was incomplete. On the same sample basis, auditors estimated that the Evidence Control Center database did not list the number of specimens in 2,791 requests and that the database disagreed with the statistical sheet and the final report in some 1,396 requests. For four requests, Information Resources was unable to locate the case files or the case files were empty. On that basis the auditors estimated that the case files were missing or empty in 931 of the 22,321 cases, more than 4 percent of the total.

It was a frightening picture of chaos in the handling, tracking, documentation of evidence as well as record retention, all issues on which ASCLD/LAB inspectors place particular emphasis. But there were many other problems. The auditors discovered there was no open proficiency testing program in either the Questioned Documents or Latent Fingerprints units. In three other units, Firearms-Toolmarks, Materials Analysis, and Hairs and Fibers, staff were not being tested according to the FBI lab's own QA guidelines. In Firearms-Toolmarks the quality control coordinator who administered the tests was not himself being tested. Unit managers also interpreted the "twice a year" testing requirement to mean that two tests could be given on the same day, rather than every six months.

But corrective action on errors in proficiency tests was even more of a problem, according to the IG's auditors. Two units had no means of taking corrective action on errors made in proficiency tests, and managers in three other units were unaware of the corrective action measures contained in their own unit's QA plans. Faced with this negligence, in January 1994, John Hicks reissued the lab's own QA corrective action policies to all unit chiefs. The truth was that many in management at the FBI lab viewed proficiency testing as a motion to be gone through, not something designed to actually improve lab performance, correct errors, or ensure accuracy.

Documentation standards were also a mess, according to the IG auditors, despite new instructions going back to 1991. The auditors decided that requirements for casework documentation were not clearly established in four units, Explosives, Chemistry and Toxicology, Materials Analysis, and Hairs and Fibers. Managers in these units stated that documentation standards were unnecessary, notes and reports being needed only to serve the examiner in court, exactly what Rudolph had maintained in the *Psinakis* case, rather than assist any other examiner or external scientist trying to check or interpret those results. This view was upheld even by section chiefs, the lab's senior management.

Three years after the ASCLD study committee's checkup, two years after the quality assurance program began, nothing had changed to correct record keeping. And all this despite the fact that documentation of lab work to a sufficient standard to allow peer review from any quarter was a very basic ASCLD/LAB accreditation requirement. Lab section chiefs made the stunning observation to the auditors, again despite both ASCLD/LAB and the FBI's own quality assurance provisions, that reviews of examiners' work by unit chiefs "would be a duplication of effort."[56] In other words, there was no need even for internal review. The auditors were blunt in stating the obvious: "In our opinion, unless unit managers review workpapers in accordance with ASCLD/LAB standards, there is a risk that errors in the examiners' conclusions will go undetected."[57]

The OGC report and the IG's audit gave Howard Shapiro and Louis

Freeh an early insight into the real depth of the problems at the FBI lab. In June 1994, Shapiro sent John Hicks a memo asking for a plan to implement solutions. Hicks retired the following month, before replying. Freeh immediately appointed Milton Ahlerich to tackle the mess. Ahlerich was a bona fide Friend of Louie and, fittingly, considering the continuing preoccupation with image, came straight from the FBI's Public Affairs Unit, where the FBI's shine was burnished every day. Ahlerich had specific instructions from Freeh: improve quality assurance within the lab and actively pursue ASCLD/LAB accreditation.

A blizzard of directives from Ahlerich in the next fifteen months would attempt to enforce some measure of compliance with ASCLD/LAB provisions. In September 1994, the new chief issued a memorandum restating policies for case review, documentation, evidence handling, and safety. In January 1995 the lab adopted revised policies for blind proficiency testing. In February there were guidelines for standard operating procedures; in July came new policies concerning the preparation of case notes and the monitoring of testimony; in September, a new open proficiency-testing program and a new policy for the control of evidence.

The truth was that by then it was too little, too late. By 1995 what the lab and successive managements had sought to avoid for years— external scrutiny—was drawing closer. The logic of outside oversight was now unassailable. For years, FBI lab managers had insisted that their work was scrutinized in court under cross-examination. For decades that had rarely happened but now, with the advent of DNA typing, some judges were upholding requests for the documentation that made real scrutiny possible. Similarly, for years, FBI lab managers had insisted their internal proficiency tests ensured high standards. Yet now it was obvious from the IG's audit that even in units where proficiency tests were being performed, they were a sham.

Following the IG audit of June 1994, Whitehurst continued to write to the IG's office with complaints. His allegations that his lab reports had been changed set new alarm bells ringing. When interviews during the first half of 1995 confirmed that two other lab employees supported some of Whitehurst's allegations, the IG started discussing the possibility of a joint IG-FBI investigation. But the idea of any FBI input in such an investigation was effectively scotched by press attention. In August and

September of 1995, Whitehurst's allegations, including the charge that previous FBI investigations had been a whitewash, became public.[58] On September 18, the Department of Justice announced that the IG would conduct its own investigation, aided by a panel of scientific experts. That investigation would, eighteen months later, produce the IG's 517-page report, a full investigation of Whitehurst's charges.

As of December 1997, seven years after beginning the process of self-scrutiny designed to lead to ASCLD/LAB accreditation, the FBI lab has still not been inspected. "I'm really surprised it's taken that long," says former lab chief John Hicks.[59] Indeed, it is now known that the FBI lab may be unaccreditable. Even if the lab sorts out its protocols, procedures, and proficiency-testing problems, it may have an insurmountable problem: its location. Space, safety, and security concerns in the laboratory's area in the FBI's headquarters are such that the Laboratory Division currently may be breaking fire and safety regulations as well as compromising the results of its forensic examinations.

ASCLD/LAB accreditation criteria cover three areas. The first, laboratory management and operations, concerns planning, organization, direction, and control, including quality control, evidence control, and proficiency testing. The second area covers personnel qualifications in all the separate areas of forensic expertise. The third area concerns physical plant, which covers space, design, security, and health and safety in the laboratory itself. Even a cursory comparison of the ASCLD/LAB stipulations in the last category and the FBI lab's layout demonstrates what may be insurmountable obstacles.

As long ago as 1988 the issue of space, safety, and security were raising such concern at the FBI lab that officials called in the architectural and engineering firm Lee-Thorp Consulting Group of McLean, Virginia, to examine the problem.[60] They recommended relocation to a new facility dedicated solely to the laboratory. Nothing happened. In 1992, another study came to the same conclusion with the same nonresult.

It was not until May 1995, twenty months after he took office and with his problems with the lab mounting, that Louis Freeh went to Congress to ask for $150.2 million to construct a new lab at Quantico, Virginia, the site of the FBI laboratory's Forensic Science Research and Training Center. This was in addition to a more than 50% increase in the lab's annual budget of $60.5 million. Construction of the new lab is scheduled to be completed in the year 2000, more than twelve years after the FBI initially concluded it needed the new facility in a new location.

In fact, a new lab went on the Bureau's shopping list largely because by early 1995, in the wake of the Oklahoma City bombing, both Congress and the White House seemed determined to throw money at the FBI. Within days of the bombing, the White House had put together a $71-million special appropriation for the Justice Department and promised another $400 million in the 1996 budget. The chairman of the Senate Judiciary Committee, Senator Orrin Hatch, promised a similar package. It was in this context that Louis Freeh wrote a $1 billion wish list to take the bureau into the next century. The proposed new FBI lab and forensics spending was just one fifth of this.

In his testimony to Congress in support of the request, Freeh was quite blunt: "We have stripped away equipment, research, and development over the past ten years to make payroll, which is important, but we need some mechanics."[61] Ironically, the need to make a strong pitch for the money for a new laboratory meant the submissions to Congress had to make it clear how outdated and inadequate the current laboratory was even in 1988. Worse still, such submissions had to show that forensic work was being affected. "Recent safety inspections by the National Institute of Safety and Health and General Services Administration have identified inadequacies in the exhaust and ventilation systems which, again, are difficult or impossible to remedy in existing space. Evidence examination and storage facilities are inadequate, and, in many areas, not immediately accessible to examiners. Irreplaceable reference files and collections cannot adequately be secured," noted one paper.[62]

The document went on to detail difficulties with the fume hoods vented to the outside—hoods needed to examine items in a putrefied condition or for handling noxious and/or highly volatile chemicals and industrial-type solvents used in processing evidence.[63] The fume hoods could not be maintained, the FBI admitted, because the air-handling capacity of the building was inadequate. The FBI lab's "recycled air," rather than the "once-cycled air" preferred by laboratories, increased the risk of contamination, and the absence of "clean rooms," sealed areas to accommodate trace analysis away from bulk-evidence analysis, carried the same risks.

The use of new instruments in the lab could be compromised because they could not be ventilated or cooled properly, the FBI concluded. Apart from the potential danger to defendants in terms of incorrect forensic results, a series of dangers to those working in the FBI facility and even in downtown Washington were listed. The FBI appropriations submission states somewhat prosaically: "The explosive bunker in the basement is inappropriate in an office facility. . . . The shipment of hazardous and explosive materials to an office building located in a major urban area is inappropriate."[64] It was also noted that the disposal of waste chemicals into neutralizing tanks adjacent to office space was unsafe and that the indoor firing range used by the laboratory's Firearms-Toolmarks Unit and the office space next to it had become contaminated with lead.

Once again, such problems were well-known and had been widely reported years earlier. Fred Whitehurst had been raising safety issues for years; the IG audit of 1994 had noted major problems too.[65] On safety, the IG noted, there were, yet again, plenty of policies and rules—most notably the FBI's Chemical Hygiene Plan (May 1991)—but they were, once again, often ignored. Compressed gas cylinders were not labeled or stored separately; protective attire, such as lab coats, safety glasses, and gloves, seemed to be optional in many units. Chemicals with flash points below two hundred degrees Fahrenheit were not stored in "FLAMMABLE" storage cabinets as policy required. Indeed, three lab units had no such cabinets. The authors have learned confidentially of at least one fire that has occurred in the FBI lab.

Space was a key problem, compromising both the safety and integrity of examinations. Numerous individual units within the Scientific Analysis Section are in split locations. "Evidence must be transported through public access hallways. . . . Evidence processing rooms are crowded."[66] As the FBI document admits: "The current laboratory layout was originally designed with the interests of the public tour route foremost. The result has proven to be terribly inefficient through the years and poses significant problems attendant to security and unauthorized access to controlled space from the tour route."[67]

Behind the document's vague terms, such as "unsafe," "overcrowded," "inefficient," "difficult unit management," and "inadequate storage space," were specific pitfalls, some of which were made clear to us privately by lab employees. "It's not just that the lab fails to check for contamination, it's simply that in many areas it is just impossible to do so," says one. "Machines are so close together—or even on top of each other—anything could be there." Four people working in space designed for two inevitably increases the risk of commingling or cross transfer. "You could put a beaker down. Your colleague might then pick it. Before you know it, trace evidence has been transferred between you. It's all pretty high risk," complained another examiner.

Despite the squeeze on government spending and the trend toward balancing the budget, Louis Freeh has now secured everything on his $1-billion shopping list. The FBI's budget has risen by nearly half since Freeh took over, from $2.1 billion to $3 billion in fiscal year 1997. Spending on the FBI's Laboratory Division has virtually doubled in just three fiscal years, rising from $60.5 million in 1995 to $112.8 million in 1997. "So much for reducing costs by employing civilian scientists rather than agent-examiners," observes one former lab manager.

What has all this bought? Because more money has not been accompanied by any commensurate increase in accountability, the truth is, we simply do not know. There is absolutely no evidence that it has bought better forensic science or that a new crime lab will bring new attitudes, new approaches, or a new culture. In the past, all efforts to impose meaningful change or enforce some accountability in the FBI lab have failed. Compliance with everything from court orders to congressional exhortations that the FBI did not agree with has been minimal, begrudging, or nonexistent.

One thing, however, is clear. The soaring budget has increased the FBI's power enormously. A drift toward the federalization of law enforcement at home and the globalization of FBI activities abroad has been one important consequence that has been reported extensively.[68] In the forensic arena, as elsewhere, the equation has been very simple. More money equals more power—for investigations, for training, for personnel, for research. And it was, after all, the arrogance of power that got the FBI lab into trouble in the first place.

The budgets have soared, but not on the condition that the FBI lab put its own house in any sort of order or, even more important, address the underlying causes of the problems, in particular the culture and attitude that pervades the lab. The money has poured in before any mechanisms to ensure radical improvements—and to monitor their enforcement—are in place. The risk is obvious: given all the circumstances, pumping more money into a fundamentally flawed organization may only serve to reinforce those flaws and their impact. That, as the remainder of this book shows, is a frightening thought and a very dangerous development.

2

THE UNABOMBER: CLUELESS

What is most remarkable about the Unabom case is not that the FBI appears to have gotten their man. Rather, it is that it took so long and in the end only happened as a result of a tip-off. When in early April 1996, an FBI agent and a Forest Service official knocked on the door of a 10-foot-by-12-foot plywood cabin on the edge of Scapegoat Wilderness in western Montana, it looked like another masterful piece of detection by the G-men. As the two, helped by another FBI agent who had been hiding nearby, wrestled briefly with their unkempt suspect amid the wood smoke and smell of drying clothes, the longest, most expensive manhunt in U.S. history seemed to have been brought to a successful conclusion.

Theodore Kaczynski was soon charged with being the Unabomber, the shadowy "mad genius," as the press had dubbed him, who had mailed or deposited a total of sixteen bombs over eighteen years. This unlikely looking fifty-three-year-old, with his torn jeans, graying beard, and little more to his name than a gearless bicycle, a .22-caliber hunting rifle, and the small plot on which his shack stood, was the most wanted man in

America. Kaczynski was a ruthless bomber who had killed three and injured and maimed another twenty-two, the government charged.

The suspect had been a particular embarrassment for the FBI. A keen letter-writer, the Unabomber had taunted the feds about their inability to track him down. He had used a nine-digit code and the letters FC on his more recent bombs to ensure his Improvised Explosive Devices (IEDs) were attributed to him and him alone. "It doesn't appear the FBI is going to catch us any time soon. The FBI is a joke," the suspect(s) had concluded in a letter to *The New York Times* less than a year before the stakeout and arrest at the small cabin, five miles west of Lincoln, Montana.[1]

On the face of it, state-of-the-art technology had played a big role in tracking down a man whose professed motive for bombing had been the destructive effects of science and the Industrial Revolution. From the high-power eavesdropping devices used before the arrest at the remote Rocky Mountain cabin, to the Unabom Internet Web site the FBI task force had created in 1995, the hunt for the Unabomber seemed to cross new thresholds in sci-crime detection. Here apparently was a wonderful juxtaposition. On the one hand, an isolated hermit tapping out his anarchist philosophy on a manual typewriter and recording his daily hunting or vegetable gardening with a ballpoint pen. On the other hand, there was the FBI's computerized ten-thousand-name database at task force headquarters in San Francisco and the detailed analysis of the Unabomber's IEDs based on the FBI lab's painstaking reconstructions in Washington.

Yet it was not sophisticated forensic science or state-of-the-art technology that had led FBI agents to Lincoln, Montana, and Ted Kaczynski's shack. It was actually the oldest sort of assistance, a human source. In September 1995, *The Washington Post* and *The New York Times* had decided to print a thirty-five-thousand-word manifesto written by the Unabomber, in the hope that the bombings would stop or more leads would emerge. Ted Kaczynski's younger brother, David, a social worker in upstate New York, had recognized some of the wording and phraseology.

Some of it was too close for comfort. "You can't eat your cake and have it too" was a phrase their mother, Wanda, a second-generation Polish immigrant had used when they were growing up in Chicago during the 1940s and 1950s. It appeared in the manifesto and in a letter from

Ted, as the family knew him. Later David would find papers that seemed to be early drafts of the manifesto when clearing out the family house in Evergreen Park, Illinois. Indeed, by the time the FBI actually was called in, the Kaczynski family had virtually solved the case for them, hiring one of the country's premier private investigative agencies. A psychiatrist, a linguistics expert, two specialists in cultural communications, and a retired FBI behavioral specialist had all strongly suggested the Unabomber was Ted Kaczynski before the FBI even got a phone call.

In fact, much of the FBI's own investigation had been a mess. Forensic evidence had been lost and misinterpreted. Turf wars between the FBI, the Bureau of Alcohol, Tobacco and Firearms (ATF), and the U.S. Postal Inspection Service had diverted energies from the main task. Disputes and disagreements among FBI personnel had been common, nowhere more so than between the psychological profilers and the agents, those who dealt with the hard evidence of witnesses, victims, and debris versus those who dealt with what many regarded as the pseudoscience of intuition.

Even the FBI's sting and the aftermath were botched. Press leaks forced the G-men to arrest Ted Kaczynski before they were ready. According to David and Wanda Kaczynski, FBI agents misquoted witness statements to help secure their search warrant for the shack; the Kaczynskis eventually filed to exclude some of the evidence seized.[2] Constant leaks after the arrest reportedly drove FBI director Louis Freeh to distraction, but as The Washington Post noted, raised the question of whether the authorities were "using the media to convict Kaczynski in the court of public opinion—and, not coincidentally, burnish the FBI's image after years of setbacks and scandal."[3]

On the other hand, things were not quite what they appeared with the suspect either. If he was the Unabomber, Ted Kaczynski was not quite the antiscience Luddite he had proclaimed himself. In fact, he was a product of the world of science. A former assistant math professor with a near genius IQ, it was his scientific methodology and attention to detail that had been largely responsible for enabling him to stay at large since the middle of Jimmy Carter's presidency. By leaving no clues—scratching trade names off batteries, using only old fuse wire, sanding his bombs down so that he left no fingerprints—and targeting a broad range of targets—academics, executives, stores, and even an aircraft—in jurisdictions from Connecticut to California, the Unabomber had spread the FBI's investigation very thin. He seemed almost invisible, and perhaps invincible.

By the mid-1990s, the Unabomber had been around so long that he had seen off a number of the original law enforcement officials who had begun the hunt for him in 1978. Many had been transferred to other duties or retired frustrated. One such was Chris Ronay, the head of the FBI lab's Explosives Unit and the FBI lab's principal examiner (PE) on the Unabom case for nearly a decade. On his retirement from the FBI in September 1994, he reflected the general lack of leads and hope when he told the press that he thought the bomber might never be caught: "You have to find physical evidence, or someone has to tell you where to look. If he doesn't give us anything and luck doesn't intervene . . . I don't see on the horizon anything leading to him."[4]

The contents of the shack the FBI now began searching overcompensated for the lack of hard evidence over all those years. It was such a treasure trove that the authorities immediately considered airlifting it by helicopter to somewhere more accessible. A thirty-three-page inventory the FBI was ordered to release later listed some 569 items. It included bomb-making components, a partially completed bomb, ten notebooks full of bomb sketches, and papers detailing pipe-bomb experiments, plus a manual typewriter that seemed to match the typeface of that on which the manifesto had been written.

On the shelves of the shack were many of the raw ingredients of bomb making: cans, bottles, and plastic containers of potassium nitrate, copper sulfate, sodium chlorate, lead chloride, ammonium nitrate, sulfur, silver oxide, and iron oxide, mostly marked by their periodic formulae. The containers showed a meticulous attention to detail, in the form of notes to the user about the purity of the contents, which were often homemade. "$BaSO_4$ may be contaminated with a little $MgCl_2$ and smaller amounts of $MgSO_4$," said one label. "Na_2CO_3 from Red Devil lye. Should be reasonably pure if Red Devil lye is. (No not very pure)," read another. As Louis Bertram, a former member of the Unabom task force, told the press: "This cabin was not a home. It was a fully-equipped laboratory."[5]

The humble cabin may, in fact, have been better equipped and more effectively manned as a lab by Ted Kaczynski than the FBI lab was by those hunting him. For the story of the Unabom investigation at the FBI lab is a forensic nightmare. In the eighteen years that the Unabomber haunted the Bureau, the lab repeatedly lost documentary evidence, failed to do the tests that might have been expected to generate leads, and then covered up the fact that things had been botched. Eventually, an FBI lab internal audit of the explosives-residue analysis of Unabom attacks by Steve Burmeister, an explosives-residue expert working with Fred Whitehurst, would reveal that much of the data on the evidence was simply missing.[6]

The main culprit was Terry Rudolph, the subject of Fred Whitehurst's original complaints about the FBI lab. Steve Burmeister's audit of the six Unabom cases Rudolph had examined in the ten years that he was the lab's senior explosives-residue analyst would prove two things. First, Rudolph's inadequacies in the *Psinakis* case were not an aberration. Second, Rudolph's legacy did not leave the FBI lab when he did to take up a teaching appointment at the FBI's Forensic Science Research and Training Unit at Quantico, Virginia, in 1988. The effects of Rudolph's work lingered dangerously in case after case.

Indeed, in the eight years following his departure, Rudolph's work and methods would cause so much controversy that they would be subjected to the scrutiny of seven separate inquiries. Many of these investigations would be the direct result of a woefully inadequate previous investigation. For each time Rudolph's work was found wanting in some way, FBI lab management would ignore the findings as well as the causes —namely, lack of scientific protocols, an abysmal record-filing and retention system, and woeful supervision of staff by management. Thus, as they strove to avoid embarrassing the bureau, management managed to ensure that eventually, that is precisely what they did.

Burmeister's audit of the Unabom cases raised serious issues about the government's forensic case against Theodore Kaczynski. Without work notes, charts, or details of how the evidence had been processed— all omissions repeatedly noted in Burmeister's audit memo—the evidence linking the bombs to the contents of Kaczynski's cabin or indeed to each other might not have stood up in court. Without full analysis of all the explosives residues identified, confirmatory tests, and sufficient data to support the stated conclusions—features missing from several files in the series of attacks—the eighteen-year search for Kaczynski might have proved to have been in vain.

But the lab's internal audit raised another frightening question: How long might a successful conclusion to this massive manhunt have been delayed by such sloppy forensic work? Had leads, so few and far between for so many years, been overlooked? Had the FBI lab's incompetence and negligence had an indirect hand in the killing and maiming of victims, rather than in bringing their assailant to justice? Even if, as in other cases, the FBI lab protested that the inadequacies of its own forensic investigations had had no adverse impact on the case, how could anyone be sure? Above all, how could something like this happen, not once, but repeatedly, and not in any old case but in the most expensive manhunt in U.S. judicial history?

The answer was the management and culture in the FBI lab. The reaction to Burmeister's audit was the same as the reaction to the investigations spawned by Whitehurst's complaints. Nothing was done. Indeed, Tom Mohnal, the principal examiner on the Unabom case who actually commissioned Burmeister's audit, claimed he never saw the critique until over a year later. When he did, he went to lab chief Milton Ahlerich, only to be told to write a response to Burmeister's charges. His memo, completed in October 1995, was little more than a defense of Rudolph's work. Once again, answering the charges, rather than dealing with the problem, became the objective. It was not until the inspector general, spurred on by Whitehurst's complaints, investigated the whole saga that the real sorry story emerged.

————

Terry Rudolph, a man with a Ph.D. in chemistry and extensive experience in private industry, had qualified through the FBI's examination and moot court system as an explosives-residue analyst in December 1978. It was less than a year before a loud implosion and toxic fumes forced American Airlines Flight 444, a Boeing 727 en route from Chicago to Washington, D.C., to make an emergency landing at Dulles International Airport. Chris Ronay, one of the FBI's leading explosives experts, recovered a nearly intact homemade amateur pipe bomb, made from a juice can and enclosed in a wooden box and mail packaging. Terry Rudolph was quickly asked to examine its contents.

Ronay's was a crucial recovery. The device, demonstrating many of the Unabomber's bomb-building techniques, would allow the FBI lab to make the link with two earlier IEDs and start a hunt for a serial bomber.

Both previous devices had been deposited at Northwestern University in Evanston, Illinois, in May 1978 and May 1979. The first was a postal package left in a parking lot, the second a bomb in a cigar box left between study cubicles. In all three devices, the loop switches were the same; the initiators, made from lamp cord, similar; the wooden dowels and filaments, almost identical. Everything in the American Airlines bomb—wire, screws, can, wood, hinges, nails—everything except the batteries and low-explosive powder had been used before or had been handmade. From now on, the FBI lab would know the suspect as "the junkyard bomber," the man who recycled everything.

The airline bomb also demonstrated another Unabomber trait: in the crafting and design of the device, the bomber had put in a lot of fail-safe devices. A cheap barometer had been converted into an altimeter switch with a piece of metal designed to stop the needle and close the electric circuit as the cabin became pressurized. But in case the bomb did not go off in midair, a pull-loop switch ensured that the electrical circuit would be closed and the bomb would go off when the lid on the box was lifted.

Reviewing the files of Terry Rudolph's work, Steve Burmeister wrote in his 1994 audit memo that Rudolph's findings indicated that smokeless powder was removed and that smokeless powder and match heads had been identified. However, there was no data in the files to review and no information on how the evidence had been processed, he noted. Mohnal, having spoken to Rudolph, added to this minimally in his later memorandum. Smokeless powder had once again been identified by the vague terms Rudolph had used in the *Psinakis* case—"physical observable characteristics" and "instrumental technique."[7]

Even this inadequate elaboration seemed improbable. Interviewed by the inspector general's investigative panel in 1996, Rudolph could not recall what instrumental technique he had used and could not explain the absence of any charts relating to such tests. Rudolph added that when the work was done in early 1980, there was no set protocol for identifying smokeless powder.[8] So much for the first big break in the Unabom case.

The next device Rudolph examined was the Unabomber's fifth, a shoe-box-size pipe bomb in the now traditional handcrafted wooden box left in a business studies classroom at the University of Utah in Salt Lake City on October 8, 1981. Again it should have yielded vital clues, having failed to go off and been dismantled by John Wooten, an ordnance disposal technician from a nearby army base. Incredibly, after X-raying it, the ATF ruled it a hoax, meaning Chris Ronay and the FBI lab did not even hear about it until April 1982. When he did, Ronay had no doubt. The components, Ronay said, bore the marks of having been put together and taken apart repeatedly. "It's not just that he's creating something carefully. He's played with it for a while. He marks things with numbers so he can put them together again right. He's leaving a little of himself at each crime scene."[9]

As a result of the delay, Terry Rudolph did not file a lab report on the explosive analysis until thirteen months after the discovery of the bomb. Once again, when Steve Burmeister looked back into the file in 1994 he found no data to review or indeed any evidence that any work had been done by the FBI lab at all. Tom Mohnal agreed there had been no tests on the unconsumed smokeless powder, although instrumental analysis of a powder found in the debris of the IED "determined it was composed of a match-type formulation," something the ATF had determined more than a year before.[10]

Rudolph later suggested to the inspector general that he might have done X-ray powder diffraction testing to look for potassium chloride, the combustion product of matches. But it was only a suggestion. As he told the IG in something of a contradiction given the inadequacy of his testing: "Even by then, I mean, Unabom was a pretty big case, so, I mean, we were doing a reasonably thorough job looking at those kind of specimens. So, I mean, that typically would have been X-ray."[11] Rudolph's work was not, however, "reasonably thorough" enough to include proper documentation of any test. The IG concluded that Rudolph's answers to them "strongly suggest a lack of competence." They added: "His work is of little value if the files do not document the basis for the stated conclusions and Rudolph must rely on his uncertain memory of what he 'probably' did in the particular case."[12]

Two days before Independence Day in 1982, Diogenes Angelakos, the vice chairman of the department of electrical engineering and computer science at the University of California, Berkeley, was badly injured in the face, hand, and arm when he picked up what looked like a can in a tiny faculty coffee room in Cory Hall. The pipe bomb, suspended in an innocent-looking gasoline container, had the trademark wooden handle linked to loop switches and lamp cord. The only difference was the batteries, D-cell this time, and a note, enclosed inadvertently perhaps: "Wu—it works! I told you it would—R.V.".

In his review of the files on this case, Burmeister noted that Rudolph did some ion chromatography tests in an effort to identify chemical components of the explosive residue left by the bomb. However, he complained that no standards tests had been run on the machine for comparison purposes, that some peaks on the charts used to identify substances were unidentified, and that no confirmation tests had been done. Rudolph had, as a result, failed to identify potentially key chemical components, such as sulfate. Once again there were no notes or data in the files to establish how smokeless powder was identified and no records of comparisons with that found in other Unabom IEDs.

Rudolph complained to the inspector general that this was all standard practice at the FBI lab and that it violated no protocol. "It was not uncommon not to have a standard in the file and it was not uncommon not to identify those peaks. I mean, I just run the chart and throw it in there. I mean, I'm going to be the only person that's going to identify them."[13] Rudolph claimed that his expertise made confirmations unnecessary. The failure to identify sulfate and other substances? It was "not significant in my view," Rudolph insisted several times. It was an extraordinary defense that he later amplified: "The fact that I didn't mention chloride. I didn't mention potassium. I didn't mention ammonium. That was not significant in my view." A key chemical component, maybe more than one, had been missed by the examiner. How were comparisons of Unabom IEDs ever going to be possible if everything that was in them was not even identified?

For more than three years, the Unabomber was silent. Then, as if thumbing his nose at the FBI and the university authorities, he struck the same target again, Berkeley's Cory Hall. On May 18, 1985, John Hauser, an air force pilot and aspiring astronaut studying electrical engineering, picked up a small white box in the computer lab, topped by a three-ring binder, all bound with an elastic band. When he lifted the binder, Hauser sustained the worst injuries yet in the series of attacks. He lost parts of several fingers and partial vision in one eye. He was quickly hospitalized with a hole in his right arm and two severed arteries.

This bomb was more devastating because the Unabomber had substituted the relatively low-powered smokeless powder for his own blend of explosive charge, a mixture of ammonium nitrate and aluminum powder. However, Rudolph did not allow this curious new development to be the beginning of a hunt for new leads. Steve Burmeister noted no confirmation test for ammonium nitrate, no confirmatory test for aluminum, and no tests for organic explosives by means of organic extraction, a method of isolation by means of dissolution in solvents. Rudolph later claimed that organic extraction during residue examination was not part of the FBI lab protocol in 1985. Burmeister disputed this, pointing out that Rudolph himself had written a paper published in 1983 advocating it.[14] Rudolph told the IG that the 1983 paper was a "suggested guide for inexperienced examiners."[15]

On June 13, 1985, the ninth known Unabomber device was found in a corner of the mail room at the fabrication division of the Boeing aircraft company in Auburn, Washington. If it was unusual in that it was not addressed to anyone, it was all too usual in design—a paper-wrapped wooden box containing a pipe bomb. The local bomb squad that dismantled it revealed that it had two spring-driven sticks fashioned as pop-up switches and D-cell batteries. The lab quickly identified it as a Unabom IED with another ammonium nitrate–aluminum main charge.

Chemically the bombs were becoming more complex—and more deadly—but Rudolph's testing hardly kept pace. Burmeister's main complaint this time was that Rudolph had found potassium sulfate and jumped to the conclusion—without confirmatory testing—that the device contained black powder, a key combustion component of which is potassium sulfate. Rudolph insisted that Burmeister was "dead wrong," resorting once again to his personal experience. "There is no chemist I know that when they're dealing with pipe fragments, explosives-type residues, if they don't find potassium sulfate, would not make a finding of black powder," Rudolph told the IG.[16] However, the IG's scientists decided that it was Rudolph who was dead wrong: "As we have observed earlier, an examiner's subjective or impressionistic 'experience' is no substitute for scientifically valid procedures."[17]

Two weeks before Christmas 1985 the Unabomber claimed his first fatality. Leaving his computer rental store, Rentech, in Sacramento, California, one evening, Hugh Scrutton bent down to move what looked like a bundle of wood with protruding nails. The resulting explosion tore through his chest, exposing his heart, killing him. The deadly extra power owed much to the bomber's latest design modifications. This was three pipe bombs in one, each exactly the same length fitting into each other concentrically, like Russian dolls. Each end of the pipe was now fitted with a steel rather than wooden dowel and fixed in place by steel pins. The thicker the containment pipe, the more gas pressure buildup during ignition and the stronger the resulting blast. Once again the device boasted the wooden box, the D-cell batteries, the lamp cord, and in the rubble, apparently designed to withstand the blast, the hand-carved letters, FC.

Burmeister's review of Rudolph's chemical analysis followed as familiar a pattern as the bomb's design. "Data not complete and hard to review, no confirmations," he concluded on looking at the files.[18] The significance of the presence of sulfates had been glossed over again and ammonium nitrate residue had been identified on two specimens without confirmatory tests. The peaks on the ion chromatography charts were also unlabeled and thus could not be matched with specimens. Admitting all this to the IG, Rudolph's cavalier attitude was unchanged: "This [the unidentified peaks] is nitrate and sulfate, and I would know that. I'm going to be the guy testifying to it." Later he added: "Nobody ever told me that, you know, fifteen years later I was going to have a review, that people needed to know in the review what those things were."[19]

What damage had been done to the investigation and how, if at all, could it be repaired or limited? Surely Rudolph's work might impugn or at the very least raise serious questions about all the forensic work done by the FBI lab on the Unabom case. Indeed, might it not completely derail the government's case against the fifty-four-year-old mountain recluse, Theodore Kaczynski, if only by means of a technicality? How could such evidence, or lack of it, be presented in court? How could the chemicals in the mountain shack in Montana be linked to the residues or explosive mixtures in the bombs if Rudolph had not filed positive identifications of them in the first place?

Burmeister put it all in a nutshell, when the IG's investigators asked him about his concerns. "If, in fact, this stuff goes to trial, where each one of these cases are brought out and Terry has to go and testify. . . . I'd just love to run and hide my head underneath a rock for the days that he's on the stand," Burmeister said. "If you have a good defense attorney who knows what he's looking for, he's going to tear it to bits. . . . He has nothing to take and show [to a jury]. . . . [H]e had no way to support that he's done [the work] properly."[20]

By mid-1993, the Unabomber had been silent for more than six years. The bureau had been as puzzled by his silence as they had been by his attacks. Was he in jail for something else? Was he dead? In a mental hospital? Or had he just given up? The psychological profilers at the FBI's Academy at Quantico were not optimistic. They believed he had simply gone to ground. His twelfth attack in Salt Lake City, Utah, six years earlier had been a close call. On February 20, 1987, a secretary at CAAMS, Inc., a computer store at 270 East 900 South in Salt Lake City, had seen a man deposit a white canvas bag beneath the wheel of her car in the parking lot. When the secretary yelled to a colleague to come to the window, the man looked up, stared back briefly through a pair of aviator sunglasses, and ambled away. "Nice butt," the secretary joked before the phones rang and the two moved away from the window and back to work.

When Gary Wright, the owner of CAAMS, parked the company service truck an hour later he stumbled across the bag that, with bits of two-by-four boards protruding, looked like a road hazard. There was a huge explosion, which tore into his face, arms, and legs. He survived. But from the incident, the first known sighting of the Unabomber, a composite drawing emerged. He had a thin, light mustache and, although wearing sunglasses and cloaked in a hooded sweatshirt, he seemed to have a ruddy complexion, blond or light brown hair, and a square, jutting jaw. The eyewitnesses, working with the police, put his age at twenty-five to thirty and his height at five-feet-ten-inches to six feet.

The composite went out across the country. For the first time, the Unabomber seemed to have slipped up. The FBI's psychological profilers proved to be right—the result was that he simply hid himself for a long time. Then, in mid-June 1993, he struck twice in two days. Maybe it was losing the limelight to the World Trade Center bombing investigation or the FBI's standoff at Waco; maybe he sensed the hunt for him was being wound down. Whatever, he announced his return by going back to his tried and trusted method: mail bombs.

On June 22, 1993, geneticist Charles Epstein lost several fingers and was injured badly in the stomach by a package bomb mailed to his home in Tiburon, California. Two days later, David Gelernter, a Yale University computer science professor, staggered into the university health clinic bleeding profusely from an arm, the chest and the stomach. He had lost part of his right hand, the hearing in one ear, and the sight in one eye after opening a package containing what he thought was a dissertation.

The resumption of the attacks just served to underline the fact that the FBI was nowhere nearer catching their man than they had been fifteen years earlier when the bombings started. Posted with the parcel bombs from Sacramento, California, was a letter to *The New York Times* making sure the FBI knew who was responsible and enclosing a numeric code for future reference. The taunting sent the authorities into proactive mode, the Justice Department announcing a million-dollar reward and establishing a telephone hot line—1-800-700-BOMB—for tips. Within days, the FBI was ordered to coordinate the establishment of an inter-agency task force based in San Francisco. Within weeks, as Director Louis Freeh took over the Bureau, the Unabom task force became a top priority. FBI managers were instructed to give its chief, FBI inspector George Clow, everything he needed—"the sharpest agents, the latest computer hardware and software, the fastest lab work." [21]

Terry Rudolph had left the lab in 1988, leaving Fred Whitehurst, who in turn had trained Steve Burmeister, in charge of explosives-residue analysis. Chris Ronay, now Explosives Unit chief, had given way to Tom Mohnal as principal examiner on the Unabom case. As the new team looked over the remains of these latest devices, it quickly became clear that the bombs were of a new order of sophistication. Copper-tube pipe bombs filled with low-explosive powder, both bombs came in rough-hewn, homemade wooden boxes glued to the inside of padded envelopes. The bombs used electrical wire, nine-volt batteries, an improvised switch, and a hot-wire initiator. Both devices were booby-trapped. When the package was opened, the spring tension applied to the switching mechanism was released, completing the electrical circuit and causing the hot-wire initiator to ignite the main charge.

In July, the FBI lab's Explosives and Structural Design units reconstructed the bombs. The devices were handcrafted, yet the bomber was certainly self-taught. Wood experts said his carpentry was unskilled, the birch, cherry, walnut, and even mahogany that the Unabomber seemed so attached to showed rough chisel edges and indentations. Metal experts said his soldering was lousy and he seemed to be casting his own aluminum for some of the components. That in itself was dangerous and could cause explosions, the lab warned the task force. Yet although rough-hewn, investigators believed the construction of the bombs was a meticulous labor. In one brainstorming session on the case, Chris Ronay was asked to estimate how long the devices took to build. "Ten hours. But I think he took hours more to make it," came the reply. "I think he gets some gratification or satisfaction in creating and manipulating these bomb components."[22]

The case was now big, and the analytical role more vital than ever. The FBI lab's main role in the Unabom investigation had always been to do comparative work, tracing similarities between devices and methods. From this they had drawn up a checklist of methods and techniques, what the FBI Explosives Unit's experts had come to call a "signature." "A signature is a sort of descriptive term for uniqueness," says Chris Ronay. "We use it as a contraction for the opinion of the expert that features of the bomb are so unusual they are not repeated singularly in other devices, and when you see them collectively they are unique."[23]

The concept of a signature, which might include such features as the way a bomb was wired, the way a bomber soldered the connections, the way holes were drilled, etc., was ultimately the only way the FBI's explosives experts had of attributing all the bombs to one person or group. Yet, unlike the chemical analysis of the contents of a bomb, which could be definitive if, unlike those of Terry Rudolph, they were thoroughly performed, a signature was a highly subjective judgment based on opinion rather than science. Even explosives experts had great difficulty describing the concept to others. Signatures were, in any case, often evolutionary. "If you took the first Unabom and the last you wouldn't be able to relate them. They're completely different," notes Chris Ronay. "You need to see them all to track the evolution."[24]

Copycat attacks or even coincidental design similarities in the thousands of bomb attacks logged at the FBI's Bomb Data Center expose the limitations of the signature concept. Similarities were always a strong possibility, especially over the length of time the Unabom investigation ran. "I'm pretty sure we got all the Unabom devices, but we had at least a couple of copycat devices with the letters FC thrown in during the investigation. In fact, I think some of those cases actually remain unsolved today," recalls Chris Ronay.[25]

It was as part of the intensified effort to generate more investigative leads in the hunt for the Unabomber that Tom Mohnal asked Steve Burmeister to review the files on previous Unabom attacks. Thus the devastating critique of Rudolph's work emerged. What became clear as Burmeister trawled through Rudolph's investigations of the six attacks between 1979 and 1987 was that the sort of comparison, the sort of chemical tracking of the Unabomber so essential to a full profile of the suspect, was precisely what Rudolph's inadequate forensic analysis made impossible.

Terry Rudolph seems to agree that chemical profiling could be very significant in the effort to build up an overall picture of the bomber. "It's one link in the case. . . . [I]t can be important, yes," he states.[26] Others agree. "Unexploded IEDs can be like a gold mine," said one explosives expert. "All kinds of things can be mixed in with the main charge. It may just be debris that can give you a good lead or it may be part of a witches' brew of explosive material that can be very personal to the individual."

Rudolph could not have known how important evidence from the early attacks, perhaps by a less skilled, less wary Unabomber might turn out to be. Neither could he know that the fairly low-grade early devices built around match heads would by December 1985 have developed into a three-pipe device that would kill. The truth was that the relatively low-key investigation he worked on in the late 1970s had by 1994 become the biggest manhunt in U.S. history, precisely the reason preservation of the evidence, meticulous recording of examinations, and scrupulous attention to detail were essential in every case.

By the time the inspector general's report investigating the scandals at the FBI lab was published, Kaczynski had been under arrest for more than a year. Yet despite Burmeister's 1994 critique, apparently little or nothing had been done to address his complaints. On April 15, 1997, the day the report was issued, a Justice Department spokesperson told the Associated Press: "We concluded that a qualified explosives examiner should review all of Rudolph's work on Unabom before it is used further in the case."[27] On page 302 of the report, the inspector general recommended that the FBI do precisely that—have a qualified examiner take another look.

Robert Cleary, the lead prosecutor in the case against Kaczynski, saw the potential impact of all this and immediately went one step further. On the day the IG's report was published he announced that he had already told the Justice Department that the prosecution "would not be relying on any of Rudolph's work in the UNABOM case."[28] One report said Cleary went further, stating: "To the extent that the government will offer explosives residue evidence in the Kaczynski case, it will be relying upon conclusions of non-FBI experts."[29]

What the IG report did reveal was that management had known for years about the inadequacy of Rudolph's work and its potential significance in hundreds of cases. It also showed how many in lab management had struggled hard to avoid a real investigation in which those consequences might be fully assessed. The IG report chronicled how, following Whitehurst's complaints about Rudolph's work in the *Psinakis* case, a series of audits, or rather halfhearted audits, had begun. What they would reveal was not only the incredible scale and truth of the allegations Whitehurst had been making about the inadequacy of Rudolph's work, but the complete inability of the FBI lab to investigate itself.

In 1989, Jerry Butler, Rudolph's former unit chief as head of the Materials Analysis Unit was mandated by Ken Nimmich, the head of the lab's Scientific Analysis Section, to review Rudolph's work in the *Psinakis* case. His final conclusion was telling: the analytical procedures Terry Rudolph had used were "weak" but were also "laboratory accepted practice in 1982."[30] Butler, himself a former explosives-residue examiner, then proceeded to review Rudolph's work in two hundred other cases. In a memo dated August 2, 1989, he listed insufficient notes, missing charts, and weak analytical procedures as the most prominent of "numerous administrative shortcomings." Alarmed by the "potential serious impact these types of weaknesses could have on the proper administration of justice," Butler recommended an in-depth review by an examiner from the Chemistry and Toxicology Unit (CTU).[31]

Unit chief Roger Martz, a nonchemist, got the job. He seemed to disagree fundamentally with Butler. Having reviewed ninety-five of Rudolph's cases, Martz found no technical errors and concluded in an

August 1989 memo to Nimmich that chemical, instrumental, or physical analyses were performed in all the cases. What Rudolph had done was sufficient to "base an opinion as to the results that were provided," the CTU chief concluded.[32] However, when interviewed by the IG investigators in 1996, Roger Martz reversed himself, admitting that he did not look at the "sufficiency of Rudolph's work to support his stated conclusions." He claimed that 10 percent of Rudolph's files lacked any notes at all and said that he told Nimmich orally that Rudolph had done a poor job of documenting his analysis and only "the very mimimum work to come to a conclusion."[33] Thus Martz's original conclusions in 1989 were not only misleading but grossly overstated—two of the very deficiencies he had been mandated by Nimmich to review in Rudolph's work.

During the IG interviews it became clear that Nimmich and Martz could not even agree on what one had asked the other to do. Indeed, the only thing that seemed clear was that there was no consensus about the definition of chemical, instrumental, and physical analyses among those doing the reviewing. With no apparent questions asked about the discrepancy between Jerry Butler's findings and those of Roger Martz, Ken Nimmich closed the investigation of Terry Rudolph's work. After all, three successive unit chiefs had rated Rudolph's case management "superior" or "exceptional" for five successive years. Challenging that assessment would be to dispute years of management's judgment.

By November 1990, as Fred Whitehurst began his week's suspension for unauthorized contact with Lloyd Snyder and the defense team in the *Psinakis* case, the incongruity and injustice of the situation was clear. As Whitehurst saw it, he had been punished for finally raising his concerns outside the FBI, largely because no one inside would listen or take action. Rudolph, the guilty party in his eyes and the cause of all his concern, meanwhile had been absolved. As Fred Whitehurst saw it the messenger had been punished, the guilty absolved, the symptoms covered up, the causes ignored. The week at home gave Whitehurst the time to write another long memo of complaint with a whole new list of allegations about Terry Rudolph and the lab.

As a result, in early 1991 the FBI's Office of Professional Responsibility (OPR) began another investigation. In addition to the repeated complaints about Rudolph's examination methods and practices, Whitehurst now alleged that Rudolph had lied to the prosecutors in the

Psinakis case and that he had admitted committing perjury on the witness stand during one case in the Southwest, testifying falsely that his initials were on a piece of evidence. According to Whitehurst, Rudolph told him that the incident was a measure of the lengths an FBI agent-examiner should be prepared to go: "[B]efore you embarrass the Bureau, you should be willing to perjure yourself." [34]

The OPR investigation quickly concluded that there was no substance to Whitehurst's allegations. Yet they failed to do even the basics, such as interview the prosecutors in the *Psinakis* case or check FBI records to determine when and where Rudolph had testified in the southwestern United States. In August 1996, John Dietz, the agent responsible for reviewing the evidence collected, was asked by the IG if he thought just asking Rudolph whether he had perjured himself, then asking a few other examiners in the lab whether they had heard of the incident, was sufficient. He replied: "Well, at the time it must have been . . . that must have been my conclusion." [35] Did he feel differently now? "Well, in retrospect, in light of things that have come to light, possibly." [36]

But if OPR was busy burying the allegations, Materials Analysis Unit chief Jim Corby was busy verifying most of them. Instructed to review a representative sample of Rudolph's cases because the OPR lacked the technical expertise to do so, he confirmed the full gamut of abuses in two hundred cases. Rudolph had repeatedly failed to follow his own explosives-residue protocol, had come to conclusions with no scientific results to draw on, had failed to run standard or confirmatory tests on the machines. He had offered opinions to "fit" the incriminating theories of investigators or other lab units, failed to label charts, and where data made assessment possible, had sometimes made technical errors, Corby concluded.

Corby felt so strongly about what he had found that he recommended strong disciplinary measures, including censorship, suspension, and probation. He further recommended the banning of Rudolph, by now out of the lab and teaching forensic investigation at Quantico, from participation in any explosives-related program or research. Nimmich, worried at the implications of what Corby had exposed, ordered a panel consisting of CTU chief Roger Martz, CTU examiner Lynn Lasswell, and Jim Corby himself to review the cases to see if any errors needed to be referred back to prosecutors or defense attorneys.

In the end the only referral back came from lab director John Hicks. Nimmich's final memo to Hicks stated that the panel had found "marginally acceptable records" in more than one hundred of the two hundred cases reviewed and that fifty-seven of these had "incomplete or missing documentation."[37] Nimmich recommended that Rudolph receive a severe reprimand. Just as Nimmich had diluted Corby's disciplinary suggestion, Hicks diluted Nimmich's. On May 18, 1992, Rudolph received what he described as "a mild chewing out" from Hicks, who at the same time handed over a five-hundred-dollar check as an incentive award for a recent good performance.[38] Even Rudolph was surprised. He had expected and thought he deserved a letter of censure, he later told the IG's investigators.

Once again the investigation raised more questions than it answered. If nearly one-third of the two hundred cases studied were inadequate, what of the hundreds of others Rudolph had worked on during more than a decade at the FBI lab? Why were no cases referred back? How could the three-member panel, Nimmich, or Hicks be sure that miscarriages of justice had not taken place, based on files that were incomplete? Why was there no effort to reeducate Rudolph on his failings, on the basics of forensic science, indeed, on scientific practice itself, especially as he was now teaching others at Quantico?

Ordered to improve the case files from memory or from notes filed away in personal drawers, Rudolph proved that his old mentality and methodology had not changed one iota. What he was being asked to do was, he claimed in a memo to John Hicks, only what an examiner might do anyway before going to court. Rudolph termed it "sprucing up the file," labeling, clarifying, and adding to the original findings, although there was apparently no obligation at the lab to note and date these additions as nonlab FBI case agents were required to do when they made changes to a case file. Asked to place a standard memo in each lab file documenting that changes had been made, Rudolph resisted. That would, he said, "only serve as a red flag in any future defense subpoena."[39] Inhibiting the defense rather than documenting scientific truth still seemed to be the overriding objective for Terry Rudolph.

Corby was far from happy. He believed his review had revealed the true extent of the problem. He was convinced there would be repercussions in court sooner or later, which, if they demonstrated the inadequacy of the internal investigations, would eventually be far more embarrassing to the Bureau than admitting any mistakes now. Besides, there was the ethical consideration. Rudolph's work raised serious questions about the reliability of the evidence the FBI was presenting and thus possibly the guilt or innocence of those being prosecuted. Throughout 1993, Corby continued to press for a comprehensive review through James Kearney, who in 1993 replaced Nimmich as section chief. But John Hicks, the lab chief, concluded the Terry Rudolph matter was closed.

In February 1994, Whitehurst's attorney, Stephen Kohn, wrote to the FBI reiterating various long-standing allegations, including those against Rudolph. Federal law dictated an investigation, completed in the spring of 1994 by John Sylvester and Steve Robinson, two lawyers from the FBI's office of general counsel (OGC). One conclusion of the OGC team was that none other than Jim Corby should undertake a final, more comprehensive review of all of Rudolph's cases. Such a review would "most likely reveal they [the cases] are sloppy and that his [Rudolph's] conclusions are not supported by the appropriate documentation," an OGC memo concluded.[40]

Sylvester recalled that the Laboratory Division, led by John Hicks, was "furious" at the thought of another review.[41] The issue that so many in FBI lab management had tried so hard to bury was back like a ghost. The best they could do was slow it down. They did. It would be more than a year—June 1995—before Jim Corby got the go-ahead to begin the comprehensive review of Rudolph's work that he had been advocating for years. By then, many of the managers likely to be in the firing line— Chris Ronay, James Kearney, John Hicks—had left the FBI lab.

Jim Corby finally got specific written instructions for his review, in itself a major development. All Rudolph's cases, more than 650 of them, were to be classified into four groups. Category one was to be all cases sufficiently complete. Category two was to be all cases that were "administratively incomplete," lacking labeling of charts and notes but containing "enough documentation to support the stated conclusions." Category three was to be cases that were administratively and technically incomplete, lacking sufficient documentation, notes, charts, graphs to support the conclusions drawn. And category four was to be cases that contained omissions or technical errors.

On November 30, 1995, Jim Corby reported his conclusions. He had placed 20 cases in category four, 137 in three, 76 in two, and 421 in category one. Corby concluded that 24 percent of Rudolph's cases, those in categories three and four, "did not meet the administrative or technical guidelines at the time the cases were worked."[42] But a complete picture was even worse. Include category two, cases that were "administratively incomplete," and it was clear that Rudolph had failed to keep adequate records in nearly 36 percent of his cases. The findings were a ticking bomb, or rather dozens of ticking bombs, at the heart of the FBI lab. In Corby's opinion, all 157 cases in categories three and four "would not be acceptable under close judicial scrutiny, or past or present peer review."[43] In other words, the FBI lab was vulnerable to defense challenges, appeals, maybe acquittals in any of these cases that might have come to trial.

In his report, Corby listed all the now familiar complaints about Rudolph's work while highlighting further deficiencies. In particular, Rudolph often failed to report results that might have been significant in the overall context of a case. In claiming that he could judge what was significant, Rudolph was in effect setting himself up as judge and jury, ignoring potential evidence as he saw fit. This was precisely what Burmeister had complained about with his failure to test for potassium sulfate in two of the Unabom cases.

The inspector general's report itself added another concern, one Whitehurst had raised: contamination. During an IG interview, Rudolph admitted most of what Whitehurst had alleged. He did not always wear gloves in the lab, place paper on his workbench when doing examinations, take contamination control swabs of his work area, or swab himself down before entering the lab on his return from the FBI's explosives range at Quantico. He admitted that a messy work space was his trademark, joking at one stage with IG investigators that his former professor had told him that if his work area was clean and tidy he knew he was not busy.

Another issue the IG raised was file management and retention at the FBI lab. Rudolph claimed he kept the files for many cases in his own filing cabinet because he did not trust the FBI Records Division to be able to recover individual files when he needed them. Rudolph recounted how when preparing for one particular trial in 1984, Records had been unable to locate the file. With the prosecutor threatening to subpoena the record keeper and his flight to the trial due to leave in three hours,

Rudolph went up to the records room. "There were actually several piles of files taller than this room that were unfiled. . . . I mean there was stuff coming out—stuff on the floor."[44] Having eventually found his file, Rudolph said he decided to keep the files of "his" cases.

The dire state of the filing system was confirmed by the lab's ex–section chief, Ken Nimmich, who said he found it impossible to know how much of Rudolph's missing documentation was attributable to the examiner and how much to the filing system. "Examiners in the laboratory have gone to court to testify without the case working notes because they could not be found in the files," Nimmich told the IG.[45] The former section chief said he had advised Rudolph to look to see if there were staple holes on worksheets or reports, to send out search slips to see if charts that should have been attached had been returned to the file, or inquire whether "somebody had found an envelope somewhere else."[46]

Missing documentation was certainly common at the FBI lab. The IG's investigators got direct experience of it themselves in both their 1994 audit and their 1995–96 inquiry, when files they asked to inspect could not be found. The scale of some of these losses were staggering. When the IG discovered that Wally Higgins, an Explosives Unit examiner, had been altering Fred Whitehurst's lab reports, the Records Division was unable to locate twenty-one of the relevant reports. They were just missing. Moreover, it could have been willful tampering. The system was completely insecure. Although it would be "improper," the FBI admitted to the IG, an employee could have removed reports from files.[47]

The IG inquiry also raised the issue of dealing with employees like Rudolph. In 1988, some in management seem to have thought that they could resolve the Rudolph problem by what was referred to by some at the lab as "rustification"—sending him to teach at the Forensic Science Research and Training Center at the FBI Academy in Quantico. The IG report noted that some witnesses stated that Rudolph had been "punished" by being transferred to Quantico. "Rudolph, however, told the IG that he requested the transfer and viewed it as a promotion, which is consistent with the relevant FBI records," the IG states in a footnote in its report.[48]

However, what the IG did not report is what Steven Robinson, one of the two OGC lawyers who conducted the spring 1994 investigation into Rudolph, told them. In a record of an interview Robinson gave the

IG, obtained under the Freedom of Information Act, Robinson said he got a "general understanding" from interviewees in the lab that Rudolph had been transferred because of his poor work. Robinson, who by the time he spoke to the IG had left the FBI, stated this would never be a matter of record. "That's not how the Bureau works. There will be the official record and what everyone knows [to be the true reason]," he explained.[49]

Robinson went on to recount how the FBI does not document poor work performance but transfers poor performers to other duties. The interview notes record Robinson relating how such employees are told that they are not performing well, and the employee responds by requesting a transfer, which is granted. He added that, as in the Rudolph case, the transfer may even be a promotion. Many transfers because of poor work are in fact to headquarters, where the lab is, and Quantico, where the Forensic Science Research and Training Center is, Robinson stated.[50]

Robinson's revelations raised serious issues. What he was alleging might be a crucial explanation for the poor quality of management at the FBI lab and their inability to make basic scientific judgments. Promotion of examiners like Rudolph, with no real grasp of the fundamental principles to which the lab should have been adhering, would help explain why the FBI lab was in such a state. Such a promotional system was likely to compound and reinforce problems rather than resolve them, with those who proved incompetent, or toed the line in hiding such incompetence, rising to the top.

Sending Terry Rudolph to teach would similarly compound the problem. Hundreds of examiners from crime labs all over the United States were from 1988 onward being trained by someone who clearly did not understand the basic principles of forensic science and whose work would ultimately be labeled incompetent, inadequate, and sloppy. A little insight into what bad practice might be perpetuated came when Rudolph was asked at the evidentiary hearing in the *Psinakis* case in May 1989 how he could remember what tests he had done without taking notes. Rudolph said he used his work in the *Psinakis* case as an example in his teaching. It was a case study of nothing more than how not to run a forensic case—being used in classrooms.

The lack of any assessment of the damage done to the Unabom case by Rudolph's work highlighted the limitations of the inspector general's investigation of the lab. Their mandate was to look into Whitehurst's charges, and although Whitehurst had made general, wide-ranging allegations about Rudolph's work, he often did not know the details of specific cases. Furthermore, Whitehurst also reported, as hearsay, what he had been told by colleagues, many of whom were too intimidated to make complaints themselves, he insisted. This would allow critics to claim he made wild allegations, although all too often the substance of what he alleged proved to be too true.

The investigation by the IG in the Unabom case was only prompted by Whitehurst's allegations about an article Tom Mohnal published in *Crime Lab Digest* in July 1994. Whitehurst claimed the article contained false information and that the lab's management should have addressed Burmeister's concerns about Rudolph's work in the case before publishing it. Whitehurst further claimed that Burmeister was rebuffed by Mohnal and Chris Ronay, the head of the Explosives Unit, when he attempted to raise those concerns.

These were strictly limited charges that the IG could not substantiate. Yet what they uncovered in investigating them was actually far more important: the evidence against a suspect in the country's biggest manhunt to date had been so mishandled by the lab that the prosecutor considered it unusable in court. Although Burmeister's review of Rudolph's Unabom work was studied by the IG, it was only to assess it against what Mohnal had written in his October 1995 memo refuting as many of Burmeister's findings as possible, at Rudolph's behest. Through no fault of the IG, its limited mandate meant that the real issue went uninvestigated.

As a Ph.D. graduate in analytical chemistry, Terry Rudolph had little excuse, except, as he kept insisting to both the IG panel and the authors in subsequent conversations, that he did not believe he had actually broken any rules. There was some truth in this assertion. There were virtually no rules, no written scientific rules at least, to break at the FBI lab. Rudolph was insistent and—in contrast to many—refreshingly honest about this: "I would have lived by those rules they kept referring to if those rules had been in place at the time."[51]

Moreover, the few rules, procedures, protocols, and standards that were in place during the 1980s were often not enforced by a shockingly negligent management. Many managers were not qualified to conduct the peer review essential to scientific work in a crime lab, the sort of review ASCLD/LAB rated as essential for accreditation. A number of FBI unit chiefs admitted this during the various reviews of Rudolph's work. Yet such a management, vulnerable as it was, had no quality assurance program, no external inspection system, no peer-review scheme to back it up. The sad truth was that at the time he worked at the FBI lab, Rudolph's output and methods were never questioned by his unit managers, as he kept pointing out during his IG interviews. Successive unit chiefs signed off on reports that were later viewed as totally inadequate, even by the lax standards of the time.

Since there were so few agreed upon, accepted protocols or procedures at the FBI lab during the 1980s, there was little need for structured training. Rudolph's training had been inadequate, so his training of Fred Whitehurst, the cause of Whitehurst's very first complaints, had also been inadequate. It was just one demonstration of how the culture of negligence and deficiency at the FBI lab could be perpetuated, handed down from one examiner to another. In his interview with the IG's investigators in February 1996, Terry Rudolph revealed a shocking picture of a sort of teach-yourself training scheme in which trainees learned what they could when they could before being submitted to the moot court process. After a year on the job, Rudolph explained, unit examiners "would kind of vote on whether or not they felt you were qualified." The picture painted really did seem to resemble the private club, Don Edwards, the former representative from California, had depicted.

When considered qualified by his peers in December 1978, Rudolph had been put in charge of the explosives-residue analysis for which, as he described it, "there was essentially no organized procedure or protocol." As he told the IG: "I hesitate to say, dumped in my lap, but it was kind of like that."[52] With Ed Bender, a chemist hired as Rudolph's technician in mid-1979, Rudolph described how the two of them essentially went on to evolve their own "philosophy" of explosives-residue examination.

One telling example Rudolph gave was their practice of not bothering to examine everything. If twenty specimens had come in from an IED, predecessors had tended to examine all of them, Rudolph observed from the records. Wanting to speed things up and noting that typically the same residue was present on every fragment, Bender and Rudolph decided to be more selective. Similarly, chemical tests became less necessary as they grew confident that they could just visually recognize substances such as black powder. Work would halt with a positive identification. "If we found some evidence of an explosive, then that's all we would do on that case." [53]

Today Chris Ronay and Terry Rudolph, both now retired from the FBI, insist that there were no problems with explosives-residue work in the Unabom case. "Terry Rudolph's work was not faulty in that case. Technology has moved on. You cannot judge yesterday's work by today's standards," Ronay says. [54] Ironically, Ronay says he would not discount other mistakes made in the Unabom investigation. He said that one mechanism the investigators used to guard against error was to "take the files, do a review, then hand it to the next guy to do a review of your work." [55]

The method begged the question as to why that had not happened with Rudolph's work, why the inadequacies of the explosives-residue work in the Unabom case took fifteen years to uncover from the time of the first case Rudolph handled. Rudolph himself is adamant: "You can't work as many cases as I did for ten years, keep working them pretty much the same way, and be consistently right. If what they were saying was true I'd have to be making a lot of mistakes. I would have to be coming up with the wrong answers." [56]

But that is precisely what Terry Rudolph and the FBI lab may have been doing. One recent incident from Lane County, Oregon, highlighted the sort of case that should probably have been referred back. In June 1983, Eric Proctor and Chris Boots were arrested for the murder of Raymond Oliver, a 7-Eleven store clerk. The case against the pair was soon dropped for lack of evidence, and Proctor and Boots filed to sue for wrongful arrest. Three years after the murder, having recently attended Rudolph's training course in explosives-residue analysis at Quantico, Lieutenant Paul Vaughn, a local state examiner, wrote to Rudolph asking for his help. His own tests on the explosives residues had been inconclusive, he noted, mentioning the lawsuit.

Breaking the FBI lab's rule that it will not look at evidence already examined by another lab, Terry Rudolph and his colleague Ed Bender repeated the chromatography tests already done, according to lawyers close to the case. They issued a lab report, signed by Rudolph, saying that they had identified a microscopic fleck of explosives residue found on Proctor's pants as double-base smokeless powder by means of isolating one of its key components, nitrocellulose.

Charles Calfee, the Materials Analysis Unit chief and Rudolph's immediate boss at the time, testified to that identification at two trials in 1986 and 1987. He stated that the identifying chemical, nitrocellulose, had been consumed by the test according to lawyers who have seen the files—apparently inconsistent with Rudolph's statement in his lab report. Proctor and Boots were both jailed for life, the indictment and conviction automatically negating their false arrest lawsuit against the state. The defendants served eight years in jail before Ricky Kuppens was identified as the killer.

According to one lawyer who has reviewed the files but requested anonymity, one of the earlier reviews of Rudolph's work had picked up the case. "The file includes documentation that says the work is sloppy, that the standards for a confirmatory test were not met," he says. That seemed to be confirmed by a report in *The Wall Street Journal*, which stated that explosives experts who had reviewed the files at the newspaper's request had a number of problems, including the fact that the same test that had been deemed insufficient initially had eventually been used to secure the convictions.[57] These experts also raised questions about the way the evidence had been handled.

Terry Rudolph told the authors that he "vaguely remembered" the case, claiming he had used a different technique from that used by the lab in Oregon to identify the smokeless powder fleck, merely confirming their results. "I understand the guy was wrongly convicted. To me the issue is, how did the powder get on his clothing. We're only examining what they send us. We didn't take it off, the Oregon people took it off," he told the authors, adding somewhat bizarrely: "There's more to this than just the FBI lab was wrong, Terry Rudolph was wrong."[58]

There may well be. Released in November 1994, Eric Proctor and Chris Boots are now suing the state of Oregon for $42 million, raising the prospect of legal action against the FBI and its lab as part of the process.

3

VANPAC: EXPRESS MAIL JUSTICE

Helen Vance was wrapping Christmas presents in a bedroom when she heard her husband, Robert, return from his Saturday errands through the back door. Coming down the stairs of the colonnaded, mock-colonial house that they had shared for twenty-seven years, she collected two packages that the mailman had delivered earlier to their Shook Hill Road address in the heart of the country club suburb of Mountain Brook near Birmingham, Alabama. "I guess Pete's sending me more horse maga-zines," said Robert Vance, glancing at the name and return address of his colleague, a fellow judge serving on the Eleventh Circuit Court of Appeals.

Cutting the white twine, Robert Vance began to peel back the layers of brown wrapping paper and tan adhesive tape. As he lifted the lid of the packing carton inside, two slivers of an aluminum pie plate made contact, sending a current powered by two flashlight batteries into a detonator—an old ball-point pen barrel packed with explosive. The homemade detonator was crammed through a hole in one of two end caps screwed onto a five-and-a-half-inch steel pipe. The inside of the pipe was

95

packed with explosive powder. On the outside, rubber bands held eighty nails. It was a crude but efficient bomb.

The blast hurled Robert Vance across the room, jagged pieces of steel and nails tearing through his torso. Within seconds, he was dead. His wife, just feet away, was knocked to the floor. Cut and bleeding, she staggered to the phone. Was it dead or had she been deafened by the noise? Help, she had to get help. Into the family van, down the long driveway to the neighbor's house opposite. "Would you call the police? A bomb has gone off!" she told an aghast Margaret Ashby. Sirens, paramedics, ambulances, St. Vincent's Hospital. It was worse than Helen Vance had had the chance to feel—internally, a nail had sliced through a lung and lacerated her liver; externally she was cut all over, especially across the stomach.

Soon there were the inevitable questions from FBI agents surrounding her hospital bed. Through the pain she told them about Bob Vance's long track record of support for liberal causes, opposition to George Wallace when her husband had become chairman of the Democratic Party in Alabama back in the 1960s, support for integration and desegregation, discreet efforts on behalf of the National Association for the Advancement of Colored People (NAACP). But as an Appeals Court judge for the past eleven years, Bob Vance had kept a low profile on such issues. Surely this was an individual with a judicial grudge, someone who had gone one murderous step further than those who had made the odd threatening phone call to their Shook Hill Road home over the years.

The following Monday morning, security guards at the Eleventh Circuit U.S. Court of Appeals in Atlanta, Georgia, X-rayed a package wrapped in brown paper with white twine and discovered a bomb. After evacuating the courthouse, members of the Atlanta police bomb squad disarmed the device. Just before five in the afternoon, NAACP member and civil rights attorney Robbie Robinson opened a similar package at his townhouse office in Savannah, Georgia. The explosion blew off his right arm and left hand, and he died within hours on the operating table. At 6:00 A.M. the next morning, Willye Dennis, president of the local branch of the NAACP in Jacksonville, Florida, got a telephone call from a friend telling her about Robbie Robinson's murder. She remembered a brown-paper package she had left unopened at her office the day before.

Could it be a bomb? She called the sheriff's office, and the bomb squad discovered a fourth explosive device.

Back in Washington, FBI supervisory special agent and leading explosives expert Tom Thurman was soon examining the bloody nails that the coroner had removed from the body of Robert Vance—shiny finishing nails with toolmarks just below the shank. The nails were due to go directly to the FBI's only metallurgist, Bill Tobin, but as the designated principal examiner in what looked like a serial bombing case, Thurman was completely in charge. He could dispatch the individual pieces of evidence at will. This was now a major case with an FBI code name. VANPAC, as the four mail bombings had been baptized (after Judge Vance's murder), was one of those cases of a lifetime. Tom Thurman was going to make the most of it.

If Thurman's approach was typical of one of the "bombers" in the Explosives Unit (EU), Frederic Whitehurst's was that of the scientists of the Materials Analysis Unit (MAU). Thurman made observable judgments on the physical debris he could see, often making rough comparisons to sample IEDs he had collected and displayed in the glass cabinets that lined the walls of his unit. The "bombers" relied heavily on oral tradition, their own experience, and memory—their own or that of colleagues in sister organizations such as the ATF.

Whitehurst and his colleagues, on the other hand, made objective observations of the microscopic particles of substances or things left behind at the scene of a crime—anything from explosives to soil, the traces that no one could see. Trace analysis, as this is known, sought to link or clear a suspect microscopically, microchemically, or instrumentally. MAU keeps definitive database sample collections of everything from car paints to domestic plastics. Any match had to be confirmed by proven research using two different scientific methods. Written reports and scientific protocols were as essential in MAU's world as they were dispensible in the world of the EU.

Whitehurst offered his services to Thurman, knowing that proper explosives-residue analysis would be essential if the bomber was to be found and prosecuted. He also knew that MAU was the only unit in the lab properly equipped to do such work and that he was the only one formally qualified to do a complete analysis, having gone through the FBI lab's yearlong training and proficiency exam in explosives-residue analysis.

As John Hicks made clear in a memo shortly afterward: "He [Whitehurst] is the only qualified explosive residue examiner in the Laboratory at the present time."[1]

Thurman chose not to use Whitehurst. Thurman needed to build a case as quickly as possible against a suspect who was obviously one of the most daring bombers the country had ever seen. It was pretty clear to him just from looking at the two sets of remains and the two intact pipe bombs that the same person had made them. He needed to prove it. He made his explosives analysis decision accordingly, dispatching samples to his friend Roger Martz, head of the lab's Chemistry and Toxicology Unit. He asked Martz to confirm the presence of the Red Dot smokeless powder explosive he was convinced he had seen in the remains of the bombs. It was a suggestive request.

A former judge himself, FBI director William Sessions quickly made solving the mail bombings the Bureau's top priority. Hundreds of special agents from the FBI, the ATF, and the U.S. Postal Service spread across the South to investigate racist and right-wing extremist groups. They were the obvious targets, given the victims and the tone of four separate notes in the bombs, all claiming to be from a group calling itself Americans for a Competent Judicial System. Even President George Bush confirmed the general suspicion. "I've been appalled at the recent mail bombings across this country. Every one of us must confront and condemn racism, anti-Semitism, bigotry, and hate. Not next week, not tomorrow, but right now. Every single one of us," he declared in his State of the Union speech on January 31, 1991.

But the bomber or bombers were not intimidated. Letters began arriving at the offices of federal judges and civil rights groups threatening to kill them because of the federal courts' "calloused disregard for the administration of justice." Then a letter was received by an Atlanta television station purporting to be from the same group that claimed responsibility for the two killings and blamed the Eleventh Circuit Court for stressing minority rights at the expense of "innocent" white women who were the victims of "savage acts of violence" by black men. The letter also warned that two more NAACP members would be "assassinated."

Down the hall from Tom Thurman at the FBI lab William Bodziak of the Questioned Documents Unit had donned his white cotton gloves and begun examining these typewritten letters and the red-and-white priority mail address labels removed from the packages. He noticed that the numeral "1" resembled an inverted uppercase "L" and concluded that the Pica 10-pitch of the characters belonged to the typeface of a Brother manual typewriter, a model introduced in limited numbers in 1961. Within hours, ten FBI agents were combing through the thousands of legal documents filed in the Eleventh Circuit Court in Atlanta looking for a match with the 1961 Brother typeface.

On January nineteenth, FBI lab agent Bob Thompson found a legal brief written by Robert Wayne O'Ferrell, acting as his own attorney. The court had dismissed his claim for employee benefits after he was fired from an insurance company. As Thompson read the brief, he became increasingly excited. "The law and court system in these United States is corrupt," wrote O'Ferrell, of New Brockton, Alabama. Sirens wailing, Thompson raced to the Atlanta airport to personally deliver O'Ferrell's court documents to the FBI lab in Washington. Analysis quickly concluded that two notices of appeal—signed by O'Ferrell—had come from the same typewriter as that used for the labels on the four mail-bomb packages and the threatening letters enclosed with the bombs. A quick phone call to the county sheriff's office established that O'Ferrell ran a secondhand-goods store, Old and New Surplus Salvage, in Enterprise, Alabama. It was a big break. In forensic terms it seemed almost as good as a fingerprint.

Swapping his lab coat for a gun, Tom Thurman led a posse of agents in a search of O'Ferrell's house. Dozens of other agents turned his junk store upside down, the whole episode covered by dozens of reporters and cameramen crowding around outside. The press had been tipped off by none other than Attorney General Richard Thornburgh, who at a White House meeting with NAACP officials earlier that day had announced that a major development in the case "was imminent." The search yielded nothing. "We even drained his sewage system to see if he'd flushed pieces of the typewriter down there," Thurman recalled later. "But we didn't find a single thing that would connect him to the bombs."[2]

The trouble was, Wayne O'Ferrell had sold dozens of old typewriters from his shop. He managed to give the agents a couple of names, and the FBI, the ATF, and the media circus moved on, leaving a trail of devastation behind them. Wayne O'Ferrell suffered stomach ulcers, lost his business, and ended up divorcing his wife—all, he claims, as an indirect result of coming under suspicion in the VANPAC investigation. Five years later, when lawyers for Richard Jewell, the hotly pursued then cleared suspect in the Centennial Olympic Park bombing in Atlanta, obtained FBI investigative files in an effort to determine why their client had been targeted, William Gill, Wayne O'Ferrell's attorney, decided to follow suit, requesting and obtaining the documents examined by the FBI lab.

John Phillips, an independent typewriter expert with over fifty years experience, quickly established no match between the typeface of the package labels, the threat letters, and O'Ferrell's legal brief. Indeed, they could not have been more different, he stated. Phillips concluded that O'Ferrell's court documents had been typed on a new electric typewriter with Elite 12 pitch not the old manual with Pica 10 pitch, that the bomber had used. "No reasonably competent and qualified typewriter examiner could be of the opinion that all of these three documents were produced using the same typewriter," Phillips added. "As a matter of fact, the difference in type is so significant that the difference should be readily apparent to even a nonexpert."[3] If there was no match, there was no probable cause for the issue of a search warrant for Wayne O'Ferrell's home or business. O'Ferrell is currently suing the FBI.

Six weeks after the bombings, the VANPAC investigation had a false start, political pressure, media overkill, and forensic errors to its credit, yet no real leads. Frank Lee, a twenty-five-year veteran of numerous ATF arson and explosion investigations, was about to change all that. Thickset, with a complexion burnished by the outdoor sports he so relished, he was the senior ATF agent in Savannah and had been first on the scene when the parcel bomb had exploded in Robbie Robinson's office. It was Lee who had organized the collection of the debris from the Savannah bombing—the debris that Thurman had examined. Now, amid the disappointment of the raid on O'Ferrell's house, Lee took Tom Thurman aside. "We've been looking at another suspect, a guy named Moody in Georgia," he confided.

Lee pointed out that Thurman's descriptions of the four bombs matched that of a bomb linked to Walter Leroy Moody seventeen years earlier. In 1972, Moody's first wife, Hazel, had been hurt badly when she opened a package bomb that Moody allegedly intended to mail to an auto dealer who had repossessed his car. Roy Moody, as he was known, an eccentric loner and compulsive tinkerer with machines, had been con-victed of possessing—although not of building—the bomb, and had served three years in jail. Since his release, the litigious Moody had been obsessed with trying to reverse his conviction. One reason had been his desire to become a lawyer—convicted felons cannot be admitted to the bar in Georgia. Moody's latest appeal had been rejected by the Eleventh Circuit U.S. Court of Appeals, one of whose judges was Robert Vance. In the absence of any other leads, it looked like a motive.

Lee's information had come from Ryan's Steakhouse on Jimmy Car-ter Boulevard in the heart of Gwinnett County, just north of Atlanta, Georgia. A hangout for the "good ol' boys," as they called themselves—an informal group of local, state, and federal bomb technicians and explo-sives experts who met once a month to swap war stories and intelligence —the restaurant had a partition for turning one end into a meeting room. The Metro Bomb Meeting took place on December 19, 1989, three days after the murder of Judge Vance. Bob Holland, who had pulled the trigger to disarm the Eleventh Circuit Court bomb at the police range, described its unusual design—square end-plates, a threaded rod running its entire length, the flashlight bulb igniter. Holland, a crusty, crew-cut ATF veteran who had begun his career chasing moonshiners thirty years earlier, passed around photographs of the device. Among those looking them over was Holland's old friend, ATF agent Lloyd Erwin, another twenty-five-year veteran, who worked in the ATF's Atlanta lab.

With the photo in front of him, Erwin grabbed a leaflet announcing Holland's upcoming retirement party, flipped it over, and sketched a sim-ple diagram of the device the ATF had reconstructed in the Moody case seventeen years earlier. "Flashlight bulb igniter," he wrote, drawing an arrow at one end of the pipe. "Metal plates." Two more arrows. The final sketch, however, had four threaded rods running through it, not one.[4] Erwin claimed that the 1972 device was the only one of its kind among the more than three thousand bomb cases he had handled at the Atlanta lab. As the meeting broke up, Erwin took aside Holland and ATF assistant special-agent-in-charge Rich Rawlins: "I don't know where he's at, but I know he's got to be out of prison because it's such a long time ago. His name is Roy Moody. It happened in Macon, sometime in 1972."[5]

Rawlins took the sketch back with him to his office and showed it to Brian Hoback, the agent in charge of the ATF side of the VANPAC investigation. He was unenthusiastic. "That's not your bomb," he said glancing at the sketch on the back of the retirement party leaflet. "Bullshit. It's got the square end plates and it's got the rod," Rawlins shot back, ignoring the fact that the sketch showed four threaded rods running through the pipe bomb.[6] Rawlins told Hoback about the Moody case and asked him to find out what he could. A few hours later, Erwin also called, suggesting that Hoback investigate Moody. "Okay," replied Hoback perfunctorily. "No, no, no, I'm telling you, you need to look at him," insisted Erwin.

Unable to find the case file at the lab, Erwin picked up the phone and called Chet Bryant, a former colleague. Like Erwin, Bryant had started out chasing bootleggers. In 1972 he had been the ATF's Agent of the Year in Georgia, responsible for the seizure of forty-two illicit distilleries and seven firearms and for solving one explosive case. The sole explosive case was Roy Moody's bomb. After spending seven years as a whiskey chaser, Bryant spent a few weeks being trained in explosives at the Redstone Arsenal in Huntsville, Alabama—then took charge of the Moody investigation the Monday morning he returned to work. Although there had never been enough evidence to convict Moody of anything more than "constructive possession" of the bomb, neither man, however, had any doubt that Moody had built the bomb and intended to mail it. "The guy was never out of my mind. I thought he would do anything," Bryant recalled. "I don't know why the judge did not give him more time."[7]

Using nothing more than Erwin's sketch and the ATF's long-buried photos of the 1972 device, Thurman and his ATF colleagues managed to construct a full-scale model. Thurman quickly concluded the same person probably had made all five IEDs—the 1972 bomb and the four 1989 devices. "One means we use to identify a bomber is through his 'signature.' People learn how to make bombs one way, and no matter how sophisticated they get, they continue to repeat certain techniques," Thurman later told author David Fisher. "That technique is almost as unique as a fingerprint, and it makes very strong evidence that two or more bombs were made by the same person or group. When I saw this, I smiled and said, 'Yeah, this looks really good.'"[8]

A bomb signature is a pseudoscientific term pioneered by Tom Thurman's FBI unit chief, Chris Ronay. Describing distinctive features of a bomb in court one day a decade earlier, the prosecutor had suggested to him that what he was describing was like a signature. "After that we talked about the concept, wrote about it in publications, and it became accepted in the courts," recalls Ronay. "It's the things that cause me to believe that the same guy made the bombs. If you believe in my credibility as an expert then it's up to the court, the jury, to accept my word. . . . [I]t is in the end opinion testimony."[9] Ronay insists that expertise is the key and subjective judgment the rationale. As such a signature seems to be whatever an explosives examiner says it is, sometimes one feature, sometimes a whole range of features. "It could even be better than a fingerprint," Ronay claims.[10]

Most fingerprint experts would feel insulted by the comparison. Fingerprints are a distinct characteristic, genuinely unique to every individual; bomb construction is not. Comparing one to the other lends explosives experts and the idea that bombers can have signatures a pseudoscientific validation. "It's just a comparison technique. Given that, the question is, how individual can you get with something like bomb construction. The answer is, not very," says one explosives expert. "I'm very uneasy every time I hear the expression. It's so subjective it's ripe for abuse. Remember how easily signatures are forged." In any case, signature or no signature, valid concept or invalid concept, the premise was flawed crucially on two counts in this case. It assumed Moody had built the 1972 bomb, and it assumed that all the devices, the four posted in 1989 and the 1972 model that had exploded in Moody's home, were the same.

In the first place, the ATF had singularly failed to prove that Moody had built the 1972 device. There was no forensic evidence, and there was nothing unique about the design that linked it to Roy Moody. Welded end plates, threaded rods held in place by bolts at either end, a battery power source, an improvised lightbulb as an initiator, smokeless explosive powder, these were features common to a number of pipe bombs, according to the ATF's own surveys. Moody had always insisted that the parcel bomb had been delivered to his house. Second, even if Moody had constructed the 1972 pipe bomb, there were numerous differences between it and the four 1989 devices.

Even Thurman knew he had to do some more work. "ATF built us a demonstration bomb duplicating Moody's bombs. We constructed a room similar to Judge Vance's office on our range at Quantico. We used bobber targets, cardboard cutouts, to represent Judge Vance and his wife. Then we opened the box. Remotely," Thurman recalled. "It blew our room apart and destroyed the bobbers. You look at the photographs of the bomb scene and compare them with the results of this test and it's about as close as you can get. When I saw this, I said, 'Now I can testify that the same person made all these bombs.' " [11]

Such reconstructions and blast damage comparisons are a legitimate and well-established means of working in the field of bomb investigations. But to draw such definitive conclusions from such gross observations is just not possible. "It's in the nature of explosions. These things can't be that exact, even if investigators get into the crime scene immediately and record it all perfectly accurately in the first place," says one explosives expert. "The fact is, many devices and explosives can do similar damage." Fred Whitehurst agrees. "This is just plain garbage," he wrote in a confidential memo to his boss, Scientific Analysis Section chief James Kearney. "The blast damage which Thurman sees could have come from any number of mixtures of explosives." [12]

With no serious progress and several failed leads, the inclination to work backward in the investigation—to look for the evidence to fit the theory of Moody's guilt—started to emerge in an affidavit Thurman now contributed to, one of several that served as a basis for a search warrant of Moody's house. Thurman cited ten similarities between all five explosive devices—the 1972 pipe bomb and the four from December 1989—and claimed that the FBI had never encountered other similar devices. That was enough. On February 8, 1990, Tom Thurman, Frank Lee, and Lloyd Erwin led a phalanx of agents through a garden littered with the debris of unrepaired machines and do-it-yourself construction projects at Roy Moody's home in Rex, Georgia, some fifty miles southeast of Atlanta. At five-feet-eleven-inches and 160 pounds, the fifty-five-year-old Moody, a former army and air force man, was striking, with deep-set, piercing green eyes and luxuriant jet-black hair. An intelligent but deeply flawed man, Moody was always dreaming up business scams. Several such schemes had involved brushes with the law—one in Florida had ended in a triple-murder charge that was dropped after a jury failed to reach a verdict.

The agents had a shopping list: the everyday hardware items that could have been components of the parcel bombs, the typewriter, packaging materials, the legal documents that littered Moody's house and might link him to the victims. A place like Moody's should have been a treasure trove, and the agents certainly carried enough away with them. Documents, tools, stationery supplies, hardware items, metal, nails, paint. The floorboards were lifted in a front bedroom that had been newly decorated; the yard, the vehicles, even the boat were searched. Floors, walls, even ceilings were vacuumed for trace evidence.

But Tom Thurman quickly realized there was nothing. The search party found every type of paint except the black latex that had been used to line the inside of the steel pipes that contained the explosive; every type of tool, except those that would have been needed to make the bombs. "We never found a single thing in that house that we were able to connect to the bombs," Thurman recalled later. "It was as if Moody knew what we would be looking for and had taken those things out of the house." [13] This curious line of reasoning would actually be invoked repeatedly at Roy Moody's trial, and now became a reason for stepping up the investigation of Moody.

Back at the VANPAC investigation's special makeshift office, FBI agents were soon going through the items they had hauled in from Moody's home. Hoback and Lee felt overwhelmed and outnumbered. "FBI now believes in Moody, wants to take over," Brian Hoback wrote in his diary. [14] Tom Thurman, already responsible for persuading Washington that a search of Moody's house was justified, was the chief cheerleader. "He was convinced and went back and convinced the FBI," recalls Frank Lee. "Everything changed from February ninth. From then on they wanted us to work out of their office, send things to their lab." [15]

By March, despite the best efforts of Tom Thurman and others, investigators lacked a single piece of physical evidence against Moody. It was clear that it would be a long haul, and with four FBI field offices within the jurisdiction of four U.S. attorneys now involved, the case was crying out for central direction. Having decided to appoint an inspector —an FBI term that gave a special supervisory agent the temporary status of a deputy assistant director—William Baker, the head of the Criminal Investigation Division in Washington, opted for Larry Potts. He was told to report to Atlanta in three days. "You are to stay there until it is solved," he was told. [16] The effect was to focus the investigation on Moody further.

Until Potts's arrival, William Hinshaw, the head of the FBI's Atlanta field office, had thought headquarters wanted him to focus on the Ku Klux Klan, the most obvious target.[17]

Pushing the Moody theory involved pushing aside other leads referred to in teletypes between FBI headquarters and field offices that were subsequently released to the authors under the Freedom of Information Act. Although heavily redacted, one teletype shows that threatening letters arriving in Texas contained the same numerical code—010187—used in the letters accompanying the VANPAC bombs.[18] Another teletype informs FBI field offices and headquarters of three unexploded IEDs attached to electricity power poles in Los Angeles in March 1990: "All three IEDs bore a characteristic that had previously been unique to three of the four VANPAC bombs and a bomb that detonated in Macon, Georgia in 1972, which VANPAC suspect Walter Leroy Moody Jr. was convicted of possessing, i.e. they had threaded rods extending through each end-cap which were secured by nuts at each end."[19] The FBI seems to have failed to follow up the lead, declining to send Tom Thurman or anyone else from the lab to California.

One new strategy was to bug Moody's ranch-style home. On the day Potts took charge of the investigation, an affidavit requesting permission for electronic surveillance was submitted to a judge. There were no other investigative techniques reasonably available, the affidavit claimed, "other procedures having been tried and failed." While Roy and Susan Moody were away in Florida, agents entered the house, bugging it, a pickup, and Susan Moody's 1972 Volkswagen Beetle, giving an added poignancy to her customized license plate, which read BUGGED. Moody was actually surprised his place was not tapped already, but as he was soon telling the media, he could be sure it was when he returned home to find a muddy footprint in the bathtub.

FBI agents listened in from a nearby surveillance van, but under the circumstances, it was hardly surprising they picked up nothing incriminating. After a month, Larry Potts decided to close down the operation. The only thing of interest that emerged was that Moody talked to himself, the sort of eccentricity that seemed to confirm to the agents that he was their man. But knowing how easy it can be to miss something on such tapes, Potts turned everything over to John Crisp, an agent with a reputation for hearing things his colleagues could not pick up. After a few weeks,

Crisp claimed he had something. Through the static he said he could hear Moody whisper: "Now you've killed two . . . now you can't pull another bombing."

This tape would later be played at Moody's trial with the FBI helpfully providing members of the jury with a transcript due to audibility problems. "Now you've killed two (unintelligible) (pause) Now you can't pull another bombin', . ." ran the transcript.[20] No one ever explained how this quote was obtained from the seemingly inaudible tape. "It was obviously a pretty devastating statement," recalls Potts.[21] It was also pretty essential. More than four months after the bombings, little else justified the continuing focus on Roy Moody.

Having proved to his own satisfaction that the four December mail bombs had been built by the same person, Tom Thurman had to do more to definitively link the four IEDs to Moody's 1972 device. With the help of his full-scale replica, he needed to expand on Lloyd Erwin's assertion that the ATF lab had never seen any other IEDs like it until the December mail bombings. Thurman had agents check the design of all five devices against thousands of registrations in the FBI's computerized bomb database and those of the ATF and U.S. Postal Inspection Service and against IEDs recorded by 217 crime labs around the country. There were no matches. "Moody's design is unique," he reported to the VANPAC task force in Atlanta.[22]

There were a few problems with this. First of all, to what were the IEDs on file being compared? A four-rod aluminum pipe bomb with welded end plates like that of 1972? Or a one-rod steel pipe bomb, like three of 1989 devices? Or even a steel pipe bomb with cast iron end caps like the mail bomb that had killed Judge Vance? What about all the other major differences between the 1972 and 1989 bombs? The sizes were different, the triggering mechanisms were different, the charges were different. But there was another serious problem. Fred Whitehurst claims that Michael Fanning, Thurman's technician in the FBI lab, later told him that the Explosives Unit had no such computerized database in 1990.[23] Whitehurst claimed that Fanning stated that the FBI subsequently created its computerized bomb database as a specific response to the VANPAC investigation.

The issue remained unresolved by the IG's inquiry into the VANPAC investigation. The IG interviewed Steve Schied, an intelligence research specialist who had overseen the ATF's rather than the FBI's bomb database since 1975 and confirmed that its Explosives Incident System, or "Exis" database, had nearly sixteen thousand entries in early 1990.[24] The IG thus absolved Thurman of any wrongdoing in stating in court that his survey and examination of databases had taken in more than sixteen thousand devices. However, the IG report does not indicate whether they spoke to Michael Fanning or others in the FBI who may have known if the FBI even had one of the basic tools of explosive investigations—a computerized bomb database.

Back in Atlanta, Larry Potts was as convinced as Thurman and the ATF agents that Moody was the mail bomber. The "unique" design concept would help, but it was not the forensic evidence he needed. Potts decided to step up the tedious process of checking into every aspect of Roy Moody's background and by mid-April had some promising leads that might provide leverage. Obsessed with clearing himself in the 1972 bombing case, Moody, it seemed, was paying witnesses to lie in court. Julie Linn-West, a disabled single mother in her thirties, admitted taking fifteen hundred dollars in bribes to say that she had ridden to Moody's house with a man to deliver a package shortly before the 1972 bomb exploded. With a federal grand jury date approaching, Linn-West agreed to have her wheelchair wired to video record meetings with Roy Moody and his wife. Although Moody was careful, often writing notes rather than talking, agents soon thought they had enough.

A strategy now seemed possible for Ray Rukstele, the prosecutor heading the case. In late April, he outlined a plan to government officials and prosecutors from Georgia, Alabama, and Florida at the Justice Department in Washington. Prosecute Roy and Susan Moody for conspiracy, Rukstele suggested, charging obstruction of justice, perjury, subornation of perjury, all based on the evidence from Julie Linn-West's meetings. This would put Moody out of commission and prevent further mail bombings while giving agents scope to try and "turn" Susan Moody into a witness against her husband. Rukstele pushed for the use of RICO—the Racketeering Influenced and Corrupt Organizations—law. The legislation had been intended for use against the mob, but by 1990 it was being widely used in other alleged conspiracy cases.

Rukstele left the Justice Department meeting disappointed. The petty rivalries of the provincial prosecutors had been a major obstacle.

Everyone wanted such a prestigious case prosecuted on his patch. Indeed, the petty squabbling made it clear to the attending Department of Justice officials that the case needed a prosecutorial supremo—a legal equivalent of Larry Potts—and they were not sure Rukstele was the man to bang a few heads together. In May, Attorney General Dick Thornburgh picked up the phone to speak to an assistant U.S. attorney in New York with plenty of experience in bringing charges under RICO. Louis Freeh came on the line and into the case as a special prosecutor or, more formally, special assistant United States attorney.

Within days, Freeh, who quickly invited Howard Shapiro to second-chair him, was settling into Larry Potts's offices on the fifth floor of 77 Forsyth Street in downtown Atlanta. As he discussed the case with Potts in his staccato, New Jersey tones, it became clear that Freeh was going to adopt Rukstele's strategy wholesale. It also became clear that Louis Freeh was going to function as the FBI investigator he had once been. Potential conflicts of interest did not come into it. "That's the new Bureau. We used to have the attitude 'We investigate, you prosecute,' Larry Potts would later recall. "Now we feel it's important to have prosecutors who are involved all along." [25]

By early July, Freeh was ready to move. On July 12, 1990, both Susan and Roy Moody were in court in Macon, Georgia, charged with obstruction of justice. Freeh had the evidence; the key was convincing the judge Moody should be held without bail pending trial. With the help of accusations of how Moody had allegedly tried to drown three employees off the coast of Florida in a supposed effort to collect on life-insurance policies, the judge was convinced. Moody was jailed and the pressure on the investigators redoubled. David Hyche began "turning" Susan Moody, a manipulated wife showing all the signs of battered woman syndrome, according to a social worker, and logged thirteen consecutive seven-day weeks. Back at base, many were working sixteen-hour days. FBI director William Sessions called repeatedly to ask about progress and needs. "Talk about pressure on a case. It's relentless," recalled one agent of the investigation: "When we get rolled up on one of those, we're going to get the guy. There's just no doubt about it." [26] Larry Potts felt the pressure too—but from another perspective. "One pressure was knowing there is nothing you can ask for that you won't get. It was almost frightening. . . . This was not a case you would want to lose." [27]

Louis Freeh had no intention of losing. But when on November 7, 1990, a federal grand jury handed down a seventy-one-count indictment charging Moody with the murders of Vance and Robinson, attempted murder, possession and manufacture of an explosive device, and the mailing of four parcel bombs, the evidence submitted was only enough to get an indictment. Freeh knew he had some time. He, Potts, and their dozens of investigators, in particular the examiners in the lab, would need it. The trouble was that when Walter Leroy Moody's first trial began in St. Paul, Minnesota, in June 1991 the case was still weak. Indeed, Freeh was going into the courtroom without a single eyewitness or piece of physical evidence tying Moody to the bombs or bombings, despite an eighteen-month FBI investigation. Fortunately, for him, cases could depend as much on the performance of lawyers and their clients as on the evidence. This was certainly going to be one of them.

Edward Tolley was a clean-cut Southern patrician with a solid legal record, especially in capital crime cases, who had been drafted at the last minute to represent Moody in his obstruction of justice case in December 1990. In the following six months, Freeh and Tolley became quite friendly, with regular negotiations taking place. The FBI's premise for these meetings was simple: Moody was the mail bomber. The investigators believed that Moody had bought a four-pound tin of Hercules Red Dot smokeless explosive powder and wanted Tolley to quiz Moody about where the remaining explosive was or if he had premade bombs that were primed and ready to be detonated. The FBI argued it was a public safety issue, but any recovered explosive powder would also coincidentally be the physical evidence Freeh needed so desperately to crack the case against Moody once and for all. Tolley confirmed the regular meetings with Freeh, but unlike other aspects of the case, was guarded about what transpired, saying: "I'm not at liberty to discuss it."[28]

No remaining explosive powder emerged. The most logical explanation was that there was none. But Tolley was pretty acquiescent on other fronts. Freeh wanted him to agree to allow Tom Thurman to testify about all the lab results, including those in purely scientific areas and beyond Thurman's explosives expertise. The proposal was portrayed as an administrative issue. Thurman had been the principal examiner, he was in charge, why not let him confirm the results of the auxiliary examiners? It would save time, resources, and inconvenience. It was a crucial step in allowing weak lab evidence to be described in court as more convincing than any expert's inevitably qualified testimony.

The arrangement, which Tolley agreed to in a legal stipulation, and was confirmed subsequently in affidavits from both Tolley and Thurman, solved a couple of problems for Freeh. First, Thurman was a true believer in Moody's guilt and organized the evidence around it. He could be relied on to testify accordingly, and thus help downplay any exculpatory evidence. Second, Thurman testifying for others would help disguise the sheer lack of forensic evidence. By 1991, for instance, it was clear that there was no DNA evidence against Moody. In fact, the DNA extracted from the saliva on two of the Yosemite National Park stamps on the packages excluded Roy Moody completely.[29] There was no hair or fiber evidence, no explosives-residue match, no fingerprint evidence, and nothing from questioned documents. Despite the examination of hundreds of legal documents belonging to Roy Moody, there was not even a typewriter match. Freeh faced the prospect of marching up to the stand a line of FBI lab agents who would testify that they had found nothing. It would not look good.

In his affidavit Edward Tolley is quite specific about the arrangement. He states that "in order to reduce the number of witnesses and laboratory personnel who would need to testify at trial" he and Freeh had agreed that Thurman "would be allowed to testify as a summary witness about the results of any and all examiners who were deemed to be nonessential to the fact-finding and the defense theory in the case."[30] Thurman states in his affidavit: "At the time of my testimony, I was aware of an agreement . . . in which I would be permitted to testify as the Principal Examiner about laboratory results that were obtained by any or all of the Auxiliary Examiners."[31] The only party to the agreement with no recollection of it is Louis Freeh. Notes on his interview with the IG investigators, obtained under the Freedom of Information Act, read: "Director Freeh stated that he had no recollection of any particular discussion(s) about which agents or how many agents would testify and reiterated that he did not recall any agreement."[32]

The arrangement could hardly be said to violate FBI procedures—there were none, at least, no written ones. However, John Hicks, the head of the FBI lab during the Moody case, was adamant when asked about this: "In all the training programs we did with our people, we always hammered that into them over and over again—stay within the bounds of your expertise. So, for example, maybe a blood expert would get on a stand testifying, and one of the attorneys might want to bring out some information about a fingerprint. The expert would have to say, 'No that's outside the area of my expertise.' "[33] Hicks also confirmed that Thurman was not a scientist or an analyst. "Thurman's role as an explosives expert was not to be a chemist or a technical expert," says Hicks. "Thurman was supposed to act as a sort of facilitator, an agent, in that he would send out all these parts to different experts in the lab and have testing done."[34]

It was thus somewhat ironic that Howard Shapiro would open the government's case against Roy Moody in the Minnesota courtroom on June 4 with a grandiose broadside that might have applied to the way his own side, the FBI laboratory in particular, had conducted the Moody investigation. Shapiro spoke of someone who "specialized in subverting, undermining and abusing the legal system"; who waged "war against the courts."[35] But Shapiro was also careful to prepare the jury. "Now you won't see a photo or a videotape of Walter Moody constructing the bombs," he continued half in jest. "You won't find his fingerprint or anyone else's for that matter on the inside of the bomb devices. It was part of his scheme, part of his method of operating. . . ."[36] Tolley riposted by comparing what was about to unfold to "a good historical novel." The government's case, he said, "will track closely historical fact, but when the facts are missing, will rely on raw conclusion."[37]

The government had three main witnesses and major problems with all three. The first was Paul Sartain, a well-built father of five who had retired from Ford Motors on medical disability and now worked voluntarily at the Shootin' Iron, a gun shop in Griffin, Georgia. Sartain lumbered to the witness stand to recount how he had sold a four-pound keg of Hercules Red Dot smokeless explosive powder and some number 65 CCI handgun primers to a gentleman on December 2, 1989. He remembered the encounter in detail, having asked the customer if he would prefer four one-pound cans—once opened the powder can be ruined by moisture—but the customer indicated he was going to use it all at once.

Sartain described the man as having "dark, reddish brown hair" that was "kind of kinky and wavy around the edges. . . . [I]t looked like it had just come out of a beauty shop."[38] He also described tinted, plastic-framed glasses "which looked like something that came from [a] drugstore" and "magnetic eyes—just stare through you."[39] Sartain identified a blue jacket recovered from Moody's home as "identical" to the one the customer was wearing, and finally identified Roy Moody, jet-black hair and no glasses, in the courtroom. "May the record reflect that the witness has identified the defendant, Walter Moody," intoned Louis Freeh with due gravity.[40]

In reality, Paul Sartain's identification of Moody had been a little more convoluted than that scripted for the courtroom. Sartain had failed to pick Roy Moody out of two separate sets of six photos—one black-and-white set, one color—on two separate occasions. It was only when he saw the suspect's picture attached to an *Atlanta Constitution* newspaper story about Moody's objection to FBI surveillance that Sartain had decided that Moody was the man who had bought the explosive and primers. After that, Sartain had not surprisingly had no problems picking out suspect number 4, Roy Moody, in a lineup at Atlanta's city jail. It was suggestive identification at its absolute worst. Dyed hair and glasses may have fit the government's version of a deceptive, clever murderer who took every precaution. But why, if this was the case, would Moody have bought the most essential ingredient for the mail bombs in person?

It was a question that loomed larger in the context of Susan Moody's testimony. She related how Moody had dispatched her on numerous errands, many of which the prosecution alleged were linked to the mail bombings. It was all supposed to show the extraordinary lengths to which Moody was prepared to go to avoid detection. Susan was told to go in disguise, pay cash, wear gloves, and park away from the stores she visited. In the summer of 1989, she claimed, she had made six to eight such trips with shopping lists that included items such as boxes, tapes, string, wire, solder, Playtex rubber gloves, and trash bags. To the government's delight, Susan had kept a cache of receipts.

The key trip in the prosecution's view was in November 1989, to Florence, Kentucky, far enough away from their home in Rex, Georgia, to satisfy Roy Moody's supposed paranoia. Moody wanted photocopies of several originals—the threatening letters the prosecution alleged—priority mail labels, a two-dollar and a forty-cent stamp, aluminum cake pans, a pad of self-adhesive mailing labels, and mailing boxes similar to the ones that contained the bombs. Susan had never read the photocopied document—she had been told not to and her obedience bolstered her image as the dutiful, subservient wife—but she was trying so hard to go incognito in scarf, sunglasses, and gloves, that employees at the store remembered her. More important, one latent fingerprint on the letter in the Jacksonville bomb corroborated her story, the prosecution claimed. It belonged to a youth who swept the floor at the photocopying store. He had refilled the machine with paper just before Susan had come in.

It was good circumstantial stuff, and after eight rehearsals, two of them in the courtroom itself, Susan Moody performed well on the stand. But she had nothing concrete. She admitted to Moody's defense lawyer, Ed Tolley, that she had never seen Roy Moody with a bomb, that she had never seen him with reddish-brown, wavy hair. He had never mentioned Judge Vance, Robbie Robinson, or the race issues to which the victims seemed to be linked. And Susan Moody's credibility was poor—something Ed Tolley hammered away at in cross-examination. She had lied in a sworn statement to a court in Florida in 1983, had lied under oath to a grand jury in Atlanta in July 1990, and was testifying under the shadow of a plea bargain deal on the obstruction of justice charge.

There were others to support Susan Moody, but with similar problems. The most notable was Ted Banks, also a self-confessed liar, a convicted felon, and another testifying under a plea bargain deal. Banks, a rough-hewn boatbuilder, had met Roy Moody in prison while serving six years for counterfeiting and, over the years, had gotten involved in a number of Roy Moody's business scams. Banks testified that in the fall of 1989 he had cut three lengths of steel pipe, welded end plates on both ends of each, and cut three pieces of all-thread—rods with thread down their whole lengths—for Moody at White House Marine, the boatbuilding company where he was a plant manager, in Titusville, Florida. He also said he had asked a friend to get some gunpowder for Moody and had been suspicious, repeatedly asking Moody if the pipes were for bombs.

This was actually a change of story that had followed charges of being a convicted felon in charge of a firearm, a charge that itself was the result of a search of Banks's home and a storage locker in the hunt for evidence in the mail bombing case. Until then, Banks had always said that the welding he had done for Moody had been for a metal bender, had insisted that he thought Moody was innocent, and said he had never heard him make racist remarks. Indeed, until being turned as part of a plea bargain, Ted Banks had intended to testify *for* Roy Moody. Even on the stand, he seemed a bit of a liability for the government. Shown pictures of the bombs in court, he claimed the welding was not his. Finally, even if the story he told was all true, it still left unresolved the issue of the fourth pipe bomb, the Birmingham bomb that killed Judge Vance. That bomb had had end caps rather than welded plates to seal it.

Banks stayed out of jail as a result of his testimony and plea bargain —but not for long. In February 1995 the old boatbuilder went back to his earlier story, retracting his court testimony in an affidavit submitted as part of Moody's motion for a new trial. Banks claimed he had been coerced by Freeh and FBI agents into lying about anything pertaining to the mail bombs, claimed he had never cut or welded the pipes and never spoken to Moody about bombs. Banks had absolutely no motive to retract his testimony from the 1991 trial and go back to his original story. As his lawyer pointed out at the time, he faced perjury charges for doing so. In 1996, perjury charges were indeed brought against him, and Banks pleaded guilty. It seems incredible, but today the man whose testimony Louis Freeh was later to describe as "the single and most probative evidence of Moody's guilt"[41] is serving forty-four months in a Florida jail for lying.

When Tom Thurman took the stand on June 14, Louis Freeh and Howard Shapiro still had a lot of heavy lifting to do. Having established himself as an explosives expert, he started by going through the recovered bomb parts piece by piece, the steel-pipe shrapnel lacerated by the force of the nails, the timers, the flashlight batteries, the explosive, the wiring —the nuts and bolts of a bomb for the layperson. He was a practiced expert witness, and having built, exploded, and examined the remains of thousands of IEDs, Tom Thurman was good at making such observations. Prompted by Howard Shapiro, the way they had gone over it beforehand, Thurman concluded the bombs were "ingenious, imbued with extreme craftsmanship."

On the surface, Thurman had to do two things: show that the four IEDs were from the same source and demonstrate that the 1972 and 1989 devices were built by the same person. Under the surface, Thurman had to do two other things: gloss over the fact that all such links were extremely tenuous and avoid the reality that the government had very little else in the way of a forensic case. Thurman began his task by stating of the four bombs: "There were lots of similarities that just, if you will, jumped right out at you on the laboratory bench."[42] With one word, Thurman gave the impression that there was a scientific basis to his assertion. It was a time-tested, coded device used by forensic experts to impress the juries, and Thurman was to repeat the insinuation of science in different ways many more times over the course of two days of testimony.

Thurman then moved on to the contents of the four 1989 devices. Obviously, to compare bombs for similarities and dissimilarities, one has to determine the entire contents. Homemade bombs, or IEDs in particular, often contain all kinds of foreign elements—wood, filings, dust, residues—that are essential not just for comparison to other devices, as in this case, but for clues as to the origin of the bombs. Roger Martz's cyanide poisoning case in Washington State had been solved by tracing exactly this kind of clue—the pieces of green algicide in the poison lacing the Excedrin tablets (see Chapter 1). Full chemical profiling and trace analysis is essential, experts agree, especially when one is attempting to compare detonated and unexploded bombs, as in the Moody case.

Thurman saw what he thought was Red Dot smokeless powder and told the court how he had sent the samples to Roger Martz to confirm it. Not surprisingly, Martz found Red Dot smokeless powder in all four devices by means of a standard mass spectrometer identification. With no other instructions, and using the Chemistry and Toxicology Unit's limited protocol for the detection of smokeless powders and nothing else, Martz apparently did not look for the presence of other explosives or substances in the samples. Anything more might complicate an investigation going in only one direction. Any search for other ingredients might prove differences.

In fact, Martz did not have the training or equipment in the CTU to identify inorganic explosives or fillers, according to Whitehurst. The IG's report agreed that the analytical tests performed by Martz may not have detected certain substances. "There was no clear delineation of the respective responsibilities of each unit. Moreover, because the units did not share a common protocol, the tests might vary according to which unit received the evidence," concluded the IG.[43] "The Materials Analysis Unit would be able to give you the overall picture, the CTU could give you one part of it," says Whitehurst. "The best analogy I can make is a car repair. If you want your tires fixed you might choose to go to the best tire place—a specialist. But if you want a general service or a mechanical defect dealt with you'd have to go to someone who could give you an overall picture."[44]

Partial, selective answers were precisely what Martz resorted to during his own testimony in the Moody trial. Asked if he had tried to compare a sample of Hercules Red Dot smokeless powder from a can obtained from the Shootin' Iron gun shop with the powder retrieved from the IEDs, Martz said he had been unable to "successfully compare" them. He cited degradation once smokeless powder is exposed to air. In fact, Martz did compare a sample from the can, from the Jacksonville device, and some known samples from the laboratory, according to the IG's report, finding both differences and similarities. "Martz was ambiguous . . . he should have stated more directly that he found differences and similarities," the report concluded.[45]

Thurman had excluded Whitehurst from the Moody case in December 1989, and Whitehurst had forgotten all about it until one day in 1995, when Roger Martz boasted to him that he had been doing explosives-residue analysis for years and that one of his greatest successes had been the VANPAC case. Whitehurst was appalled. To his mind Martz had not been trained in explosives-residue analysis, even by the dubious standards of the FBI lab. So in 1995, five years after the trial in Minnesota, with Walter Leroy Moody facing the prospect of going on trial for his life in the state of Alabama, Frederic Whitehurst dug out the files, found the lab reports, wrote off for a set of the court transcripts, and began a forensic science critique of the VANPAC case—an investigator investigating the investigators.

The resulting twenty-six-page memo was one of Fred Whitehurst's most detailed complaints ever, a forensic line-by-line analysis of the court testimony of Tom Thurman and Roger Martz. His analysis alleged many of the most serious abuses possible in forensic science: overstating results, drawing false and selective conclusions, incomplete testing and the use of unvalidated or unwritten testing procedures, testifying beyond a given area of expertise, and inadequate documentation of results. At the very least, he claimed, it was misrepresentation and falsification. In the four years between the end of the Moody trial and the start of his own investigation, Whitehurst had gathered what he considered plenty of corroborating evidence about Roger Martz and Tom Thurman. He noted in his memo that Roger Martz had "on a number of occasions in the past signed off on analytical reports which gave incorrect opinions concerning the content of multicomponent explosives mixtures. In those reports smokeless powder was the only material found and yet reexamination noted other components."[46]

Thurman, he noted, had shown similar scientific limitations while they were conducting tests on the range at Quantico, Virginia. "Both I and SSA [Supervisory Special Agent] Steven Burmeister had to explain to SSA Thurman in the most elementary terms the significance of the presence of nitrate oxidizers in explosives. SSA Thurman had no idea what an explosive material was composed of or how the different components functioned in the chemical reaction of the explosion," wrote Whitehurst.[47] It confirmed what Whitehurst had always said: Thurman's training and experience qualified him as nothing more than an explosives technician, able to make gross observations or comparisons on bombs but not qualified to carry out the detailed scientific analysis.

In his memo, Whitehurst argues that the incompleteness of the testing meant that Thurman and Martz never scientifically proved that the main charge was a double-base smokeless powder (Hercules Red Dot) in the four explosives. Thus they could never be certain that all four devices were the same or dissimilar. Thurman also undermined his own contention that the main charge in all four devices was Red Dot smokeless powder by testifying that one of the powders contained "black appearing round dots." According to Whitehurst, "The FBI Laboratory often identified mixtures or combinations of powders" in IEDs. The "black appearing round dots" that Thurman is looking at may have well been another type of smokeless powder, he wrote.[48]

Thurman testified that the bombs that killed Judge Vance and Robbie Robinson were "essentially identical." Then he said that all four 1989 devices were identical. "The conclusion I reached is that these devices were . . . made by one individual, working off the same plans, using essentially the same type of materials," he pronounced to the court.[49] Yet as we have seen, one of the bombs sported such an obvious difference that a child could have remarked on it. The Birminghan bomb that killed Judge Vance had no welded end plates but cast iron end caps on the end of the steel tube. It was cut from a different piece of tube, being 1½ inches in diameter, not 2 inches, and was shorter than the other three, 5½ inches rather than 7 inches.

Having "proved" that the four explosive devices all contained Red Dot smokeless powder as the main charge, the prosecution and Thurman then moved on to argue that the four devices were so unusual as to be of a virtually unique type. Thurman was asked by Shapiro whether the design of the four devices was common. "They are very uncommon," he replied. "Are there aspects of them that are particularly unusual or unique?" Shapiro continued. "Yes, sir."[50] Thurman went on to list the high-explosive detonator—a ballpoint pen tube pushed through the pipe bomb's end caps—the steel end plate, electrical wiring, and the threaded rod, which when all combined in a mail bomb made them unique. The detonator was "a type of modification that I have never seen before in the hundreds of bombs that I have examined and been privy to review."[51] The electrical wiring was "so specific that it shows the same hand, what I referred to as a bomber's signature."[52]

You don't have to be an expert to realize that electrical connections made of the same type of wires and materials are hardly of a unique type. But in even discussing the electrical wiring, Tom Thurman was beginning to demonstrate a tendency to wander off into a subfield of expertise. Having established that his role at the lab was limited to general bomb comparisons, Thurman now took the court on a tour of a variety of different fields of forensic expertise. Nails and shrapnel from the bomb, DNA in the saliva on the stamps, analysis of the paint used to line the pipe-bombs, the rubber and adhesives used in the packaging, Thurman commented on them all. Only when asked to comment as a toolmark examiner on the gripping-tool marks left on the bomb tubes did he show any hesitation.

Thurman's case for the similarity of the mail bombs was flawed, but his pseudoscientific jargon about detonators, explosive powders, and electrical wiring, whose combined form somehow produced the alchemy of a signature, made it difficult to cut through. Not so the comparison of the everyday packaging items that surrounded the explosive. On the two-inch-wide packaging tape that bound the parcel bombs, Thurman told the court: "We determined in the laboratory that this tape was from the same source, the same manufacturer. We are not really sure what the manufacturer is, but we know it is from the same source."[53] Same on the black latex paint, which Thurman asserted had been hand-painted onto the inside of the tubes making up the body of the bombs. "All of this paint is from the same source. Again the manufacturer was not identified, however it is the same chemical composition."[54]

Thurman does not say how such deductions were made. The reason is simple. The FBI data did not support Thurman's assumptions. The Materials Analysis Unit (MAU), the FBI lab unit responsible for analysis of both products, had no adequate databases for either tape or paint at the time. Tracing the manufacturer may have made a more valid comparison possible. But Thurman is unequivocal; this was not done in either case. The FBI paint protocol at the time did not classify paint by chemical composition. The reason was simple—there were a strictly limited number of formulae for paint at the time, many different paints from different manufacturers having the same chemical composition. So even if the black paint in the four bombs had been proven to be chemically identical that would not have proved that it came from the same source.

Thurman's testimony illustrated the pitfalls of the agreement Tolley and Freeh had struck. He was completely out of his depth on the paint and tape evidence because he was testifying from the lab report of Robert Webb, an auxiliary examiner on the case. Webb, an agent in the MAU, had examined the tan tape, the black paint, the RTV white sealant, and the glue used in the bombs and their packaging. But the tests he had done, microscopic, so-called "wet chemical" analyses, infrared spectroscopy, and gas chromatography, were not capable of determining what he concluded, the IG's investigation decided. Webb had in reality overstated his results, working from an unwritten protocol for such tests that, in the words of the IG's report, "had not been validated by the FBI or, to our knowledge, any other laboratory, with regard to their ability to determine if samples could have come from the same source."[55]

The IG's forensic scientists totally rejected what they termed Webb's "working proposition" that the examinations he performed would have necessarily revealed some differences if the materials had come from different manufacturers. Yet when examining the charts of Webb's tests, differences is precisely what the examiners found. In six cited cases, charts for paint, glue, the tape, and the RTV sealant from the four devices and packages revealed very different peaks or patterns, the basis for chemical comparison. Charts for tests on the tape from the Atlanta and Jacksonville devices could not even be located. Webb blamed the differences on contamination, variations in sample preparation, or machine calibration. He acknowledged that certain discrepancies in the test results were significant enough to require further explanation but then, completely illogically, did not retract his conclusions about the common origin of the samples.[56]

But all this was just a warm-up for the spuriousness of the link Thurman and the prosecution now developed between the 1972 bomb and the 1989 devices—the link that was essential for Roy Moody's conviction. In the afternoon of his first day on the stand, Howard Shapiro asked Thurman whether he had come across a bomb similar to the four 1989 devices. "Only one," answered Thurman. "Is that the device recovered from Mr. Moody's home?" Shapiro asked. "Yes, sir."[57] Back at the beginning of the case, ATF agent Rich Rawlins had noted the obvious differences between the 1989 devices and the 1972 bomb. Now two bomb experts, Robert Rush, a former FBI bomb technician, and Don Hansen, the former head of the San Francisco Police Department bomb squad listed numerous other dissimilarities in written reports.

With access to the photos, drawings, FBI and AFT lab reports, affidavits, bomb surveys, and even a videotape of the reenactment of the Birmingham bomb explosion Thurman had staged, Rush listed ten major differences.[58] Hansen settled for nine.[59] The differences, listed in the sort of detailed reports that contrasted sharply with so many FBI lab reports, ranged across every conceivable area—construction, design and types of materials used. Some of these were as obvious as Rawlins had pointed out. The 1972 device was constructed of pieces of aluminum tube with square aluminum end plates held in place with four threaded bolts, whereas, the 1989 bombs were made of galvanized pipe and end caps or steel plates welded to the pipe with one threaded rod. The 1972 device was much smaller, just $2\frac{1}{2}$ inches by $1\frac{1}{2}$ inches, and less powerful. Hazel Moody had been injured in the 1972 bomb; Robbie Robinson and Judge Vance both had been killed.

The 1972 device used no nails for "additional fragmentation," as Rush put it, was not secured inside the box, and the tube had not been painted with black latex paint. Moreover, the explosive charge had been different. "This device [the 1972 bomb] utilized a mixture of double base gunpowder as the explosive charge unlike the 1989 device which had a signal type of smokeless double base gunpowder (Hercules Red Dot) which was utilized in all four items," concluded Rush.[60] His comment was ironic in view of Whitehurst's observations. In looking for only one explosive, the Hercules Red Dot that Sartain said he had sold, and ignoring the possibility of other explosives in the 1989 devices, Thurman and Martz had denied themselves a possible link to Moody and the 1972 bomb.

Both Hansen and Rush noted major dissimilarities in mechanical design. "The triggering switch in the 1972 bomb was totally different in design and function than that which was employed in the 1989 series. The paper clips, for instance, were employed in a different manner and for a different purpose," Hansen noted.[61] "The 1972 device did not use a detonator of any kind as a means of igniting the explosive charge. A modified flashlight bulb was used as the sole source of initiation," added Rush.[62] Both men noted the absence of an improvised battery holder in the 1972 device and the fact that two C-cell batteries had been used in 1989 and a single D-cell power source in 1972.

It hardly added up to a signature—a giveaway that was "almost as good as a fingerprint" in Tom Thurman's eyes. Yet, incredibly, given the nature of the defense experts' evidence and the fact that the government's case hinged crucially on the connection between the 1972 and 1989 devices, neither Rush nor Hansen testified to challenge Thurman. "To this day I don't know what happened," Rush says. "I turned up in St. Paul one day as instructed ready to testify, introduced myself to Ed Tolley, who then went into a huddle with Louis Freeh, the prosecutor. When he came back a few minutes later he told me I wouldn't be needed to testify."[63] When asked, Ed Tolley justified the decision by saying that both Rush and Hansen sat through the cross-examination of Thurman. "They sort of guided me with the technical questions," he claimed.[64]

Tolley certainly challenged Thurman himself on the differences between the 1972 and 1989 devices, as he had Lloyd Erwin of the ATF earlier in the trial. Indeed, Tolley got Thurman to admit that there were many differences between the devices. However, Thurman quickly fell back on his experience and expertise, claiming the similarity was such that it constituted "a signature" tying all the bombs to Moody. He was not challenged to define or specify what this significant similarity or signature was because Ed Tolley did not ask. Indeed, Tolley did not inform the jury specifically of his experts' findings, except by implication in some of his own statements and questioning. "I do not suggest to you that Agent Thurman intentionally misrepresents evidence to you," he said in his summation. "But, I do suggest . . . that Agent Thurman is result oriented in this regard, and in this case. There are by my count, 16 to 23 major differences between the '72 device and the four '89 devices."[65]

Tolley never explained those differences. Questioned further, Tolley was quite defensive: "If I sound like a fan of Thomas Thurman, that's not intended to be. What Thurman did that I thought was so effective on the stand was, instead of trying to make a case that they were identical, he accepted the fact that they were dissimilar. And then he turned around and hooked us by pointing out to the jurors that there were certain things that were the same, and those certain things were so unique that they constituted a signature." He confides, "I've got to give credit to the devil . . . he was very effective in turning that back around on us. And hell, it wasn't much. It was just good testifying by him."[66]

Or perhaps a poor defense. Both Rush or Hansen would have denied that there were any similarities so unique as to constitute a signature, whatever that was. In fact, documents indicate that the government knew there were crucial differences and expected cross-examination on the subject. A teletype from the FBI's Atlanta field office dispatched sometime in 1990 refers to charts that show "how Moody improved his techniques between 1972 and 1989 bombs and will also show steps taken to defeat evidence used against him in [the] 1972 trial."[67] Hansen's report in particular pointed out that, according to the results of the FBI's own research, none of the features cited by Thurman as adding up to uniqueness were actually unique. Of the fifty-three pipe bombs mailed in the ten years through 1989, seven had welded end plates, forty-six a hinged lid/booby-trap triggering device, twenty-seven contained a threat letter, and seven used black paint inside the pipe.[68]

When Tolley leaned over the defense table and told his client that he was not going to call Hansen or Rush, Roy Moody quickly realized he had lost his best chance. "I was just so shocked," Moody says from Death Row in Alabama. "If there were going to be no experts to show that the evidence was fabricated, that the testimony was perjured, I knew I had to get up there."[69] Moody insisted he take the witness stand immediately.

Tolley objected vehemently, telling the judge that Moody might perjure himself and believing Roy Moody would do himself a lot of damage. On the latter point, Ed Tolley was right. On the stand, Roy Moody outlined an elaborate story that accused Mike Ford, his former lawyer, of sending the bombs, demonstrated a knowledge of physics and chemistry that would at least have enabled him to make the bombs, and made clear his obsession with clearing himself of his earlier conviction. Worse still, under cross-examination from Freeh, Roy Moody justified lying under oath in court.

"If the government wanted to prove Roy was angry and embittered at the legal system, they could hardly have scripted a better speech," wrote Mark Winne, an Atlanta-based author of a book about the VAN-PAC case. "Roy finished at the end of the day, the only witness for the defense, perhaps one of the most effective for the prosecution."[70] While Freeh called a string of rebuttal witnesses, including Mike Ford, to bolster the image of Roy Moody as an obsessed liar, Ed Tolley canceled the court appearances of the more than half a dozen witnesses he had subpoenaed. None of their testimony was compatible with the defense Roy Moody had just posited.

Not surprisingly, it was all downhill from there. Many of the key issues were now lost in the drama of the trial and were skimmed over in the summing up. There was little reference to the forensic science and "expertise" that underpinned the government's case, even less to Roy Moody's supposed motive or lack of it. What reference there was to the forensic evidence was punctuated with errors. Freeh said the black paint inside the pipe bombs had been sprayed, rather than hand-applied as the FBI lab had decided. Some of the eighty nails attached to the bomb that killed Judge Vance had been traveling at thirteen thousand feet per second, Freeh stated, citing a figure that had not been mentioned either in direct testimony or in lab reports.

Such mistakes and the fact that they went unchallenged were by now just symptomatic of the case. The IG's interview with Freeh on the matter noted: "He commented that no one objected to the statement during the trial and they certainly do not have the right to do so now."[71] In his own summation, Ed Tolley hammered away at what the government did not have. "We can send a man to the moon, ladies and gentlemen, and we just about have in this case. But with all their technical expertise . . . there has not been found one nail . . . not one nail in any car, any home, any storage locker . . . of Walter Leroy Moody. There has not been found one grain, . . . not one grain of smokeless powder in any-thing connected to Roy Moody. Nobody is that much of a master crimi-nal, ladies and gentlemen."[72]

Moody was, the jury decided. The government, they thought, had proven its case beyond a reasonable doubt. As he left the courthouse, Ed Tolley blamed the defeat on Roy Moody's refusal to proceed with a mental illness defense and his insistence on taking the stand. Judge Edward Devitt, suffering from terminal cancer, was quickly hospitalized. When Ed Tolley and Louis Freeh met up again in St. Paul later, they smuggled a bottle of whiskey into Devitt's hospital room and drank a toast.[73] Roy Moody was sentenced to seven life terms plus four hundred years. There was to be no parole from the maximum-security jail in Marion, Illinois.

There were congratulations, and promotions, all round. Tom Thur-man recalls being at his laboratory bench when he took the phone call that informed him that Moody had gone down. When Chris Ronay, his boss, retired in 1994, he became head of the FBI's Explosives Unit and Bomb Data Center. Roger Martz became acting head of the Scientific Analysis Section of the lab in 1995 on James Kearney's retirement. Larry Potts was soon promoted to the plum job of assistant director of the Criminal Investigation Division at the FBI. Within a month, Attorney General Dick Thornburgh had made Louis Freeh a federal judge in New York. In less than two years, Freeh was named director of the FBI, Howard Shapiro again following him, this time as his general counsel at the J. Edgar Hoover Building in Washington, a position created especially for him by Freeh.

The IG's office was still investigating Whitehurst's charges about the VANPAC investigation, Tom Thurman, and Roger Martz as Roy Moody went on trial for his life in a subsequent state prosecution in Alabama in October 1996. It was not prosecutor Robert Morrow's job to tell the jury that Roger Martz and Tom Thurman, the men who trotted out their evidence again at the state trial in Birmingham, were under investigation for serious professional misconduct in this case and many others. And Louis Freeh, director of the FBI, the original prosecutor, the man whose career had been lent a meteoric boost by his success in the VANPAC case, was not going to stand in the way of his friends and employees testifying before the IG's investigation had reached a conclusion. The FBI took just one precaution before the trial. Roger Martz and Tom Thurman made blanket denials of Whitehurst's charges in sworn affidavits.

With Ted Banks refusing to testify against Moody, despite being hauled up from jail in Florida and invited to tell his story again, the case was even thinner than five years earlier in Minnesota. Few worried. Moody had already been found guilty and he had no lawyer, having decided to represent himself. It seemed to be just a question of going through the motions. On November 4, 1996, Walter Leroy Moody was found guilty of the package bomb murder of Judge Robert Vance in the state of Alabama. On February 10, 1997, he was sentenced to die in "Big Yellah Moma," Alabama's electric chair, notorious for failing to kill a victim with its first embrace of current. Awaiting sentencing, prosecutor Robert Morrow was handed a handwritten fax from Louis Freeh, congratulating him.

Less than three months after Moody's second trial ended, Roger Martz and Tom Thurman were transferred to FBI duties outside the lab. The IG's draft report had been submitted to Louis Freeh and the FBI's top brass. The conclusions were damning and dangerous. Ironically, although being implicated in major failings in many other cases about which Whitehurst complained, both Martz and Thurman were censured only modestly for their conduct in VANPAC. Martz, the IG stated, had been ambiguous in stating that he had been unable to "successfully compare" the Hercules Red Dot smokeless powder from the Shootin' Iron shop and the bombs. Thurman, meanwhile, overstated results by drawing conclusions only on the basis of what Robert Webb had written in his auxiliary examiner's report but that were scientifically unjustified.

The IG's conclusions were far too narrowly based. Because the IG only investigated Whitehurst's specific charges, there is no analysis of Thurman's flawed comparison of the IEDs and his subjective concept of a signature. There was no scrutiny of William Bodziak's typewriter comparisons. There is no real investigation of why documentation was missing from the VANPAC files, documentation on which Webb's overstated results were based. Above all, as with so much of the IG's report, there is no context. No effort to examine the shortcuts and flaws that justified focusing solely on Roy Moody as a suspect from an early date, why such a focus took place to the exclusion of other leads, why working backward from the assumption of Moody's guilt was automatic in the VANPAC investigation.

This is all the more surprising in that many of the issues the IG report seems to gloss over on the VANPAC investigation were heavily criticized in the remainder of the report. For, as the IG's report itself noted, the VANPAC case highlighted numerous serious inadequacies in the FBI lab. These included the absence of written and validated protocols for standardized procedures, file review by unit managers to ensure conclusions were supported by appropriate analysis and data, proper record retention and retrieval systems, clear guidelines on the respective responsibilities of individual units for examinations and a strict policy on testimony in court and a system for monitoring such testimony. All these deficiencies and many others would become even more obvious in the high-profile cases that now followed.

4

RUBY RIDGE:
SCREW-UP, COVER-UP, CONSPIRACY

Press, lawyers, jurors, no one could believe it. Summoned to the sixth floor of the glass rectangle that was the Boise Federal Courthouse by Judge Edward Lodge, they were told that what was already one of the longest jury deliberations in Idaho state history would have to begin anew. Cyril Hatfield, the seventy-two-year-old World War II veteran and securities salesman who had been elected foreman when deliberations began two weeks before, had been taken to the hospital with a chronic heart condition. Doctors wanted him excused from any further stress. Judge Lodge had agreed and, after receiving assurances from Anita Brewer, one of the two alternate jurors, that she could be fair and impartial, he had sworn her in. It turned out to be just the last of many reversals for the government in the case of USA v. *Randy Weaver and Kevin Harris*.

It would be another nine days before anyone would know it, but Anita Brewer was to change the whole dynamic of the jury. First, the man she replaced had been a mainstay of a proconviction faction of what had begun to look increasingly like a hung jury. Second, as a medical technician she would introduce an element of scientific logic to the debate, not only in reasoning, but in focusing on the forensic evidence in the case. In her job, lab samples were handled with infinite care, test results handed to doctors were checked and rechecked if necessary, she told her fellow jurors. Yet here was the government trying to convict two men to long prison terms on the basis of evidence that had been lost, mishandled, and collected in a way that would not stand up to the rigors of a high school science class. "She was very persuasive. I wish we'd had her on the jury before," says John Harris Weaver, the forty-three-year-old printer who was elected to take Hatfield's place as foreman. "I think Anita gave real meaning to the word 'deliberate.' "[1]

Just one example of what Anita Brewer was talking about had arisen during closing arguments when Kevin Harris's defense attorney, David Nevin, announced that he had new evidence. As a fascinated audience strained to hear, he brought out the regulation-issue backpack that U.S. Marshal William Degan had been wearing on the August morning in 1992 when he had been shot dead on Ruby Ridge, a remote, heavily wooded mountainside in the panhandle of northern Idaho. He showed the jury the bullet hole the FBI lab had identified as an exit hole. But then he showed the increasingly incredulous five men and seven women another hole in the fold of the backpack, a hole the FBI lab in Washington had ignored.

Although Nevin had up to this point claimed self-defense for his client, it was good theater and potentially vital evidence. If the second hole was the entry hole, Nevin argued, as he strolled around the courtroom, Marshal Degan must have been shot from behind by one of his fellow U.S. marshals. And that meant he could have been killed by one of them, too, absolving his client, Kevin Harris, and his coaccused, Randy Weaver, of the most serious of several charges they faced—murder. Nevin reminded the jury that it was only the second FBI lab test of the bullet fragments found in Degan's body that had found them to be "consistent with" those fired by Kevin Harris's old bolt-action 30.06-caliber hunting rifle. That was not proof. Indeed, in the light of the performance of the FBI lab throughout this case, it raised reasonable doubts.

With Anita Brewer on board, the jury acquitted Kevin Harris and Randy Weaver on all but two minor charges. Their decision put the laboratory, along with the rest of the FBI, in the dock as never before, in what *The Washington Post* soon labeled "one of the worst law enforcement debacles of recent years." In fact, as the months and years went by it would turn out to be much more than a debacle. The very questions now being asked would, for the first time, place the FBI lab's performance and the Bureau's own internal investigation of it under detailed scrutiny. First a Justice Department report by a task force, then a Senate subcommittee investigation would make stinging criticisms and lead to the opening of a criminal investigation of senior FBI officials. The deputy director of the FBI, Larry Potts, Director Louis Freeh's friend and golden boy, would be suspended, pending criminal charges, then resign from the FBI, having been promoted personally to the number two post by Freeh while still under investigation. But by then it would be clear that what happened at Ruby Ridge and then back in the FBI's headquarters in Washington was a cover-up of a screwup by means of an institutional conspiracy.

Investigators of the lab's role in the Ruby Ridge inquiry uncovered some of the most serious offenses in forensic science—loss of evidence, failure to do tests, destruction of evidence, and a complete failure to search or log a crime scene properly. When the government's own prosecutors decided to hire independent experts, the Firearms-Toolmarks Unit, a key plank of the myth that the FBI's lab was the best in the world, would have its reputation blown away. Finally, and most important, there was the posing and destruction of incriminating evidence.

The Justice Department investigators in particular were deeply shocked, raising a question in their final report that should have set alarm bells ringing throughout the criminal justice system of the United States. If what they had uncovered was happening in such a high-profile case as Ruby Ridge, what might be happening in "matters of less importance," they asked?[2] To this day, it is hard to say. The Senate subcommittee linked their own conclusions about the lab's inadequacies with the serious criticisms of the inspector general's 1994 audit. Among many other things, the whole of the Ruby Ridge incident demonstrated that the FBI could not police itself, the subcommittee concluded, confirming the opinion of one FBI veteran that investigations were "run backwards" to reach predetermined outcomes.[3] Nowhere was this truer, it seemed, than in the lab.

What led to the siege at Ruby Ridge was not in dispute. In 1989, an ATF informant had entrapped Randy Weaver, who had agreed to supply him with two shotguns with illegally sawed-off barrels. The charge was designed as leverage. The ATF wanted Weaver, a white separatist Christian Identitist, to become a source of information on the Aryan Nations, a leading white supremacist organization based on a forty-acre compound in Hayden Lake near Coeur d'Alene, Idaho.

Weaver had refused and, although not a member of the Aryan Nations, had rung the compound to tell them of the infiltration effort. After being charged, Weaver was issued a court summons citing an incorrect date. When he did not appear, a warrant was served, and his wood-framed cabin high on a mountainous promontory known as Ruby Ridge was put under surveillance by means of two hidden solar-powered video cameras. By August 1992, the humble cabin, built with two-by-fours, plywood, and scraps from a nearby sawmill, was being staked out by six U.S. deputy marshals belonging to the elite, heavily armed Special Operations Group.

On the morning of August 21, the family Labrador, Striker, started barking and dashed off into the dense pine, larch, and maple woods that surround the cabin. Kevin Harris, a close family friend, and Sammy Weaver, Randy's fourteen-year-old son, picked up their hunting rifles in pursuit of Striker, hoping it was a deer. When the dog discovered the U.S. marshals, a gunfight broke out. Who shot first was the first key issue of the trial; ballistics can often indicate or even prove many things but could not answer the million-dollar question in this case: Why what took place happened.

What was evident when the smoke cleared at what was known as the Y, the intersection of an old logging road and the trail that led up to the cabin, was that Striker, the dog, lay dead, Sammy had been injured in the arm and then, having started to run home, had been shot in the back, and Kevin Harris had fired at least twice at the U.S. marshals. By the time Harris made it back to the cabin to tell Vicki and Randy Weaver that their son was dead, William Degan, one of the most heavily decorated men in the U.S. Marshals Service and the father of two sons, was bleeding to death from a gunshot wound to the chest.

Within hours, the story that the law enforcement agents had been ambushed and were still under fire from the cabin had reached FBI headquarters in Washington. The crack Hostage Rescue Team was flown to Sandpoint, Idaho, and their rules of engagement were controversially changed while the team was still in the air. When in the early evening of

August 22, Randy Weaver, his sixteen-year-old daughter Sara, and Kevin Harris ventured out of the cabin to visit the shed where they had managed to lay out Sammy's body, several teams of snipers had the whole area covered.

One shot from FBI sniper Lon Horiuchi hit Randy Weaver under the arm as he lifted the latch on the shed door. As all three ran back to the cabin, Sara trying to shield her dad, the presumed target, Vicki Weaver opened the cabin door, carrying her ten-month-old baby, Elisheba, in her other arm. As Weaver, Harris, and Sara tumbled through the door, Horiuchi pulled the trigger of his bolt-action sniper's rifle a second time. The bullet hit Vicki Weaver in the forehead, severing her carotid artery and taking away half her face before going on to hit Kevin Harris in the upper arm and chest. Vicki fell to the floor screaming, clutching the uninjured Elisheba to her chest. Within seconds Vicki Weaver was dead. Kevin Harris and Randy Weaver surrendered more than a week later, and were quickly charged with various counts of murder, conspiracy, trafficking in illegal weapons, resisting arrest, and stockpiling weapons.

Firearms—rifles, shotguns, submachine guns, and pistols, from the old, iron-sighted hunting rifle carried by Kevin Harris to the silenced submachine gun carried by Marshal Larry Cooper at the Y—were at the center of all the charges. Who shot first and why, who killed who and how, and above all, why a crack FBI sniper had killed a mother with a baby in her arms inside her own home when aiming at someone else outside—these were the key questions.

The FBI seemed to stake out its case from the moment its agents allowed the television cameras to film the fourteen weapons and some of the forty-five hundred rounds of ammunition they discovered in the cabin. This, the prosecution would allege, was a veritable miniarsenal stockpiled to confront and deter law enforcement officers from entering the Weaver "compound." Allegations that there were tunnels and booby traps added to the image. According to the official version, the fanatical Weaver family first had ambushed, then pinned down, the U.S. marshals for more than twelve hours, firing hundreds of rounds at them from the cabin. Lon Horiuchi, the FBI's sniper, had been aiming at Kevin Harris with both shots, even though both had missed. He had shot under the rules of engagement he had read before going to his position: armed males outside the cabin "can and should" be shot if the shot could be taken without endangering children.

As for what happened at the Y, the government's line was simple if unconvincing. Marshal Degan saw Sammy Weaver and Kevin Harris coming, rose onto one knee, identified himself, and told them to freeze. Harris shot Degan and Marshal Art Roderick shot the dog. Marshal Cooper saw Degan go down and fired at Harris. Somehow Degan fired seven shots after he was hit, one of which hit Sammy Weaver in the arm. Sammy was then shot and killed while running away. The U.S. marshals claimed none of them had been aiming at him. Harris and his defense team's story was even simpler and made much more sense. According to them, Roderick shot Striker, a furious Sammy Weaver, who did not know who the marshals were, fired at Roderick and missed. Degan shot Sammy in the arm and Sammy turned to run home. Kevin Harris shot Degan to protect Sammy, but Cooper finished him off with a bullet through the back.

Ballistics would need to determine who had fired what by matching bullets or fragments to the firearms involved and the holes in clothes, accessories, or wounds. Lines of fire would need to be established; distances, often determined from the gunshot residue or bullet wipe surrounding a wound or clothes, would need to be ascertained as part of a reconstruction of events. Within days, Supervisory Special Agent James Cadigan, a sixteen-year veteran of the FBI lab's oldest and best-known department, had been made principal examiner for the Ruby Ridge case.

To the visitor, Firearms-Toolmarks is probably the most spectacular unit of the FBI lab. The microscopic comparisons of Hairs and Fibers or the trace analysis of Chemistry and Toxicology and Materials Analysis are largely invisible and often unintelligible to the nonscientist. The five thousand–reference arsenal of guns collected by the firearms experts— everything from the largest caliber, precision-engineered machine gun to the oldest homemade pistol—is the most jaw-dropping display at the lab. Here are the personal weapons of some of America's most notorious gangsters: John Dillinger's .45-caliber Smith & Wesson and the assorted rifles that once belonged to Bonnie and Clyde. For most visitors, the highlight of the FBI lab tour is the demonstration of shooting at the ominous black silhouettes that make up the targets at the indoor range where the FBI does its test firings.

The basis of firearms identification is forensic science's Holy Grail of individualization—in the case of firearms, relating a particular bullet to a particular gun. The starting point is the FBI's General Rifling Characteristics File, a database detailing the general rifling or bore characteristics of the barrel of nearly twenty thousand different weapons. But while the characteristics file can associate a bullet with a make or several different makes of weapon, only the striations or other marks on a bullet—surface indentations, usually scratches—produced by the spiral grooves cut into every gun barrel to give a bullet the spin essential for its direction, will associate one gun with one bullet.

Given a gun, and a bullet suspected of having come from that gun, FBI firearms examiners fire the weapon into a water tank, recover the bullet, and make a comparison. The theory is simple: Every barrel is unique. The instruments used to bore the barrels are worn down minutely with every cut, changing microscopically, and thus leaving the gun with a metallic "fingerprint." Still, the practice of firearms identification is tricky. An examiner can make the match only by lining up two bullets under a comparison microscope. The $64-million question is: what constitutes a match? How many striations will suffice to be certain?

As with so much else in forensic science, there is no universal agreement on this even among firearms examiners. Making "matches" is put down to experience. There is no science to it. And as if striation comparisons were not enough of a minefield, there are all kinds of other considerations. The firing pin, the extractor, and the ejector post of a gun may all etch marks on the casing of a bullet as it is ejected. All have to be considered in any potential identification. Then there is the impact. A bullet that hits a hard target, or even something as relatively soft as human tissue or bone, may have its shape altered radically.

The controversy of the shootings, the difficulties involved in firearms identifications, and the relatively large area over which the shooting at Ruby Ridge took place made the thorough sealing and searching of the crime scene more essential than ever. Yet the FBI could not have gotten off to a worse start. Overlooked evidence, posed evidence, tainted searchers, inexact marking and measurement—the searches of the Y and the Weaver cabin at Ruby Ridge would make a good forensic science textbook case study of how not to do it. Every move the FBI made seemed to hand a grenade to Harris and Weaver's defense lawyers. As Justice Department investigators noted in 1994, even FBI personnel were highly critical of the way the search was done.[4]

The crime scene at the Y was supposed to be subjected to a thorough search, first on August 24, then over the six days from August 27 to September 1. The reason for this was simple: there seemed to be a lot to find. The U.S. marshals insisted that they had been in a major firefight and had exposed "hundreds" of rounds of fire. In fact, no more than nineteen rounds were fired at the Y, seven by U.S. marshal William Degan from his 5.56-millimeter M-16 rifle; six in two three-round bursts by U.S. marshal Larry Cooper from his Colt Commando 9-millimeter suppressed submachine gun; one by U.S. marshal Art Roderick from his 5.56-millimeter M-16 rifle to kill the dog, Striker. In addition, no more than three rounds were fired by Kevin Harris from his 30.06-caliber bolt-action rifle and probably two, but possibly only one, by Sammy Weaver from his Ruger Mini-14 hunting rifle.

Yet despite the supposed throroughness of the FBI search in looking for the evidence of this alleged turkey shoot, much was left behind. On March 22 and 23, 1993, a team composed of prosecutors, local deputy marshals, Boundary county deputy sheriffs, and independent forensic experts revisited the scene, and despite up to two feet of snow in places, discovered several bits of possible evidence, including major items such as a bullet and part of the butt plate of Sammy Weaver's rifle. Worse was to come. In November 1995, Boundary county sheriff Greg Sprungl led another team to the scene, more than three years after the event, and uncovered several more bullets among more than forty possible pieces of evidence.

The truth was it was hard, difficult work. "Looking for a needle in a haystack would have been easier," Sprungl told the press. "This was more like looking for a needle in a hayfield."[5] Guided by a crime scene metal detection expert, Richard Graham, Sprungl's team spent five weeks at the Y, the scene of the shootout. "The only way you could do it properly was inch by inch, going over every bit several times. We took tree stumps apart, the lot," recalls Sheriff Sprungl.[6] The thoroughness paid off. By May 1996, one of the bullets recovered had been identified as a 9-millimeter Winchester SilverTip. It soon became clear that it was the bullet that had killed Sammy Weaver.

The crime scene problems at Ruby Ridge were not unique. There had been plenty of problems with the FBI's handling of crime scene searches before. The Evidence Response Team (ERT), the new specialist squad which included lab personnel from a spectrum of disciplines, was the FBI's response to this criticism. It was on standby, expecting to be dispatched, as soon as FBI headquarters heard about the death of Marshal Degan, according to the Bureau's own Strategic Information and Operations Center log. Somehow, Special Agent in Charge Eugene Glenn, the man in overall command at Ruby Ridge, had not been told. He later told the Justice Department that he would not have used the ERT anyway. He saw Ruby Ridge as a "normal murder crime scene."[7]

Even if three deaths, including that of a U.S. marshal, were normal, the investigation was not. In the first place, the first two searches of the area around the Y took place while the siege of the cabin was still underway. In the second, the area around the Y was densely forested, with abundant undergrowth. Agents often had to rake through six inches of leaves, pine needles, twigs, and branches to locate the cartridge casings, bullets, and other evidence that would be the basis of the forensic case.

Apart from the failure to find evidence, mapping what was discovered was bungled badly. Triangulation is the standard method of fixing the location of evidence at a crime scene. High school geometry teaches that measuring from two fixed reference points rather than one is more accurate. Yet at the Y on Ruby Ridge, triangulation was not used. The FBI co-case agent, Joe Venkus, designated a burned tree stump as the sole reference point, with miniature flags or index cards being used to mark the spot of any evidence. Measurements were taken with a three-hundred-foot tape borrowed from Idaho state police, with FBI agent Mark Thundercloud marking the spots on a hand-drawn map that was not to scale.

The result, according to Kim Lindquist, the coprosecutor at the Weaver-Harris trial, was not accurate enough. The locations of evidence such as Marshal Degan's bullet casings, for instance, were critical to the prosecution's theory that Degan may have fired all seven rounds after being critically injured—the only theory that fit the marshals' insistence that Harris had fired first and wounded Degan. With no compass headings used, no accurate record of elevations, and no triangulation, the "precision essential for crime scene searches and evaluations was inexcusably lacking," the Justice Department task force concluded.[8] In court, the defense team had a field day. The charismatic Gerry Spence, the best-known defense lawyer in the land, used a pair of electrical extension cords to demonstrate that when only one measurement is taken, evidence can be located in a number of different spots on an arc radiating from a fixed point.

But all this paled in comparison to what Spence was to label the "magic bullet," evoking the one discovered during the investigation of John F. Kennedy's assassination. Despite five days of searching by dozens of agents and the use of three metal detectors, one bullet, labeled exhibit L1, was not found at the Y until August 31, after Randy Weaver, his daughters, and Kevin Harris had surrendered. It was important. It had been fired from one of the Ruger rifles recovered from the cabin and could help prove that Randy Weaver had been involved in the firefight at the Y on August 21.

The bullet's late discovery and its relatively pristine condition—it had one dent and a few striations on it, but nothing compared to all the others fired at the Y, which had invariably hit rocks, trees, and vegetation —had always made the defense team suspicious. It could, after all, have been a bullet found lying in or near the cabin. That would explain its late discovery and its condition. On May 25, six weeks into the trial, Gerry Spence was convinced he had the evidence for his theory when the prosecution handed over a package that included photos of evidence in situ taken by FBI photographer Kelly Kramer.

One photo showed L1 pointing in one direction, another the opposite. In both cases the .223-caliber bullet was neatly positioned on top of some leaves by the side of the dirt road, making its late discovery all the more suspicious. Eventually an incredible explanation emerged. FBI agent Larry Wages, who had led several of the searches of the Y, had actually found the bullet on the morning of August 31 but was quickly ordered out of the area as Randy Weaver and his daughters surrendered and left the cabin. Unable to locate the official FBI photographer, he claims he had James Cadigan photograph it, then picked it up, put it in a plastic evidence bag, and pocketed it.

After assisting in the search of the Weaver cabin, Wages claimed he remembered he needed a photograph with letter designations on it to ensure the bullet's admissibility as evidence in court. Having found Special Agent Kramer, the FBI's photographer, he returned to where he believed he had found the bullet but was unable to remember which way around it had been facing. As a result he had Kramer photograph it facing both ways. Wages claimed he forgot to tell co–case agent Greg Rampton that the photos were posed until he was asked in October or November. Prosecutor Ron Howen admitted he had known all this but had not told the defense when he handed over the photographs six weeks into the trial.

There is little doubt that the "magic bullet" episode played a considerable role in undermining the government's credibility in the Ruby Ridge case. "I think it was a stroke of genius by Gerry Spence, labeling it 'the magic bullet,' " says David Nevin, Harris's defense lawyer. "That one piece of evidence was a perfect reflection of the case, the incompetence, the untrustworthiness, and the real possibility of a conspiracy."[9] In fact, the bullet was matched eventually with Sara Weaver's Ruger rifle, so if it was a conspiracy, it was also a bungled one.

Randy Weaver did own a Ruger rifle, but the bullet had not come from his gun's barrel. And no one, not even the FBI or the U.S. Marshals Service, was claiming that Sara, Randy's sixteen-year-old daughter, had been anywhere near the Y during the shootout on August 22. As for the bullet's condition, Larry Wages, who had some ballistics training, was quite helpful under cross-examination by the defense during the trial. He suggested that it looked like a bullet that had been pushed through a rifle barrel with a rod.

The Justice Department's investigation concluded that the FBI agents had not used the metal detectors at Ruby Ridge properly. Given these difficulties with such low-tech, it was perhaps understandable that the real high tech should give the FBI even bigger problems. On August 31, two visual information specialists from the FBI lab, Cyrus Grover and Michael Taister, started surveying the crime scene with a theodolite system—essentially a laser beam that measures distances from a fixed point. With much of the evidence removed and a number of the marker flags now out of place, a very inaccurate computer-generated map of the crime scene emerged. It was in fact so inaccurate that it could not be correlated with the basic hand-drawn diagram done by FBI agent Mark Thundercloud.

The FBI's Shooting Incident Review Team (SIRT) had even more problems with the theodolite system. Measurements were taken using two fixed points: FBI sniper Lon Horiuchi's firing spot and an outhouse in the cabin's yard known as the birthing shed—the place where Sammy Weaver's body had been laid out. Both were wrong. James Cadigan, a key member of the SIRT, could not relocate the spot on the mountain that Lon Horiuchi had shown him to be his firing point when the FBI sniper had returned briefly to the scene after the incident. In the end, Cadigan guessed, and guessed wrongly. The outhouse, meanwhile, had been moved by the Hostage Rescue Team during the standoff. No one had bothered to tell the SIRT team.

The result was that the FBI lab's computer diagram of Horiuchi's shooting trajectory was off by about 45 degrees. Eventually the lab's Special Projects Section acknowledged the error and corrected the trajectory—after Horiuchi had been summoned to the lab to locate his real firing spot on the diagram. However, in changing the angle, the technicians apparently forgot to change the distances. The result was that measurements on the final diagram were off by up to fifty feet.[10]

Despite the failure to collect or locate so much of the evidence, the FBI laboratory in Washington did receive a total of 199 items from the Ruby Ridge crime scene and performed 350 examinations, generating 12 lab reports. From Firearms, the hub of the investigation, requests for tests and analysis went out to units ranging from Serology to Hairs and Fibers. Yet in the coming months, the Ruby Ridge forensic work would turn out to be such a long catalog of incompetence, inefficiency, and foot dragging that, as with the collection of evidence at the crime scene itself, observers were soon asking whether what went on in this case was part of a conspiracy rather than just the sort of screw-up that the lab had proved itself to be perfectly capable of in the past.

After all, when the siege at this beautiful spot—an arm's reach from heaven as one local journalist put it—was over, there was a lot to hide. A fourteen-year-old child running away from the scene had been shot dead, as had a mother with a babe in her arms trying to shelter her family in her own home. All this was in aid of the arrest of a man who, as he admitted later, may have been a bit stupid, but certainly was not, by any reasonable definition, dangerous. As a result, what happened at Ruby Ridge has been subjected to more investigations by more departments of government than any other law enforcement incident in recent times.

There have been five internal FBI reports investigating what happened at Ruby Ridge, the last three at least the result of the inadequacies of previous reports. None have been made public, but they have been described collectively by a Senate subcommittee as "variously contradictory, inaccurate and biased."[11] There has also been a 542-page report by a task force set up by the Department of Justice under Barbara Berman at the Office of Professional Responsibility. Completed in June 1994, Berman's report, or the Task Force Report, as it became known, was never released formally, but eventually it was leaked.

The Task Force Report includes two particularly critical chapters on the performance of the FBI lab and the collection of evidence. One damning comment on the FBI lab said it all: "If the response in this matter is typical of high-profile homicide cases involving the death of a federal law enforcement officer and two citizens, we wonder about the response to matters of less importance."[12] The last two of the five FBI reports were respectively a submission and a response to the Justice Department's task force. The first of these, known as the Walsh Report, was supposed to be a detailed factual account to the task force. Instead, it became an exercise in justification with "members of the Walsh team going out of their way to solicit legal and forensic opinions supporting the FBI's actions at Ruby Ridge."[13]

Hearings before the Subcommittee on Terrorism, Technology and Government Information, part of the Senate Committee on the Judiciary, followed in the fall of 1995. The senators reiterated the findings of the task force, and expressed particular frustration at the FBI lab's James Cadigan's stonewalling when he appeared before the subcommittee. His answers to critical questions were described as "unsatisfactory" by Chairman Arlen Specter and "an embarrassment" by the Idaho senator, Larry Craig. One Senate aide went further when recalling the testimony later. "It was just insufferable arrogance, sitting there and maintaining everything they did was perfectly correct. It was actually revolting."

The subcommittee astutely linked the criticism of the lab in the Ruby Ridge case with other complaints, in particular the "serious questions" the Justice Department's inspector general (IG) had raised in the June 1994 audit of the lab (see Chapter 1) and the criticisms just beginning to be made public in the summer of 1995 by Frederic Whitehurst. But the senators also made another connection: their general observations about the FBI's inability to investigate itself adequately seemed particularly pertinent to the lab. The subcommittee noted that in August 1992, the exact time of the Ruby Ridge incident, the FBI's inspection division had concluded that the FBI laboratory was operating "efficiently and effectively."

One of the most startling facts about the hearings was the refusal of five FBI agents to testify. For the first time in the FBI's eighty-seven-year history, agents took the Fifth Amendment. It only could add to the suspicion that a cover-up into the killings of Sammy and Vicki Weaver as well as the death of Marshal William Degan was in process. In August 1995, the month before the Senate hearings had begun, Eugene Glenn, the FBI's special agent in charge at Ruby Ridge, sent a stinging twelve-page letter to the Department of Justice's OPR.

One of twelve agents rapped over the knuckles with sanctions imposed by FBI director Louis Freeh for failings in the Ruby Ridge affair, Glenn said the FBI investigators of the whole episode needed to be investigated themselves. He refused to take the blame for changing the rules of engagement, claiming they had been approved by headquarters. Senior people, including the deputy director of the FBI, Larry Potts, were being absolved, he insisted.

As a result of this charge, yet another inquiry, a criminal investigation under the U.S. attorney of Philadelphia, Michael Stiles, was eventually begun. In October 1996, Michael Kahoe, the deputy chief of the FBI's Violent Crimes Unit, pled guilty to obstruction of justice in destroying an internal critique of what happened at Ruby Ridge, known as the After Action Report.[14] Kahoe destroyed the document rather than hand it over to prosecutors in the Weaver-Harris trial, knowing that if he did it would have to be revealed to the defense under discovery rules. In October 1997, Kahoe was sentenced to eighteen months in jail; this came two months after Stiles announced that the available evidence did not support further criminal prosecutions against four others, including Deputy Director Potts.

The whole Ruby Ridge affair became such an embarrassment for the FBI because of a desperate effort to preserve the image of an infallible agency. This involved a multilayered cover-up to hide the original embarrassment, the mistakes made in conducting the siege at Ruby Ridge, which in fact just involved more mistakes. Nowhere was this more obvious than in the FBI lab, as the prosecutors' complaints make plain. The lab refused to do tests and provide expertise, was incompetent when it did, lost evidence, showed absolutely no initiative in the investigation, and refused to hand over exculpatory material, the prosecutors alleged. This helped sabotage the case, by providing endless evidence for the defense team's argument that the operation was bungled and that the incompetence was now being covered up.

It all started appropriately enough with a refusal. More than six months before the trial began in April 1993, U.S. assistant attorneys Ron Howen and Kim Lindquist told FBI case agents Greg Rampton and Joe Venkus that the prosecution would need a "shooting reconstructionist" to corroborate the marshals' testimonies about the firefight at the Y. According to Lindquist, the agents insisted there was no such thing as a shooting reconstructionist, but after some discussion Joe Venkus did call the FBI lab, only to be told precisely that—there was no such forensic discipline.[15]

This is patently untrue. Exasperated, Lindquist told the U.S. marshals to find one of the best shooting reconstructionists in the country. Within twenty-four hours the name of Dr. Lucien "Luke" Haag, a widely respected expert from Arizona, was on his desk. When Lindquist spoke to him, Haag was surprised it was a request from the prosecution. Why were they not using the FBI lab? He knew they did shooting reconstructions; indeed, he had worked with an FBI expert on a previous case.

Cadigan now blames a misunderstanding. He claims that he told the prosecutors that no one single person could testify about bullet trajectories and the positioning of the participants in the shootout. The FBI did not offer shooting reconstruction as a "single discipline" and he had doubts that it was possible in such a wide open area as that at the Y. "Normally crime scene reconstructions that I have been involved in were in—usually occurred in closed spaces, closed areas in which there were holes in walls, et cetera, to establish lines of bullet trajectory," he told the Senate subcommittee in October 1995.[16]

Lindquist says that Cadigan's attitude changed when he heard that Luke Haag was to be involved. Cadigan claims he consulted his boss, the head of the Firearms-Toolmarks Unit (FTU), Jack Dillon, and called back to say that he would be available to attempt a reconstruction. When Lindquist said he would continue with Haag, Cadigan asked to accompany the prosecutors to the crime scene for the reconstruction. Lindquist agreed. In reality it was Haag's name that had spurred the FBI's FTU into action. He was very good and had testified against the FBI lab before and embarrassed it. Lindquist was disgusted. He knew there was no miscommunication and was convinced that this was simply another effort by "the ever image-conscious FBI to save face." [17]

As the Ruby Ridge investigation progressed, it became clear to Lindquist and fellow prosecutor Ronald Howen that Cadigan was out of his depth. When it was all over, the case lost, and the prosecution's evidence in tatters, the two prosecutors sent a scorching thirteen-page memo to Barbara Berman, the head of the Justice Department's task force investigation. "With all due respect to the supervisor [Cadigan], it was quite obvious that Mr. Haag was quite out of the supervisor's league when it came to not only shooting reconstruction but ballistic and firearms identification," the prosecutors stated. [18] The FBI lab, they concluded, was "out of touch with forensic reality." [19]

The bullet that killed Sammy Weaver passed right through him, leaving investigators with the difficult but not impossible task of trying to ascertain what caliber of projectile had killed the fourteen-year-old as he ran back up the trail toward the cabin. This, according to Kim Lindquist, the FBI laboratory refused to do, Cadigan asserting that no test recognized by forensic science enables an examiner to determine with any certainty the caliber of a bullet puncturing clothing. There was no offer from the FBI to proffer an opinion on the basis of elimination. After all, there were a strictly limited number of weapons at the Y during the shootout. Residues from some of the radically different types of bullets being used could have been expected to be found on the thick sheepskin jacket Sammy was wearing when killed.

Eventually the FBI lab did do tests that included some for gunshot residue on Sammy Weaver's jacket. There was no "definitive" conclusion, Cadigan told the Senate subcommittee. Dr. Martin Fackler, an independent wound ballistician from Florida, a surgeon and thirty-year military veteran, did not agree. Dr. Fackler, recommended by Dr. Haag and the second of the independent experts the prosecution decided to recruit in the face of the FBI lab's intransigence, took the witness stand for the government to testify that in his opinion Sammy Weaver was killed with a 9-millimeter bullet.

When at the Senate hearings in the fall of 1995 the U.S. marshals came up with another theory—that Randy Weaver had accidently shot his own son with his 9-millimeter Tanfoglio TZ-75 pistol—Senator Arlen Specter asked Haag and Fackler to take another look. With full cooperation ordered, the two experts received everything from the local FBI office in Phoenix, Arizona—the lab notes, the weapons, the cartridges, the spent bullets, and the sheepskin jacket, long-sleeved shirt, and T-shirt that Sammy Weaver had been wearing when killed. Even though the key bullet had not at this point been recovered by Sheriff Sprungl from the Y, the two experts were to embarrass the FBI lab further by concluding that a 9-millimeter Winchester SilverTip jacketed-hollow-point bullet fired from Deputy U.S. Marshal Larry Cooper's Colt submachine gun was "the single source of the fatal wound to this decedent."[20]

The report, and the range and thoroughness of the tests it detailed, put the FBI lab to shame. Luke Haag outlined how the weapons were tested, the retrieved bullets and casings matched, the bullet speeds measured. Then the holes in the clothing were measured. Although a bloodstain surrounded the hole in the sheepskin jacket, infrared photography revealed what appeared to be a partial ring of "bullet wipe," or residue around the blood. But it was the test firings that would provide the proof.

Backing test areas cut from the three items of clothing with seven-inch-long blocks of gelatin and a 0.060-inch piece of rubber to simulate flesh and skin respectively, three types of bullets were fired from Larry Cooper's Colt SMG, Randy Weaver's TZ-75 pistol, and a civilian version of the M-16 used by the other deputy U.S. marshals. Only the 115-gram, 9-millimeter Winchester SilverTip bullets made entry holes anything like the dimensions of those in the original clothes, left no fragments in the "wound track" of the gelatin, and exited cleanly. Indeed, the 124-gram 9-millimeter FMJ-RN Norinco bullets fired from Randy Weaver's pistol failed to cut significant holes in the clothing at all.[21]

Within days of conducting his tests, confirmation of Luke Haag's complete upstaging of the FBI lab became possible when a 9-millimeter silver-tipped bullet was found at the scene by the Boundary County Sheriff Department's search team. Although the bullet was badly damaged, it was dispatched to Haag, and in May 1996 Sheriff Greg Sprungl announced that it had been matched by means of "trace evidence" with one of the weapons from the scene. Although he refused to give details, few who had followed the case had much doubt. The bullet had been matched to Marshal Larry Cooper's Colt submachine gun, either by means of striations or fibers from Sammy Weaver's clothing or possibly both. Not only had the FBI lab not needed the bullet to prove who shot and killed Sammy Weaver in the back as he ran home, but it could have found the confirming evidence if the crime scene had been properly searched in the first place.

But the refusal to provide expertise or do tests, however minimal their value compared to what was available from private experts, was only one aspect of the pattern of complaints about the FBI lab in the Ruby Ridge case. Foot-dragging was the norm throughout. Indeed, the trial of Randy Weaver and Kevin Harris was delayed twice in part as a result of the lab's failure to do tests on time. Tests designed to determine whether two pieces of metal were once part of Marshal Degan's canteen clip (requested August 27, 1992), a blood sample comparison for both Vicki and Sammy Weaver (September 9, 1992), and tests designed to show if holes in Degan's backpack and the clothing it contained were caused by a bullet (October 28, 1992) were all still outstanding by Christmas. The first lab test results did not reach prosecutors until late November or early December. These were basic tests on evidence collected as early as August.

The request for the crucial tests on Degan's backpack was not answered until January 22, 1993, in a lab report that came only after several follow-up requests. Even then the report was virtually useless. An "exit" hole in the backpack and holes in the clothing inside had a "linear relationship" that "could" have been caused by a bullet or fragments," the report stated. Furthermore, as junior defense attorney Kent Spence was to discover by accident only days before the end of the trial, Cadigan's report addressed only one of the two bullet holes in the backpack. Cadigan has no explanation for this, insisting to Justice Department investigators that he had examined the backpack "closely."

The FBI lab made the usual complaints about a backlog of work and lack of adequate resources in apparent justification. Yet by their own criteria they had failed, as even the Bureau recognized in its own internal administrative review report on the performance of the laboratory in the Ruby Ridge case. The FBI's investigators concluded that the effective priority for lab tests was established by trial date, something confirmed by James Cadigan. The Senate subcommittee decided that this had simply just not happened. "Any formal prioritization progam in place at the FBI Laboratory yielded, at least in the Weaver case, to a situation where only the squeaky wheel got the grease," the senators concluded.[22]

But if a trial date is the effective priority criteria, it seems incredible that FBI evidence transmittal forms to the lab have no location to insert one. Sometimes trial dates are just written on or added to covering notes, but not always. As a result, James Cadigan was able to claim he had no knowledge of the Weaver-Harris trial date until November or December. FBI case agents refuted that vigorously, saying they referred to it in many telephone conversations with Cadigan. The pace of lab testing did pick up, but lab tests requested weeks earlier were still being done during the pretrial hearing and even during the trial itself.

Requests for a number of examinations were simply ignored by the FBI lab. Samples were returned, spoiled, or simply lost. In September, blood samples from Randy Weaver and Kevin Harris were sent to the lab. With no specific instructions, according to Cadigan, and given "insufficient space to maintain items of evidence," the samples were returned to the FBI field office in Boise, Idaho. Packed with other items and with no indication that perishable blood samples were included, the blood spoiled, and fresh samples had to be taken. The lab managed to lose, ignore, or refuse a range of tests on samples from Sammy Weaver, Vicki Weaver, and Bill Degan. On September 3, the lab was asked to compare blood samples from Vicki and Sammy with the blood found on jackets and a pair of pants. When there was no response to this request in the first composite lab report dated December 23, Greg Rampton, the FBI's co–case agent in Boise, complained. The laboratory was adamant that no blood and hair samples had been received, despite records to the contrary.[23]

It all added up to a lack of "coordination, communication and cooperation" within the FBI lab, the Justice Department's Task Force Report concluded. The delays had a serious impact on the prosecution's discovery obligations and the way the government was perceived by the court and at trial, the task force decided. Gerry Spence, all fringed buckskin jacket and cowboy boots, was, as ever, more adamant. In more than forty years in the courtroom, he told Judge Lodge, he had never seen a prosecutor work so hard to hide evidence from a jury. Hiding information or, as the Justice Department's Task Force Report put it, a serious failure to comply with discovery obligations, was the order of the day. Whenever the lab did comply, it was either reluctantly or incompetently.

One instance was the defense team's request for James Cadigan's lab notes and records of the test firings of all the weapons, a request made sometime in the first ten days of May, the third and fourth weeks of the trial. Cadigan was reluctant to hand them over, later claiming that Joe Venkus, one of the case agents, had advised him to delay until a court order forced him to submit them. On May 13, Cadigan received an angry phone call from Joe Venkus's immediate boss, the man in charge of FBI activities throughout Idaho, Special Supervisory Agent Michael Dillon. He demanded to see the test firings immediately.

Cadigan faxed his notes to Boise and followed up by express mailing the original notes and the test-fired bullets, securing each, he claims, in a separate envelope with sticky tape before placing them in a box for shipment. That was not how they arrived. The next day Cadigan took a phone call from Boise telling him that three of the envelopes had opened during shipment and that the contents had commingled. Back to Washington the bullets went, back under the comparison microscope, and back to Boise.[24]

The prosecutors are also adamant that the lab withheld so-called *Brady* material, or exculpatory data which by law must be supplied to the defense—the same allegation Fred Whitehurst was making about the lab. One good example was the erroneous shooting diagram and map of the location of the evidence prepared by Grover and Taister. "The Bureau vehemently argued that mistakes are not subject to discovery. They failed or refused to acknowledge that the defense and the Court are not obliged to accept our explanation of mistake and that the erroneous diagram was clearly Brady material," noted the prosecutors in their memo to the Department of Justice.[25]

What the Senate subcommittee decided constituted willful and repeated failure to abide by discovery rules ended with Judge Lodge, the presiding official in the Boise courtroom, finding the FBI in contempt of court for obstruction of justice. The government's actions "evidence[d] a callous disregard for the rights of the defendants and the interests of justice," he concluded, fining the government the cost of the defense attorneys for one day. "We made no effort to collect it and predictably the United States has made no effort to pay it," noted Gerry Spence.[26]

From the moment the United States attorney's office in Boise, Idaho, decided to adopt a modified "open file" discovery policy, there always were going to be problems. The FBI always had been horrified by prosecutor Ron Howen's decision to throw the book at Harris and Weaver. Senior FBI officials knew that the conspiracy charges in particular would open up the whole case, including the death of Vicki Weaver, to defense and public scrutiny. Documents and reports would be demanded; senior FBI officials might even have to appear. Why not just charge Harris with the murder of Marshal Degan and Weaver with the shotgun charge and failure to appear in court?

When Howen persisted with his sixteen-page indictment, listing ten separate but interlinked charges, even minimal cooperation became highly dangerous for the FBI. It assumed "the role of an adversary," in the words of the Justice Department task force's report. As a result prosecutors soon felt they were fighting on two fronts, holding off both the FBI and the high-powered defense team. "It was ironic really. We chose to pursue a complete disclosure policy in an effort to disarm the defense and the accusations of cover-up that were flying our way. Even now I'm convinced that we never saw everything from the FBI," says Maurice Ellsworth, former U.S. attorney of Idaho.[27]

Thus, just as the lab has to be seen as part of the FBI machine, James Cadigan's approach to the Ruby Ridge investigation was part of a much broader institutional attitude. "I don't think anyone in the FBI was operating in isolation on the Ruby Ridge case. The lab was being dictated to like everyone else," says Ellsworth.[28] The denigration and the undermining of the prosecutors became the norm in the bureau, with Cadigan at one point complaining of the range and number of the investigations having to be done to fit the prosecutors' apparent "theory of the week." Ironically, one reason for extra requests to the lab—a number of which were, in any case, ignored—was that conflicting testimony and late disclosure made new tests inevitable.

In 1995, even FBI director Louis Freeh concluded that he had never encountered a situation in which the relationship between the FBI and government prosecutors was as "chronically bad and abrasive." He omitted to say in his submission to the Senate subcommittee hearings who he felt was responsible. The Justice Department and Senate subcommittee had no such hesitation. "Primary" responsibility, both bodies concluded, lay with FBI headquarters. The manner in which such noncooperation became public of course simply added to the defense case that a cover-up, and not a very good one at that, was in process. Indeed, like all bad cover-ups, the authorities' tale of what had happened came apart—in this case, on an almost daily basis—in the Boise courtroom under the weight of a steady stream of contradictory, incredible, and delayed evidence.

Why would U.S. marshals bother to kill a family dog after they had come under fire from Sammy and Kevin Harris if, as they maintained, Harris had shot at them first? Marshal Roderick said the dog was running toward him, yet the autopsy showed the bullet entered Striker's rump and traveled through him parallel to the spine. Surely it was more likely that Sammy Weaver, having seen Striker shot by a man in full camouflage with no identifiable markings, had fired back, been wounded in the arm, and that Harris had opened fire on Marshal Degan to protect Sammy as well as himself, the story Harris actually told.

How could Degan's colleague, Marshal Larry Cooper, be so convinced that Degan had never fired his weapon, when ballistics had matched seven bullet casings scattered over more than twenty feet at the Y to Degan's gun? If Degan really had been hit by the first shot from Harris could he really have fired seven rounds while bleeding to death from a mortal wound in the chest? And if Harris had fired first, why had Frank Norris, another of the U.S. marshals, recalled that the first shot he heard that morning was the "distinctive sound of a .223," the caliber of the M-16 rifles carried by Marshals Art Roderick and William Degan, not Kevin Harris?

None of this answered the inevitable questions about the technical competence of these law enforcement marksmen. If, as the marshals insisted, they had shot at Kevin Harris, how had they managed to hit Sammy Weaver, obviously a child, less than five feet tall and eighty pounds, and hit him not just once but twice? The bullet that killed him struck him full in the back and penetrated his heart. How much of a threat was a child running away? He was obviously running home. Indeed, he had announced it, shouting, "I'm coming, Dad," when Randy Weaver shouted to him to come home moments before he was killed.

Similar questions faced the FBI's sniper, Lon Horiuchi. He said he had been aiming at Harris when he wounded Randy Weaver with his first shot at the birthing shed on August 22. Then he had been aiming at

Harris when he killed Vicki Weaver with his second shot. These were men who were supposed to be able to hit a dime at two hundred yards. At the very least, there seemed to have been some terrible marksmanship at Ruby Ridge.

Numerous skirmishes over discovery obligations ended in near farce when on June 4, 1993, barely a week before the end of the trial, Ron Howen returned to his downtown office in Boise to find a thick package waiting for him. The documents inside included the FBI's Shooting Incident Review Report, notes of the investigators' interviews with members of the FBI's Hostage Rescue Team and perhaps most crucially, two matchstick sketches by Agent Lon Horiuchi, the FBI sniper. The documents came with a covering note from an FBI agent saying the enclosed were in response to a defense subpoena of April 13—nearly two months previous. Howen turned the envelope over. It had left the FBI mailroom on May 21, more than five weeks after the request, traveling to Boise via fourth class mail.[29]

The documents, obviously essential to Lon Horiuchi's cross-examination, were handed to the defense lawyers only hours after he had left the stand under heavily armed escort. A furious Judge Lodge ordered that Horiuchi return from Washington. Having already failed to justify shooting into the cabin in violation of the rules of engagement, the taut, unemotional West Point graduate now struggled to explain a sketch of what he had seen of the Weaver cabin door as he pulled the trigger to fire the shot that killed Vicki and injured Kevin Harris.

The defense said two semicircles at the window of the cabin door Vicki Weaver was holding open were obviously heads, proving that Horiuchi had known two people were crouching behind the flimsy door. On the WestCoast Hotels notepaper Horiuchi had drawn on, the position of the "mildot"—the dot seen through the ten-power scope that places the crosshairs of a gun's sights ahead of any moving target—seemed to confirm that he was aiming at Vicki Weaver.[30] Horiuchi claimed he could not see through the window of the door because the curtains were drawn. He had drawn in the two peering heads to show the shooting-review officers where he thought family members "might be."

Yet again, the delay in handing over the FBI evidence in the hope of preventing too close a scrutiny backfired hopelessly. The sketch simply reinforced defense allegations of a conspiracy and a cover-up to hide it.

Gerry Spence believed that Vicki Weaver had been targeted. It seemed preposterous, at first, but the theory did have some credibility. Vicki was the real strength of the family, more outspoken than Randy and perhaps more certain of her antigovernment beliefs. It was she who had written two somewhat threatening letters to the local prosecutor concerning the original weapons charges. Randy, she insisted, would not surrender "to your lawless government."

The court had already heard how the U.S. marshals and the FBI had been told that Vicki was the key to Randy's surrender. Michael Weland, a reporter for the local Bonner County *Daily Bee*, the only journalist to interview the Weavers before the standoff, had explained how he had even contacted the FBI's psychological profile division to tell them that if they really wanted to get Randy Weaver to come down from the cabin they would have to separate him from his wife.[31] Somehow the threat assessment of Vicki Weaver had taken on a life of its own. Just as Randy was supposed to have been involved in several armed bank robberies before retreating to his booby-trapped heavily fortified compound on the ridge, the authorities had incredibly come to believe that Vicki Weaver would kill her own children rather than surrender.

But some Ruby Ridge document discovery requests never produced what was probably the most damning evidence. And they probably never will. On March 6, 1993, following repeated unanswered requests from the prosecutors' office in Boise, the Justice Department ordered the FBI to release all the "core" documents on the Ruby Ridge affair. These included such crucial evidence as the After Action Report, an internal critique; the handwritten or typed versions of Larry Potts's notes concerning his discussions of the rules of engagement; and the handwritten notes of Deputy Assistant Director Danny Coulson.

It was probably already too late. Sometime between January 7 and the first week of April 1993, all copies of the first After Action Report, on paper and computer disk, the product of a November 1992 roundtable case conference of all the FBI participants in the Ruby Ridge debacle, were destroyed. The report was believed to be the ultimate embarrassment, showing serious discrepancies between the bureau's official version and what its own inquiries had determined.

It was against this backdrop that the new director of the FBI, Louis Freeh, inherited the aftermath of events at Ruby Ridge, successively re-

viewing the internal reports and the conclusions of the Justice Department task force in mid-1994. By the end of the year, Freeh had completed
his review of the fifth and final internal FBI report into Ruby Ridge. The
administrative review, or Matthews Report, as it is known, after author
Charles Matthews III, was supposed to be a response to the Justice Department task force's report. That had concluded that portions of the rules of
engagement had not only departed from the FBI's standard deadly force
policy, but had also contravened the U.S. Constitution. The depth of the
investigative penetration of the Matthews Report was reflected in its
conclusion on this, the central issue: "The rules of engagement are considered unconstitutional; therefore, there is no need to discuss them further."[32]

That seemed to set the tone. On January 6, 1995, Freeh announced
that twelve FBI agents would be censured: the maximum penalty was a
fifteen-day suspension for Eugene Glenn, the minimum, a letter of censure
for firearms examiner James Cadigan, Larry Potts, and most of the others.
Despite having demonstrated "inadequate performance, improper judgment, neglect of duty, and failure to exert proper managerial oversight,"
according to Freeh, the twelve agents "did not commit any crimes or
intentional misconduct."[33] A letter of censure was the same punishment
Freeh had once suffered for losing a mobile phone. And with Deputy
Director Floyd Clarke now retired, Freeh had Potts in mind for a promotion.

In fact, Freeh already had effectively promoted Potts. On December
6, 1994, one month before he made his recommendation on censure and,
indeed ten days before Charles Matthews had even reported back, Freeh
had announced the promotion of Larry Potts to acting deputy director,
effective January 3, 1995. Yet in making the announcement about the
letter of censure, Freeh said Potts had failed to provide proper managerial
oversight with regard to the rules of engagement. "As head of the Criminal Investigative Division, Potts had overall responsibility for the crisis
incident and the FBI participation in the subsequent prosecution," Freeh
concluded. Potts was in charge but was not, it seemed, to blame.

Even to the Bureau's friends and supporters this looked like tailoring
the punishment to the circumstance, not the crime. Deputy Attorney
General Jamie Gorelick wrote to Louis Freeh advising him that she
wanted a thirty-day suspension for Potts, something that effectively would

have ended the acting deputy director's chances of assuming the position permanently. On March 7, Louis Freeh wrote an extraordinary four-page memo to Jamie Gorelick and her boss, Attorney General Janet Reno, showing just how far he was prepared to go in supporting Potts.

Freeh opposed any suspension of Potts out of concern about how the change to his recommended punishment would affect his "personal credibility" as director. He further cited the personal effect the suspension would have on Potts in that, as Freeh readily admitted, he could not then be confirmed as deputy director, and because it would imply that the FBI and the Department of Justice "dispute the credibility of the employees involved in the creation and implementation of the Rules of Engagement." [34] Once again the obsession with image was paramount. The memo warns about how the media will see it, and how Freeh's own rank and file will view the issue. In closing, Freeh almost seems to threaten: "It is my view that the increased discipline is so divergent from my recommendation that it is likely to do profound damage to the relationship between the Department and the FBI." [35]

On April 5, Jamie Gorelick caved in, despite the fact that she was later to tell the Senate subcommittee that she considered Potts's failure to determine what the rules of engagement were "appalling" and a "major failing." Freeh issued a letter of censure the same day and recommended the promotion of Potts to deputy director the day after that. Janet Reno approved the promotion on May 2, 1995. Freeh was right about the rank and file, but wrong about what would outrage them. It was Potts's promotion, not his suspension, that would now become Louis Freeh's biggest problem since he took over the bureau. Eugene Glenn, one of the twelve agents originally disciplined, was particularly angry.

Within days, a detailed twelve-page letter was on the desk of Michael Shaheen, head of the Office of Professional Responsibility (OPR) at the Department of Justice. Glenn alleged that the Matthews Report was designed to cover up the responsibility of higher level FBI officials at headquarters for what had happened at Ruby Ridge. He claimed that Potts had told him during the standoff that he had approved the rules of engagement personally and that Danny Coulson had at one point reminded him to act in conformity with them. Glenn demanded a real inquiry, saying Matthews was a close associate of Coulson and that it was inconceivable that an FBI agent with twenty-five years of experience could have "inadvertently presented such an incomplete, inaccurate document."[36]

By going outside the Bureau to complain, as Fred Whitehurst had done about the lab, first in the Steve Psinakis case, then on a whole range of related issues, Eugene Glenn, the special agent in charge of the operation at Ruby Ridge, knew he had committed a cardinal transgression of the FBI's internal code. He also knew, like Fred Whitehurst, something would finally have to be done. It was. OPR began investigating. On July 14, 1995, Louis Freeh personally told Larry Potts that the controversy meant he would have to reassign him on an interim basis. The deputy director was stripped of his responsibilities and shunted down to the Bureau's training division in Quantico. On August 11, 1995, Potts was suspended indefinitely, along with four others, including Danny Coulson. Criminal referrals now were made, and United States Attorney Michael Stiles began investigating.

Now it was Freeh who was in trouble. Everything he claims he sought to avoid in Potts's censure—media criticism, congressional fury, rank-and-file outrage—had come to pass. He eventually admitted that the recommendation to promote Potts while disciplining him was a grave error. But Freeh seemed to blame his own investigators, pointing out that he was "obviously" not given the full facts in the Matthews Report on which he based his recommendation. That raised a number of questions. How good were his own investigators? Did this not prove that they could not investigate themselves or their colleagues? And if they would keep information away from their own director, surely they would not think twice about keeping information away from external scrutineers, whether prosecutors, staff from the Department of Justice's Inspection Division, or ASCLD/LAB laboratory inspectors.

In October 1996, Michael Kahoe, the head of the FBI's Violent Crimes and Major Offenders Section, entered into a plea bargain with Stiles's investigators and admitted to obstruction of justice in destroying all copies of the After Action Report. Larry Potts, then head of the Criminal Division, Danny Coulson, then deputy assistant director of the FBI's Criminal Division, and Gale Evans, Kahoe's immediate subordinate all remained suspended indefinitely. It was not until August 1997 that the Department of Justice announced that after two years of investigation, the longest ever investigation of the FBI, Michael Stiles and his team had recommended against criminal prosecution.

The Department of Justice's press release stated that "the available evidence does not support further criminal prosecutions of FBI officials." The key word was "available." The fact that Kahoe had agreed to cooperate in a plea bargain suggested at the very least that investigators believed there was more to learn, but that in the end they could not get the physical evidence to corroborate it. But Stiles's investigation did make one thing clear: Other crucial evidence—evidence from the FBI lab— had, like the After Action Report, been destroyed.

This came to light when, within weeks of the establishment of the criminal inquiry, Stiles's team sent George Michael Baird, a senior FBI official who had worked on the Walsh Report in 1993, a letter warning him that he was a target of their investigation. As part of the FBI's internal inquiry, Baird had asked FBI visual information technician Cyrus Grover to produce a "pictorial," a technical drawing estimating Vicki Weaver's position relative to the cabin door when she was killed. Baird gave Grover a batch of new forensic evidence from which to work: the entry angle of the bullet that pierced the glass and Vicki Weaver's face, the location of the bullet hole in the curtains on the window of the cabin door, and the scatter pattern of the shattered glass from the window.

Grover drew up the pictorial from Horiuchi's vantage point, looking northward toward the cabin, and concluded that Vicki Weaver, 646 feet away by his estimate, would have been visible to Horiuchi. He told Baird of the drawing and his conclusions in a telephone conversation. Baird responded: "We don't need it, get rid of it," according to two federal law enforcement officials familiar with the investigation.[37] It could have been an innocent comment. But Grover did not take it to be. Indeed, he was so troubled by Baird's instructions that he reported the incident to the Department of Justice's OPR. Baird became the sixth FBI official to be suspended in October 1995.

But apart from the evidence that may not have been available because of such cover-ups, there remain significant questions about the methodology of the criminal investigation. Its conclusions may well have been compromised. Michael Stiles's team conducted more than 600 interviews with 378 witnesses, searched FBI offices, and reviewed more than half a million pages of documents, including "previously unreviewed files containing the bulk of FBI headquarters records relating to the crisis."[38] Yet, as the press release goes on to make clear, most of the people doing all this were themselves FBI agents. This despite the inadequacy of all the previous internal investigations by FBI agents, despite the fact that they were investigating allegations of a cover-up by other FBI agents, their superiors, and despite previous protests during the Ruby Ridge inquiries about the conflict of interest involved in FBI agents investigating FBI agents.

Maurice Ellsworth, the U.S. attorney in Idaho responsible for the Ruby Ridge prosecution, was so concerned about such a conflict of interest that in 1993 he had hesitated about even being interviewed by Barbara Berman's task force, which, like Stiles, had used FBI agents as investigators. "I do not question their desire to be objective, only their ability," Ellsworth wrote in a letter to Janet Reno.[39] Eventually, convinced that the FBI had "no horse in this race," despite the fact their institution was the main target of the investigation, Ellsworth submitted to the interview, only to have all his fears confirmed. "More than once when I expressed frustration at the way the FBI had done things in the case, the two agents interviewing me interrupted to explain or even rationalize FBI policies or procedures," he says.[40]

But the methods of the Stiles's investigation threw up even starker conflicts of interest in relation to the lab. Given that the Berman task force had chronicled the woeful performance of the lab when faced with a conflict of interest in the original Ruby Ridge investigation, given that the Baird-Grover incident made the destruction of incriminating documentation from the lab part of the inquiry, and given that some of the most senior officials at the FBI were the targets of the investigation, it seems extraordinary that Stiles's team would even consider sending exhibits they wanted examined to the FBI lab. Yet this is exactly what happened. A total of 143 pieces of evidence, "physical exhibits" according to Stiles, who refuses to say any more, were sent to the FBI lab for forensic examination. "I don't see that there was any reason not to use the FBI lab. We thought it was appropriate," Stiles opines.[41]

In Michael Kahoe someone had now been charged and sentenced for a cover-up, but it was those higher up who needed to hide what he had destroyed. Few FBI insiders believe that Kahoe, a middle-rank official, would have acted without orders in the fiercely hierarchical FBI. Everything pointed to a broader cover-up, as Eugene Glenn originally had charged. After all, the resistance to releasing the information Kahoe had destroyed had come from the very top. As the Senate subcommittee had concluded on the subject of documentation in 1995: "There is no question that this resistance came in large part from Headquarters and the Section of the FBI headed by Potts and Coulson, high-ranking officials of the FBI who were themselves intimately involved in the FBI's conduct at Ruby Ridge."[42]

The recommendation that there be no prosecutions was far from the end of it. Sources in the Justice Department confided that Michael Stiles's team had written a blistering report on the conduct of Potts and Coulson, and there were reports of recommendations of "aggressive disciplinary action" within the FBI, including possible termination.[43] In the end, Potts avoided the possibility of sanctions or dismissal by retiring from the FBI almost as soon as he became eligible for a full pension, at the end of August 1997. In October, *The Washington Post* reported that he had found gainful employment in the private sector, joining the Investigative Group International as executive vice president.[44]

Other leaks from the Stiles inquiry seemed to raise real questions about the lack of "available evidence" against Larry Potts. During the investigation, the former deputy director had belatedly produced an undated memo that laid out a far more restrictive deadly force policy, which he claimed he had dictated to an FBI secretary. He offered this as proof that he had never signed off on the shoot-to-kill rules of engagement. In September 1997 it was reported that investigators, doubting the document's authenticity, had submitted it to forensic testing.[45] The result strongly suggested that the memo was fabricated after the event, a belief reinforced by the fact that the secretary concerned had no recollection of ever typing it.

But the cover-up and who ordered it is one thing; what is being covered up remains the key issue. When would anyone be charged with the crimes Kahoe, and maybe others, have been covering up? The most obvious is a possible murder or manslaughter charge. Lon Horiuchi's second shot, the one that killed Vicki Weaver, was determined by the Justice Department task force to be unconstitutional. Even under the amended rules of engagement, themselves now determined to be unconstitutional, but the ones that Horiuchi was operating under, the sniper was allowed to fire only at armed males outside the cabin if the shot did not endanger children.

Even if he was shooting at Kevin Harris and not Vicki Weaver as he insisted, his second shot hit them both inside the cabin and certainly endangered children. At one point the FBI tried to justify the shot on the grounds that Horiuchi was operating under the FBI's standard deadly force policy, where immediate threat is the key determinant. But that too was an uphill argument. Three civilians, running for cover to their own home without having fired a shot or even raised a gun, and all more than two hundred yards away from the FBI snipers? It hardly seemed to constitute an immediate threat.

Within a week of the announcement that Michael Stiles's investigators would recommend that no charges be brought, Boundary County prosecutor Denise Woodbury took the opposite course in Idaho. On August 21, five years to the day after the shoot-out at the Y, she announced charges of first-degree murder against Kevin Harris and involuntary manslaughter against Lon Horiuchi. As The New York Times put it: "Ms. Woodbury gave few details on how her two-person prosecutorial staff planned to do what a multi-million dollar Federal task force could not do: get convictions." [46]

The answer, of course, was proper investigation. Woodbury herself revealed at the press conference that her staff had uncovered new forensic evidence, but she, like others involved, would say no more. In fact, by August 1997, Luke Haag had been working on the case for the Boundary County Sheriff's Department for four years. One source says anonymously that by the time the local prosecutor made her move, a total of five bullets had been recovered from the Y, all of which had been examined by Luke Haag. Whatever the outcome of another trial, it seems certain, once again, to expose the woeful incompetence of the FBI lab in both the collection and examination of evidence.

That was, also of course, one of the key lessons of the Ruby Ridge investigation. Even in basic disciplines such as ballistics, it was clear that the FBI lab was not the best, it was just the best at promoting and protecting its image of being the best. Moreover, in believing no one could do a better job, in believing it was exclusive and superior, the FBI lab cut itself off from external expertise such as that of Luke Haag or

Martin Fackler, external expertise from which it evidently could learn. The results were inevitable. Bad habits had become entrenched as a result of a failure to keep up with the latest best-practice procedures and protocols. Worse still, new techniques or methods in the rapidly developing world of forensic science were often ignored or learned poorly. As a result, the FBI lab had fallen behind and was "out of touch with forensic reality," as the Ruby Ridge prosecutors had realized quickly.

It was precisely such arrogance that made the Bureau incapable of investigating itself. The Senate subcommittee was unequivocal: "The authors of every [FBI] report we read were looking more to justify agency conduct than to follow the facts where they lead."[47] This Orwellian world of institutional bias led "investigators" to some extraordinary conclusions. The Shooting Incident Review Team with James Cadigan of the lab assessing everything from the wrong firing position, concluded of Lon Horiuchi's second shot that "the use of deadly force was justified in that she [Vicki Weaver] willfully placed herself in harm's way."[48] The subcommittee concluded that was "frighteningly wrong." One early FBI report concluded that the FBI's Ruby Ridge operation was a "success"; other agencies such as the U.S. Marshal's Service were, however, heavily to blame.[49]

All this was nothing new to agents themselves. "It has been an open secret for years that . . . internal investigations are generally run backwards," wrote Christophir Kerr, a veteran FBI agent and executive board member of the seven-thousand-strong FBI Agents Association. "The facts are often 'developed' to support a predetermined outcome. In the perhaps apocryphal exhortation attributed to J. Edgar Hoover, 'Fire that man! No. Get the facts. Then fire him!' " Kerr went on to describe how probes were run by officials in the career path, "a relatively insular, 'close-knit' group . . . beholden to an 'Old Boy Network' that takes care of its own in matters large and small."[50] Kerr concluded, as Eugene Glenn had, that getting the facts as a result of internal investigations was "at best unlikely." To outline what he called "incestuous entanglements" Kerr wrote: "Imagine the likely result if the old Rose Law firm assigned a junior associate to investigate alleged misconduct by Vincent Foster, then presented the case to Webster Hubbell for recommendations with adjudication by Hillary Rodham Clinton."[51]

This inability to investigate or self-regulate, the conflicts of interest thrown up by the Old Boy or the Friends of Louie network, the lack of accountability in the FBI, all these problems were becoming obvious in the lab during the ongoing Ruby Ridge inquiries. In fact, the parallels were uncanny. Convinced his allegations were not being properly investigated by the Office of Professional Responsibility within the FBI, Fred Whitehurst had, like Eugene Glenn, gone to an agency outside the FBI. In both cases, something approaching a real investigation only took place when a senior FBI agent broke ranks. And although the problems both investigations revealed were systemic, none of them had been picked up previously by the FBI's internal agencies.

In 1997, three years after he had taken the same steps as Glenn, Whitehurst would be fully vindicated on the inadequacy of the internal investigation of the lab. Both James Maddock, deputy general counsel of the FBI, and Mike Bromwich, the inspector general at the Department of Justice, admitted as much before Congress on May 17, 1997. "The lab's inability to resolve in a timely way serious and credible allegations of incompetence . . . allowed the problem to fester for almost six years," admitted Bromwich. "There were a number of internal reviews that failed to go far enough, which failed to recognize the seriousness of the issues presented, and I can offer no excuse for that," admitted Maddock.[52]

Another parallel between the Bureau problems highlighted by Ruby Ridge and what was happening in the lab was the promotion of Friends of Louie or Old Boys while under investigation. Larry Potts was promoted during and after an investigation that turned out to be totally inadequate. In July 1994, Tom Thurman was promoted to acting head of the Explosives Unit in the lab while still under investigation for allegedly making changes to Fred Whitehurst's lab reports. In 1995, Roger Martz, head of the Chemistry and Toxicology Unit, was promoted to acting chief of the Scientific Analysis Section in the lab while under investigation by both the IG and the OPR on a number of charges made by Whitehurst. Like Potts, both Martz and Thurman would ultimately have to be reassigned when many of the complaints against them were verified.

Ultimately, what Ruby Ridge made clear was two things. First, the problems that Whitehurst perceived in the lab reverberated throughout the FBI. Institutional bias was generic, the bureau's inability to investigate itself pervasive, the absence of written protocols and procedures common, the failure to file vital documentation or even destroy incriminating paperwork not abnormal, and an unwillingness to hand over discovery or exculpatory information was understood. For most agents, both in the lab and beyond, loyalty to the Bureau came first; the truth, the facts, or justice might have to wait or even be ignored if there was a conflict of interest.

The second thing Ruby Ridge made clear was that Whitehurst's reported inadequacies about the FBI lab stretched beyond his own work sphere. He had nothing to do with the Firearms-Toolmarks Unit, yet many of the problems he complained about in Explosives, Chemistry and Toxicology, and Materials Analysis were obviously of the same ilk. Loss of evidence, inadequate reports, sloppy procedures, lack of management oversight, inability to handle a crime scene or do the basics of forensic science well—everything he was alleging in units he had direct experience with was evident in yet another lab unit, in the Ruby Ridge case. By 1995, it was just a question of when and how all this would come to light.

5

WORLD TRADE CENTER:
THE EXPLOSIVE TRUTH

When Judge Michael Mukasey came into court at 9:40 A.M. apologizing for the malfunctioning of the air-conditioning and promising to break at 3:00 P.M. to "limit the misery," there was no indication it would be anything but a normal, if bakingly hot, August day in the Manhattan courtroom. The charge sheet listed twelve suspects, headed by the partially sighted Egyptian cleric Omar Ahmad Ali Abdel Rahman, known to those who read the inside pages of the New York tabloids as the "Blind Sheik." The eleven Arabs and one American were accused of a wide-ranging conspiracy to blow up the World Trade Center and several leading New York city landmarks, including the Holland and Lincoln tunnels and the United Nations.

But throughout the summer of 1995 the trial, based on the testimony of a dubious informer, seemed to have been going nowhere. Four other Arabs had been found guilty of the actual bombing of the World Trade Center eighteen months earlier, in March 1994. This case, World Trade II as it had become known in legal shorthand, seemed like a mopping up operation of assorted Islamic fundamentalists. The evidence, beyond the defendants' obvious anti-American sentiment, seemed at best vague, at worst, incomprehensible.

Yet Frederic Whitehurst had taken a particular interest. Having worked hard at the painstaking forensic detective work that had brought the first World Trade Center bombing case to court he knew a thing or two about what had happened at the scene and back at the FBI's lab in Washington. He was worried, particularly about the conduct of his boss at the crime scene, the case agent and principal examiner on the bombing, David Williams. Learning of his criticisms, Valerie Amsterdam, a court-appointed defense lawyer for two of the defendants, had subpoenaed him as a material witness. It was she who now accepted the judge's invitation to start the morning's proceedings.

What Fred Whitehurst, chemist, explosives-residue analyst, FBI special agent, and now defense witness was about to say publicly for the first time was to rock the FBI lab in Washington to its foundations. His FBI restriction on discussing individual cases effectively broken by the subpoena, his commitment on the stand "to tell the truth, the whole truth, and nothing but the truth," would lead to prime-time television appearances, an appeal to allow him to testify in the still ongoing O. J. Simpson case, and a major eighteen-month investigation of the FBI lab by the inspector general of the Justice Department.

Within eighteen months of Whitehurst's appearance in the New York courtroom, David Williams would be ousted from the FBI lab and be investigated for potential criminal charges for his conduct in the World Trade Center bombing investigation, while defense lawyers would start filing appeals on the basis of the revelations about the lab. But by then Fred Whitehurst would be facing the fate of so many whistle-blowers: placed on indefinite "administrative leave" and preparing for a long legal struggle just to get his job back.

What Whitehurst claimed on the stand was that attempts had been made to alter his lab reports to exclude scientific interpretations other than David Williams's assumptions, which were in turn tailored to match the existing evidence. Determined to present the court with irrefutable evidence that the bomb had been composed of urea nitrate, large quantities of whose constituent chemicals he believed he could tie back to the defendants, Williams had tried to cut out alternative explanations for the presence of two naturally occurring chemicals at the bomb scene.

When he failed to secure the deletions in the lab reports, Williams developed other nonscientific misinterpretations of data to achieve the same ends.

The alteration of scientific lab reports, especially by someone without chemistry qualifications like Williams, went to the heart of ethics, best practice, and impartiality in forensic science. There may be little or no agreement on ethical standards in the profession, but the alteration of lab reports was the one thing that all forensic scientists interviewed, including those who have worked for the FBI, agree is totally unacceptable. If true, Whitehurst's charges seemed to epitomize the repeated allegations of pro-prosecution bias in the FBI lab.

The allegations raised a myriad of issues in one. There was the question of unqualified staff being in management positions of authority; the issue of the pressure examiners came under from their own bosses inside the lab as well as prosecutors beyond it; and the whole question of overstated results and selective analysis. For good measure, Whitehurst's testimony also raised the issue of exculpatory evidence, evidence or conclusions from crime scene material that under the *Brady* ruling had to be handed over to the defense if it might play a part, however slight, in exonerating a defendant.

Given all these issues, and the fact that Whitehurst indicated that this was part of a broader battle that had erupted in other cases, the press was not slow to pick up the trail. Within a month, Brian Ross, chief investigative reporter for ABC's *PrimeTime Live*, was ready to run a groundbreaking piece that was to set the issue alight. "Until tonight, the FBI had tried to keep secret what agent Fred Whitehurst had to say, tried to keep secret the fact that one of its own agents, a highly respected and distinguished one, was alleging an ongoing pattern of criminal misconduct inside the FBI itself," announced Ross on the air on September 13, 1995. With the FBI refusing to put anyone up as a spokesperson for the program, a whole range of defense lawyers found themselves in a prosecutorial role.

"I've never seen an FBI agent ever take the stand and say that his superiors told him to lie and to frame defendants at a trial," concluded John Jacobs, Valerie Amsterdam's defense colleague. "This is startling evidence. It's evidence of fabrication, of misleading jurors, of basically committing perjury," concluded Johnnie Cochran, taking a brief time out from the ongoing O. J. Simpson trial in Los Angeles. "In more than thirty-two years of practice, I've never seen anything quite like these documents."[1]

Cochran was referring to several of Fred Whitehurst's memos to his superiors in the FBI lab that ABC had obtained. Armed with these, Brian Ross was able to broaden the attack, showing that Whitehurst was alleging that Tom Thurman, his old nemesis, had been altering his reports for more than five years, "apparently to slant the conclusions and opinions in favor of guilt." Reading a Whitehurst memo, Ross continued: "He had altered the reports. I had the evidence. I presented it to the section chief and nothing has been done to repair those reports. They sit in the files of the FBI without the slightest effort to change what they are: in places, incorrect opinions." For good measure the *PrimeTime* story included a sideswipe at Roger Martz as "one of the FBI agents who pressured Whitehurst to go along with allegedly altered test results."[2]

With Martz having just testified at the O. J. Simpson trial, and the defense team in Los Angeles increasingly reliant on raising reasonable doubt about the handling of forensic evidence in the case, Cochran had already asked to be allowed to call Fred Whitehurst as a witness. When asked by Brian Ross about relevance, given that the Whitehurst memos said nothing about the O. J. Simpson case, Cochran raised the issue that was at the back of everyone's mind. Just how far might this go? How many cases, how many FBI lab experts did it involve? "When you have an agent who has a propensity, a proclivity to testify falsely, to perjure him- or herself, to fabricate evidence, they don't just do that in one high-profile case, whether it's Waco or the New York Trade Center. It becomes a pattern because they can get away with it. Once they determine who the bad guy is, they can go after that person, and the end justifies the means," Cochran told Ross.[3]

Just hours before the *PrimeTime* show went on air, the FBI had faxed ABC with a statement. They claimed that the Bureau had investigated Whitehurst's "concerns about forensic protocols and procedures" vigorously and had "reviewed more than 250 cases involving work previously done by the Laboratory." The statement continued: "To date, the FBI has found no evidence of tampering, evidence fabrication or failure to report exculpatory evidence."[4] The statement was ingeniously worded, separating general concerns about procedures and protocols from the more serious charges.

In fact, even the FBI's own investigators had upheld some of Whitehurst's general concerns and what the Bureau might consider lesser charges as much as four years earlier. Though still prohibited by the FBI from talking about specific cases, Whitehurst commented on the FBI's investigation of his allegations during the *PrimeTime* broadcast. He dismissed it out of hand as inadequate. In doing so he raised another issue publicly for the first time. Was the FBI up to investigating its own lab? Did the Bureau have the motive and means? Had the issues Whitehurst had raised been brushed under the smothering carpet of internal investigation? The inspector general (IG) of the Department of Justice seemed to be asking itself the same questions.

Until the summer of 1995, the IG had been involved in a fairly limited investigation of the alteration of lab reports and the testimony of examiners in court, allegations that had arisen from its own very critical audit of the lab in June 1994. The remainder of Whitehurst's many other charges had been left to one branch of the FBI's internal investigative arm, the Office of Professional Responsibility (OPR). But by May 1995, the IG office was becoming alarmed at what it was hearing. Other scientists, in particular Whitehurst's colleague Steven Burmeister, an explosives-residue analyst, were confirming some of the allegations. Worse still, these allegations went back a long way. They had not been adequately investigated in the past, one reason they were coming to public notice with such explosive potential now.

It was something the FBI was to recognize in a rare moment of contrition nearly two years later in May 1997. Grilled by members of Congress about the adequacy of these investigations, James Maddock, the deputy general counsel of the FBI, admitted: "There were a number of internal reviews which failed to go far enough, which failed to recognize the seriousness of the issues presented, and I can offer no excuse for that."[5] The IG put it this way: "It became clear that a more global, comprehensive investigation was warranted."[6] However, despite the inadequacy of its previous investigations, the FBI firmly intended to have a hand in this one. An internal letter released under the Freedom of Information Act in January 1997 shows that in June 1995 the IG and the FBI's OPR agreed to "jointly investigate this matter from this point through its resolution."[7]

The letter from David Ries, the inspector-in-charge of the OPR, to

Thomas Bondurant, deputy assistant inspector general, makes it clear this might actually be a violation of operating procedures. It was certainly completely counterproductive from Fred Whitehurst's point of view. He had taken his complaints to the IG's office, an external, independent agency as he saw it, precisely because of the FBI's failure to correct serious failings in the past. Yet here was the bureau trying to get in on the same investigation, confirming a "sharing of our respective investigative product to date."[8]

It seems to have been only the glare of publicity and Whitehurst's emphatic rejection of the FBI internal investigations that saved the day. After *PrimeTime* came *Larry King Live,* the *Today Show,* and a feature in *Newsweek.* As Whitehurst completed two days of deposition by lawyers in the "trial of the century" in Los Angeles, the IG's office prepared to announce a major investigation into all his allegations. It would be conducting it alone. The Department of Justice began assembling a team of U.S. assistant attorneys, investigators attached to the IG's office, and five internationally renowned forensic scientists, three of them foreigners. For the first time ever, the policies and procedures of the FBI lab would be subjected to external scientific review. Independence was a slightly trickier issue. FBI director Louis Freeh pledged complete cooperation. It was a necessary reassurance, given that any investigation would depend crucially on documentation in the FBI's control and that the bureau was not beyond refusing, losing, or even destroying embarrassing paperwork, as the Ruby Ridge investigation was about to confirm.[9]

Encouraged by the IG's announcement, Whitehurst began work on an eighty-page critique of David Williams's testimony in the first World Trade Center bombing trial. In the document, Whitehurst drew on his direct experience of the crime scene investigation, the test explosions, the report alteration episode, and his chemical expertise to conclude that Williams had "misrepresented the truth," testified beyond his area of expertise, and presented testimony "biased" in favor of guilt.[10] The IG's report would, when published sixteen months later, agree. Their review of what had happened in the World Trade Center bombing investigation would be the most critical chapter of a stinging 517-page document.

Curiously, in finding so much merit in Whitehurst's complaints about the World Trade Center bombing investigation, the IG's office would seem to have been guilty of one of the few things they exonerated the FBI of in their report—the failure to hand over exculpatory evidence. Only a fraction of what Whitehurst chronicled—speculative and unscientific testimony, potential contamination, misrepresentation—came out in court on August 14, 1995. Yet his memo to the IG was apparently not handed over to the defense lawyers in both World Trade Center bombing cases until more than a year after the IG received it in January 1996.

By then it was all too clear that government prosecutors had probably not had the forensic evidence they appeared to have had in securing the convictions. Were four men in jail unjustly? If ever there were a case for an appeal on the grounds of misrepresentation, possible perjury, and new evidence, the first World Trade Center bombing trial was it. "I truly believe that if the appellate division really scrutinizes this case and the law means anything, there's a good chance of reversal," says Hassen Ibn Abdullah, one of the defendant's lawyers. "However, I can't say I'm that optimistic about our judicial system anymore. And there's just too much politics in this case."[11]

———

When his pager went off just before lunch on February 26, 1993, David Williams sensed his round of golf that Friday afternoon might have to be postponed. He was right. Explosives Unit chief Chris Ronay told him there had been a big explosion in the parking lot under the 102-story twin towers of the World Trade Center in Manhattan. Initial reports suggested a gas explosion or that a transformer had blown up, but from the moment he walked into the huge crater of twisted steel beams and huge slabs of dangling concrete, all carved out of the five levels of the underground parking lot, Williams was convinced otherwise. "I knew we had a bomb the moment I walked in. . . . In the unit we have a policy of not attributing an explosion to a bomb until we have physical evidence of that bomb but . . . when I was asked about it by Governor Cuomo I told him, 'If it looks like a duck and walks like a duck, it's a duck.' "[12]

That assumption of course put David Williams, one of the most gung-ho "bombers" in the lab, in a position of some authority, although no one at the crime scene, least of all Williams, seemed to know where that authority came from. "In the middle of all the confusion I stood up on a chair and shouted, 'Listen up everybody. My name is Dave Williams and I'm in charge here. From this point on the FBI laboratory is coordinating this crime scene investigation. . . .' Everybody went to work and we never had another problem."[13] Famous last words.

One of Williams's first tasks was to show Steve Burmeister and Fred Whitehurst, the FBI lab's two qualified explosives-residue analysts, around the scene. It was not a pretty sight. The crater was more than one hundred and fifty feet wide and seventy feet deep, running through five one-foot-thick concrete floors. Structural engineers were still busy trying to secure the safety of the twin towers and their two-foot-thick reinforced steel support columns. Wind-sheer braces would help limit the movement that became obvious as the huge cracks in the structure widened in the gusty February snowstorms. But the foundations had been weakened, and they included the seawall that kept the Hudson River's groundwater at bay.

Given the magnitude of the task, the quantity and size of rubble and debris to be screened, not to mention the transportation difficulties, Burmeister and Whitehurst quickly got permission from their bosses in Washington to set up a temporary lab at the New York Police Department's academy. FBI lab personnel were transferred, and equipment that would help identify any explosives residues, such as an ion mobility spectrometer and a high-performance liquid ion chromatography system, were purchased or leased. From the start it was obvious there would be difficulties. There were the general, traditional tensions between the scientists of the Materials Analysis Unit and the nonscientists of the Explosives Unit. But these tensions would soon be exacerbated by the particular, specific problems of the World Trade Center incident.

The FBI lab had no experience of handling an investigation into this big an explosion. The British, with their long experience of big IRA bombs, had been vital in the investigation of the downing of Pan-Am Flight 103 over Lockerbie, Scotland, in December 1993. But even airline bombings were radically different from attacks on landmark buildings in public places. If this was a bomb and mass terrorism, the FBI lab had little experience to fall back on. The rudimentary bombs of the white supremacists, antiwar protesters, the Unabomber (see Chapter 2), and the mail bombs of the VANPAC case (see Chapter 3)—the FBI's experience —just did not compare. This was a whole new ballgame.

To make matters worse, the men swabbing down the concrete in

the cavelike crater underneath the World Trade Center and their coun-
terparts testing the bits of debris hauled into the temporary lab in New
York came up with nothing specific to identify the explosive. This kind
of forensic detective work relies on coming up with unconsumed particles
from the explosive charge or distinctive byproducts in the residue of
what the explosion left behind. Here there were neither. Burmeister and
Whitehurst could detect only ammonium and nitrate ions, both of them
naturally occurring substances. Contamination at the scene was a major
problem. Ammonium ions could have been the result of the fracture of
four large sewerage pipes in the explosion and the urea salt used to grit
the ramps against ice in the parking area. Nitrates were present in the
pervasive pollutants, including exhaust fumes, of a downtown Manhattan
garage.

The uncertainty of the chemical analysis contrasted sharply with
Dave Williams's rapid progress on other fronts. Three days after the explosion, two of his team hauled a huge piece of a vehicle's rear chassis out of
the crater. By dusting with white powder, as for fingerprints, an NYPD
detective was able to come up with a vehicle identification number
(VIN), or part of a VIN, the individual identification every vehicle car-
ries. By feeding LHA75633 into the FBI's National Criminal Intelligence
Center computer, a field agent was able to identify the full seventeen-digit
VIN, 1FTHE34YOLHA75633 as belonging to a 1990 Ford 350 Econoline
van owned by a Ryder rental outlet in Jersey City. It had been rented
by Mohammad Salameh, a twenty-five-year-old Palestinian and former
student of Islamic law who had been living in the United States for five
years. Salameh had reported the van stolen from a shopping center the
day before the explosion.

Williams quickly concluded that the van had been at the center
or near the center of the explosion. Pitting and cratering, the minute
indentations caused by the force of unexploded particles or the hot gases
given off in an explosion, dotted the metalwork of the remains of the
vehicle. And the link to Salameh seemed an exceptionally lucky break.
An intense, wiry character, he was known to the FBI as an Islamic
fundamentalist who had raised money for the Afghan mujahideen and
had been close to the Egyptian religious leader, Sheik Omar Abdel Rahman. When he arrived to collect his four-hundred-dollar deposit at the
rental agency in Jersey City on March 4, he was arrested by an FBI agent

posing as an employee. "I guess I was stunned," Williams recalled on taking the phone call that told him of the arrest. "It was a tremendous feeling. But now we had to prove that he'd done it."[14]

With a premature arrest under his belt, Williams set about the task of 'proving' it with a vengeance. Phone records, business cards, and tip-offs led investigators to three associates of Salameh and a ten-foot-square storage locker near Liberty State Park in Jersey City. Here, the FBI's find included about 300 pounds of urea, a dozen bottles of nitric acid, and 12 pints of a brown liquid, homemade nitroglycerin. Within days, Peter Wolpert, president of the City Chemical Corporation of Jersey City, had told investigators that he had sold someone known to him as Kemal Ibrahim, an alias of Ramzi Ahmed Yousef, another associate, a variety of bulk chemicals. These included nitric acid, sulfuric acid, and fifteen hundred pounds of urea.

David Williams had his link. But to what? What did the chemicals mean? One suggestion came from Rick Strobel, an ATF explosives-residue analyst working on the investigation. Five years earlier he had investigated a pipe-bombing incident in Rockville, Maryland. The bomb had exploded during construction, killing four students. Residue tests suggested the main charge of the bomb was urea nitrate, a somewhat unstable white crystalline powder, which in the presence of moisture tends to disassociate into urea and nitric acid. As an explosive, urea nitrate was so rare that the FBI had no screening test for it, and checks revealed no chemical company manufactured it or sold it in the United States. Indeed, the Maryland incident remained the only known urea nitrate explosion listed in the FBI's Bomb Data Center database.

Williams sought evidence to prove it was a urea nitrate bomb and, more specifically, one about twelve hundred pounds in weight. But the scientists were cautious. They detected urea in the debris. The complication was the cracked sewerage pipes. Urea was a major constituent of urine. Moreover, despite examining every twist and fold, every cavity of what seemed to be the debris of the van, they could find no trace of any unexploded urea nitrate crystals—the vital clue they needed. There were too many unknowns, too much environmental pollution, without the evidence of control tests before the explosion to be able to say categorically what the main charge of the bomb had been.

Help was at hand in the form of Roger Martz's Chemistry and

Toxicology Unit (CTU). With Whitehurst and Burmeister both in New York, and some samples having to be returned to the lab in Washington, there were no chemists specializing in explosives residue back at head-quarters. When a tire fragment believed to be from the Ryder van was dispatched to Washington within days of the explosion, the CTU's Lynn Lasswell analyzed it for trace evidence with a solid-probe mass spectrome-ter and concluded that urea nitrate was present. Martz approved Lasswell's conclusions, which were incorporated into a composite lab report dated April 12, 1993.

Both Burmeister and Whitehurst disagreed with the conclusions, complaining they were overstated. The mass spectrometer, they asserted, could not discriminate between urea nitrate and other urea or nitrate compounds—it could only detect single elements. If the instrumental results only showed the presence of urea and nitrates separately, they could, once again, have come from any of the background environmental sources. The tire fragment needed a confirmatory backup test and, despite scouring the scientific literature and taxing Rick Strobel's memory, no one knew of a test that would confirm the presence of urea nitrate to the exclusion of everything else.

With the complaints overruled by their immediate superiors, Whitehurst wrote to John Hicks, the head of the lab. "In the rush to find the perpetrators of the crime a number of novel methods of investigation and crime scene handling were conducted and mistakes made. One of those mistakes is the identification by this laboratory by mass spectrome-try alone of urea nitrate in explosives residue."[15] With no response, Whitehurst and Burmeister devised an alternative to make their point: their own "blind" proficiency test for Roger Martz's unit. If external inspectors could not test the FBI lab's science, perhaps insiders could. Steve Burmeister brought in some commercial-grade ammonium nitrate fertilizer, which the two scientists ground up and dissolved in acetone. Whitehurst then urinated into a 250-milliliter beaker, evaporated the urine, and dissolved that in acetone.

They placed the two samples in test tubes, labeled them as if they had come from 40 Pamrapo Avenue in Jersey City—Mohammad Sala-meh's address, where urea nitrate crystals had been found—and left them for Roger Martz. The results were such that, according to both Burmeister and Whitehurst, it was impossible to tell the difference between these samples and urea nitrate. When he tested them Martz, known as the expert on the mass spectrometer, seemed elated, according to Whitehurst, effusing: "These results are blowing my machine away."[16] Martz insists he never concluded that the samples demonstrated the presence of urea nitrate, claiming that the machine detected simply urea and nitric acid.[17]

If he did, Whitehurst and Burmeister's next step made little sense. Feeling their case was proven, Whitehurst and Burmeister went straight to the Scientific Analysis Section's assistant chief, Al Robillard. On the witness stand under oath in August 1995, during the second World Trade Center bombing trial, Whitehurst recounted what happened next: "Mr. Robillard became extremely loud and extremely angry at Mr. Burmeister. He advised us that he would now have to embarrass his Chemistry and Toxicology Unit chief and that we were never, ever again to do something like that to him. I might add though that two hours later, going down the hall, he gave me a thumbs-up sign and said: 'Fred, that is what we hired you for!' "

The ruse had the desired impact—an impact that, as now seemed customary, no amount of complaining to management had achieved. Jim Corby instructed Whitehurst to review the CTU's results and write a new dictation, as a forensic scientist's findings are known. This was then incorporated into a new lab report amending that of April 12. The battle may have been won, but the war was far from over. On June 15, 1993, Whitehurst submitted his dictation to David Williams for inclusion in the main composite lab report. Among other things it detailed the examination of two samples by means of solid-probe mass spectrometry.

In both cases, Whitehurst stated, the results of the analysis were "consistent with the presence of urea and nitric acid." He added, in conclusion, the qualifier he viewed as essential: "However, these materials are also found from this analytical method following analysis of other materials such as extracts of urine and fertilizer. Therefore without a confirmation of the presence of trace amounts of urea nitrate, a conclusion cannot be rendered concerning the presence of this material on the evidence. Such a confirmation technique is not known to the examiner at this time."[18]

Sometime later Whitehurst was summoned by James Corby, the head of the Material Analysis Unit, to his office. Whitehurst recalls that Corby told him: "They—I don't know who they were—that they want me to take statements out of my report and he showed me the statements they wanted me to take out of my report and they were marked, highlighted with yellow highlighter."[19] It was the two qualifying statements that were highlighted, and Williams and the Explosives Unit who were trying to exclude them.

On the face of it it was a classic example of the pro-prosecution old guard in the lab seeking to exclude what could only be considered exculpatory data for the presence of nitrates and urea—a statement that apparently would give the defense ample opportunity to raise reasonable doubts and get the defendants off. Williams agreed that he wanted the qualifying passages deleted. "I felt that was fluff, that wasn't necessary. . . . And the fact that he's putting in any possibility of where this material could have come from was bullshit," he later told the IG's investigation with some disdain. "If he was going to go into where these chemicals could have originated from, why didn't he make an opinion that this Trade Center could have been damaged by an act of God or lightning?"[20]

Williams's attitude may have had something to do with the fact that he did not get his way on Whitehurst's reports. Jim Corby put his foot down, knowing this could be a real problem for the lab if it ever emerged in court. It struck at the heart of the lab's method of operation, having principal examiners (PE), who were often not scientists, collate final lab reports by reviewing and incorporating the specialist reports of auxiliary examiners (AE), who were often the only ones qualified in their field.

There was an unwritten rule in the FBI lab that dictation, as the word implied, was not changed, except with the consent of the examiner concerned. Yet the absence of any signature or seal on FBI lab reports meant that they could be changed without the author's knowledge. "An FBI lab report is evidence . . . unauthorized changes in these reports could have resulted in serious consequences during legal proceedings and embarrassment to the Laboratory as well as the entire FBI," Corby wrote in a later memo.[21] Altering reports might be considered tampering with evidence. And it was not the first time the issue had arisen. Indeed, both Whitehurst and Corby knew it had happened before and that altered reports remained on file.

———

It was Fred Whitehurst's technician, Kelly Mount, who first told him that Tom Thurman had told her in a casual aside that he sometimes "streamlined" Whitehurst's dictation before including them in his official PE reports. That was in November 1992. Within a month, Whitehurst had extracted from the files sixteen samples of final reports in cases where Thurman had been the PE and Whitehurst an AE. Several had been altered in a way that "changed the meaning or significantly altered the content" of the dictations, he had complained in a December 1992 memo to his unit chief Jim Corby. Corby had raised the matter with his boss, the head of the seven-unit Scientific Analysis Section, Ken Nimmich, and personally told Thurman not to alter dictation.

It may have been this admonition of his senior and mentor in the Explosives Unit that persuaded Williams to seek permission to alter Whitehurst's report in the World Trade Center case rather than to just do it. But these continuing attempts troubled Whitehurst. What might be being said in his name that he did not agree with, or that was just not scientifically valid? Might he find himself embarrassed on the witness stand someday by something he had not written? In July 1993, he addressed two memos to the head of the FBI lab, John Hicks. In the first he stated categorically that he had been told that exculpatory information was not to be included in laboratory reports and was to be "offered only in the courtroom upon appropriate questioning by defense counsel."[22] As an example, he forwarded a copy of his "Tradbom" report with the exculpatory information Williams had wanted excluded highlighted.

In the second memo, Whitehurst asked Hicks for "clarification in writing of the position of the FBI laboratory." He added: "If biasing is required, what is the legal basis for this biasing and am I in violation of any Bureau policy or Federal regulation or law if I attempt to present in my reports a fully unbiased opinion of data?"[23] In a clear reference to the Steve Psinakis case (see Chapter 1), in which he had approached the defense with what he considered exculpatory data, Whitehurst said he wanted to know if disciplinary action would be taken if he continued to present alternative explanations for scientific results in his reports. "By this time I was beginning to think that there might be something wrong with me. I was thinking maybe there was some reason for all this," he says. "I just wanted to know how I could do this properly, just what the rules were."[24]

In November 1993, Whitehurst hired the law firm Kohn, Kohn and Colapinto, who run a legal service that specializes in representing whistle-blowers (see Chapter 1). On February 7, 1994, Stephen Kohn wrote a long letter to the FBI's office of general counsel (OGC) citing the alteration of lab reports among a long list of complaints about the laboratory. Eventually the OGC recommended a review, and the new Scientific Analysis Section chief, James Kearney, assigned Jim Corby to examine all of the dictations and reports in which Thurman had been PE and Whitehurst AE. It was not until January 1995—more than two years after Kelly Mount's original revelations—that the review was completed. It confirmed Whitehurst's worst fears.

Corby found that Thurman had altered thirty-one out of fifty-two of Whitehurst's reports during a five-year period ending in 1992. Thirteen of these had been rewritten in ways that Corby considered altered the meaning of the original dictation. Kearney and Corby then analyzed the thirteen reports. Kearney determined that in twelve of the reports, Thurman "significantly altered Whitehurst's dictation," and in one other he "reported technical results without supporting laboratory analysis."[25] However, he concluded that the changes were not made to "bias the reports in favor of the prosecution" but to "clarify the reports by integrating the findings . . . into the full context of the report." He recommended no administrative action beyond another admonition to Thurman not to do it again.[26] "No doubt about it, Tom Thurman shouldn't have been doing what he was doing, but the changes did not really change the consistency of the reports, so I thought they were making a big deal over nothing," Kearney told the authors.[27]

Corby's analysis was much harsher. To him, the changes were "clearly intentional" and could expose examiners to having to effectively deny their own reports in court. Corby concluded the changes made it clear that Thurman "does not understand the scientific issues involved with the interpretation and significance of explosives and explosive residue composition. He therefore should realize this deficiency and differentiate between his personal opinions and scientific fact."[28] In short, Jim Corby was convinced that Thurman could not even understand Whitehurst's reports, let alone clarify them.

Yet there seemed to be little ignorance about Thurman's intentions. Of the thirteen cases, all but one of the alterations made the findings more definite.[29] Changing or omitting qualifying clauses such as "similar to" or "consistent with" was only part of it. In some cases whole sections of Whitehurst's reports had been completely rewritten using Thurman's own assumptions or observations. On other occasions passages were simply excluded or phrases such as "chemical analysis shows" added to give reports a more definitive scientific ring. Notwithstanding Kearney's conclusion, there seemed, in short, to be a systemic pattern of doctoring the dictations to make them more pro-prosecution.

Further evidence of the scale and significance of the alteration of FBI lab reports became evident with the publication of the IG report in April 1997. The most extreme example was laboratory case number 20624009, from 1992.[30] Three samples serve to demonstrate. Where Whitehurst had written:

> The results of chemical and physical analyses of specimen Q1 are consistent with the presence of ammonium nitrate. Ammonium nitrate is one of the two components used in binary high explosives

and

> The results of chemical and physical analyses of specimen Q2 are consistent with the presence of nitromethane. Nitromethane is one of the two components used in binary high explosives.

Thurman had replaced this with:

> Present in specimens Q1 and Q2 are the two components which comprise the Kinestik two-component explosive system. The white powder, which was identified as ammonium nitrate, for this explosive is contained within a white plastic container in specimen Q1 and is labeled by the manufacturer "Kinestik 1 Solid." . . . The second part (liquid) of this two-component system is present in specimen Q2 and contained in a clear plastic tube and labeled by the manufacturer as "kinapouch Kinestik 1 Liquid." This liquid, which is red in color, was identified as nitromethane."[31]

The first changes are obvious. "Consistent with" is forensic science's shorthand for "may," in an expert's opinion. It is an equivocal conclusion used only when an examiner has failed to identify a substance or trace definitively. The "consistent with" Whitehurst uses here allows for reasonable doubt in any trial proceedings; the "identified as" Thurman changes this to does not, a potentially vital distinction between guilt and innocence. In forensic science the use of "identified" in a lab report, particularly one from a trace analyst dealing with explosives residue, automatically assumes scientifically or chemically identified by some generally accepted form of analysis. But Thurman, as the VANPAC case illustrated (see Chapter 3), was inclined to identify by observation. Hence, his insertion of the conclusion that the Q1 and Q2 specimens were the two components of the Kinestik explosive system—a decision he told the IG he came to based on the packaging, manufacturer literature in the unit's Explosive Reference Files, and his "25+ years of explosive experience."[32]

The IG found all this and plenty of other examples totally unacceptable. But the alteration of reports was not confined to Tom Thurman. Wallace Higgins, also an examiner in the EU, had changed at least 19 of 48 dictations Whitehurst had submitted to him in less than four years, up to May 1994.[33] Higgins's changes were, if anything, more serious. In thirteen instances, more than 25 percent of the cases the IG was able to examine, Higgins omitted important qualifying language, eliminated Whitehurst's forensic opinion altogether, changed the findings, and even managed to identify the presence or absence of chemical compounds not identified by Whitehurst. Sometimes these reports appeared to be sheer fantasy. In one instance, Whitehurst wrote: "No indication of the presence of lead organic primary explosive was found." Higgins left out the sentence altogether, inserting his own: "An electrical match inside the detonator initiates lead styphnate and lead azide which in turn initiates the PETN."[34] It was real alchemy: Higgins had turned the absence of lead into a presence and detailed how he supposed it all worked.

The problem was almost certainly much more extensive. How much more extensive we will never know, for two reasons. First, Higgins and Thurman were the only principal examiners accused of changing reports, so they were the only individuals ever investigated by the IG's office. Second, in yet another extraordinary example of the FBI's inability to file or preserve crucial evidence, the Bureau was unable to locate Whitehurst's dictations in some twenty-one additional cases—more than 30 percent of the total—in which Higgins had been the principal examiner. The filing and record retention system at the FBI lab was never a subject of the IG's investigation. Yet the almost accidental discovery of the widespread loss of documentary evidence was perhaps one of the most serious revelations of the inquiry.

It struck at the heart of the negligence that underpinned the way things were being done. Potential evidence had disappeared, apparently on a massive scale. It was just one example of how the IG's thorough but strictly limited investigation raised as many questions as it answered. Who controlled these files? Who was responsible for the documentation? What if one of these cases came to court, or the file was relevant to another case, or if the case had already been to court, an appeal was lodged? How much documentation from how many files was missing overall in the FBI lab? It seemed incredible that the FBI lab, so cautious about letting evidence out or defense representatives in—all on security grounds—was busy losing evidence in the short journey between the lab and its filing center—both within the same building.

The IG's inquiry team ran into the problem of missing documentation at every turn. But lab staff reaction to this was as revealing as the discovery itself. The IG's interviews showed that many supervisors and examiners at the FBI lab clearly failed to understand exactly why files, charts, dictation, bench notes, research papers, etc., were essential for what forensic scientists call "file integrity." It went back to the basics of science: results have to be intelligible, verifiable, and ultimately replicable by another scientist in another laboratory. If files were incomplete, how could work be checked, even by FBI supervisors, let alone external examiners such as the IG's team or ASCLD/LAB inspectors?

Where were the missing dictations? Could they have been destroyed intentionally? The sheer numbers suggested something systemic. If senior examiners were prepared to tamper with reports, might they not be prepared to get rid of them altogether? Even the FBI thought this was a possibility. In a letter to the IG, the Bureau noted that any of the following might explain the absence of a document from an FBI file. "The person responsible for sending the document to the central files failed to do so; the document was sent to be filed but did not reach the file room; and the document reached the file room but was misfiled. FN: Although it would be improper for an employee to remove a properly filed document from a file, this is a possibility."[35] Given the admitted lack of security and checks on lab reports, anyone with the motive to destroy lab reports would seem to have the means.

Motive was the key issue. Somewhat curiously, the IG's final report decided that in Thurman's case, although there "seemed" to be a pattern of overstating AE dictation in a way that would "normally" be favorable to the prosecution, "we do not find that Thurman intended to write reports with a prosecutorial bias."[36] Despite cooperation, some explanation, and even a limited admission of error by Tom Thurman, it seemed a strange conclusion in the face of the evidence. Thurman had changed twelve reports in favor of the prosecution. Higgins, who refused to accept that the changes were substantive, and so resented being questioned about them that he walked out of his first interview with the IG, had altered at least thirteen reports materially, and probably more. Both had made the changes systematically over a period of years. Yet the most the IG's report was prepared to say was that both Wallace Higgins and Tom Thurman had "erred."

The question was crucial. Intent was the key to substantiating the most serious charges yet against laboratory examiners—perjury and obstruction of justice. The IG's final report glosses over the matter, saying it found no intent to commit perjury or obstruct justice. Yet the referral of the final report to the Criminal Division of the Department of Justice seemed to imply there was a case to answer. The IG's report is adamant in stating that it found no evidence to support what it termed Whitehurst's most inflammatory allegations and seemed to base much of its recommendation that he could not "effectively function within the Laboratory" on the "sweeping accusations" he had made against other examiners.[37] Whitehurst himself quite logically points out that it is his duty as an FBI agent to report all such suspicions—indeed, he was bound to report any "indication" of "possible" misconduct even if based on hearsay, both by an executive order and by the FBI's internal rulebook.[38] "I've always said I might be wrong," he says. "But, hell, this is the Federal Bureau of Investigation. If it's my job to report things, it's their job to investigate them. All I've ever wanted is a complete investigation."[39]

At a congressional hearing in May 1997, the inspector general, Michael Bromwich, was asked the crucial question about intent by Congressman Robert Wexler (Democrat, Florida). If the Explosives Unit examiners' intents were not criminal, what legitimate law enforcement purpose would there have been in changing the reports? Bromwich said that he did not know what their motives were. Later he was asked whether the "coincidence" that all but one of the dictations were changed to make them more pro-prosecution did not "get to the motive of the person doing it." Bromwich was equivocal: "It suggests things about the motives of the person doing it, and I don't deny for a moment that there may have been pressures within the lab to push evidence to the limit."[40]

As a scientist James Corby had no doubts about Thurman's intent. In an undated memo to James Kearney, written sometime in the first four months of 1995, he argued that Thurman should be censured for rewriting Whitehurst's dictations. "In conclusion," he wrote, "SSA Thurman committed errors which were clearly intentional." In the end, on Kearney's insistence Thurman was neither censured by letter nor orally reprimanded. Indeed, less than five weeks after Corby concluded that Thurman had materially altered thirteen of Whitehurst's dictations and with the review of those cases by Kearney and Corby still in progress, Thurman was promoted to acting chief of the Explosives Unit (EU).

R. Patrick Welch, who had applied for the position of EU chief, charged that the delay in the investigation, and Kearney's exoneration of him, showed that Thurman had been "preselected."[41] Welch claimed that this was in violation of internal FBI procedures. It was true that the FBI's review took over two years, but the FBI rejected Welch's contentions and appeal of the appointment. But the experience of Ed Kelso, the head of the Bomb Data Center at the time, seems to confirm that Thurman had been preselected for the job. In September 1997, he told a congressional subcommittee that he had been "ordered" by the head of the lab, Milton Ahlerich, to withdraw his application for the post.[42]

―――

Ultimately, the attempt to change Whitehurst's World Trade Center bombing report, although unsuccessful, was only part of Dave Williams's effort to make the evidence fit the crime. Since the EU was unable to link the suspects to the chemicals definitively, identifying the main charge of the bomb as urea nitrate gave him nothing more than a circumstantial case. Six months after the blast the investigation had failed to turn up a single witness. No one had seen any of the suspects load the van, drive it to the World Trade Center, or leave the scene of the crime.

If forensic evidence could not link them more certainly to the scene, the chances of a conviction would be uncertain at best. One possibility was the EU's old standby of trying to re-create the bomb. Videos of detonations always impressed juries, and the extent of any test damage should help the EU identify the bomb by means of the size and velocity of detonation, which in turn should help link it back to the missing nitric acid and urea. In fact, armed with the information from the searches in Jersey City, Williams had been working backward along this path for some time.

Within ten days of the blast, the principal examiner provided Thomas Jourdan, a forensic chemist in the Chemistry and Toxicology Unit, with a list of the chemicals missing from the storage locker and asked him to calculate the potential amount of urea nitrate that could have been produced. There were many variables: the purity of the ingredients, the conditions under which they were mixed, the volumes that were mixed, all of which would in turn affect the percentage yield of the reaction. Another factor was what is known in chemistry as the stoichiometry, the way the molecular weights of the two chemicals, urea and nitric acid, react together to form the third, urea nitrate.

In this case the molecular weight of urea is 60, that of nitric acid, 63. Therefore, even if there were an unlimited amount of urea in any mixing container, and only 63 grams of nitric acid, the reaction would only produce 123 grams of urea nitrate. Nitric acid would be a limiting reagent in this reaction. Having done his calculations, Jourdan informed Williams that, with the amount of nitric acid found as a limiting reagent the "upper limit" of urea nitrate that could have been produced was 1,821 pounds. Believing that Williams and the Explosives Unit did not understand the chemistry and concept of a limiting reagent, Jourdan wrote a memo defining it as the substance "you run out of first."

As his testimony at the first World Trade Center bombing trial was to illustrate, Williams never did get hold of the concept of the limiting reagent, but that did not stop him from going ahead with an effort to re-create the bomb. After several mini urea nitrate detonations on the FBI's range at its training base at Quantico, Virginia, in August 1993, Williams, Whitehurst, Burmeister, and others set out to mix and explode twelve hundred pounds of homemade urea nitrate at Eglin Air Force Base in Florida. It was a big job with an unstable substance. Shrouded in moonsuits, Whitehurst and Burmeister weighed the urea, dissolved it in distilled water, then mixed the sludge with nitric acid in plastic trash cans standing in ice water. The precipitate urea nitrate was then placed on drying trays and put into ovens. A white powder looking not unlike salt or sugar then crystallized from the solution.

By this time Williams felt he had the formula that the suspects had followed in building the bomb. Agents had uncovered six large notebooks that seemed to be homemade military textbooks with hand-drawn diagrams and instructions in both Arabic and English. One of the pages seemed to show how to make a small urea nitrate pipe bomb. Instructions in the text, according to an unofficial translation, read: "Boil a huge amount of urine (10 cups) until it becomes one tenth the amount. Then filter it into another cup to isolate foreign objects. Then slowly add one-third cup of nitric acid to the urine and let the mix sit for one hour."[43]

There were only two problems. First, the books had been confiscated by U.S. Customs at Kennedy airport in New York six months before the blast, and so were not in the possession of the suspects when they were alleged to have built the bomb. Second, despite Dave Williams's later claim in court that he had followed the formulas for the production of urea nitrate laid down in the notebooks, the IG decided that neither he nor anyone else at the FBI followed these formulas in making urea nitrate.[44] Given the internal battles in the FBI lab over the TRADBOM case, details of which had come to the attention of both sets of lawyers, it might have been anticipated that the trial of the six defendants eventually charged in the first World Trade Center bombing case would not go well. Indeed, long before Steve Burmeister and David Williams were to appear as the last of more than two hundred witnesses for the prosecution, the government's case seemed to have been derailed.

It was an unlikely looking charge sheet from the start. Two of the defendants, Ramzi Ahmed Yousef and Abdul Rahman Yasin, both portrayed as the brains of the plot, had never been captured. A third defendant, Ahmad Ajaj, a twenty-seven-year-old Palestinian, had been jailed six months before the explosion, having been arrested on September 1, 1992, at Kennedy airport with the bomb-making manuals he claimed were from the U.S.-backed anti-Russian war in Afghanistan. The three remaining defendants, Mohammad Salameh, Nidal Ayyad, and

Mahmud Abouhalima, were all what might be loosely termed Islamic fundamentalists, but none had been seen building the bomb, driving it to the World Trade Center, leaving it there, or leaving the scene. Moreover, the government's efforts to prove they had been seen anywhere near the key locations would soon look manipulatively contrived, as witnesses changed their stories, failed to identify the defendants, and recalled sightings months after their initial statements.

In the courtroom, the government strategy quickly became clear: overwhelm the jury with the details of this circumstantial evidence and wrap it in the emotion generated by the death and destruction of the explosion. In other words, put the crime, the outrage and the defendants' political philosophies on trial as much as the defendants themselves while avoiding any defense attorney's efforts to expose the gaps in the investigation or the FBI lab's incompetence. Before long a seemingly endless line of witnesses would be telling the story of the rescue operation, the search for evidence, the identification of the van.

Clark Anderson, the government's sixtieth witness, was the first to even mention one of the defendants by name—but not in association with any crime. Mohammad Salameh had rented the Ryder truck identified as the one wrecked in the explosion at the World Trade Center—something no one, including Salameh himself, disputed. Eventually even the judge, Kevin T. Duffy, began to lose patience. "At some point you're going to have to finish putting parts together and get down to the case against these defendants," he chided the prosecution seven weeks into the trial.

When the prosecution did get down to their case, it all came apart fairly quickly. First there was the testimony of Jan Gilhooly, a Secret Service agent who, along with two colleagues, was parking his car in the World Trade Center garage when the explosion occurred. Thrown thirty or forty feet and knocked unconscious by the blast, he had been interviewed by investigators the following day. He had made no mention of a yellow van then, but did now in court, readily admitting that he had told prosecutors about this recollection only the night before his testimony in court. Postconcussive shock syndrome, as Gilhooly claimed, or convenient amnesia, as the defense alleged?

Whatever it was, there was a lot of it among prosecution witnesses. Blessed Igiri was an assistant manager at the Space Station Storage Com-

pany, where the defendants were alleged to have stored their bomb-
making chemicals. Igiri testified that on February 25, 1993, he saw
Salameh attempt to take delivery of two tanks of compressed hydrogen
gas; these were designed to increase the force of the explosion, according
to the prosecution. Asked whether he saw Salameh again that day, he
replied with a seemingly very certain "No."

After lunch, in response to the same question from prosecutor
J. Gilmore Childers, Igiri changed his story, saying that he had seen
Salameh return later in the day with a yellow Ryder rental van. In cross-
examination, the defense attorney asked Igiri if he had spoken to Childers
during lunch. He denied that he had and confirmed that to Judge Duffy.
Duffy then asked Childers if he had spoken to Igiri, only to be told: "Yes,
your honor, we did have some words," something Igiri finally admitted
when an exasperated Judge Duffy asked Igiri a third time.

A third key witness's evidence seemed just a little tainted. On
November 18, Peter Wolpert, president of the City Chemicals Corporation of Jersey City, identified a photograph of a heavily bearded man
known to him as Kemal Ibrahim—allegedly an alias for absent defendant
Ramzi Ahmed Yousef—as the man who had paid him four thousand
dollars in one-hundred-dollar bills for three large orders of chemicals,
including urea and nitric acid. But Wolpert had agreed to testify only
after being given immunity, and after doing so admitted that his company
was under investigation by local officials on two counts: violations of fire
and environmental regulations. Was his testimony a classic trade-off, as
the defense suggested?

Two more key eyewitnesses were to have similar problems during
the trial. Willie Hernandez Moosh is a Spanish-speaking gas station attendant who had contacted the FBI after seeing a picture of Mohammad
Salameh on a news report. He said he had pumped gas for a yellow Ryder
rental van driven by Salameh sometime between 3:00 and 4:00 A.M. on
February 26 in Jersey City, nine hours before the bomb went off and only
a matter of hours after Salameh had reported the van stolen. Moosh also
claimed that Salameh was accompanied by Yousef and Abouhalima, who
was driving a blue Lincoln Town Car. It was crucial evidence that placed
three of the defendants together hours before the explosion within a few
miles of the World Trade Center. Moosh had picked out photos of
Salameh and Abouhalima from FBI spreads. His was an essential part of

the jigsaw, so essential that Moosh had been paid a total of $40,500 by the FBI so as to be able to quit his job and be available to testify.

In court, it did not go according to plan. When asked to identify the driver of the Lincoln Town Car Moosh ignored Abouhalima, with his striking orange-red hair and pointed at one of the jurors. The driver of the van, supposedly Mohammad Salameh, was another of the jurors, he claimed. It was not until the next day, during cross-examination by defense lawyer Robert Precht, that Moosh, ignoring a question, identified Salameh. On redirect, despite the protestations of the defense, Childers was allowed to get Moosh to positively identify Abouhalima. The net effect was more than reasonable doubt. Near the end of his testimony, Childers asked Moosh to clarify a minor point for the record. "The record has absolutely no clarity whatsoever, so what's the difference," interjected the judge.

The initial forensic testimony was no more definitive. On February 3 the court learned that 2,233 latent fingerprints had been developed from the more than 1,000 exhibits in the case, some 343 of the prints belonging to the defendants. Receipts, telephone records, address books, even the infamous bomb-making manuals, all had fingerprints—but these proved nothing in themselves. Yet on December 1, a New York City police detective, Ronald Alongis, seemed to be promising something big. As chief prosecutor J. Gilmore Childers took Alongis through the craft of fingerprint comparisons, a world of loops, whorls, arches, ridge characteristics, and amino acid secretions, the court waited with bated breath. Prints on Exhibit 702A, a World Trade Center garage parking stub, matched those on Exhibit 702, Mohammad Salameh's fingerprint card. The trouble was, it had been fed through the parking meter on February 16, ten days before the explosion, rather than February 26.

The DNA evidence was similarly tantalizing. On December 9, Lawrence Presley from the FBI's serology department installed a portable screen and dimmed the lights to give the courtroom a basic course in DNA typing. On March 1, 1993, a letter from the Liberation Army Fifth Battalion had arrived at *The New York Times* claiming responsibility for the blast. Presley related how he had compared DNA extracted from the envelope flap with a sample of saliva from Nidal Ayyad. "They matched," Presley told the court triumphantly. "In other words, Ayyad was a potential contributor to the saliva on the back of the envelope," he concluded.

"Match" meant probability, not certainty, he explained in another of those abuses of the most fought over word in forensic science. In fact, 3 percent of the Arab population had the same DNA profile as that extracted from the saliva on the envelope, according to Lawrence Presley. And the DNA on the postage stamp did not "match" any known sample. It was not Ayyad's.

Steve Burmeister, who took the stand to begin four days of testimony on January 20, 1994, could provide only more of the same—chemical circumstance. Yes, he had found sulphuric acid burns on a shoe recovered from the closet of Mahmud Abouhalima in Woodbridge, New Jersey, he told the prosecution. Yes, it could have been caused by spillage from a car battery, given that Abouhalima earned his living as a driver. Yes, he had detected nitroglycerin on a shirt and a piece of carpet in an apartment rented by Mohammad Salameh; but yes, no one denied he might have been in contact with nitroglycerin—it had been discovered at the storage locker.

Above all, Burmeister could not confirm what the prosecution most needed him to confirm: what made up the bomb. *The New York Times* said it all under the headline GAP IN THE PROSECUTION'S CHAIN OF EVIDENCE. Reporter Richard Bernstein, who had sat through it all, wrote: "A forensic chemist with the FBI took the stand in the World Trade Center bombing trial yesterday and said that he had been unable to form a definite conclusion about the contents of the device that shook the Trade Center on February 26. The chemist, Steven G. Burmeister, seemed to leave a gap in the chain of evidence the prosecution has painstakingly been building."[45]

Prosecutor Childers worked hard to close that "definite conclusion" gap. He got Burmeister to confirm the long list of chemicals found in the storage locker, then got him to affirm that each could be used to make a bomb, then got Burmeister to recall how he had detected all of the individual substances, at the scene or on the debris, that would have been there if a urea nitrate bomb had exploded. Eventually, having edged as close as he dared, Childers pounced: "So could you say that the lack of a conclusion is based not on a lack of indicators and more on the basis of environmental factors?" The defense's immediate objection was sustained.

Under cross-examination Robert Precht, Salameh's defense attorney seemed to score some points. He took the court through the complications of the Burmeister-Whitehurst battle with David Williams and a quick lesson in the meaning of terms such as "consistent with" in forensic science. Yes, Burmeister admitted, he and Whitehurst had exposed the inadequacy of the Chemistry and Toxicology Unit's testing at the FBI lab with samples of urine and fertilizer; yes, there had been efforts to change reports to say urea nitrate had been found at the site, a change that would have made the analysis and conclusions "misleading." Intent was, as ever, a moot issue. Burmeister thought it was a matter of presenting it "better" to the court. "To the court or to the prosecutor?" Precht shot back. "I don't know that," Burmeister replied. Neither did he know if other "errors" had crept into other auxiliary examiners' dictations presented to Williams.[46] It was an alarming but realistic possibility, a question that no one had posed to date.

As Burmeister stepped down it was clear that everything was still on the line. He had gone as far as he could both as a professional scientist and as an expert in explosives residue. It was unlikely to be enough for a conviction. Now, as a hushed courtroom looked on in awe, television monitors, wall charts, enlarged photographs, and finally an exquisite scale model of the six underground floors of the trade center, replete with removable crater, an escalator, and the red-and-yellow garage markings on the B-2 level, were carried into court. Government witness 206 or 207 —even the clerks seemed to have lost count—now walked into court to place a miniature Ryder van on the second level of the garage. It was all up to the man who now pressed a remote control to turn on a series of lights in the model—yellow for shards from the van, white for tire fragments, red for the pieces of the hydrogen cylinders that he said were packed in with the chemicals to magnify the explosion. David Williams held the floor and the prospects for conviction.

It was to be done with a combination of bogus science, baffling "expertise"—based largely on assumption and intuition—and semantic license. Given that he knew he had to be careful, that the story of his battles with Burmeister and Whitehurst had already been related to the court, it was to be an extraordinarily risky performance in the quest for a conviction. The only explanation for this was that the stakes for Williams personally were as big as they were for the prosecution collectively. This was his first big bombing case as a principal examiner and they did not come any bigger than this. It was a case dubbed the advent of international terrorism on U.S. soil, a case with which his name would always be associated if a guilty verdict was returned, "the case of a lifetime" as Williams himself later labeled it. It was to be a short lifetime. Three years later what David Williams was now about to say in a Manhattan court-room would end his career in the FBI laboratory.

The starting point for him was a very speculative estimate as to the weight of the bomb: "My initial estimate was somewhere between a thousand and 1,500 pounds. That was within a day or two after . . . as a ballpark figure, about 1,200 pounds." This initial estimate was based on nothing more than observed damage and, although Williams tried to dress the assessment up with charts on the Monroe effect—"how shaped charges work and cut the steel with opposing angles," as he put it in court—he was, as he readily admitted, speculating. "You're able to kind of estimate how much explosive," he told the court on one occasion. "These things produced an impression on me," he claimed on another.[47]

The IG's report concluded that the analysis was "intuitive, unscientific and imprecise" despite being a rough estimate. Moreover, as Tom Thurman told the IG's investigators, examiners in the Explosives Unit of the lab did not normally estimate the quantity of explosives used in any given bombing—there were too many imponderables—placement, physical confines, types, or mixtures of explosives. Thurman recounted how this was demonstrated to examiners during training, with three car-tridges of dynamite being detonated—one on the ground, one in the ground, and one buried and covered in the ground—to illustrate "vastly differing damages."[48]

The reason for going out on a limb on the quantity of explosive was that Williams, as ever, was working backward. The defendants were known to have purchased fifteen hundred pounds of urea, three hundred pounds of which had been recovered by the FBI from a storage locker in Jersey City after the explosion. Calculating the reaction with the amount of nitric acid known to be missing from purchases and assuming a "non-laboratory environment" yield of 60 to 70 percent—a figure that was somehow linked to his own urea nitrate manufacturing experiment at Eglin Air Force Base—Williams arrived at the twelve-hundred-pound figure for the size of the bomb. In explaining all this to the court he once again demonstrated that he still did not understand the concept of a limiting reagent or remember which substance it was, telling the jury it was the urea.

Some of this was shrouded in a fairly typical gimmick: a video of a white van being blown up by fifty pounds of ammonium nitrate explosive. As Richard Bernstein noted somewhat sardonically in *The New York Times:* "The purpose of the video seemed to be to show that an explosion inside a van would cause it to rupture outward in all directions."[49] The IG's report saw through all this just as easily as *The New York Times* and was scathing in reviewing Williams's testimony:

> The purpose of a criminal trial is of course to determine guilt. The issue of guilt is the ultimate question to which all others are directed. In contrast Williams began with a presumption of guilt as a foundation on which to build inferences. . . . The agent simply assumed that the perpetrators produced a 1,200 pound bomb at the Trade Center using the urea and nitric acid missing from the defendants' facility and that yield (the amount used at the bombing divided by the amount missing) informed his testimony about "non-laboratory yield."[50]

Faced with the Burmeister-Whitehurst expertise, Williams knew he needed a nonchemical means of identifying the main charge as urea nitrate. He homed in on an area where he was the supposed expert—explosives, specifically, the velocity of detonation (VOD) of the blast. Williams settled on a VOD of 14,000 to 15,500 feet per second, a figure that, in his own words to the court, limited the possibilities "to the fertilizer-based explosive such as ammonium nitrate, and also certain dynamites, the ammonium-nitrate type dynamites."[51] It also of course included urea nitrate: "Urea nitrate in smaller quantities detonates at a velocity of about 14,000 feet per second. The larger quantity . . . compacts on top of itself and may approach 15,500 feet per second."[52]

Williams's starting point for his VOD figures was once again observation—looking at the damage. He told the court that on a brief initial two-and-a-half-hour walk through the site he had the chance to inspect a lot of damaged vehicles, concrete, steel-reinforcing rods, beams, and other fragments of materials. The way steel beams had been broken off —"specific, unique, breaking," according to Williams—the direction and distance parts had been thrown, the "heaving" or pushing damage rather than the "brisance" or "shattering" damage, even the bodies of the victims, one with partially chewed food in his mouth, another with fragmentation damage in the eyeball but not on the eyelid, suggesting no time to blink, all these suggested a specific VOD, according to Williams. "By putting all these things together and looking at the size of the hole I estimated that the velocity of detonation was somewhere between 14,000 and 15,500 feet per second, with a little bit of give on each side of that."[53] Later he was to add to the IG investigators that his estimate of the VOD was somehow supported by the "pitting and cratering" he found within four feet and the evidence of "heaving" with no tearing within eight and a half feet of the seat of the explosion.

Some of these observations could have excluded the high explosives used by the military that have VODs of more than 18,000 feet per second, but the "heaving" range of such explosives has a huge range of VODs, varying from about 3,000 to 18,000 feet per second. The narrowing of this range beyond that seemed once again to be intuitive, not scientific. "I can roughly get a feel that it was a very hot explosive or not." "These things produced an impression on me," as Williams told the IG, apparently believing that a panel of international forensic scientists, including Dr. Gerard Murray, one of the world's leading explosives experts, would be as likely to ignore the complete absence of any empirical data as the Manhattan court. As Tom Thurman, the head of the Explosives Unit, told investigators, none of this was in the unit's training. Thurman told the IG that he had never estimated a specific VOD from a damage assessment; indeed, Dave Williams was the only examiner who had even tried to, as far as he knew.

A VOD of 14,000 to 15,500 feet per second was a cornerstone of David Williams's argument that it was a urea nitrate bomb, yet incredibly the figure seems to have been made up. No one in court asked where he got the figure from. Later, when the IG did, Williams claimed that he had gotten it "orally" from "knowledgeable sources within the field of explosives."[54] None of the three individuals Williams named recall talking to him. There is very little literature on the subject, with the only known source giving a wide-parameter VOD of 3,400 to 4,700 meters per second for urea nitrate, which is equivalent to about 11,155 to 15,420 feet per second.[55] The IG obtained Williams's case notes and found nothing to indicate where he had gotten the figures. After the trial, Williams detonated the homemade urea nitrate Whitehurst and Burmeister had produced at Eglin Air Force Base. He told the IG that the VOD was measured at 12,100 feet per second. In fact, even this was wrong, although not by much.[56]

It seems that, as with his figure for the size of the bomb, having estimated the VOD from the damage assessment and written this up in a lab report, Williams decided to try and remain consistent by bending the science and literature to fit his "facts"—working backward again. Even though he had the applicable page from the one standard text giving him the 11,155 to 15,420 feet per second parameter in his notes, and had consulted these notes before taking the stand, he testified without qualification to his own VOD figures—14,000 to 15,500 feet per second.

In the first draft of their report, the IG's investigators wrote the following: "Williams' Salameh [trial] testimony about the VOD of urea nitrate was at best, incomplete and, at worst, intentionally false." By the second draft, the published edition had replaced "intentionally false" with "knowingly incorrect" for what the report termed "the sake of precision."[57] What that precision was no one seemed to be able to say. The effect was that the IG once again had backed away from drawing what seemed to many people the most reasonable conclusion from the evidence —that Williams had committed perjury by knowingly lying on the witness stand. That change of words in turn allowed the IG and the FBI to continue to maintain that Fred Whitehurst's most serious charges—perjury and fabrication of evidence—had not been substantiated by the investigation.

The narrowly defined VOD speed allowed Williams to restrict options on the main charge of the explosion. "I believe urea nitrate was the bulk constituent in that bomb with other explosive materials," he told defense counsel Austin Campriello.[58] So could it have been another kind of bomb? "Not likely," Williams replied. "As I said, the bulk of the explosive material could have been urea nitrate with other things such as ammonium nitrate dynamite and certainly there was some type of initiator, but the bulk of the explosive was, in my opinion, urea nitrate."[59]

When grilled by the IG as to how he could render that opinion, Williams revealed all about how he worked: "The reason I was able to do that in testimony was because I had the benefit of the search sites, the storage sites, the bomb factory and of course viewing evidence from the crime scene." Later he added: "[H]ad I not had the benefit of any other searches, I could simply say in the Trade Center I don't know what that explosive was. I don't know what it was. I could never tell you what it was." [60]

Williams was admitting that when his reasoning had to be based on scientific analysis and data, not assumption, there was no proof it was a urea nitrate bomb. It was a perfect illustration of how a pro-prosecution bias could infect a case when the examiner knew too much about the extraneous circumstances. It also demonstrated graphically why examiners needed to be scientists—the logical reasoning of science being the platform on which forensic examination had to be built. "If the scientific link, the nexus as we call it legally, is not there, there cannot be a conviction," says Atique Ahmed, Nidal Ayyad's lawyer. "Here we had the scientist saying, no we can't draw any conclusions, and the nonscientist, the case agent, drawing conclusions and doing so with absolute certainty." [61]

What David Williams, a principal examiner in the FBI's lab, was saying in effect was that, if you assume the defendants are guilty you can prove they are guilty. The IG even outlined this reasoning in a step-by-step way in its final report. Urea nitrate ingredients were found in the defendants' storage locker; the defendants committed the World Trade Center bombing; the defendants must have used what was available to them; ergo, it must have been a urea nitrate bomb that blew up the World Trade Center. Whatever the alleged plot by the defendants, there was certainly one by the FBI laboratory: find them guilty by whatever reasoning necessary.

By the time the IG had finished investigating him, David Williams's name topped a charge sheet as long as the defendants' in the World Trade Center bombing. Concluding that they were "profoundly disturbed," the IG decided Dave Williams had given inaccurate and incomplete testimony, invalid and misleading opinions—some based on speculation—and had testified on two separate issues beyond his expertise in a way that appeared "tailored to the most incriminating result." [62] But in the World Trade Center bombing case incrimination worked. Four years before the IG was to raise these questions, questions that might have been serious enough to make an argument for reopening the case, the Manhattan jury took just four days to find all four defendants guilty. "You unjust people, you did us an injustice," yelled Mohammad Salameh as he was hustled out of court.

The defendants had not been helped by their defense team's decision not to put up any expert witnesses. British explosives expert Dr. John Lloyd, who had been instructed on behalf of Mohammad Salameh, is still mystified as to why he was not called to testify. Lloyd, who was to testify to considerable effect about the inadequacies of the FBI lab in the Oklahoma City bombing trial the following year, says the defense used the material he provided but still wishes he had been there: "I felt that the FBI would not have been able to get away with some of their claims if the defendants' attorneys had had experts in attendance."[63]

The defense lawyers felt that the government's case had collapsed under the weight of its own contradictions, with the forensics center stage. "I thought Burmeister's testimony at the end, that they did not know what caused the explosion, was enough to get an acquittal given everything else," recalls Hassen Ibn Abdellah, Mahmud Abouhalima's lawyer.[64] But it was the testimony of the last witness and the absence of any defense case that the jury remembered. One juror, noting how impressed they had been with the government's visual displays, complained to the press afterward that the defense had "presented nothing in rebuttal."

On May 24, Judge Duffy, known for his maximum sentencing, consulted actuarial tables to add up the life expectancies of the six victims. Adding on two mandatory terms of thirty years each for two separate counts, he came up with sentences of 240 years each without parole. Dave Williams dined out on the story of how he had solved the World Trade Center bombing for more than a year, lecturing all over the country to attentive audiences of students and law enforcement officials. A little over a year later he would be asked to do it again, in Oklahoma City.

6

OKLAHOMA CITY: CONTAMINATING, COMMINGLING, CONSPIRING?

The explosion at the World Trade Center was not the largest on U.S. soil for long. At 9:02 on the morning of April 19, 1995, the first reports of a massive blast at the Alfred P. Murrah Federal Building crackled over the radios of the emergency services in Oklahoma City. In a cacophony of sirens, police, fire, and medical services converged on the nine-story U-shaped structure—or what was left of it. A huge crater at the very front of the building testified to a blast that had taken what one forensic scientist was later to describe as a "massive bite" out of the front of the building. Some 168 or 169 people, investigators never have been able to say for certain, lay dead or dying beneath an avalanche of concrete and steel rubble. Fifteen of the victims were children who had been having breakfast at the day care center inside.

As an attack on a federal building it was clear that the investigation, rapidly code-named OKBOM, was an FBI job. David Williams was designated principal examiner and made crime scene manager within an hour of the explosion on the basis of his perceived success in New York in the World Trade Center bombing. As the biggest single challenge to the U.S.

government's authority in peacetime, this was yet another case Washington had to solve and quickly. This time, however, the first major FBI lab bungle did not originate from the Explosives Unit or even the Scientific Analysis Section, but from a forensic artist working in what was known as the Investigative and Prosecutive Graphics Unit of the lab's Special Projects Section, the people responsible for what are generally known as "artists' impressions." The flawed impression of a suspect produced and transmitted around the world within hours of the explosion was to haunt the investigation and fuel conspiracy theories long after the prosecution of Timothy McVeigh and Terry Nichols for the bombing.

Once again, it was an axle and a vehicle identification number (VIN) of what turned out to be a hired Ryder truck that launched the investigation. Located at the scene within hours of the start of the search, the VIN was traced to Elliott's Body Shop, a Ryder truck rental agency in Junction City, Kansas. By dawn the next morning, Elliott's mechanic, Tom Kessinger, and Ray Rozycki, the FBI artist dispatched from Washington, had produced two impressions of the men who had rented the truck. Never had the standard anonymous epithet John Doe enjoyed such publicity. Under a black-bordered headline, WANTED BY THE FBI, the brooding visages of two men soon stared out from the front page of every newspaper in the country.

John Doe I proved relatively easy. The owner of the Dreamland Motel in Junction City identified him as Timothy McVeigh, arrested some ninety minutes after the explosion and held in Noble County jail in Perry, Oklahoma, for carrying a concealed handgun and driving his mustard-yellow Mercury Marquis without rear license plates. But despite the arrest of dozens of additional suspects, including an Australian tourist in Ontario and an army deserter who had to don a bullet-proof vest to face an angry crowd in Los Angeles, John Doe II is still at large.

Tom Kessinger was never happy with the sketch of John Doe II. He had not even seen it before publication, and was relieved when the FBI, realizing they were getting nowhere, called in Jeanne Boylan, the country's foremost forensic artist. A veteran of some seven thousand investigations over twenty years and author of the only sketch of the hooded man who was believed to be the Unabomber, Boylan met Kessinger in Junction City, Kansas, in early May. "The first thing he said to me was the sketch was bad. He said, 'That's not what I saw,' " she recalled in a *Washington Post* article. "I was very casual in my response. I said, 'Okay, what did you see?' Internally, I was thinking, 'What's going on here?' "[1]

Incredibly, Ray Rozycki had produced a frontal sketch of a suspect that Kessinger had only ever viewed in profile, an impression of a bare-headed man that the forty-four-year-old mechanic had only ever seen wearing a baseball cap. After years of sketching for the FBI, including similar such remedial work, she was not so surprised. The FBI's sketch had been produced using what Boylan considers a dangerously manipulative method. The artist had shown Kessinger photographs of the 960 faces that make up the FBI's Facial Identification Catalog, asking him to point out the resemblances of separate features—chin, nose, lips, and eyes—on faces as he noticed them, before filling in a facial identification fact sheet from which to draw the sketch.

Boylan, by contrast, relies on gentle questioning and the descriptions of the witness, something that in this instance produced a profile sketch of a five-foot-ten-inch white male of medium build in his late twenties or early thirties wearing a two-tone baseball cap. It both satisfied and relieved Kessinger, who, strangely, given the FBI's efforts, was later described in court by Ray Rozycki as a very good eyewitness: "Very descriptive, able to visualize the image that he had in his head of an individual." Briefing half a dozen FBI officials after completing the sketch, Boylan recalls one of the frustrated agents muttering: "How did this happen?" She replied, "We have major problems . . . the questions were never asked."[2]

Jeanne Boylan knew what she was talking about. It is notoriously difficult to correct false starts in manhunts using bad artists' impressions. Even now the FBI refuses to discuss the first sketch other than to say it is unreliable. Boylan is more definite. "It should never have existed," she says. "Misinformation is worse than no information at all."[3] Today it is impossible to discount the possibility that the FBI never found John Doe II because they and the public started off by looking for the wrong man. Equally possible is that the hunt for the second suspect that several Oklahoma City residents as well as Kessinger said they saw was quietly ditched because of the early embarrassment. It is even possible that John Doe II died in the blast, becoming the victim number 169, completely blown away by the force of the explosion apart from a left leg that investigators have never been able to match to any of the known victims.

Evidence that the hunt was quietly ditched comes in a memo written by a San Francisco FBI agent in late May 1995. The agent notes that he is discontinuing efforts to track down a John Doe II lead as a result of a directive from the Oklahoma City command post to hold them "in abeyance."[4] In mid-June, law enforcement officials seemed to try to kill off John Doe II completely by claiming that he was Todd Bunting, a twenty-three-year-old army private stationed at Fort Riley who had rented a truck at Elliott's Body Shop twenty-four hours after McVeigh allegedly had picked up his vehicle under the alias Robert Kling. None of that explained why Kessinger had linked the person the FBI said was Bunting with McVeigh or how other witnesses in Oklahoma City shortly before the bombing recalled seeing McVeigh with someone who seemed to be an accomplice. Kessinger stuck to his story for months and in the end the government decided not to call to court any eyewitnesses who complicated its version of events with sightings of a supposed McVeigh accomplice.

Not surprisingly, John Doe II has taken on a mythical life of his own, fueling conspiracy theories that the authorities had good reason not to identify him: because he would link the bombing to government informers who had warned the ATF and the FBI. To this day the tantalizing grand jury indictment against both McVeigh and Nichols states that they conspired "with others unknown." Unknown is how the authorities seem to want them to remain.

Given such a scenario, Dave Williams was in his element. In Oklahoma, "Super Dave" (as his colleagues ironically dubbed him) had another chance to use the techniques deployed in New York during the World Trade Center bombing investigation: working backward from the evidence connected to the suspects as much as deducing from the disparate clues that might be hidden among the rubble at the crime scene. As a result, Williams, though nominally in charge of the crime scene in Oklahoma, was rarely on site, spending much of his time examining McVeigh's car or searching Nichols's home in Herington, Kansas, or his father's farm in Michigan. From the start, this was a one-track investigation.

Inspector general documents paint an extraordinary picture of David Williams's sloppy and cavalier attitude in one of the most important crime scene investigations ever launched in the United States. The documents are records of the interviews of FBI and other law enforcement personnel carried out by the inspector general's investigators for his report on the lab. Incredibly, none of these serious complaints made it into the final edition of the IG's report, lending considerable credibility to the assertion of the National Association of Criminal Defense Lawyers (NACDL) that no real judgment on the importance of the evidence assembled by the IG's team can be made until all the raw material used to write up the report is released.

Two interviewees, Ed Kelso, the head of the FBI lab's Evidence Response Team, and R. Patrick Welch, of the FBI's Inspections Division, pointed out that in the middle of the investigation the crime scene was opened to the public for a memorial service attended by President Bill Clinton. As Kelso put it, thousands of people were allowed to "tromp all over" the crime scene, calling into question the use of any evidence found afterward.[5] James Powell, a veteran bomb-squad officer working with the ATF as an explosives enforcement officer, told IG investigators that the crime scene was not adequately secured in the first place. He cited universally accepted protocols that call for the crime scene area to be measured from the center of the explosion to the edge of the most distant debris plus an additional 25 percent of that distance. This was not done. Red Cross volunteers serving refreshments, as well as military personnel, were allowed unfettered access to the area.[6]

Evidence, in particular parts of vehicles, was removed before locations were properly plotted, according to Powell, while Kelso recalled Williams telling searchers sifting through the debris with rakes: "If you can't see it at rake's length, it's not worth picking up." Later he added: "We've got thousands of pieces, we don't need to pick up any more."[7] Kelso was shocked, pointing out that the tiny piece of debris not visible "at rake's length" might well be the bit with the hole drilled through that might allow investigators to determine what sort of detonation cord had been used. Kelso described Williams as a "laughingstock" even among his own Explosives Unit (EU) colleagues and claimed that two technicians, Wallace Higgins and Jim Lyons, had walked off the site in disgust at Williams's handling of the evidence at the Oklahoma City bomb site.[8]

Williams was right about one thing. He had more evidence than he could handle, seven thousand pounds in total. LaTonya Gadson worked in the EU team processing the evidence as it arrived on Floor 1B of the basement at FBI headquarters. She told IG investigators that the shards of metal, concrete, wood, and steel that made up the evidence were a mess, with no sorting having been done on-site and no sequence recognizable in the collection. Most of the evidence had not been packed properly, with many of the bags unsealed, allowing debris to fall out and add to the confusion. Some items had not been bagged at all. Collections of items arrived in boxes with only the box labeled. On two separate occasions, Gadson recalled finding an empty bag in a box with several other bags filled with evidence.[9]

It seemed all the more incredible given that Dave Williams had started work in the FBI lab in the Evidence Control Center. But "control" was the operative word with Williams. During Timothy McVeigh's trial, Christopher Tritico, the defense lawyer who handled the forensic side of the case in court, noted that Dave Williams's initials appeared on "virtually every piece of evidence delivered to the lab."[10] Williams admitted that he had not actually checked the evidence in and that others had placed his initials on the evidence on his instructions. It was a chain of custody that meant nothing. Williams was forced to admit under cross-examination that if there were questions about contamination or tampering later he would only be able to identify the individuals who had actually handled the evidence by means of their handwriting. As the investigation got underway, there would indeed be plenty of questions about key pieces of evidence.

On September 5, 1995, Dave Williams issued a twenty-eight-page EU lab report on the Oklahoma City bombing that showed all the hallmarks of his tendency to work backward, draw unscientific conclusions, and overstate results, all in aid of the incrimination of the only suspects, Timothy McVeigh and Terry Nichols. As with the World Trade Center explosion, his report started with a specific velocity of detonation (VOD), in this case 13,000 feet per second, which was once again based on the simple observation of the crater and explosive damage to buildings, automobiles, and victims. Williams wasted no time in reaching the conclusion he needed to: "A fertilizer-base explosive, such as ANFO (ammonium nitrate and fuel oil) among other commercial and improvised explosives, has an approximate VOD of 13,000 fps."[11] Williams was only too aware that Nichols was alleged by investigators to have bought ammonium nitrate fertilizer and diesel fuel oil a few weeks before the blast. A receipt for the fertilizer had been found at his home in Herington, Kansas.

Yet even this skewed logic was flawed. ANFO has a broad VOD range. The IG's report cited *Dupont Blasters' Handbook* as listing a range of 7,000 to 15,600 feet per second and suggested that with the sort of improvised ANFO explosive alleged to have been used in Oklahoma, that range could have been even broader. But even Williams's narrow range, expanded in his interview with the IG investigators to 12,000 to 14,000 fps, could have covered a lot of different explosives. In his interview with the IG, Williams admitted to working backward, saying that it was only Nichols's purchase of ammonium nitrate and diesel oil that allowed him to conclude that it was an ANFO bomb. Based on the post-blast scene alone, he concluded, the main charge could have been a number of explosives, even dynamite. There was no mention of the suspects' purchases as the basis for his conclusions in his lab report.

Williams's conclusions as to the weight of the explosive and the containers it was carried in was even more closely based on the evidence recovered in the searches. The FBI's principal examiner claimed that he estimated the ANFO bomb to have been about 4,000 pounds "not solely on the basis of the receipts" recovered from Nichols's home. He cited the damage, the crater, and the CONWEP program, an explosives computer simulation system, which two days after the explosion actually estimated the size of the explosive as 3,000 pounds of ANFO or 2,460 pounds of TNT.

In actual fact, 4,000 pounds was the amount of ammonium nitrate purchased, according to the receipts recovered from Nichols's home, one of which had McVeigh's fingerprint on it (although only on the back, according to the FBI lab). Williams's report also stated categorically that the explosive was contained in fifty-gallon white plastic barrels, some with blue trim. Without measuring the curvature of the plastic fragments recovered at the scene, which the lab apparently failed to do, there was no way of knowing the size of the drums. However, just such fifty-gallon drums were recovered from Terry Nichols's residence.

The same pattern repeated itself throughout Williams's twenty-eight-page report dated September 5, 1995.[12] The triggering mechanism?

Either a detonator from a Primadet Delay system or sensitized detonating cord, concluded Williams. The crime scene? No evidence of either. The suspects? Primadet systems at Nichols's house and PETN, normally a component of detonating cord, on McVeigh's clothes. The detonator? A nonelectric variety, stated Williams. The fuse? "A nonelectric, burning type of either hobby fuse or a commercial safety fuse . . . the time delay was approximately 2 minutes and 15 seconds." The reason? Evidence linked the defendants to a burglary at a quarry in Marion, Kansas, where nonelectric detonators were stolen and the named fuses were found at locations linked to the defendants. No evidence of either was found at the crime scene. The two minutes and fifteen seconds had an even more curious genesis. It was exactly two minutes and fifteen seconds before the blast that a yellow Ryder rental truck appeared on a security videotape outside the Alfred P. Murrah Federal Building on April 19, 1995.

Another problem that reared its head again was the alteration of auxiliary examiners' reports. Despite the fact that the laboratory had issued a policy memorandum on September 1, 1994, explicitly requiring the verbatim inclusion of AE reports in the wake of the fight during the World Trade Center bombing investigation, David Williams admitted changing the reports of Steve Burmeister, the chief explosives-residue analyst on the Oklahoma City case. The changes slanted conclusions in favor of the prosecution in relation to two key pieces of evidence, one of which, Q18, was the knife Timothy McVeigh was carrying at the time of his arrest.

To some extent it was a rerun of the tests on the knife in the Steve Psinakis case (see Chapter 1) that had so concerned Fred Whitehurst in 1989. The Explosives Unit (EU) at the lab knew the bombers would have needed something to cut the detonation cord; confirming traces of the explosive residue PETN on this knife could be crucial evidence in a successful prosecution of McVeigh. It was what the "bombers" of the FBI's EU termed "a pressure call." Burmeister was unable to be as categorical as they would have liked. According to the McVeigh defense team's explosives-residue expert, Dr. John Lloyd, Burmeister's test results showed that the confirmation test for PETN had failed. "If the first test fails then it is entirely contradictory and objectionable to assume that first test has any remaining credibility. The overall result is an inconsistency with PETN," he points out.[13] Burmeister, however, wrote: "The results of an instrumental examination of residues removed from the blade portion of specimen Q18 was consistent for the presence of pentaerythritol tetranitrate (PETN)," but added: "The presence of PETN . . . could not be confirmed in specimen Q18." Williams changed this to: "Traces of PETN were located on specimen Q18, however could not be confirmed."[14]

The statement made no sense; once again an indefinite statement of association—"consistent with"—had been changed into a definite one of presence—"were located"—and exposed the basic inability of nonscientists to work on scientists' reports in the FBI lab. Williams insisted to the IG's panel that the statement was not contradictory. Faced with this, the IG was only able to conclude that the man in charge of the forensic science of the most important criminal investigation ever in the United States did not know what he was doing. "Williams apparently does not understand the role of a confirmation test in determining whether a substance is located on a specimen," the IG wrote.[15]

Williams claimed that Burmeister had agreed to the changes in the report "twice," saying that the chemist had looked at the first draft in which "could not be confirmed" had been completely removed. In saying this, Williams admitted that he had intentionally tried to change the sense and meaning of the report, in which Burmeister was already stretching the overall meaning of the results of the tests, according to Dr. Lloyd. Williams claimed that Burmeister had objected, so he had added the phrase "could not be confirmed" as requested and had had the final copy approved by the author. Burmeister said he did not recall discussing the statement, and since it has no meaning, it would have made little sense for him to have approved it.

But Williams was not the only target of the IG's report. The inquiry lambasted his boss, the chief of the EU, Tom Thurman, citing the FBI's own policy on supervision. Thurman, according to FBI rules, was required to conduct "a complete supervisory review" of Williams's work and reports. This review had to include "a review of all PE work notes, graphs, charts and photographs and other materials to determine if the examiners' conclusions can be supported and have been properly documented."[16] After interviewing Thurman and analyzing Williams's report, the IG decided that the head of the Explosives Unit was guilty of a complete abdication of supervisory responsibilities. In fact, of course, Thurman as a nonscientist was not capable of a scientific vetting of the report. Yet he had washed his hands of even an administrative review, approving a report with unsupported conclusions that he could not justify.

Thurman seemed unembarrassed about laying bare his supervisory attitude. "[A]s long as [Williams] portrays to me that he is in fact comfortable with that, I'm not going to change it," he told the IG's investigators.[17] Thurman admitted in an interview that he had disagreed with the report. He stated that neither the specific VOD or the weight and identity of the main charge of the bomb in Williams's report could be justified. On the fuse, Thurman admitted that the correct conclusion in the report should have been that the Primadet Delay system or sensitized detonating cord "could have been used" and that the nonelectric burning-type of fuse was one possibility "but certainly not the only one."[18]

Roger Martz did not escape the IG's censure either, but the background reason was curious. By 1995 Martz, chief of the Chemistry and Toxicology Unit (CTU), had secured responsibility for explosives-residue analysis, a somewhat "sexy" subfield at the center of some of the most celebrated investigations. In June 1994, a lab restructuring had seen Steve Burmeister and two explosives-residue technicians transferred from Jim Corby's Materials Analysis Unit (MAU) to Martz's CTU. Bizarrely, at a time when there was a need for more explosives analysis than ever as a result of a steep rise in the number of bombings, Fred Whitehurst, the lab's most senior explosives-residue analyst, did not transfer with his colleagues. He was moved to the paint and polymer section of the MAU as a trainee—something he and others saw as retaliation for his persistent criticisms and complaints.

Those best qualified to judge—in particular James Corby, head of the MAU, and Steve Burmeister, now the lab's leading explosives-residue analyst—had doubts about Martz supervising the explosives-residue program. In many ways it was a step backward. The dispute during the VANPAC investigation had shown that the less rigorous protocol followed by the CTU for explosives-residue analysis could lead to certain substances—often themselves important clues—not being comprehensively identified. Burmeister had been trained by Fred Whitehurst; Martz was not even a chemist. Even with Whitehurst on the sidelines, clashes were inevitable, as scrutiny of the lab finally intensified under the IG's gaze. The war would end with Burmeister replacing Martz as head of the

CTU within twenty months, although only because Fred Whitehurst, even from paints and polymers, would not let up.

James Kearney, the head of the Scientific Analysis Section, apparently recognized the risks of letting Martz loose. In January 1996, he told IG investigators that lab management had decided in April 1995 to hold back the Oklahoma City evidence for Steve Burmeister to analyze when he returned from the crime scene. "Kearney related that they did not want the problem they encountered in . . . again," according to a redacted record of an interview with the IG released under the Freedom of Information Act, an obvious reference to the disputes in the World Trade Center bombing investigation. Kearney goes on to tell investigators that he could not recall any work by Martz, but if he had worked on the case it was "probably only administrative work."[19]

In fact, once again, FBI lab management proved to have no control. Within days, Martz had placed himself at the center of the trace evidence investigation, starting tests for explosives residues on McVeigh's knife, T-shirts, jeans, and earplugs—the key items of evidence. The clothes, among the most important evidence in the investigation, had traveled from the Noble County jail, where McVeigh was initially held, to Washington via Oklahoma City as casually as groceries, arriving in a brown paper grocery bag with the top folded over, inside a cardboard box.

Burmeister was understandably upset. In 1995 he told the IG's investigators that Martz had "erred" in some examinations. In particular, Martz had failed to perform a microscopic examination of the clothing and knife before vacuuming and swabbing the items for explosives residue. This step, laid out in what served as the FBI lab's official explosives-residue protocol, is to permit larger pieces of material to be removed with forceps or a scalpel before vacuuming or swabbing, thus avoiding the possible commingling of two different residues.[20] Martz made a visual examination, and when asked by the IG why he had done nothing with a microscope, claimed the protocol "does not require microscopic examinations." When the IG requested a copy of the protocol, Martz retorted that "[n]o protocol in the Chemistry/Toxicology Unit (CTU) requires any examiner to perform a certain type of analysis."[21]

Martz never supplied the IG's investigators with the explosives-residue protocol, which *does* specifically require microscopic examination, first under an optical microscope; then, if any recognizable, uninitiated material is found and removed, under a scanning electron microscope. The protocol, one of the few in use by the FBI lab in April 1995, is a six-page, single-spaced document with a detailed set of instructions that includes a quick-reference step-by-step diagram, with microscopic examination at the top of the chart. Martz's failure to adhere to the protocol reflected all the concerns that Burmeister, Whitehurst, Corby, and apparently even Kearney had had about giving control of explosives-residue analysis to Martz. He was not a chemist and had not undergone the FBI's one-year training program in explosives-residue analysis, the basis on which everyone else was considered qualified to practice their specialties within the lab.

When criticized in a draft version of the IG report, Martz presented officials with what was his third version of a rationale for not using a microscope, while now admitting it was required by the protocol: "My interpretation of visual and microscopic analysis, which was part of the protocol at the time, was that if something was observed by visual examination, that microscopic analysis would be performed." [22] The absurdity of the statement was laughable, the obvious purpose of a microscope being to observe particles not visible to the naked eye rather than those that were. The IG's final report concluded rather generously that Roger Martz's interpretation of his own unit's protocol was "unpersuasive," while his explanation lacked "credibility." [23]

Other tests performed by Martz produced divergent results, again indicating the dangers of an unqualified examiner doing explosives-residue analysis, while raising the serious issue of contamination. Martz found PETN residue on McVeigh's knife; Burmeister, when he returned from the Oklahoma City crime scene, did not. However, Burmeister found nitroglycerin on the knife, although Martz had not. Martz found no PETN on McVeigh's clothes; Burmeister found PETN on both the T-shirt and trousers. But as curious as the divergent results were, there followed an even stranger set of reversals by Burmeister on the acceptability of Martz's testing.

In 1995 Steve Burmeister told the IG's investigators that Martz should have rinsed the knife rather than using a moistened swab for residues; in 1996 he said that both swabbing and rinsing were "permissible." In 1995 Burmeister described Martz's vacuuming of McVeigh's clothes as an "unqualified technique"; in 1996 he told the same investigators it was a "qualified . . . credible technique." As we have seen, in 1995 Burmeister told the IG that generally Martz "erred in some examinations" in the Oklahoma case; in 1996 this too had changed. "I don't think he erred in any of these exams. . . . I think he did an acceptable job there."[24]

Burmeister's explanation was that his initial interview had been based on Martz's "sparse" notes, and that between the first and second IG interviews he had had "an opportunity to talk with him," with Martz explaining that he had done more than was reflected in the notes. Examination notes inadequate to enable another scientist to replicate the results were in themselves a serious, although common, violation of the norms of forensic science in the FBI lab, but it was far more complex than that. It should be remembered that Martz was now Burmeister's boss. And it is undeniable that Burmeister's less critical review of Martz's work buttressed the prosecution's case in McVeigh's trial for the Oklahoma City bombing.

The IG's investigation proceeded in parallel to the prosecution's preparation for the trial of Timothy McVeigh. Indeed, the actual report was published just days before jury selection finished. From the start, Special U.S. Attorney Joseph Hartzler and his team of prosecutors knew that Whitehurst's allegations against Tom Thurman, Roger Martz, and Dave Williams might make all three FBI examiners too much of a risk. Although they kept their options open until the IG's draft report was handed to them, they knew they might have to prosecute the case without the testimony of officials who normally would have been considered key witnesses. Calling any of the three to the witness stand might invite the defense team to put the FBI lab, rather than McVeigh, on trial. It all threatened to be a rerun of the way in which Johnnie Cochran had managed to put the Los Angeles police department and crime lab as much as O. J. Simpson on trial in Los Angeles in 1995.

Thus, in a move unprecedented in a case of this size or importance, the prosecution was preparing throughout 1996 for the eventuality of having to prove its forensic case without the testimony of the crime scene chief, the principal examiner in the investigation, and the unit chiefs of the two sections of the FBI lab that had done the vast bulk of the forensic work. This decision, the timing of the IG's report, and then later a controversy over its admissibility, introduced an air of unpredictability into the case. The evidence against Timothy McVeigh was entirely circumstantial, and circumstance, it was soon clear, was now going to decide what evidence might be admissible.

With Williams, Martz, and Thurman in limbo, the forensic burden-of-proof now rested very firmly on the shoulders of Steve Burmeister. Any suggestion of unacceptable practices in the examinations of his boss could open the whole can of worms at the FBI lab. Any suggestion of divergent results between Martz's tests and those of Burmeister raised the prospect of contamination and lack of expertise. Burmeister must have been under tremendous pressure to endorse his boss's procedures—exactly what he began to do in his interviews with the IG investigators in 1996.

"I think several of us found him to change his stories a little easier than we would have liked—we did discuss the possibility that he had been under some kind of pressure," says Douglas Lucas, one of the five forensic scientists on the IG panel.[25] However, the IG did not appear to question Burmeister about his many changes of mind—changes that were confirmed in the courtroom in May 1997. When defense lawyer Christopher Tritico tried to probe the contradictions between his 1995 and 1996 statements, prosecutor Beth Wilkinson objected, an appeal Judge Richard Matsch quickly sustained.

But turnabouts in the Burmeister testimony in the Oklahoma investigation were only one skirmish in a huge war. From the moment the grand jury indictments against McVeigh and Nichols were handed down in August 1995, it was clear that the government had its work cut out to prove its case. The eyewitness testimony was confused and contradictory, not least because of the John Doe II sightings. Almost everyone who claimed to have seen McVeigh in a Ryder truck in Oklahoma City on April 19 said they had seen him with a second suspect, as had the staff at Elliott's Body Shop in Junction City. With the FBI now apparently declining to even look for John Doe II, defense lawyers could use what has become known in legal circles as the "empty chair strategy"—essentially blaming the other guy or, more generally, the "others unknown"—while claiming their client had been targeted unfairly.

Then there was the reliability of the government's key witnesses, Lori and Michael Fortier, old army friends of McVeigh, who had been the best man at the couple's wedding. Lori told the grand jury that McVeigh had told her of his plot to blow up the Alfred P. Murrah Federal Building, "an easy target," according to McVeigh, in the winter of 1994. While staying at their mobile home in Kingman, Arizona, McVeigh had arranged soup cans on the kitchen floor, Lori Fortier recalled, demonstrating what he meant by a "shape charge"—a triangular charge against the U-shaped, glass-fronted building. Lori Fortier recounted how she had helped McVeigh manufacture a false North Dakota driver's license in the name of Robert Kling, the name used to rent the Ryder truck in Junction City, Kansas. Michael Fortier testified that he and McVeigh had driven from Arizona to Oklahoma City in December 1994 to case the building and choose the alleyway where McVeigh planned to leave his getaway car.

It was compelling stuff, but the Fortiers had huge credibility problems. Both admitted to having regularly used marijuana, amphetamines, and LSD during the time these events and conversations supposedly took place; both had been inconsistent witnesses, denying to the media that they knew anything or that they thought McVeigh was involved, and both had persistently lied to FBI investigators in the days immediately after the bombing. The truth was that the Fortiers' testimony had changed since they had agreed to plea bargains. Lori was promised formal immunity the day after she testified in court, and Michael pleaded guilty to a range of reduced charges for selling and transporting stolen weapons, failing to disclose the plot, and lying to investigators, in exchange for his testimony. And Michael Fortier's real motivation seemed to have been recorded by the FBI itself in a bugged telephone conversation with his brother John, nine days after the blast. "I can tell a fable, I can tell stories all day long. . . . the less I say now, the bigger the price will be later," he said on a tape later used by the defense team in court.

With witnesses like that, the forensic evidence assumed more importance than ever. The defense knew that Frederic Whitehurst, war hero, FBI agent, model employee, and unimpeachable forensic scientist was a far more credible witness than people such as the Fortiers. If the FBI lab, along with Williams, Martz, and Thurman, could be put on trial, McVeigh and Nichols might well walk free, particularly if the IG's report, hovering over the whole pretrial preparation like Banquo's ghost, substantiated any of Whitehurst's allegations. As the trial drew closer and details of the charges and the IG's investigation filtered into the press, the media began to realize the potential of all of this to blow the prosecution's case out of the water. "Until the case goes to trial Whitehurst waits like a ticking time bomb," noted *Time* magazine in November 1996.

For nearly two years before jury selection began in a nondescript Denver courtroom, a ferocious battle raged between the government and the defense team over what information was available to be released, what should be released, to whom it should be released, and when it should be released. It seemed no exaggeration to say, as leading defense lawyer Stephen Jones did, that the case rested on the forensic evidence. Buried in the lab amid the tens of thousands of pages of lab reports, bench notes, protocols, and memos, not to mention the scores of letters of complaint sent by Frederic Whitehurst and the tens of thousands of pages of interviews assembled by the IG, was more than enough evidence to raise serious questions about the Oklahoma case. But would it come to light? And if it did, would the judge rule it admissible? Would the key issues in this case be tested by a jury or by cabals of lawyers working in the Department of Justice?

The scale of the crime, the desire to restore credibility to the judicial process after the O. J. Simpson trial, the need to start rehabilitating the FBI's reputation after a spate of bungles and unprecedented congressional criticism during 1996–97, meant that the Oklahoma City bombing case was one the U.S. government could not afford to lose. If ever there was a case with pressure for a conviction, this was it. Thus, while one arm of the Justice Department strove to get to the bottom of the allegations against the FBI lab, another arm, the Criminal Division, assembled a team to counter the impact of that investigation on the Oklahoma City bombing prosecution, scrutinizing every defense request for information in the light of the legal obligation to release exculpatory evidence. The conflict of interest was obvious; the fox really was guarding the chicken coop, as one defense lawyer put it.

Both sides assigned a lawyer full-time to the forensic aspects of the case. Robert Wyatt, one of Stephen Jones's partners, began for the defense, before Christopher Tritico, a Houston trial lawyer, went "back to school for some chemistry lessons," as he put it. The Department of Justice designated Beth Wilkinson, a young Justice Department prosecutor, to neutralize Whitehurst's allegations and the lab issue for Joseph Hartzler's prosecution team. Within a month of the grand jury indictment, Stephen Jones and his team had asked for copies of all Whitehurst's complaints and permission to interview the FBI examiner. In May, a defense motion claimed that the government's case was flawed due to "scientific fraud, misconduct and gross negligence in the administration of the FBI crime lab."

Despite the requests and filings, over the next six months much of the defense team's information would come from the press or from other lawyers dealing with cases that concerned Whitehurst's allegations. For months, efforts to interview the man himself would be blocked. As time went on and the implications of Whitehurst's charges became clearer, the defense's request lists would lengthen to include all protocols, lab reports, and records of the interviews done by the IG investigators. Never had a defense team put the FBI lab under a microscope like this, and official resistance strengthened as the discovery paper-trail lengthened. Through a series of hearings and motions of complaint to Judge Matsch during 1996 the parameters of the McVeigh trial emerged, but not before the trial had been postponed twice because of the government's failure to hand over documentation.

One central problem was the increasingly suspicious delay in the publication of the IG report. In an April 1996 hearing, prosecutor Beth Wilkinson told Judge Matsch and the defense team that she anticipated publication "some time this summer." By late June, prosecutors were saying the report was "basically complete" but would not be published until September. In fact it was not until the end of January 1997 that a draft report was finally submitted to the FBI, with the key individuals criticized invited to respond—all under the tightest security. Whitehurst himself was only allowed to peruse the report for two hours and was then ordered not to discuss its contents with anyone, including his lawyers or his wife, Cheryl, another lab employee.

There was then a further delay as the IG initially refused to release the relevant sections of the draft report to lawyers in ongoing cases likely to be affected by its findings. Fearing a rewrite and possible dilution of the findings in the wake of the FBI's critical response, the National Association of Criminal Defense Lawyers and Whitehurst's own lawyers, Kohn, Kohn and Colapinto, went to court in March 1997 to try to force its release. It was only then that a publication date, April 15, 1997—two weeks into the Oklahoma City bombing trial—was fixed and finally met.

The situation became even more dangerous for the government

during the discovery process, when it became clear that testimony from other scientists supported some of Whitehurst's charges. Most of this information remains under seal or unreleased and did not appear in the IG's report. However, Stephen Kohn, Fred Whitehurst's lawyer, claims that nine other lab personnel had supported his client's allegations about possible contamination in the lab.[26] Motions filed by the defense in September 1996 named two lab employees and summarized their statements. "Brett Mills, FBI laboratory examiner, has stated that an area in the FBI laboratory that was used to store evidence collected in connection with this case was contaminated with PETN." The motion continues: "Dr. Mary Tungol (an FBI laboratory employee) has stated that she believes that evidence taken from Timothy McVeigh's car was contaminated."[27]

The notes of the IG investigators' interview with Mary Tungol elaborate on this. Tungol recalled that Martz gave her some data from an analysis that someone else had performed on material found in Timothy McVeigh's car: "When she interpreted the data, she found calcium sulfate with a trace of freebase cocaine," the notes record. "She reported her findings to Martz who was very excited because he thought he would also get a drug charge out of the case. She explained to Martz that she believed that he may have contaminated the sample because it is unusual to see only a trace amount of freebase cocaine. "Martz said that he did not contaminate the sample and that he was appalled that she would suggest that."[28]

According to the notes, Martz later did a mass spectrometry test on the sample and found no trace of cocaine. Martz subsequently told Burmeister that Tungol did not know what she was doing because she found cocaine where there was none. Tungol responded by refusing to interpret other people's data in the future, telling Burmeister that if they wanted her to analyze samples, they would have to provide her with the evidence to allow her to run her own tests.[29]

Both incidents afford further insight into the workings of the FBI lab. Again someone was being asked to interpret someone else's data. Sources report an informal system of "internal marketing" by some unit chiefs and managers, i.e., shopping around for someone prepared to give them the forensic opinion they are looking for. Termed "forensic prostitution" by Stephen Jones and more than one examiner at the FBI lab, this might have been one example of it. Again, in both instances the issue of contamination had been raised, in particular background contamination, and now by two examiners other than Fred Whitehurst. The weakness of not doing the sort of regular background checks for contamination that Whitehurst advocated was well understood in forensic science circles. If contamination was measured before testing, its level could be eliminated statistically by discounting it in any calculations after testing. With no background measure the results could be useless.

In the late summer of 1996 the McVeigh defense team got the opinions of the forensic experts they had retained—Brian Caddy, professor of forensic science at Strathclyde University, Scotland, and Dr. John Lloyd, a fellow of the Royal Society of Chemistry in Britain and a thirty-year veteran of forensic investigation. Both men had played major roles in challenging the evidence and eventually overturning the convictions of several groups of Irish nationals who had all served long prison terms in Britain for major IRA bombings. Having examined the FBI lab reports that were released to the defense, both men expressed shock.

"If these reports are the ones to be presented to the courts as evidence then I am appalled by their structure and information content," wrote Professor Caddy. "The reports, in my opinion, are not reports as such but are a mere catalogue of items and the results of some experimentation. . . . The structure of the reports seems designed to confuse the reader rather than help him."[30] Professor Caddy and Dr. Lloyd both noted that the reports failed to explain which techniques drew which particular conclusions, mixing up various types of examinations—DNA analysis, explosives-residue analysis, and soil examinations, for instance. They also complained about the failure to qualify conclusions by noting possible alternative sources of many of the "suspect" substances detected, and with no quantitative data—measurement of the amount of the substance traced—both experts stated they could make no judgment on potential contamination. "The reports are purely conclusory in nature. It is impossible to determine from them the chain of custody, or precisely what work has been done on each item or the reliability of the reported results in terms e.g. of specificity and freedom from the effects of spurious contaminants (explosives or otherwise) or the competence of whoever was responsible for the results," wrote John Lloyd.[31]

In his one-page letter, Professor Caddy remarked that there was just not enough data in the reports for him to make any "sensible comments about the identification of trace explosives in this case." There was a strong sense that anyone asking for meaningful observations based on such "reports" was simply wasting his time. For the first time, FBI lab explosives-residue work on a major case had come under peer review from two internationally renowned forensic experts. Their verdict should have sent a shudder down the spine of everyone in law enforcement throughout the United States, from the attorney general and the director of the FBI downward. In fact, no one even blinked. Such criticism was repeatedly portrayed as an arcane scientific dispute that no layperson could really understand or, in the case of Whitehurst's complaints, the outpourings of a disgruntled employee. For now, every question was swept under the carpet of the IG's apparently endless ongoing investigation. For the government, a successful prosecution in the Oklahoma City case and the credibility of the U.S. judicial system were far more important priorities.

Professor Caddy's and Dr. Lloyd's expert opinions underscored the objections of the defense team. "The way they write their lab reports is just incredible," Christopher Tritico told the authors. "They will just say, this piece of evidence was tested by one or more of the following methods. Then they list every test they have at the FBI lab so you've no way of knowing what they actually did. Down at the bottom of the page it will say that it's been confirmed. The result is, you don't know what they did, how they did it, or who did it."[32] Even without the help of experts, the defense team had noticed other scientific shortcomings. In particular, screening tests often were being used as confirmatory tests—the sort of thing one lawyer compared to getting a blip on an airport metal-detector and concluding that the passenger in question was carrying explosives. "It was a bit like looking at an audit without seeing the accounting slips or checks," one defense team member reports. "We encountered incredible resistance trying to get the checks and deposit slips to see if they matched the stated result."

In his affidavit, Dr. Lloyd listed seventeen sets of documentary material he said he would need to make meaningful comments. They included such basic items as a specimen list, which he said should include the nature of each item, where and when it was found, who found it, and to whom the item is attributed, and chain-of-custody statements dealing with the transfer of the items to the laboratory. He also asked for copies of all laboratory working papers, notes, instrumental data, and charts for all the items examined for explosives traces, along with a list of all results, positive or negative, from each laboratory test, with both the identity and quantity of the substances detected.

Other requests dealt with manuals and protocols, the results of all quality assurance work, and the raw data on which those results were based, by which the efficacy of all lab operations, scientific and nonscientific, were tested routinely. Finally, Lloyd requested all the results, along with the original data, working papers, and notes of all monitoring for contamination of the laboratory and the individuals involved in explosives examination since January 1, 1994. He wanted to know about the physical structure of the laboratory, whether the air was filtered, whether a positive air pressure was maintained, and the provisions applied as a safeguard against contamination "by explosives traces."

These requests were for information about standard requirements for any crime lab's accreditation by ASCLD/LAB. Indeed, it was clear that the requests addressed virtually all of Whitehurst's concerns about methods and means at the lab. But, unsurprisingly, it was equally clear that the lab could not come anywhere near meeting these standards. It was known that the air supply was not filtered at the lab. It was known that the storage of bulk items in trace analysis areas was customary, and that as a result contamination was almost certainly a problem. It was also known that the only check for background contamination since January 1994, and possibly since 1986, had been done by Frederic Whitehurst in May 1996, after the key evidence in the Oklahoma case had been through several separate units at the lab.

Eventually sixty-three pages of what the lab used as explosives-residue protocols were submitted to the defense, virtually all of them drawn up by Burmeister and Whitehurst in an effort to remedy what they saw as perhaps the most serious deficiencies in the lab. However, many were handwritten and several were incomplete, as Steve Burmeister admitted in a letter to Donald Thompson, the acting chief of the lab, when responding to the defense request.[33] None of the protocols were completely adequate, according to Dr. Lloyd: "None of the documents I reviewed could have been reasonably considered to be a protocol in the normal sense."[34]

On August 30, 1996, McVeigh's and Nichols's defense lawyers filed a request for the "production of examinations and tests and underlying data, methodologies and protocols" under Rule 16 of the federal Rules of Criminal Procedure, the discovery rule for federal courts. At the beginning of November, just eight days before they were due in court again to press their discovery case, the defense received more than five thousand pages, unsorted, redacted, and much of it poorly photocopied. It was shipped to Britain for Dr. Lloyd to sift through. "Most of what we had asked for was missing, but what was there was quite revealing about the overall performance," he reports. "There was a general pattern—the use of degraded, unchecked equipment, the reporting of positive results when they hadn't done the tests to draw any such conclusions—a whole range of problems." [35]

Releasing so much so late was an old trick. But within days, the defense team was able to make it clear they had not received what they needed. "The material which is absolutely necessary to determine whether the analysis is accurate is missing," Stephen Jones told the hearing on November 13. "Now it's either missing because it doesn't exist, which is a damning indictment, or we simply haven't been furnished with it." With the FBI lab and prosecution probably unable and certainly unwilling to provide the essential information to allow defense experts to make a judgment, Stephen Jones and his team decided to go for broke— dismissal of the core of the forensic evidence against McVeigh.

Seeking a pretrial hearing on the issue would force the FBI lab to prove that appropriate scientific methods were applied properly before the results could be admitted as evidence. The defense had a long charge sheet, citing the "possibility of contamination of the items tested and the testing equipment; that the FBI laboratory lacked proper protocols and prescribed procedures; that the testing methodologies used were inappropriate and that unqualified persons participated in performing the tests."

As worded it was difficult to argue with any aspect of the motion. The question in legal terms was a more technical one: was all this covered by the *Daubert* v. *Merrell Dow Pharmaceutical, Inc.* ruling, a 1993 Supreme Court decision that had become the litmus test for the admissibility of forensic evidence for the past four years. *Daubert* had supplemented the *Frye* standard of a procedure having to be "generally accepted" by a meaningful segment of the relevant scientific community. *Daubert* created broader guidelines about what constituted acceptable science, something which was now to be interpreted more flexibly by individual trial judges. Many saw it as having opened the courtroom door for "junk science." That was certainly true in this case.

On February 26, 1997, Judge Matsch used his discretion—and ruled against the defense. "The challenged evidence does not involve any new scientific theory and the testing methodologies are neither new nor novel," he wrote. "The government intends to prove that particular chemical elements were found on or in the items tested. . . . [T]he government will, of course, be required to establish the relevance of such evidence by proof of a chain of custody linking these items to persons, places and times of significance to the issues in this case." [36] It was a burden of proof that the government would have great difficulty with at trial. Judge Matsch went on to state that "the necessary foundation for admission of evidence should be presented to the jury," and the defense could challenge that by asking what are known as voir dire questions, essentially challenging the expert or the expertise at the time, with the jury making up its own mind in the course of its deliberations. [37]

That was exactly what the defense wanted—the chance to put the matter before the jury. There was just one problem: who and what would appear? It seemed unlikely that anyone was going to argue with Steve Burmeister's qualifications or methodology, although that too was ultimately a matter for the jury. Roger Martz was the potential problem with the admissibility of Burmeister's results; his testing could have raised serious doubts about the validity of anything Burmeister had done once Martz had handled the crucial items. By February 1997 it was clear that Martz was highly unlikely to appear in court, having been removed from his position in the lab along with Dave Williams and Tom Thurman in response to the IG's draft report in January. The big question was the final IG report. Judge Matsch did ultimately have the power to rule out evidence on the basis of relevance or reliability. Would the jury see it?

Leaks to the press had made it clear that the IG's report, although still unpublished, was pretty damning. Front-page stories and editorials in leading newspapers posed the obvious question: Where now the Oklahoma City bombing trial? In mid-March, two weeks before trial, McVeigh's defense team secured court-ordered excerpts of the draft version of the report. "It was less than 20% of the total and redacted to the point where it was virtually useless," one member of the defense team told the authors. "Because it was only a draft and names and specifics were blacked out, there was no chance of using it to file motions, our main interest."

One final pretrial matter that had been winding its way through the legal process simultaneously showed just how frayed the prosecution's nerves were by this point. The defense had been asking to depose Fred Whitehurst for more than a year. Whitehurst and his attorneys took the line that he was perfectly willing to be deposed but on the same terms as he had been at both the World Trade Center bombing trials, with lawyers for both the prosecution and the defense present, along with his own counsel.

With his whole career now on the line, Whitehurst feared intimidation and retribution—he had, after all, been punished before for speaking to the defense. Unsurprisingly, the prosecution got access to Whitehurst first. In July, Joseph Hartzler phoned him personally. It was all very friendly, Whitehurst reminding the prosecutor that he worked for the government and hoping that "he would not regard him as the enemy," according to Hartzler. Later Whitehurst sent the U.S. special attorney a scientific textbook with an inscribed note directing him to specific pages and wishing him "luck and success" in seeking justice.[38]

It could not last. On September 9, 1996, James Maddock, deputy general counsel at the FBI, wrote to Whitehurst's attorney, Stephen Kohn, to tell him that Joseph Hartzler and Beth Wilkinson would interview Whitehurst in three days' time in Room 7426 at FBI headquarters. Maddock enclosed a nondisclosure agreement for Kohn to sign. When Kohn refused to agree to this, Maddock and Hartzler said they would make the "voluntary" interview "mandatory." Kohn replied that since Whitehurst's job assignments in the Oklahoma case were very limited, he feared that much of the questioning would be about Whitehurst's whistle-blower disclosures to the Department of Justice, a violation of federal law and potential witness intimidation.

When there were no concessions from the FBI, Kohn filed and secured a temporary restraining order on September 12, the day before the proposed interview. Judge Matsch ordered the government to show by September 16 why he should not make his order against the interview permanent. "The court is confronted with an emergency involving the possibility of irrevocable adverse effects on the integrity of the evidence," he stated in his ruling.[39] It was not until October 29 that the judge lifted his restraining order, saying that the prosecutors could talk to Whitehurst if the FBI examiner set his own terms for the interview and he was accompanied by his attorney.

The deposition did not actually take place until a few days before Christmas. It was a bitter three-day affair, with objections every few minutes. Maddock refused to allow Whitehurst to answer a number of questions on the grounds of national security, FBI privilege, or FBI rules. These included questions such as the layout of the lab, much of which hundreds of tourists walk through every day. But the intimidation beyond the proceedings was even more real, according to Stephen Kohn, who cited two instances of specific threats.

Kohn claimed that during a break in the proceedings, Hartzler cornered him in a corridor to say that he should be "concerned about potential administrative action that could be taken against Whitehurst due to some of his testimony which was exaggerated or wrong."[40] Hartzler later claimed he was referring to a statement Whitehurst made to Mike Tigar, Terry Nichols's defense lawyer, when, seeking to illustrate how easily innocent people could be convicted, Whitehurst stated that Tigar could probably be found guilty on the basis of residue on his hands now. It is a point Whitehurst frequently makes in interviews and has been borne out by the series of convictions in Britain of innocent people for IRA bombings, several of which were based on "explosive" residue traces that turned out to be the result of handling innocent, everyday items.

Kohn also complained that he and his client received an even starker threat from James Maddock during the deposition. "Maddock expressed disgust with the IG . . . and stated he was one of the officials who would determine Dr. Whitehurst's further employment status with the FBI," Kohn wrote in a written complaint.[41] Kohn added that Maddock said he would take into consideration Whitehurst's "willingness to . . . work with the prosecution in the Oklahoma City bombing case when he and the FBI decided what personnel action would be taken with respect to Dr. Whitehurst."[42]

Challenged with these statements, Maddock questioned Kohn's contemporaneous notes and blamed Kohn for a tendency to create a "hostile" environment. "I've never made a statement of disgust with the Inspector General; we've cooperated fully with him," he told the

Associated Press, neatly avoiding the allegation that he had linked administrative action against Whitehurst with cooperation with the prosecution. "I've suggested he [Kohn] should consider a more cooperative spirit."[43]

There was little chance of that, given that the really adversarial part of the proceedings, the trial itself, was only just about to start. In his opening statement, Prosecutor Joseph Hartzler addressed the jury with the heady brew of emotional witness statements, dubious forensic evidence, and sometimes contradictory eyewitness testimony that would make up his team's circumstantial case. "Now you will undoubtedly hear criticism of the FBI laboratory, especially the explosives unit of the lab," he warned the jury on April 24. "None of the people who have been criticized for their work at the FBI lab will be witnesses in this case."

That was certainly true. The prosecution would lean heavily on Steve Burmeister, whose credentials seemed difficult to challenge. An FBI special supervisory agent, but also a chemistry graduate and qualified explosives-residue analyst, Burmeister had been trained by Fred Whitehurst, who described him as "an exceptional scientist." He would be backed up by Ron Kelly, a veteran laboratory examiner, in training, although not yet qualified, to be an explosives-residue expert in the Chemistry and Toxicology Unit at the time of the explosion, but nevertheless assigned to accompany Steve Burmeister to the crime scene in April 1995.

The external expertise would come from Vivian Dewyse, a chemist working for Imperial Chemical Industries in Montreal who would testify about the composition of the ammonium nitrate fertilizer alleged to have been purchased by McVeigh and Nichols to build the bomb. Underpinning all this would be Linda Jones, a principal forensic investigator at the ministry of defense's forensic explosives laboratory in Britain with extensive experience of ammonium nitrate bombs planted by the IRA.

Lining up for the defense would be Fred Whitehurst, John Lloyd, a former colleague of Jones, and a British pathologist, Thomas Marshall. The defense would also reserve a walk-on role for none other than Dave Williams to address a few of the obvious questions about his investigation. There would not be many. Eventually Judge Matsch would rule that only six pages of the IG report, less than a quarter of the chapter on the FBI lab's role in the Oklahoma City bombing investigation and just a fraction of the total 517-page report as a whole—all of which was arguably necessary to put the lab's performance in context—were admissible as evidence.

The exclusion of the real forensic inadequacies, press leaks about a supposed confession by McVeigh just days before the trial began, and the gut-wrenching testimony of the surviving victims would make the defense team's task an uphill struggle. Now, in his opening statement however, the slightly studious-looking Stephen Jones raised all the obvious reasonable doubts. "The question is, did they get the right man?" he asked the jury. "You'll see the investigation lasted two weeks. The investigation to build the case against Timothy McVeigh lasted about two years." The case against McVeigh was as strong as the full might of unlimited FBI and U.S. government resources could make it. Yet it still looked flimsy on the basis of Williams's efforts to work backward and make the facts fit the suspects.

Despite the discrediting of Dave Williams's logic in concluding that McVeigh and Nichols had built, transported, and detonated an ammonium nitrate fertilizer bomb using fuel oil as an initiator, this remained the government's case. Incredibly, given that a man's life was at stake, the jury would never hear the IG's debunking of Williams's investigative method. Instead, the defense team would be left to challenge the forensic case with strong but less concrete allegations of dubious methods in collecting evidence and possible, even probable, contamination of such evidence. Despite this, revealed during the case would be destruction of evidence, inadequate testing to draw the conclusions made, woeful record keeping, and a hopeless lack of supervision and management control. Equally significant, FBI lab employees would deny the alteration of reports and contradictory test results despite the IG's systematic documentation of both.

Ron Kelly was the first forensic witness to take the stand for the government. His testimony was to introduce an exhibit with an extraordinary history and significance—a book-sized, oblong piece of the Ryder truck, red-and-yellow-painted fiberglass and filler on one side and plywood, part of the skin that lined the interior of the van, on the other. Found in the parking lot across from the Murrah building, this was Exhibit 664 in court; Q507 to the FBI lab. Kelly claimed to have found Q507 on the morning of April 21, when searching the parking lot with Steve

Burmeister and FBI photographer special agent Alton Wilson. Kelly described to prosecutor Beth Wilkinson how he had had this item, one of fifteen of interest recovered that morning, photographed, and had then bagged it, marking it with his initials and the number CT-4/21-06.

Although the lab managed to produce a wide-angle shot of a section of the parking lot that was said to include Q507, there was no standard evidence photo of Q507 center frame, in the place where it was discovered. "The photograph they produced was a general shot," Dr. Lloyd says.[44] "It was obvious to me looking at the photos that no photograph of Q507 in place was ever taken," concurred Chris Tritico.[45] Under cross-examination, Ron Kelly admitted that Q507 had not been photographed in place before being recovered. He also admitted that another piece of the van had actually been bagged, logged, and moved before being replaced for photographing "as closely back to the original location" as possible. Kelly admitted that there was no record of either the discovery of Q507 or the strange method of the second item's recovery in either the evidence log or in any other documentation. He also admitted that this was a violation of written rules in both the FBI's general administrative manual and the manual of instruction governing the collection of evidence.

Thus began a train of events that were to call into question the origin and chain of custody of the most important piece of evidence in the government's whole case against McVeigh. It was Ruby Ridge and the "magic bullet" all over again (see Chapter 4). Q507, it turned out, was the only piece of evidence to have what the FBI claimed were ammonium nitrate crystals on it, the crucial proof that the cause of the explosion was an ammonium nitrate bomb. In December, during his pretrial deposition, Fred Whitehurst had told both sets of lawyers that Dave Williams had told him not to bother analyzing the red and yellow paint on Q507 because it had been "turned in by a civilian." As a result, Whitehurst said, Williams told him that Q507 would not be used as evidence. On the witness stand, Ron Kelly twice denied that the piece had been handed in by a civilian, insisting he had found the item.

However, given the absence of an evidence photo and the inconsistencies in his other testimony about the collection of evidence, Kelly was not totally convincing. Williams, in his brief appearance on the stand, recalled talking to Whitehurst about Q507 but could not recall telling him it had been handed in by a civilian. Perhaps more cautious as a result of the now published attack on his forensic reputation in the IG's report, Williams was distinctly guarded when questioned by Christopher Tritico in court on May 27. "Is it true, sir, that Q507 was found by a citizen and not by Mr. Ron Kelly?" "I don't know that answer," Williams replied.[46]

If the chain of custody was crucial yet dubious before Q507 left Oklahoma, it became even more so in the FBI lab. Q507 turned out to have had two evidence collection bags, one of which was marked with initials that, as Ron Kelly stated in court, looked like a "P and an M or an R and an M." Roger Martz, it seemed. Had he handled Q507 as well as McVeigh's clothes, knife, and earplugs before Burmeister? Burmeister claimed Martz had not. But how was he to know, carrying out a crime scene investigation in Oklahoma City, then in Kansas, for days after the blast? Moreover, it soon became clear that Steve Burmeister had every reason to believe Roger Martz if he had told him that he had not handled it. The prospect of Q507 being tainted was too potentially damaging to the government's case to contemplate.

Almost a month after its discovery, Steve Burmeister claimed to have found ammonium nitrate crystals embedded in Q507. Inadequate notes made it impossible for John Lloyd or others to check his procedures but, far more important, Burmeister failed to preserve the crystals, some of the most important evidence in the whole case. "It's not normally a procedure that I follow," Burmeister told the court, offering inconclusive photos as evidence of his discovery. "I'm sure that there is a special packaging I could have done to preserve them for the future, but I feel that I've documented them enough that there was no need to do that."[47] Once again, crucial evidence had been discarded in a crime lab, one of the most common complaints by defense lawyers. "It happens time after time," moans Professor James Starrs at George Washington University in Washington, D.C. "Evidence should not only be offered to the defense, but preserved until all appeals have been exhausted. I'm ashamed to say that that often does not happen."[48]

John Lloyd pointed out that the crystals need only have been placed in a desiccator to have been preserved. But there were other inconsistencies. The photographs showed what seemed to be scorching of the plywood. In court, Burmeister said he discovered the crystals embedded in the burned wood. Burmeister's handwritten notes, however, referred to a glaze of crystals: "Microscopic portion of wood [see photo] has glaze of crystals," they read.[49] It was an important distinction. A glaze could have been added, brushed on; crystals that were embedded had to have been driven into the wood by force.

No one could say how crystals, embedded or glazed, could survive such a blast. The heat at the center of an explosion was simply too great. Neither John Lloyd nor Linda Jones had ever recovered ammonium nitrate crystals from an explosion in this form. Burmeister himself agreed it was "rare"—none of the test explosions of ammonium nitrate fertilizer he knew of had ever left residues that included complete crystals. His theory was that this particular piece of the Ryder truck had collided with the crystals in midair, some distance from the source of the explosion. "We're talking about amazing things at very split-second opportunities," Burmeister told the court.[50]

Yet that was not the end of the amazing features of Q507. Ammonium nitrate easily absorbs moisture, any moisture—rain, humidity, even dew—and rapidly liquefies. Q507 was not recovered until the morning of April 21, more than forty-eight hours after the blast. Yet the night of the bombing there was a torrential thunderstorm in Oklahoma City. The storm was so violent that the flight Ron Kelly and Steve Burmeister were traveling on to Oklahoma City was forced to land overnight in Little Rock, Arkansas. How had the crystals on Q507 survived the deluge? The FBI argued that Q507 was bent at either end to form a sort of concave shape, with either end lifting it off the ground. The crystals were protected from the rain and all other elements, "glazed" or "embedded" as they were into the wood on the underside.

With no photographs of Q507 in place, or of the crystals themselves, it was impossible to tell. Fred Whitehurst, for one, just could not believe it, relating how hygroscopic—water absorbing—ammonium nitrate crystals were even in the controlled humidity of the FBI lab. "I don't believe that the crystals on that wood subjected to a deluge could survive," he told the court of Q507.[51] But even if the FBI lab had "proved" this was an ammonium nitrate bomb, the link to McVeigh was weak. The ingredients were cheap, readily available, and easily purchased in agricultural areas such as Oklahoma, Kansas, and the surrounding states. The government's contention was that McVeigh and Nichols had purchased two thousand pounds of fertilizer from a farmers cooperative in McPherson,

Kansas, which in turn had been supplied by an Imperial Chemical Industries (ICI) plant in Joplin, Missouri. The fertilizer comes in the form of prills, tiny white balls no more than one or two millimeters in diameter, coated with chemicals partly to protect the ammonium nitrate from moisture until use.

ICI prills manufactured in Joplin in 1994–95 had one internal additive, aluminum sulfate, and three particular chemicals in the external coating. The chemistry of the missing crystals that would have linked the bomb back to the ICI prills had always been a problem for the prosecution. Burmeister's reports said he found traces of aluminum, sulfur, and silicon—all naturally occurring and all present in both ICI's and other manufacturers' ammonium nitrate prills. Burmeister found no magnesium, magnesium silicate, or talc, a good absorber of moisture, that was a key ingredient of the external coating of ICI's prills.

There are many unanswered questions about the government's efforts to establish that the bomb was composed of the same prills as those found at Nichols's house. Burmeister, to his credit, concluded that the elements he found in the ammonium nitrate crystals that he did not preserve were only "consistent with" ICI prills. However, he tried to prove more. Indeed, he traveled to Montreal to visit ICI, taking Q507 with him. Somehow there were no crystals on or in the wood when he arrived. "That piece has gone through a lot of hands since the times that I've seen it," he told the court. "I can't speak to how they would have disappeared."[52] It seemed incredible. Had Burmeister really set out to travel all the way to Montreal without checking that he had the crystals he was taking for testing? "The magic crystals, the crystals that so magically appeared, have so magically disappeared. They're gone," as Christopher Tritico told the court. The implications were clear. "ICI doesn't get to test them. Dr. John Lloyd doesn't get to test them. Linda Jones doesn't get to test them. There is only one person on the face of the earth that got an opportunity to test the crystals of ammonium nitrate on Q507: Special Agent Steven Burmeister."[53]

Tests were certainly done for the FBI by ICI in Montreal. A report listed tests on both crushed and whole prills and on some unidentified crystals. The government claimed the latter had nothing to do with Burmeister's famous crystals. One of the three ICI scientists who had done the tests was due to testify but was scratched, presumably because the findings did not support the prosecution's contention about the prills or the crystals or both. Whether he tested the crystals or not, he may have told the court that he would have expected to find magnesium traces on them if the prills were indeed ICI's. John Lloyd told the court this for the defense. The scratched witness, meanwhile, being in Canada was beyond the reach of any subpoena from the defense.

In the end, the forensic science of the explosion was as circumstantial as everything else in the case. As Steve Burmeister admitted in court, even allowing for the evidence of the now missing crystals, the prosecution could not prove it was an ANFO bomb, let alone that the bomb had been built by McVeigh and Nichols using ICI ammonium nitrate fertilizer as the main charge. McVeigh's T-shirt, jeans, boots, and earplugs, the key personal items that might also be expected to carry explosives residue, yielded little more. In fact, given Martz's handling and testing of them, they simply raised more questions. Whitehurst confirmed in court that Burmeister seemed to realize the consequences when he returned from the crime scene investigation: "Mr. Burmeister was angry that Mr. Martz was working on it, working on evidence and rendering opinions, because he didn't think Mr. Martz was qualified to do that."[54]

On the stand, Burmeister took his retraction of earlier testimony about Martz's work to the IG's investigators one step further. He claimed he had been supervising Martz on April 22, when Martz had begun the tests on the key items of evidence. Martz had been "serving as a technician . . . under my direction," he told the court. Yet he was hardly supervising his boss's work in person; Burmeister was nowhere near the FBI lab in Washington on April 22. He was in Oklahoma City before moving on to Kansas before returning to the lab to do examinations on April 28. It was in this context that Beth Wilkinson moved on to the key question: "In [reviewing Martz's work personally], did you compare Agent Martz' work to the additional tests that you conducted?" Burmeister: "Yes." Wilkinson: "Were those results consistent or inconsistent with one another?" Burmeister: "They were consistent with one another."[55]

Yet almost every test Martz and Burmeister had conducted separately had produced different results: Martz found PETN explosive residue on McVeigh's knife, Burmeister did not, possibly because Martz had swabbed it rather than rinsed it; Martz did not find PETN on McVeigh's T-shirt, Burmeister did; Burmeister found nitroglycerin on the knife,

Martz did not; Martz found RDX, another explosive residue in the pockets of McVeigh's pants; Burmeister found none. Consistent?

Anyone who sat in court to hear how the FBI had handled McVeigh's personal effects, how the defendant, a known gun enthusiast, handled weapons constantly—possession of an illegal weapon was the original reason for his arrest—and how easily explosive residues permeate the atmosphere would have had to conclude that any FBI lab tests were at best questionable. First, there was the grocery bag enclosed in a cardboard box in which the clothes arrived. Fatal, said John Lloyd, relating how even sealed Ziploc plastic bags had been shown to be permeable to explosives residues. Paper or cardboard was just asking for contamination. The only safe methods were nylon film bags, metal-foil-lined bags, or metal containers, Lloyd claimed. But in trying to avoid contamination, it helped to start with the real basics. What were two or more items doing traveling to the FBI lab in the same container, even if it was a paper bag? Was cross-contamination the intention?

Second, there was the treatment of the clothes when they reached the FBI lab. Brett Mills told the court how he had taken the cardboard box to the Explosives Unit, placed it on the floor, then moved it onto a table, unpacked its contents, repacked them in individual polyethylene bags, and carried the individual items to various departments of the lab: Chemistry and Toxicology for Martz's initial testing, Special Photo Section for photographs, Hairs and Fibers for examination. The items had been all over the lab before being returned to Burmeister for the second stab at trace analysis.

Questioned by Christopher Tritico about this, John Lloyd described best practice in Britain by way of contrast. Floors, he said, were inevitably the most contaminated parts of labs, particularly in explosives units. He described how the premier labs in England and Northern Ireland banned anyone who had had contact with bulk explosives from access, described how disposable booties and overalls were mandatory for all others and how contamination monitoring took place on a weekly basis. Trace analysis should take place first; evidence for such analysis should always be unpacked by the person about to perform that analysis; repackaging, particularly in an explosives unit, was unacceptable.

John Lloyd's testimony might have been the ASCLD/LAB inspector taking the FBI lab apart—it was basic science, delivered with scientific clarity and reason in layman's terms. The whole point about contamination, Lloyd said, was that assumption and speculation about it were pointless. "If it [contamination] is not determined by experiment, then any test result that you get on a specimen is meaningless," he told the court.[56] Scientific logic dictates that quantitative contamination checks are essential—if you know how much background contamination you are living with you can take that into consideration in assessing any results. Ten nanograms, or ten billionths of a gram, of PETN residue was irrelevant if monitoring revealed ten nanograms of background explosives-residue contamination.

For the first time the issue of potential contamination and its implications in the FBI lab had emerged in a major way in open court. There was no general scheme for regular testing and no written protocol, Steve Burmeister admitted. The only tests that seemed to have been done were periodic studies by Fred Whitehurst, the most relevant of which, when about seventy-five swabs were taken, was done on May 8, 1995, during the period in which Oklahoma City evidence was being handled. Whitehurst found PETN residue on one bench in the Explosives Unit (EU), and PETN and traces of another high explosive in the EU-evidence-handling area in the basement of FBI headquarters. Previous studies had shown glassware to be contaminated, despite repeated washing with soap, water, and acetone.

At the FBI's training facility in Quantico door handles had proved to be a particular risk in transmitting contaminating residue. In his testimony, Whitehurst cited other contamination concerns. Carpets that were vacuumed but never shampooed or checked; doors to trace analysis areas that were left open and unlocked, giving everyone access; prestige tours by visiting dignitaries walking through working areas; and evidence often left out on workbenches or in hoods overnight, leaving it exposed to contamination or even tampering.

But all this was general observation. Burmeister's tests on McVeigh's clothes and earplugs, however, were real results. Burmeister identified PETN residues in the right pocket and residues consistent with PETN in the left pocket of McVeigh's jeans. The same results came from the upper half of the two McVeigh T-shirts and his earplugs. But it meant little. McVeigh carried ammunition in his pockets and his side arm in a shoulder holster. As far back as 1979, PETN had been listed as one of twenty-three organic compounds that might occur in smokeless powders used in ammunition. The earplugs, for use at the range, might be expected to test positive for such residues. In the absence of corroborating evidence—no explosive residue on the steering wheel or gearshift of McVeigh's car, in the two storage lockers where the bomb material was allegedly stored, under McVeigh's fingernails or in his hair—the results were hardly incriminating.

No other forensic evidence was any stronger. FBI fingerprint technician Louis Hupp testified that there were no McVeigh fingerprints on the Ryder truck rental agreement or Ryder truck key and admitted that the FBI had failed to find any at Elliott's Body Shop, despite tearing out the counter. Indeed, all the evidence linking McVeigh to "Robert D. Kling," the man who had rented the truck in Junction City, was particularly weak. Eyewitness evidence was contradictory and the handwriting analysis of the three samples of the signature inconclusive. Tire tracks from Nichols's home in Herington, Kansas, were equally indeterminate. They could not be linked to the Ryder truck, FBI examiner William Bodziak told the court. He had not even tried to match them to any other type of vehicle.

It did indeed seem to be a one-track investigation, as Stephen Jones had alleged. And hanging over the whole inquiry was the specter of John Doe II. Was his the missing leg? The real bomber might have died in the blast, the defense suggested. The embalming fluid used to bury the leg when it was originally misidentified had stymied all FBI lab efforts to get a DNA match or profile. The rest of the body could have been blown away, Thomas Marshall, a British forensic pathologist testified. He had experienced the phenomenon before in Northern Ireland, he told the court on May 22.

In his summation, Chris Tritico described what the FBI lab did as more like a Stephen King novel than chemistry. He hammered away at the incredible saga of the nine-inch piece of the van, Q507, the inconsistencies in the story of its discovery, the "embedded" or "glazed" crystals that could never be checked, their miraculous survival of the heat of the explosion, then the rain and wind of the April 19 storm; the equally miraculous way the crystals disappeared before they and their sole witness, Steve Burmeister, reached Montreal. Real or unreal, Tritico suggested an alternative origin. The Oklahoma firefighters may have used ammonium phosphate–based extinguishing substances. Burmeister himself had said ammonium and nitrate ions could naturally bond together to form crystals.

The defense team also hammered away at the prosecution's failure to put Roger Martz and Dave Williams on the stand. But having been prevented from introducing the evidence against them, all Chris Tritico could do was plant the seeds of doubt with the jury. "Ladies and gentlemen you have to ask yourself . . . why didn't Roger Martz testify? Why is Roger Martz the *former* chief of the Chemistry and Toxicology Unit? Why didn't Roger Martz come and tell you about the testing he did on the clothing?" The defense's overriding theme in summation was that the inconsistencies, inadequacies, and incompetence of the FBI lab were not accidental. There was one central aim—to make the evidence fit an explanation for the bombing that had evolved within days of the explosion and had not changed one iota since, even when facts and forensics pointed in contrary directions.

McVeigh and Nichols had plenty of motive, but so did thousands of other government-haters. If ever there was a case where there was an almost primeval need for someone to be found guilty, this was it. In Oklahoma City, the blood really did cry out. "I'm afraid that it's generally true that the more emotion you have the less evidence you need," one legal commentator told CBS while waiting for the verdict. Having heard Judge Richard Matsch warn them specifically to consider the case on the evidence alone, the jury did at least deliberate for three days. On June 2, 1997, Timothy McVeigh was found guilty on all eleven counts. Eleven days later the same jury opted for the death penalty.

7

O. J. SIMPSON:
DIRTY HANDS, BAD BLOOD

Ask Americans why they were so riveted by the O. J. Simpson case, the investigation and two trials that gripped the nation for nearly two years, and you will get many answers—wealth, celebrity, race, sex, jealousy, the sheer mystery of a real life "did he do it?" Ask them what it was about and they venture the slow-motion chase of Simpson's white Bronco, the drama of O. J. trying on the bloody glove discovered behind his Brentwood estate, the endless media hoopla both inside and outside the courtroom. But ask one of the lawyers and they will tell you that the trial was about blood and DNA. They might also tell you that DNA—shorthand for deoxyribonucleic acid—is a unique genetic "fingerprint" that can be extracted from human cells, allowing the police and prosecution to place suspects at the crime scene with scientific certainty.

In fact, DNA typing or profiling is *not* a genetic fingerprint, and to portray it as such is scientific fraud. Fingerprints are an individual characteristic; everyone's are unique; DNA profiles are not. DNA typing produces what is known as a random probability match—sometimes as high as one in several million or even billion, sometimes as low as one in dozens. As such it represents the probability of a match between a sample left at the crime scene and a suspect, not a definitive match itself. To pretend, as some proponents seem to, that DNA profiling, this sci-crime wizardry, is infallible is a gross distortion of the truth. No one disputes the science; the practice, however, is another matter. There are essentially three problems.

One, though DNA typing came out of the regulated, pristine environment of medical labs, it was adapted to forensic science and the unregulated crime labs. In the United States in particular, it was pushed onto the crime-fighting scene without the publication of validation studies, protocols, and procedures for external scrutiny. As such, it is constantly subject to challenge in the courts. Second, making a match is far from scientifically certain; it is in fact sometimes highly subjective. Different methodologies produce different results, and it ultimately depends on the DNA examiner comparing two sets of bands or spots—one from the control sample and one from the actual sample—on an X-ray printout. It is the human factor again, and all the usual biases in making matches have come into play in a number of cases challenged in court. Third, even the means of computing the statistical probability of a match was in dispute at the time of the O. J. Simpson case. The choices of population databases and the method of mathematical calculation make huge differences in the probabilities presented to juries.

In short, when O. J. Simpson came to trial, DNA typing was not the clean, clinical, definitive crime-fighting tool—the Holy Grail of "individualization" of which every prosecutor dreamed. After more than sixty books, thousands of hours of television, and miles of newsprint it seems extraordinary that there is another side to the O. J. Simpson trial, a story that has never really been told. Yet there is. The reason there was no conviction in the O. J. Simpson trial was that the defendant's "dream team" managed to put the Los Angeles Police Department (LAPD), the LAPD's crime lab, DNA testing, and forensic science more generally all on trial. All were found guilty.

In winning, the O. J. team managed to take a broad sideswipe at the FBI lab. Although the Bureau was not center stage in this case, the O. J. Simpson case echoed every complaint Fred Whitehurst and others had ever made about crime labs in general and the FBI's in particular. By specifically putting DNA typing procedures on trial, the defense called into question the whole lack of regulation, proficiency testing, and administrative control of the most powerful forensic tool since fingerprinting. It was a control that the FBI had fought tooth and nail to exercise, a control formally legitimized by means of congressional legislation the year O. J. Simpson was charged. The result was that the woeful standards in DNA typing, the subjectivity involved, the lack of proficiency testing, and the statistical arguments, all had their origins in the FBI lab.

There were three great ironies about this. The first was that one of the most thorough examinations of a crime lab and forensic procedures ever conducted in a U.S. court all happened by accident. There was no congressional hearing, FBI inquiry, or Department of Justice investigation. O. J. Simpson just happened to have the motive and means to fight. Few if any defendants charged with murder have the money to conduct their own forensic examination. O. J. Simpson's team took the LAPD crime lab, the oldest in the country, apart, fiber by fiber, cell by cell. In doing so they proved the truth of a phrase that a number of California forensic scientists had long used to depict the LAPD lab—"from first to worst."

The second irony was that nothing really changed as a result of this challenge. Although this case was fought in the press as no other before it, the media found the DNA evidence unintelligible, and so they largely ignored it. Ultimately, crime labs seemed to pay no attention at all to one of the most public exposures ever of their inadequacies. In October 1995, at the end of the trial, one of their most potent critics, Paul Giannelli, a professor of law at Case Western Reserve University in Cleveland, warned that police departments might try to rationalize the status quo, realizing that a case like O. J. Simpson's is the exception not the rule. He was right. For crime lab directors as well as the public this really was the trial of the century. There was no need to worry until the next one.

The third irony was that in a bizarre kind of way, this case seemed to illustrate what critics of crime labs had been saying for years—lack of regulation threatened to let the guilty go free as well as lock up the innocent. In the end, any examination of the evidence could leave only one impression: the LAPD and its lab had the evidence to secure an easy conviction. Yet any reading of the defense's analysis and exposure of what was done with the blood evidence gives scope for reasonable doubt. Evidence could have been both contaminated and planted. If the LAPD had had a decent lab, followed proper procedures, and guarded against contamination, there could have been no such defense. The truth was that DNA, the cutting edge of biochemical genetics, the most sophisticated sci-crime weapon in history, was useless when grafted onto crime labs that cannot even keep their glassware clean.

The lineup that started to assemble in Los Angeles in the summer of 1994 under O. J. Simpson's lead lawyers, Robert Shapiro and Johnnie Cochran, read like a who's who of forensic science in the United States. Barry Scheck and Peter Neufeld were New York lawyers who had come to specialize in using DNA to clear defendants falsely imprisoned on rape and murder charges as part of a scheme known as the Innocence Project. In the two years prior to August 1994, they had already secured the release of eight men, one from Death Row in Virginia. Flawed forensic evidence all too often proved responsible for the miscarriages of justice they dealt with; the failure to preserve evidence from crimes all too often meant there was nothing they could do to clear others. "We see this case as a means of educating the public, for perhaps generating legislation, to generate a major change in the way crime labs do business in this country," Peter Neufeld announced.[1]

Lining up with Scheck and Neufeld were others from the East coast. They included Dr. Henry Lee, who had run the state police crime lab in Connecticut for more than twenty years and has a reputation for being one of the best criminologists in the United States, a man who can read a crime scene like Sherlock Holmes and rivet juries as he tells them how he did it. Above all, Lee is known for his scrupulous scientific integrity, advocating that examiners take on cases for the defense as well as the prosecution. Lee frequently threatened to leave the O. J. Simpson case in the first few weeks when he felt subtle pressures to compromise scientific facts. "Nothing to hide. I give both sides exactly the same thing," he emphasized in one defense case conference.[2] Lee's expertise proved invaluable. From early on he found inconsistencies. Impressions in the pools of dried blood at the scene suggested two different shoe-prints. Two murderers? The blood drops down the pathway to Nicole's front door showed no splatter. Were they placed? "Something's wrong here," Lee would tell the jury, one year on, a subtle variation of "Something is fucked up here"—his initial reaction after studying the crime scene photos with his huge magnifying glass.

In the end, it was Lee's treatment at the hands of the LAPD that riled him more than any pressure from the lawyers. He felt intimidated, obstructed, and demeaned on his visits to the LAPD lab, where on one particular visit he was kept waiting, given no protective clothing, then told to use a microscope with which he could not focus. For months the LAPD refused to allow Lee and others to examine evidence, finally responding to a court order only after the trial had begun in January 1995. When thirty boxes of evidence arrived in New York for examination, Lee's team could not believe the state it was in. Blood samples had been transferred to the bindles—the envelopes they are transported in—while still wet; one lens from Nicole Brown Simpson's eyeglasses was missing; and there were undocumented hairs on both victims' clothing.

In fact, the LAPD seemed more interested in investigating Lee and his forensic colleagues on the defense team than the evidence itself. Lee eventually accused the LAPD of going to extraordinary lengths to dig up dirt in an effort to discredit them, charges that were supported by at least two other experts. "If the LAPD spent as much time investigating homicides as they spent investigating us they would solve every murder," Lee later told Cyril Wecht, one of America's best known forensic pathologists and a former president of the American Academy of Forensic Sciences.[3] In the LAPD's eyes, Lee, a police forensic scientist, had simply crossed the line in working for the defense. "One week we are testifying for the prosecution and we are fine. The next week we are testifying for the defense and we become the great evil," Lee complained.[4]

Lee had been brought into the investigation by Michael Baden, the former New York City medical examiner, forever famous for finding the bullet that killed Marlon Brando's daughter's lover under a rug a week after the LAPD's search had ended. Also in the lineup was Ed Blake, an independent forensics expert who ran his own lab in California and brought to the case an encyclopedic knowledge of DNA and its use in the courtroom. Having worked with the Los Angeles prosecutor's office many times—indeed, he was hired by the defense minutes before the prosecution tried to retain him—his ability to read the opposition proved invaluable. Others with a specialist interest in DNA followed, including William Thompson, a criminology professor at the University of California at Irvine, and Robert Blasier, a defense lawyer from Sacramento who had successfully argued the first extended challenge to the admissibility of a particular and less reliable form of DNA testing, known as PCR, in California courts.

Facing them alongside Marcia Clark and Christopher Darden were Rockne Harmon and George "Woody" Clark, California's two most experienced DNA prosecutors. Acerbic, prickly, and uncompromising, there is nothing Harmon liked more than going head-to-head with DNA naysayers. He took reverses in court, particularly those based on DNA, personally, and was outspoken when he thought the courts were in error.[5] His acerbic wit was to give the case one of its best media sound bites, when he rebutted the defense's contamination contention by asking DNA analyst Gary Sims: "Can DNA fly?"

So if the defense team had a mission, so did Harmon and Clark. In 1992, the California Appeals Court had challenged the admissibility of DNA random probability matches in two separate cases. In one of these, the FBI lab had claimed that there was a one in 200 million chance among the African-American population that Kevin O'Neal Howard had not beaten and strangled his landlord, Octavia Matthews. But the defense had appealed on the basis of the statistical probability estimates, saying there was no general scientific acceptance of the methodology. The appeals court had agreed and the case had now gone to the California Supreme Court, which had agreed to rule on the validity of the FBI statistical methodology.

The second case demonstrated that the FBI lab could not even agree on its own DNA estimates. In 1990, the district attorney in Sacramento brought rape and murder charges against Jeffrey Hronis and John Bertsch on the basis of an FBI lab report in April 1989 that both defendants matched the physical evidence with a probability of 1 in 8 million (Hronis) and 1 in 12 million (Bertsch). In early 1992, shortly before the preliminary hearing, the FBI lab's DNA unit retested and recalculated. Hronis's random probability-match profile dropped to 1 in 16,000 for Caucasians, 1 in 41,000 for African Americans, and 1 in 19,000 for Hispanics. Bertsch's was an even more alarming change: 1 in 200 for Caucasians, 1 in 200 for African Americans, and 1 in 100 for Hispanics.[6] Eighteen months later, the FBI reported that there was "a difference of opinion among its scientists" about whether there was a match at all.[7] District Attorney Steve White had to drop the case.

Harmon and Clark both understood only too well that the O. J. Simpson trial could be a vital battle in the long struggle to get DNA science and procedures, in particular FBI procedures and statistics, accepted in California courts. Exclusion—results that cleared a suspect —were one thing. Inclusion—the incrimination of someone on a random probability-match statistical method that was in dispute, even among the technicians doing the tests, not to mention lack of agreement on the testing methodology itself—was something else, particularly in California, where skepticism dated back to the very earliest days of DNA typing.

In 1987, the California Association of Crime Laboratory Directors had sent fifty DNA samples to the three private commercial labs doing DNA forensic typing in the United States at the time. Although analysts knew they were being tested, two of the three labs mistakenly matched unrelated samples. Cellmark Diagnostics, a company that was to perform much of the DNA typing in the O. J. Simpson case, made two false matches, an error they attributed to cross-contamination during DNA extraction. The results demonstrated the scope for human error. They also illustrated the need for the full details of a lab's DNA-typing protocols and the scientific data underlying them to be made public for peer review by other scientists.

Another factor was the image of DNA typing. What was by 1994 the most commonly used form of DNA testing, polymerase chain reaction (PCR), had actually been devised and patented by a brilliant but unconventional California geneticist who listed drug-taking, surfing, and womanizing as his main activities when not researching. Kary Mullis had won the 1993 Nobel Prize for chemistry for a simple method of duplicating DNA strands, thus solving criminologists' two major problems: quantity and time. Often a crime scene yielded too little body fluid in too degraded a form to prove testable, and the standard DNA test, restriction fragment length polymorphism (RFLP), took months. PCR, "genetic xeroxing" as it is sometimes known, needs less original sample and takes only a matter of days or weeks.

Ironically, Mullis did not see his PCR method as reliable enough to be applicable to crime fighting and was prepared to go on the witness stand and say so in the O. J. Simpson trial. Mullis was one of a number of PCR exponents who were very concerned about its application outside the clinical, regulated atmosphere of medical labs where it had been devised. PCR is undoubtedly a less definitive DNA typing method, producing random-match probabilities in the hundreds or thousands rather than the millions, and was only being refined and honed at the time of the double murder in Brentwood, Los Angeles. It, like O. J. Simpson, was on trial.

But beyond the biochemists, geneticists, and lawyers were a jury, judge, and public who were unlikely to understand a word of PCR science. It was rammed home to Michael Baden one day early on when the lead defense counsel, Robert Shapiro, asked him: "You mean you can't see DNA in a bloodstain?" Not everyone was a scientist, Baden had to remind himself.[8] It was little easier for the judge, Lance Ito. Although in January he boasted he had spent two weeks reading up on DNA in preparation for an admissibility hearing, one close observer of the trial, Cyril Wecht, said he knew there would be problems with the DNA evidence when he noticed Judge Ito studying the autoradiograms, the DNA X-ray charts, upside down.

Yet the evidence itself was becoming more overwhelming by the day. To combat any threat of a defense based on contamination, the prosecution quickly dispatched more than two dozen separate blood samples to three different laboratories. It was an unprecedented move. Some lawyers and scientists had recommended having DNA tests performed by two laboratories, but now the prosecution in the Simpson case had gone one better. A further innoculation against defense challenges was to get all three labs to use both available DNA testing methods, the lengthier, more reliable RFLP method as well as the newer, less certain PCR test.

One reason the FBI lab seems to have missed out on sharing the DNA analysis in the "trial of the century" was because of concerns about defense challenges. First, the Kevin O'Neal Howard case had demonstrated the absence of "general scientific acceptance" of the FBI method of statistical computation of DNA random probability matches. This had been underlined by a population geneticist who had surveyed thirty of his colleagues. He discovered that nineteen of them did not accept the way the FBI was calculating random probability matches; only eleven did.[9] Second, Judge Ito had ruled that defense representatives, in particular DNA expert Ed Blake, could be present during testing, something Milton Ahlerich, the FBI lab chief, categorically ruled out.

Third, another court ruling, this one by a Los Angeles trial court in

1991, meant that California had become just about the worst state in the union for the FBI and its DNA typing evidence. In *People* v. *Halik* it was not just the FBI's statistical method that had been challenged, but its matching criteria, the means by which a match of the two sets of DNA bands on the X-ray printouts was declared by the DNA examiner. The defense contended that the FBI was being far too liberal in its subjective declaration of a match, and there was no general acceptance of its criteria by scientists.

In response, the court assembled what it called "perhaps the most comprehensive compilation of judicial and scientific materials ever assembled for a pre-trial hearing on these issues."[10] Using the complete records of admissibility hearings from previous cases in a number of states where the FBI's DNA typing methods had been scrutinized, the court ruled in favor of the defense. No general acceptance; no admissibility, and this referred to the method itself, not just the statistical calculations. It was a landmark ruling that made the FBI's DNA-typing matching techniques vulnerable to exclusion from courts throughout California.

As a result, no blood samples in the O. J. Simpson case went to the FBI lab for DNA testing. Four blood drops from Nicole Simpson's pathway, thought to have been shed by the killer as he walked or ran away, and one drop from the driveway went to three laboratories—the LAPD lab, the California Department of Justice lab in Berkeley, and the private lab of Cellmark Diagnostics, based in Germantown, Maryland. Three separate bloodstains from the black metal rear gate at Nicole's home went to the lab in Berkeley, as did most of six bloodstains, a bloody partial footprint, and three stains not collected until August, all found inside Simpson's Bronco. Four bloodstains found in the driveway, foyer, and master bathroom went to Cellmark and Berkeley, as did two dark dress socks, one later discovered to have a large bloodstain, and the famous leather glove smeared with blood found in the alleyway that ran alongside a guest house at the Simpson estate.

The DNA typing results of all this were pretty alarming for the defense. The most incriminating blood drops, those on Nicole's pathway and driveway, matched O. J. Simpson's—the former with a 1 in 240,000 PCR probability match and the latter with a 1 in 170 million RFLP match. All were collected on June 13, the day after the murders and before blood was drawn from O. J. Simpson's arm. The large bloodstain on the gate produced a 1 in 57 billion RFLP match to O. J. Simpson, the smaller two, a 1 in 520 match using PCR, but all three were not collected until July 3, apparently having not been spotted until three weeks after the murders. Most of the blood in the Bronco was Simpson's, but Nicole's DNA was found in the partial bloody footprint on the driver's side, and a stain on the center console contained Ron Goldman's blood.

The three stains collected in August, six weeks after the murder, contained DNA matching those from all three individuals, the defendant and both victims. At the Rockingham estate, all the DNA matched Simpson's except that in the large bloodstain on the dress sock, again overlooked by the LAPD until weeks after the murder. The sock showed DNA matching both Simpson, a 1 in 57 billion RFLP match, and Nicole, with a 1 in 7.7 billion match. The Aris Isotoner Lights leather glove found in the alleyway was smeared with blood containing DNA matching all three individuals, Simpson, Brown, and Goldman.

Blake, Scheck, and Neufeld told the defense team that they had to accept these results—three labs, two distinct DNA testing methods— and move on. The PCR testing results might be challengeable but the RFLP results were not. If Simpson's blood was at the crime scene, Nicole's blood on the glove and sock, and Ron Goldman's blood in the Bronco, what next? It was Scheck, scientifically scrupulous but working as a defense lawyer on the assumption of O. J. Simpson's innocence, who devised a strategy. What evolved was a defense based on the planting and contamination of evidence.

In August 1994, the defense team discovered that the LAPD had no standard system of record collection for evidence. LAPD criminalists Dennis Fung and Andrea Mazzola, the latter a trainee with only four months' experience, had collected bloodstains on gauze cotton swatches without numbering them or tagging them. The swatches varied in size, shape, and number. Some had as many as seven stains, others as few as three, presenting endless possibilities for mixing, substituting, or even planting swatches. The LAPD criminalists had ignored the basics of preserving blood, using plastic bags and leaving samples in a police truck for the whole of a boiling day in June. Degradation was inevitable. And since the stains on the gate, in the Bronco, and on the sock had been missed until three weeks after the murders, the defense could argue that they had not been there during the initial searches. They could have been planted.

Throughout the summer, that scenario became more plausible by the day. Barry Scheck calculated that blood was missing from O. J. Simpson's reference sample. Thano Peratis, a police nurse, testified that he had drawn between 7.9 and 8.1 milliliters on June 13. The LAPD used 1 milliliter on June 14, yet on June 21 the toxicology unit measured only 5.5 milliliters in the vial. What had happened to the missing 1.4–1.6 milliliters? Three more withdrawals totaled 1.6 milliliters, and the defense was given 1 milliliter for its own tests. Yet the log showed only 2.6 milliliters remaining in the vial at the end of June. If the 1.7–1.9 milliliters unaccounted for had spilled, then tests could be said to be invalid through contamination. But it could also have been part of a conspiracy. Someone may have had the means—blood—to frame O. J. Simpson.

And the opportunity seemed to be there too. Detective Philip Vannatter and lab examiner Dennis Fung had had Simpson's blood for much of June 13, the day after the murders. Peratis had given it to Vannatter, who instead of taking it to the lab and logging it in, took it up the Santa Monica Freeway to Simpson's Rockingham estate and gave it to Fung sometime that afternoon. No records, no times. In court, Fung was to say he could not remember when he had placed the sample in the van. One way or another Simpson's blood was not checked into the LAPD lab until June 14. Moreover, the next day Vannatter handled both victims' blood, picking up samples at the coroner's office and delivering them to the LAPD serology unit for DNA tests.

In January 1995, Barry Scheck laid out to his defense colleagues a scenario dealing with every single piece of DNA evidence. It ran to forty single-spaced pages. The key was pinning everything down to the LAPD lab, whose crime scene criminologists and lab technicians could be shown to have been negligent, sloppy, and inept. All the evidence that had gone to Cellmark and the state lab in Berkeley had been handled, unpacked, stored, and in some cases tested in the LAPD's lab first. The contention would be that it had been degraded, contaminated, and switched in a lab Scheck now labeled "a cesspool of PCR contamination," before getting anywhere near its final destination. In other words, tests done elsewhere, whatever the results, were irrelevant. In another sound bite that would come to crystalize Scheck's forensic case, any testing done after the LAPD had handled anything was "garbage in, garbage out."

The key now was showing this had probably, not just possibly, happened. Although the defense team was confident that they could impeach the LAPD criminologists and the DNA technicians individually, they needed to show that the problems in the lab were systemic. Ed Blake immediately suggested recruiting an expert defense witness to study the LAPD lab, its procedures and processes, in detail. The man chosen was Dr. John Gerdes, a microbiologist from Denver, Colorado, a scientific purist who ran a tissue-typing lab and had made previous studies of crime labs.

When the O. J. Simpson trial finally got underway in January 1995, several prosecution witnesses could not have helped the defense more in their overall strategy. Indeed, on April 17, Judge Ito was to observe during a sidebar that he had never seen a witness so thoroughly destroyed as Dennis Fung, the first forensic scientist to take the stand.[11] Scheck's cross-examination set the tone for the whole trial, establishing Fung, and by implication the investigation, as inefficient, incompetent, and inaccurate, yet not so inept as to be beyond a criminal conspiracy.

Fung admitted possible cross contamination of the right-hand Aris Isotoner Lights leather glove found at Nicole Brown Simpson's condominium—LAPD Detective Tom Lange had asked Fung to move it into the center of the crime scene. Confronted with photographs of his trainee assistant, Andrea Mazzola, working on her own, Fung confessed that he had not always supervised her as he had claimed. Fung also readily admitted that he had handled evidence without gloves and left the blood swatches in plastic bags in the heat of his van for seven hours because the vehicle's refrigerator did not work properly.

In one glorious moment, Scheck read from Barry Fisher's *Techniques of Crime Scene Investigation:* "It is a certainty that wet or damp bloodstains packaged in airtight containers such as plastic bags will be useless as evidence in a matter of days." But the pièce de résistance was when, having gotten Dennis Fung to admit that he did not see blood on the gate on June 13, the day after the murders, Scheck produced a photograph to show the large bloodstain on the gate before it was collected on July 3. When Fung confirmed that was what he had seen on the day he finally collected a sample of the blood, Scheck projected a photograph of the same gate taken on June 13. "Where is it, Mr. Fung?" Scheck demanded, referring to the bloodstain. "I can't see it in the pic . . . photograph," Fung stammered.[12] Neither could anyone else in court. The seeds of doubt had sprouted. How had the blood suddenly appeared, if it had not been planted?

After Andrea Mazzola came Gregory Matheson, the LAPD's chief chemist and serologist. Cross-examination by Bob Blasier was a forensic dissection of LAPD lab procedures that produced one important admission—the LAPD kept no accurate records of sample blood. More could always be drawn from the suspect, Matheson argued. Then came Dr. Robin Cotton, a petite, studious-looking woman with wire-rimmed glasses. As the director of the lab at Cellmark Diagnostics, Dr. Cotton had the job of explaining the ABCs of DNA to the court and presenting the official results. With her charts, slides, and bar charts she was a practiced, professional witness used to guiding lay juries through the scientific morass.

DNA, and its four chemical bases, adenine, guanine, thymine, and cytosine, was described as a sort of recipe for the creation of every human from the time each one is a single cell, a fertilized egg. Every cell has a complete copy of an individual's DNA that lays down his or her genetic blueprint; it determines if he or she will have blue or brown eyes, or be fat or thin, tall or short. DNA is arranged in two strips called chromosomes that are wrapped around each other like a pair of twisted ladders, one from our mother and one from our father. Each chromosome is actually a long string of genes that would be six feet in length if it could be stretched out.

All this has been known for some time. DNA typing, what was actually going on in the laboratory, became possible with the discovery in the early 1980s of variable number tandem repeats (VNTRs), areas of DNA where there is a great deal of variation, and thus a low probability of two people matching if fragments are compared at four, six, or more specific locations along the chromosomes. Thus typing or profiling is based on comparing what DNA extracted from crime scene tissue or body fluid, usually semen, blood, or saliva, looks like against DNA extracted from a sample, usually blood, from the suspect. The DNA typing looks for matches in these lengths of DNA, known as alleles or bands.

There are two types of test, Dr. Cotton explained. In RFLP, the more reliable typing test requiring a larger sample, the DNA is cut into fragments chemically. These are then pushed through a gel by means of an electric current, as if through a sieve, and transferred to nylon membranes, which then have radioactive DNA probes applied to them, binding them to matching DNA sequences. X-ray film is placed next to the membranes, the film developed, and a pattern of bands is revealed where the radioactive probe is bound to the DNA fragments. The final DNA-typing autoradiogram is a picture of light and dark bands—sometimes compared to supermarket bar codes—with the DNA typing of the crime scene samples being compared to the DNA typing of the suspected source alongside.

In PCR typing the crime scene sample is treated with a chemical solution to inhibit degradation and boiled to remove the DNA. This is then combined with short fragments of known DNA, called primers, and with other chemicals that stimulate replication by means of a polymerase chain reaction, which mimics the natural processes by which DNA copies itself. Small quantities of replicated DNA are then applied to 8 or 10 spots on reagent strips. Each spot contains a different segment of the other known DNA. If the replicated DNA contains a segment matching the known segment, a blue color appears on the spot. The comparison here is matching the pattern of spots from the sample from the crime scene to that taken from the suspect that has been through the same process.

The principle behind the PCR test—to identify an area of DNA where there tends to be variation from one person to another and amplify it—is sound. The practice is another matter. In the first place, there is an ethical issue. The amplification of DNA in the PCR test effectively involves manufacturing evidence before it could be examined. Second, contamination is much more of a threat in PCR testing. The process is sensitive, complicated, and delicate, especially during the amplification stage. Third, there is the issue of the accuracy of the amplification. It is known that some alleles or variants amplify more efficiently than others. As a result, PCR amplification could be qualitatively faithful but quantitatively unfaithful.

Dr. Cotton outlined all the lab results that incriminated O. J. Simpson. She dealt powerfully with the issue of contamination, explaining that degradation or exposure to heat or humidity would never alter DNA results. But the matching statistics that Cotton outlined did seem open to challenge. One in 170 million for whites and African Americans for one of the blood drops on the condominium pathway; 1 in 1.2 billion if you added "Western Hispanics." The figures for matches of Nicole Brown's and O. J. Simpson's blood found on the socks seemed even more unreal. One in 6.8 billion for Western Hispanics, 1 in 9.7 billion for whites, and 1 in 535 billion for African Americans—one hundred times more people than there were on earth.

The numbers sound ridiculous, and many scientists allege that they are. For this is where DNA typing crosses into other fields, namely population genetics and statistics. After determining a match, analysts first estimate the frequency with which each allele or variant occurs in the individual's DNA by determining its frequency in a database containing DNA profiles of a reference population of the same ethnicity. It's a process of rapid multiplication, the frequency times the number of specific locations on the chromosomes, usually four or six, at which the DNA of the individual has been typed. The problem is that if the lab gets the initial frequency estimate wrong, the error is multiplied rapidly and thus magnified. In one early DNA case in New York, for instance, a defense expert had calculated that a private DNA lab, Lifecodes, had exaggerated the random probability match by eight thousand–fold.

One key issue here was the population database on which the DNA frequency figures were based, both its size and its relevance to the particular ethnicity of the suspect. In his two-day cross-examination of Dr. Cotton, Peter Neufeld, Barry Scheck's partner, went to the nub of the issue: What were these figures based on? Not much, it turned out. A DNA-typing database of blood donated by 240 African Americans at a Red Cross clinic in Detroit. In questioning the database, Neufeld was stoking the flames of one of the great scientific debates of the 1990s in the United States.

Inevitably, the FBI lab was at the center of the whole fight. For by 1995 it was the Bureau's blueprints for both statistical calculations and the typing methodology itself that had become the basis for national DNA criminology. And how that had happened was quite a story.

———

DNA typing, developed in Britain in 1984, became the Wild West frontier of U.S. forensic science when it crossed the Atlantic. Three private labs sprang up, but because there was no regulatory mechanism for forensic science in the United States, the varied techniques, the ethics of the process, and the accuracy of testing procedures were never monitored. Yet in DNA typing there was more need for scientific validation and proficiency testing than ever before. The implications of the new science were just too enormous for anything less. DNA results alone could jail someone for life or even take away their life. Yet the technique had already been used in more than one hundred criminal cases before coming under real scrutiny for the first time during a murder trial in New York in 1989.

Congressional hearings chaired that same year by Don Edwards, himself a former FBI agent, soon brought calls for licensing and regular proficiency testing. But by whom? The FBI started maneuvering for control. The stakes in terms of power in the war against crime were enormous. DNA typing tended to deal with the most serious felonies—rape and murder. A national database like the FBI's fingerprint depository was a necessity, the Bureau argued, but it could only be based on some agreed national standard, something it should determine. The Bureau's position was soon bolstered by the lobbying of the private labs, who saw enormous profits in an endorsement of their technology by the FBI.

The Bureau itself had started slowly on DNA typing, with a small group led by Dr. Bruce Budowle, a Californian biologist with a Ph.D. in genetics, traveling to Europe and the private U.S. labs to study methods, then researching for two years at the FBI lab's research center in Quantico. The result of what the Bureau termed "numerous experiments" to "increase efficiency or increase reliability" was the FBI's own RFLP method of DNA typing. The data and results that underpin them have never been fully published and the resulting methodology has never been independently validated. The outcome was inevitable. The FBI's methodology and techniques have not been accepted by the scientific community as a whole and have become the cause of huge dissension.

Two rather instructive articles were published during this period, both printed in *Crime Laboratory Digest*, the joint quarterly periodical of the FBI and ASCLD. Although distributed to crime labs and a few academic institutes, it is hardly a scientific journal; its contents are not peer-reviewed and its editors are hardly independent. The first article described the DNA research being done but not the results obtained or the protocols used, although this article has in itself since been portrayed as validation for FBI methods of DNA analysis.[13] The second article, entitled "Validation of the FBI Procedure for DNA Analysis," was just as flawed in its basic premise.[14] It described a procedure validated by the same lab that devised it.

In 1988, the FBI began typing DNA samples in real cases as the "validation" article went to press. The conflicting pressures of the need to bring a new technology into the fight against crime as rapidly as possible and to ensure that that technique was scientifically sound was a dilemma that had already been resolved in favor of law enforcement. Ironically, one of the most salient features of the FBI's new DNA-typing program was the number of suspects that it cleared immediately, up to one-third of all cases referred. It was a reassuring statistic that was soon being used to counteract critics of the lab's DNA techniques. The awkward question of how many innocent people had had cases built against them before the FBI started DNA typing was ignored.

In 1988, a National Academy of Sciences (NAS) study due to be carried out by the National Research Council to look into standards and make recommendations on DNA typing was postponed. Both the FBI and the National Institute of Justice—a sister agency of the Bureau within the Department of Justice—could not find the funds. Critics charged the FBI had no need of the study in the first place; the Bureau's standards and statistical computations were becoming the norm among the country's state, county, and city crime labs. The FBI's rationale for pushing out its own RFLP test and methodology before any real validation study was done was clear: They were in a hurry to produce a national index of DNA types. In other words, the end justified the means.

In the first nine months of 1989, the FBI trained sixty technicians in DNA-typing techniques. The next year the number doubled to 120.[15] The Bureau was quickly stuffing the DNA-typing industry with its own men and women and with them came the FBI's own DNA image-analysis computer software for analyzing RFLP autoradiograms. There was a corresponding explosion in demand for DNA typing from the FBI lab itself. By December 1990, the FBI lab had received 13,378 DNA profiling requests as the message spread about the wonders of this new technology.[16] There was no competition. Federally funded, the FBI offered the tests and training, free; private labs such as Lifecodes and Cellmark charged.

The Bureau's role as a proselytizing missionary for the benefits of DNA typing, or rather its version of it, was symbolized by the International Symposium on the Forensic Aspects of DNA Analysis in June 1989. More than 350 invited guests, the mainstays of the country's crime lab establishment, heard FBI director William Sessions bang the drum at a dress dinner. But the higher profile of the Bureau and the postponement of the NAS study only spawned more criticism and more challenges in court. Faced with the need to be seen to be doing something, the FBI set up its own group to look at methodologies and establish guidelines.

The Technical Working Group on DNA Analysis Methods (TWGDAM) was composed of thirty-one scientists, representing sixteen forensic laboratories in Canada and the United States—all law enforcement labs—and two research institutes. It met for the first time in November 1988 at the FBI lab's research center under the chairmanship of the FBI's James Kearney. As strange a creature as its acronym suggests, TWGDAM had many uses for the Bureau, all of which might loosely be described as pseudovalidation. On one level it was designed to build consensus: "sharing protocols" was among its written purposes. But its first meeting also set up a subcommittee to formulate guidelines for a DNA-typing quality assurance program.

The subcommittee, chaired by James Mudd of the FBI, produced guidelines in April 1991. Included was a whole new concept of self-validation, a concept pioneered in the very testing that led to the evolution of the FBI's DNA-typing methodology. Every lab should validate DNA procedures internally, the guidelines ruled. There was no obligation to publish or even report the results of any such processes, so there was no way judges, courts, or other scientists could determine proficiency, errors, or deficiencies. Thus in redefining and coopting the concept of validation, the FBI-led group dispensed with the need for the external scrutiny that was ostensibly its whole purpose.

There was, however, a clear rationale to self-validation. By 1991, the courts were demanding validation studies and the data that underpinned them in order to satisfy what some judges ruled were the legal standards of admissibility. Self-validation methods were something that could be passed off as validation without giving many details to defense experts. The net result was clear. "FBI crime lab analysts are now going to court armed with FBI self-validation publications asserting the reliability and validity of FBI research and methodology," one expert concluded.[17] Worse still, so were the hundreds of DNA-typing analysts that the FBI had trained. By 1991, bad science was sweeping through the DNA-typing labs and the courts like a plague.

All this would be highlighted before the year was out. In the case of *United States* v. *Yee* in Ohio, three defense experts, all highly qualified scientists, launched the most concerted challenge yet to the FBI lab's way of doing science. Recruited by Scheck and Neufeld, the three experts managed after much litigation to force the FBI to release the research and experimental data underlying its DNA-matching methodology. In lengthy analytical reports, the experts argued that the FBI's validation research was inadequate and many of the conclusions in several key articles in *Crime Lab Digest* were groundless or wrong. They concluded that the findings the FBI had published could not be replicated and that the bureau's DNA-typing system could seriously affect the sizing of bands and thus make matches unreliable. In sum, pro-prosecution bias had been built into the FBI lab's DNA-typing system.

Dr. Peter D'Eustachio, a defense expert and molecular biologist at New York University, challenged some crucial FBI lab assertions on how DNA typing was unaffected by contamination. The court ordered the release of the base data and Dr. D'Eustachio received two unpublished manuscripts describing a single set of experiments. D'Eustachio concluded there was no scientific basis for the conclusions, claiming that the experiments were "badly designed and poorly executed" with "failed controls, inadequate sizing, failure to assess all probes, and significant misinterpretation or misreporting of key experimental results."[18] When Dr. D'Eustachio sought to obtain the data that formed the basis of a table comparing the measurement of DNA fragments in different samples known to have come from the same person, the FBI could not produce it.

The Bureau confessed that it had not kept adequate scientific records, but it did hand over more recent data of the same type. Yet these data could not replicate the original findings. Dr. D'Eustachio concluded: "This unrepeatable bias means there is no objective, reproducible standard for comparisons of known and questioned DNA specimens."[19] As such, it was perhaps unsurprising that one memo released as part of the discovery process in the *Yee* case showed that in an earlier case in Des Moines, Iowa, the FBI had contemplated destroying DNA proficiency-test data rather than hand it over to defense lawyers.[20] This stuff could be highly embarrassing.

But the comprehensive demolition of the FBI's DNA-typing methodology did not stop there. Dr. Paul Hagerman of the University of Colorado Medical School saw an FBI lab notebook including a protocol used in the study. He became worried about a phenomenon known as "band-shifting" and the consequent problems of interpretation to make a match, arguing that the FBI match criteria, which allowed a 5 percent difference in size between two bands before a match could be declared, was much too broad. It was certainly much broader than that of Lifecodes or Cellmark, the main private DNA labs. The likely result was obvious, Hagerman noted. The match window being used by the FBI was likely to produce an "excessively high rate of inclusions."[21]

Professor Daniel Hartl, a geneticist from Washington University Medical School in St. Louis, agreed, and went even further. He said the 5 percent window "should be scaled down by approximately half" to be consistent with accepted scientific practice. But for Hartl it was one unpublished FBI study that epitomized the inadequacies of the FBI's DNA-typing techniques. Some 225 FBI agent trainees had been typed twice in late 1988 and early 1990 during what seemed to be a quality control study. It was a crucial study. Here there was no question of sampling variation or statistical complications. All the FBI DNA protocol had to prove was that it was sufficiently reliable to identify the same individuals on two different occasions.

It could not. Indeed, the results were extremely alarming. "Unless I had been told that these bands were from the same individuals, I would have been forced to conclude that the sampled individuals were different," Professor Hartl concluded.[22] The results showed that using the FBI's techniques and DNA protocol, 12 percent of the agents did not match themselves on two different occasions just fourteen months apart. "In a research laboratory such quality control would be totally unacceptable, and in a medical diagnostic laboratory it would be criminally negligent," Professor Hartl concluded.[23]

The FBI never managed to refute these criticisms directly, and the magistrate in the Yee case noted "the remarkably poor quality of the FBI's work and infidelity to important scientific principles."[24] He appeared somewhat alarmed at the arrogance of Bruce Budowle, who had appeared in person in Ohio to justify the FBI's DNA-typing methods: "Dr. Budowle did not respond persuasively to Dr. D'Eustachio's criticisms, and he refused to acknowledge the potential significance or merit of a competent scientist's critique and to consider the desirability for further experimentation and confirmation."[25] It was an attitude of mind that was pervasive among senior management at the FBI lab. As John Hicks, the lab's director, had retorted when asked why the FBI did not estimate an error rate in tests. "We think we get them all right."[26]

The number, position, and clarity of DNA bands on an autoradiogram can vary a little depending on the quality of the sample or the testing conditions, all of which made objective matching criteria more essential than ever. In theory, the bands were "scored" by computer-imaging techniques, part of the DNA software the FBI was dispensing. Yet the *Yee* case illustrated how liberally the FBI was scoring its bands, while another case revealed that examiners could override the computer's results when they chose to produce completely subjective matches, by sight alone. In *State* v. *Despain* in Arizona in 1991, a court ordered the FBI to rescore the autorads that had incriminated a defendant by means of the manual override.[27] The results were very different. Had the computer's results been accepted, the FBI would have reported an exclusion rather than a match, according to defense expert Dr. Simon Ford.[28]

Hartl, Hagerman, D'Eustachio, Ford, Thompson, and Lander were all members of a growing band of scientists, geneticists, statisticians, microbiologists, and criminologists who throughout 1990–91 effectively dismantled the credibility of the FBI's RFLP procedures and protocols. The whole experience demonstrated the pitfalls of not following proper scientific procedures by submitting them to critical evaluation. Yet, ironically, these cases also illustrated precisely why the FBI was so reluctant to do so, why it refused to let defense experts oversee tests, why it bitterly contested court orders to hand over data, why it never willingly published its research. The procedures and personnel just would not withstand any real scrutiny. "It's just not science as any other scientist understands it," notes Bill Thompson. "When you show scientists the details they realize what you mean."[29]

With pressure from both Congress and the courts intensifying, the National Research Council (NRC) formed a panel under the chairmanship of Victor McKusick, a geneticist at Johns Hopkins University, to look into the whole mess. Just weeks before it was due to report in April 1992, one aspect of what was now an unholy scientific battle about standards, validation, methods, and statistics burst into flames. Forget about bands and overrides—the FBI's math, critics now claimed, was as bad as its science.

In the fall of 1991, the magazine *Science* accepted for publication an article demolishing the FBI's statistical methodology as "unjustifiable and terribly misleading"[30] Authored by Richard Lewontin, from the Museum of Comparative Zoology at Harvard, and Daniel Hartl, it was based on arguments both had made for defense lawyers in a number of DNA cases, including *Yee*. Lewontin and Hartl argued that the FBI's multiplication method assumed that their population divisions—African Americans, Caucasians, and Hispanics—were homogeneous populations mating randomly—an unsupported and unsupportable assumption.

In reality, Caucasians come from many different countries in Europe, comprising numerous subpopulations. Ditto for African Americans, who come from West Indian, African, and genetic American pools. Hispanics, most of all, are an umbrella ethnic group composed of very diverse subpopulations. All three FBI population divisions, African Americans, Caucasians, and Hispanics, tend to intermarry among each other, making their genes and DNA much more similar than the FBI and other DNA labs were allowing for. Lewontin and Hartl argued against the multiplication method and advocated "ethnic ceilings," in essence using broader based genetic databases from different subpopulations within the major racial groups to estimate random probability-matches in DNA profiling.

The fight about the article's genesis was almost as vicious as that about the facts. Entitled "Population Genetics in Forensic DNA Typing," Hartl and Lewontin's piece appeared with a rebuttal article.[31] *Science* also ran a three-page summary of the controversy, which included a justification sidebar with a quote from one of the rebuttal authors, Kenneth Kidd, a Yale geneticist. "I felt publishing the article would create a very serious problem in the legal system," he claimed. This sidebar article included a curious observation by its author, Leslie Roberts: "Academic scientists were not the only people concerned about the paper. Rumors abound that unnamed people from the FBI said they would make sure the article was killed. John Hicks, director of the FBI's Crime Laboratory, says he heard the rumor, questioned his staff, and could find no evidence for it."[32]

Hicks' disclaimer mattered little. What was clear was the FBI did not want to change its DNA-typing methods or statistical sums and it was prepared to apply enormous pressure on those who advocated that it should. Peter Neufeld would later chronicle some of this protracted campaign against critics in an article appropriately entitled: "Have You No Sense of Decency?" [33] Meanwhile, John Hicks started to insist that the FBI lab was the victim: "This is no [longer] a search for the truth, it is war the way people are behaving," he told *Science*. [34]

Hicks seemed oblivious to his own role in all this. One good example came in April 1992, when a judge in Seattle ordered the draft of the NRC's report released as part of a case in which DNA-typing methods were being challenged. Dated October 15, 1991, "DNA Technology in Forensic Science" did not, among other things, endorse the multiplication technique the FBI was using to arrive at its DNA random probability-match statistics. Indeed, the draft report seemed to take Lewontin and Hartl's side, warning: "Neglecting population substructure plays the same role in genetics textbooks as neglecting friction and air resistance in physics textbooks." [35] Sciencespeak for: It's important.

There was only one problem. The final NRC report, not the draft, released just a few days later, said nothing about multiplication and population substructures. And John Hicks had submitted a lengthy critique of the draft report's population genetics chapter sometime earlier. Victor McKusick, the chairman of the NRC panel, insisted that the changes "came out of the review process not Hicks' letter." [36] McKusick added that as a sponsor, the FBI could not dictate the product, but it was not "inappropriate" for scientists to offer "expert advice." Indeed, the preface to the report thanked Hicks for his assistance. According to Victor McKusick it was just unfortunate that the draft report got such wide distribution. [37]

Just weeks before the final report was due to be issued, news leaked out that the FBI was dispatching researchers on a worldwide hunt for better data on the genetics of ethnic subpopulations, just what Lewontin and Hartl had said was needed. FBI employees set off for Denmark, Spain, France, Italy, Germany, and Britain. Not for the first time, while lambasting critics publicly, the FBI lab had decided to do exactly what they were advising, or to gather the material to do it, anyway. "We want to see if there is any great divergence from the kind of distribution of [DNA] alleles we see in the United States," said FBI lab chief John Hicks. "We've assumed that there isn't." [38] Assumption, anathema to science of course, was the main problem at the FBI lab, where the assumption that lab examiners were always right, that there was no need for validation, that external proficiency was unnecessary ruled.

On April 14, 1992, the DNA controversy made the front page of *The New York Times*. "The new report . . . says courts should cease to admit DNA evidence until laboratory standards have been tightened and the technique has been established on a stronger scientific basis," ran the story. A hastily called press conference chaired by McKusick that same day was followed by a page-one retraction by *The New York Times* the day after. According to the paper's science editor, the original story had not been based on any splits in the panel or disinformation. It was based on "interpretation."

Several law professors had told the newspaper that the panel's call for laboratories to meet "high standards" was "tantamount to saying that DNA evidence should not be admissible at this time." That opinion spoke volumes about the law professors' view of the current standards of the nation's crime labs. It was Neufeld and Scheck's view as well. The fact was that no crime lab performing DNA profiling for forensic purposes in April 1992 met the standards the NRC report was endorsing. Even McKusick admitted that the facts in *The New York Times* article were "basically correct"; it was the "misleading interpretation" he disputed, in particular the assumption that hundreds of cases in which DNA profiling had played a major role in convicting people would have to be reopened.

Such an assumption was perfectly logical as the recommendations of the published report now made clear.[39] The multiplication that produced the huge statistical odds juries were hearing was to be curtailed, although not eliminated, by imposing an "interim ceiling" on such calculations. Noting that the technology was evolving all the time, the committee recommended the creation of a standing National Committee on Forensic DNA Typing. It should be convened under the auspices of a government agency with a scientific, not law enforcement, mandate, the report concluded, recommending the National Institutes of Health or the National Institute of Standards and Technology. The FBI's efforts at self-regulation of DNA typing through TWGDAM did not go far enough, the report stated. Finally, the committee recommended blind external proficiency testing for crime labs doing DNA typing and said the results of such testing should be disclosed to juries so they could assess the likelihood of error.

Even some opponents of the report's recommendations seemed to agree with *The New York Times*'s original interpretation, complaining that the panel had not understood the implications of what they were saying. Yet the NRC report was actually a very balanced document, which in the words of one panel member, Dr. Eric Lander, had sought to ensure the admissibility of DNA evidence by defining "common ground" with a conservative standard that would satisfy the criteria that it was "generally accepted in the scientific community." In other words, it was an effort to ensure DNA evidence got into court, not the reverse, as the FBI and its supporters kept claiming.

The concern of the committee, as it had been of critics from the very beginning, was not the science but its practice and interpretation. "They keep branding us as some sort of Luddites," complains Bill Thompson, who has been at the forefront of the battle throughout. "I think it is simply a reflection of their lack of understanding of science and what its role should be in criminalistics that prevents them from really comprehending what we are saying."[40] That sentiment was underlined by a comment from Dr. Eric Lander on the logic of external proficiency testing for DNA typing: "It is simply crazy and scientifically unacceptable to agonize over the exact population frequencies which might be one in a million, or one in a hundred thousand . . . and yet not have the actual data for the accuracy, the proficiency of a laboratory's handling of samples."[41]

The NRC's report had said what you would expect a scientific body to say; the FBI lab reacted as you might expect a law enforcement agency to react. The report had not endorsed FBI practices on DNA; indeed, some of its recommendations—an advisory committee controlled by another body and blind external proficiency testing—were anathema to the Bureau's lab. The report was a challenge, and any challenge, however merited, well argued, or justified, was to one degree or another a threat. A firestorm of debate erupted as the FBI lab redoubled its efforts to lobby academics and Congress. A broad coalition of prosecutors, scientists, and academics, as well as FBI agents themselves, attacked the report. This was a battle the FBI lab seemed determined to win at almost any cost. If there was to be any consensus, it would be the Bureau's consensus.

And there was a considerable cost, in the short term at least. Before the NRC report was published, California courts had allowed the FBI's DNA-typing statistics to go to juries. Now the state's First District Court of Appeals used the NRC report as the standard, the "common ground." It was as a result of this that the FBI's figures, and thus the Bureau's whole DNA-typing evidence, were ruled inadmissible in the case of Kevin O'Neal Howard in 1992. Eight months later, in early 1993, the same California judge, Ming Chin, wrote another decision, this time bemoaning the continuing DNA-typing dispute. Chin lambasted the critics of the NRC report, saying they should shut up or they would lose the admissibility of DNA-typing evidence altogether.

The battle was being fought in the courts for one simple reason: the absence of any regulatory authority, any referee, in the world of forensic science. By 1994, even Congress thought it was all getting out of hand. The idea of DNA-typing legislation, which had been tabled every year since 1990 as part of larger crime bills, was pushed forward one more time. Once again it looked possible that DNA might become the first area of forensic science to be formally regulated by legislation. It was, but hardly as expected. In fact, the way the legislation was adopted took on an uncanny similarity to the production of the NRC report.

Back in 1990, Congress had proposed legislation that would have placed responsibility for obligatory testing and mandatory standards in the hands of the National Institute for Standards and Technology (NIST), a move the NRC report endorsed in 1992. But in the intervening four years legislators had been submitted to an avalanche of lobbying by the FBI even more overwhelming than that unleashed on the scientific community and the courts. The Bureau had a fair wind. Its prestige and reputation had rarely been higher on Capitol Hill; the perceived threat from crime and domestic terrorism rarely greater.

The FBI was being invited by many representatives to take a more leading role in national law enforcement—and being given the money to do so during the early 1990s. "I talked to a lot of congressional aides on this issue at the time and watched the gradual dilution of the proposed DNA legislation. The fact is, no senator or congressman wants to be seen to be soft on crime. The result is, no one had the balls to stand up to the FBI, even on such an important issue as this," says Professor Bill Thompson.[42] "If you discount a few rapists and murderers I suppose there are no votes in opposing the law enforcement establishment," notes leading forensic scientist, Robert Ogle.[43]

Thus the DNA Identification Act of 1994 made the FBI, the law enforcement organization with the most prominent, unaccredited, and unmonitored crime lab in the country, responsible for training, dispersement of funds, and proficiency testing for DNA typing. The Bureau was authorized to institute a quality assurance, quality control, and, if a study proved it to be feasible, a proficiency testing program that crime labs practicing DNA typing would have to participate in to be eligible for any of the $4.5 million in grants to be allocated each year through 1998 for DNA analysis. An advisory board, appointed by the director of the FBI, would develop and recommend the quality controls and proficiency-testing standards for the director to review and implement.

In the meantime, until the new advisory board reported and the FBI director acted, the quality assurance guidelines adopted by TWGDAM would be the "interim national standards." Four years later those interim standards, the FBI's standards, are still the national standards. As part of the deal, the FBI got the go-ahead to establish and administer a national DNA database, the Combined DNA Index System (CODIS). Even members of the forensic science profession questioned all this. IS THIS THE FOX WATCHING THE HENHOUSE? one headline in a specialist journal asked.[44] As Bill Thompson put it: "Having the FBI Director appoint the DNA Advisory Board is a bit like having the president of the Oscar Meyer Company appoint a board charged with regulating the content of bologna."[45]

What had happened to NIST, recommended in the NRC report and proposed as the regulatory authority in the original legislation? For many of the small but growing band of reformists in forensic science, not to mention other scientists, defense lawyers, and civil libertarians, this was important. NIST was the natural organization to regulate forensic science; monitoring DNA typing could have been the start of a move toward real regulation. "What we ended up with was a legal framework for ensuring a monolithic FBI perspective on the way things must be done. That's very, very dangerous," complains Ed Blake. "It doesn't have the kind of evilness of the Gestapo in Germany in the 1930s, but it's not really any different in intent."[46]

Shortly after the DNA Identification Act was passed another article appeared in *Nature*. It seemed to herald a truce in the DNA war, or perhaps the FBI's victory, for by now the Bureau was, in one author's words, "the genetic equivalent of the only guy left standing after a barroom brawl."[47] The article was jointly authored by Eric Lander, a member of the NRC panel and longtime critic of DNA typing standards, and the FBI's Bruce Budowle, the midwife of the very same standards and methods. "The DNA fingerprinting wars are over," these two principal antagonists declared. In the light of what they termed "extraordinary scrutiny," they said, it seemed "appropriate to ask whether there remains any important unresolved issue about DNA typing."[48]

The article included what seemed to be an extraordinary mea culpa: "DNA typing was marred by several early cases involving poorly defined procedures and interpretation. Standards were lacking for such crucial issues as: declaring a match between patterns; interpreting artifacts on gels; choosing probes; assembling databases; and computing genotype frequencies. There is broad agreement today that many of these early practices were unacceptable, and some indefensible."[49] It was only a few lines further into the article that it became clear that this did not apply to the FBI. These were the faults of a few "biotech start-up companies" with no "track record" in forensic science. Indeed, in contrast, the authors declared: "The US Federal Bureau of Investigation (FBI) moved much more deliberately in developing procedures, sought public comment and opted for conservative procedures."[50]

Such a deflection of blame could be guaranteed to get the DNA war going again, and Lewontin and Hartl did not disappoint. In long letters to *Nature* they both pointed out the reality.[51] Lewontin noted that the reliability of laboratory practices had been dismissed in just two paragraphs. The very idea that DNA lab practices were being overseen by the FBI, an agency that had failed so spectacularly to match the DNA samples of its own 225 agents, was just "ludicrous" he wrote.

Lewontin said the problem of crime lab reliability in DNA typing had been greatly exacerbated by the increased use of PCR technology. Large fresh samples of blood were often examined in the same area as minute samples from the crime scene by the same technician—an argument that Barry Scheck and Dr. John Gerdes would soon make forcefully in the O. J. Simpson trial. The chances of error by mislabeling, mix-ups, or contamination from aerosols, unchanged pipette heads, or similar sloppiness had grown significantly and was "many orders of magnitude greater than the tiny match probabilities calculated for forensic purposes." [52]

———

Hartl and Lewontin were convinced that the public reconciliation between Lander and Budowle just weeks before the start of the O. J. Simpson trial was a deliberate effort to clear the air. The first two paragraphs of the original article seemed to make that clear. The authors said the trial was likely to feature "the most detailed course in molecular genetics ever taught to the U.S. people." What should be cause for celebration was obviously one of deep apprehension for Lander and Budowle. "Already the news weeklies are preparing the ground with warnings that DNA fingerprinting remains 'controversial,' being plagued by major unresolved scientific issues," they noted. [53]

In fact, at this point Budowle, a friend of prosecutor Rockne Harmon, was expected to take the witness stand for the prosecution. He never appeared. Instead, Barry Scheck had to be content with savaging Collin Yamauchi, the LAPD's key DNA technician in the O. J. Simpson case. Like Dennis Fung he was no match for the Brooklyn bombshell. Armed with a photograph showing the test tube containing O. J. Simpson's sample blood covered in stains, Scheck forced Yamauchi to admit to the kind of contamination threat that Lewontin had outlined in his letter to *Nature:* he had spilled some of O. J. Simpson's blood onto his lab gloves when he opened the reference sample. This could account for the missing blood. It also raised the prospect of contamination of all the other samples.

Although Yamauchi insisted he had changed his gloves, the fact that he had not recalled the blood spill in preliminary testimony left plenty of room for doubt. By reconstructing each step of his tests, Scheck was able to show that the quantity of DNA consistent with that in O. J. Simpson's blood in the swatches collected from the crime scene declined in the order in which Yamauchi handled them. Tracking contamination through the evidence? And the leather glove found at Nicole's condominium which Yamauchi had handled first and cut small rectangular samples from: might it not have been contaminated from the stains on the reference tube? It was an intriguing prospect. The DNA allele matching Simpson's was only found in samples from the wrist leather where Yamauchi had written his initials to signal who had made the sample cuts.

Yamauchi's testimony contrasted sharply with that of Gary Sims, the DNA analyst at the California Department of Justice lab in Berkeley. That too was part of Scheck's strategy. If the source of contamination was the LAPD, procedures there needed to be shown in the context of what should and could happen in a DNA lab. So Sims answered countless questions about procedures, safeguards against contamination, and how blood was handled at the Berkeley lab. However, Scheck pounced when he came to planting evidence, in this case on the famous pair of dark dress socks found in O. J. Simpson's bedroom.

Dennis Fung had seen no blood on the socks when he bagged them as evidence on June 13; LAPD lab supervisor Michele Kestler, and defense experts Michael Baden and Barbara Wolf, had seen no blood on them when they examined them on June 22; no one had seen blood on them when they were examined as part of an inventory of evidence on June 29. Then somehow on August 4, a large stain, nearly an inch in diameter, appeared, providing enough DNA for a definitive RFLP test. As Barry Scheck showed the sock to the jury, no one had any problem noticing the bloodstain.

Dr. Lee and Professor Herbert MacDonnell, the defense's blood-splatter expert, concluded that the bloodstain had been pressed into the sock while it was lying flat—it was a "compression transfer." The blood had soaked through the outside of one side of the sock and left a wet transfer on both inside surfaces. Had the blood splashed onto the sock while O. J. Simpson had been wearing it, his lower leg would have blocked any such transfer. In a desperate effort to counteract the now strong possibility that evidence had been planted, samples of blood from the sock and the condominium gate were sent to the FBI lab in Washington. The control samples of Nicole Brown's and O. J. Simpson's blood would have had the preservative EDTA (ethylenediaminetetraacetic acid) in them. Would the stains?

The FBI's answer came in the form of charts that were confusing and vague. There was some EDTA. Bob Blasier, the lawyer handling the EDTA issue, visited the FBI lab and talked to Roger Martz, the head of the Chemistry and Toxicology Unit, who had handled the tests. Blasier sent the results to Dr. Frederic Rieders, a top toxicologist. Spikes on the FBI data charts clearly showed the presence of EDTA, but not much, single-digit parts per million. The significance of this was questionable:

Most people's blood is believed to contain a residue of EDTA from the chemicals used in food preservatives.

The problem for the defense was that definitive results—results that showed comparable levels of EDTA in the blood in the reference tube with the bloodstains on the sock and the back gate at Nicole's condominium in Bundy—were impossible. The tests for EDTA were new, so new in fact that Roger Martz had actually devised them himself. Moreover, in the case of the stain on the gate, the EDTA had bonded chemically with the metal, reducing the amount that could be traced. Dr. Rieders did however tell the court the one thing the defense needed him to say. In his opinion, based on the FBI lab's test results, there was EDTA in both the bloodstains that had been found after the other evidence.

Roger Martz was called as a witness for the defense on July 25. Relaxed and self-assured as usual, he claimed he had not positively identified EDTA but admitted the test results were consistent with EDTA. It all hinged on the interpretation of the results. Both Martz and Rieders agreed that the liquid chromatography–mass spectrometer tests gave peaks on the charts that showed the presence of 293 and 160 ions, two components of EDTA; they disagreed on whether another peak demonstrated the presence of a 132 ion, the third constituent needed to show that EDTA was present.

After lunch on the first day of his testimony, Martz was much more aggressive and emphatic; the defense eventually had him declared a hostile witness. During the lunch break Martz had called Washington and spoken to someone in the research unit in Quantico, where Budowle worked.[54] When Blasier asked him about his change of demeanor, Martz responded with the telling comment: "I think I decided I had to be more truthful. I was not telling the whole truth with yes and no answers. . . . I decided that I wanted to tell the whole truth."[55]

As Bob Blasier began a series of questions about the raw data, it became clear it no longer existed. Martz had erased it after he had finished testing. "We only have so much computer space," he complained.[56] The admission allowed the defense to suggest more dubious practices. As part of his testing, Martz had analyzed his own blood but made no notes and prepared no report, even though this was to be part of his evidence in court. Martz claimed this was research, not case work, and thus did not count. However, the IG's report found once again that it was just symptomatic of all Martz's records on the case: notes were not numbered and initialed, the case number was unidentified in some, and procedures went unexplained in others.

Martz became steadily more flustered on the stand. This was one of the most experienced expert witnesses the FBI lab could offer, yet Martz was "unprepared, ill-at-ease and defensive—characteristics that undermined his effectiveness as a witness" according to the IG's report.[57] It was clear that Martz could not match the toxicology expertise of Dr. Rieders. "Martz's poor preparation, his lack of a toxicology background and his maladroitness as a witness were evident when he misstated the value for pi, admitted that he was unfamiliar with the word 'pharmacokinetics,' commented about the need to tell the 'whole truth,' and appeared to boast that he was the foremost expert in EDTA testing."[58]

By the time Roger Martz made it to the witness stand, the final blow to the DNA evidence had already been delivered. On June 22, the prosecution brought one of the key protagonists in the DNA numbers war to the stand. Dr. Bruce Weir, a professor of statistics and genetics at North Carolina University, was a key "pro-admissibility," anticeiling man, who advocated and used the FBI's method. Putting Weir in front of the jury allowed the whole issue of statistics to be aired. Worse still for the prosecution, the O. J. Simpson case now became the first trial in which a serious debate took place about the probabilities of matches in samples involving mixtures of blood, a new twist that multiplied the disagreements between the two sides in the numbers war.

The mixed blood samples from inside O. J. Simpson's Bronco, particularly those containing Ron Goldman's blood, were among the most incriminating evidence against Simpson. But there was a problem. In the PCR test being used by the prosecution, one of the alleles found in Ron Goldman's blood tended to mask one of the alleles found in O. J. Simpson's blood when the two were mixed. "You can infer that this allele, the 1.2, is there when dealing with blood from a single person but not when it's mixed," explains Bill Thompson. "Weir assumed it was, something he admitted in court."[59]

Peter Neufeld was merciless in cross-examination. "The numbers on that board are biased against Mr. Simpson, isn't that correct?" he insisted. "As it turns out, it looks that way, yes," Weir replied.[60] It illustrated the difficulty of a statistician dealing with figures derived from molecular genetics. A recalculation by Weir reduced a 1 in 3,900 probability that a stain on the Bronco's steering wheel contained a mixture of Ron Goldman's and O. J. Simpson's blood to a 1 in 1,600 chance. It was another turning point in the trial. If the results had been proven wrong once, were they worth considering at all?

With cross-examinations like those of Fung, Yamauchi, and Weir, Barry Scheck, Peter Neufeld, and Bob Blasier had, among them, virtually demolished the prosecution's forensic case before calling a single witness of their own. The prosecution wound up with key elements of the defense's case unrebutted. The missing blood, the sock, the famous glove that did not fit—all served to make the defense's theory of contamination and framing at least possible. Many of the prosecution witnesses had undone themselves, a combination of sloppiness, overconfidence, and brinkmanship brought on perhaps by the sheer quantity of evidence they had against O. J. Simpson. But in the end it was forensic science's DNA typing that was put on trial and found wanting.

The witness who did most of the job for the defense was Dr. John Gerdes, a microbiologist from Denver. Gerdes looked the part of a scientist; solid and bespectacled, he was a medical lab director inclined to apply the standards of the rigorous government regulation of the Clinical Laboratories Inspection Act to forensic labs. As such he was the perfect candidate to set about a thorough study of the LAPD lab. He was also the perfect candidate to impress the jury. His solid image was reinforced by a dramatic style of delivery.

Reviewing test materials covering fifteen months of examinations from May 1993 to August 1994, Gerdes concluded that the LAPD lab had a contamination problem that was "persistent and substantial . . . month after month." He rammed home his point by saying a responsible oversight agency "would shut the lab down."[61] That statement served to make the key point: There was no oversight agency; the FBI had persistently blocked the establishment of one for DNA testing. The lack of external proficiency testing was just one of a number of areas in which John Gerdes and Barry Scheck, questioning him on direct, were able to use the National Research Council (NRC) report to nail the LAPD lab, forensic science, and the prosecution—all at the same time.

More than three years after the NRC report had recommended blind external proficiency testing for DNA-typing labs, no such testing was being done, due in large part to the FBI's opposition. Indeed, just weeks before Gerdes took the stand in Los Angeles, a representative of the National Institute of Justice (NIJ), charged by Congress under the 1994 DNA Identification Act with examining the possibility of establishing a testing program, reported that the NIJ was leaning toward the conclusion that it was not feasible.[62]

Using the NRC report's dire warnings about the possibility of contamination and errors "even in the best laboratories when the analyst is sure every precaution has been taken," Gerdes reviewed more than a thousand examples of PCR typing done by the LAPD lab. Gerdes said he found five typing errors in these tests and numerous examples of contamination. Displaying sample test strips on the overhead projector in the courtroom, he pointed out several faint dots among the dark dots identifying specific allele. Seeking to make the connection to the O. J. Simpson case, Scheck then put a set of Cellmark PCR test strips up in court. They showed the same faded dots. Gerdes concluded that the faded dots suggested alien genes in the sample. The LAPD lab had either mixed O. J. Simpson's blood with Ron Goldman's and Nicole Brown Simpson's or Cellmark had somehow introduced "contaminants and artifacts."

———

As Gerdes finished testifying, a major fight about Martz's performance in Los Angeles was erupting back in Washington. After hearing Martz's testimony, Bruce Budowle was furious and complained to training center chief Kenneth Nimmich that Martz had not credited Budowle's research team with developing and validating the EDTA testing procedures. Actually, the research unit and Martz had worked on devising the EDTA tests separately but contemporaneously. However, when asked who had validated the test, Martz had chosen to articulate the FBI lab's self-validation thesis on DNA rather than mention the center's work. "The test validates itself basically," he had told Bob Blasier.

Budowle's cry of "foul" meant that for once it was not just Whitehurst making the complaints about Martz's credibility, although it was only Whitehurst's reporting of what he says he heard of the matter that led the IG's office to investigate the whole affair. Ken Nimmich sent a memo to lab director Milton Ahlerich on August 30, 1995, passing on Bruce Budowle's complaints and recommending an oral reprimand. The memo cited two reasons: Martz's failure to credit the research unit's role in passing on data and performing the validation study, a matter about which he had been "less than candid," and his failure to keep notes.[63]

On the latter point, the memo quoted the FBI's *Manual of Administrative Operations and Procedures:* "An Agent's notes of a precise character, made to record his/her own findings must always be retained. Such notes include but are not limited to accounts, work papers, notes covering such matters as crime scene searches, laboratory examinations, fingerprint examinations. If a doubtful situation arises, resolve the question in favor of keeping notes."[64] It was a curious effort to apply the norms of the FBI in record keeping and note taking to the lab, which for years had studiously ignored them.

Martz refuted these specific complaints in two memos to Ken Nimmich. In his reply, Nimmich accepted all of Martz's points; indeed, he seemed to bend over backward to justify his acceptance.[65] Martz had not erased digital data improperly. All pertinent data had been printed out and it was not practical to save it all. Nimmich further agreed that by the end of his testimony Martz had acknowledged the role of the research unit. A memo to Milton Ahlerich dated September 18 emphasizes that the phrase "less than candid" had been used to imply a posture of enhanced self-importance rather than a misstatement of factual data. Milton Ahlerich memoed back immediately to Scientific Analysis Section chief Randall Murch, saying that he viewed it as a performance issue, not misconduct. Murch agreed with his boss. Martz was "counseled" about lack of precision when testifying and the need to give credit to others.

What was going on here? The bald facts are stated in the IG's report, but as so often there is no context or interpretation. It is difficult to avoid the conclusion that Ken Nimmich's sudden change of heart and the paperwork that articulates it were, as O. J. Simpson's defense lawyer Bob Blasier described them to Judge Ito, "Let's circle the wagons" memos.[66] By September 1995 the real enemy—Whitehurst—was back. Just as the issue of Martz's testimony arose, Whitehurst's allegations about the FBI lab suddenly went mainstream on the back of his testimony in the second World Trade Center bombing trial and the nation's obsession with the O. J. Simpson trial.

The appearance of Whitehurst and his lawyer, Stephen Kohn, on ABC's *PrimeTime Live* on September 13 included comments on memos containing complaints Whitehurst had made about Martz and others.

Johnnie Cochran quickly announced that he was going to ask Judge Ito for permission to recall Roger Martz, and to call Fred Whitehurst as a witness. Whitehurst's allegations were a perfect fit for the dream team's defense case. Here apparently was more suspicious law enforcement behavior to graft onto that of the LAPD. Whitehurst, Budowle, and three colleagues were essentially alleging that Martz was not credible, on the stand and in the lab.

Thus by mid-September the FBI lab's senior management faced the very real prospect of one of their own, Roger Martz, being recalled to the stand to answer questions about his prior testimony, why he may not have told "the whole truth" the first time around. Aside from casting obvious aspersions on the rest of his testimony about EDTA, this nightmare scenario would have included the prospect of Whitehurst being called to state that Martz's testimony was, in his opinion, part of a pattern. Whitehurst certainly had plenty of other credible examples. It was bad enough that Martz had testified while under continued internal investigation on serious charges—Whitehurst's charges. But worse, the original memos from Budowle and Nimmich indicated that others were backing Whitehurst's charges about Martz's credibility, albeit in a different case. By mid-September, Bob Blasier and the O. J. Simpson defense team had copies of these original memos.

This was explosive stuff. Martz was not only head of the Chemistry and Toxicology Unit at the time he testified in the Simpson trial, but he was acting head of the seven-unit Scientific Analysis Section, a very senior position supervising scores of staff. The wagons did indeed have to be circled. Damage limitation and plausible deniability were the order of the day. Memos were written, including the one from Nimmich to Ahlerich accepting all Martz's responses and Ahlerich's reply about it all being a performance matter. These memos, both dated September 18, arrived on the defense team's desk in Los Angeles within hours of being written, on September 19, the day Judge Ito conducted his hearing on whether Whitehurst and Martz should testify. There were no discovery delays on this matter.

After two subpoenas, Fred Whitehurst was deposed in Los Angeles at the same time as the Department of Justice began to pour more oil on the bonfire of the FBI lab's credibility. The IG's office announced on September 18 that it was launching a major inquiry into Whitehurst's allegations about the FBI lab. External forensic scientists, including three foreigners, would advise the investigators, a Department of Justice press release announced. Coming just days after the FBI had faxed ABC television with a statement saying it had investigated all of Whitehurst's charges and decided they were unfounded, the implications were clear: even the Department of Justice thought the FBI's internal investigation had been a whitewash.

On September 20, Judge Ito ruled that neither Martz nor Whitehurst would be allowed to testify. Ito must have had at least one eye on the widespread criticism of him for letting the trial drag on for nearly eight months and his own promises to the jury to wind up the trial. Whitehurst's testimony about the FBI crime lab would only "aggravate and confuse" the jury, Ito ruled. "The issue of whether Martz was qualified to conduct explosives and bomb residue testing in other cases has no direct bearing upon the [blood preservative] testing in this case," he wrote.

The same day, Fred Whitehurst and Stephen Kohn held a news conference in the Criminal Courts Building in Los Angeles. Whitehurst defended his criticism of the FBI lab and commended the Justice Department's decision to launch its inquiry. The person Johnnie Cochran had portrayed to the press as a "mystery witness" was a mystery no more. However, what he would have said on the witness stand freed from the FBI's gag order that prevented him from talking in any detail outside the courtroom remained a mystery. With Kohn having to act as his mouthpiece in response to a number of questions, the press became more curious than they might have been had he actually testified. From now on, the FBI lab was a story on the national news agenda.

In the end, the DNA and blood evidence only came up once in the jury's short deliberation in the O. J. Simpson trial, a measure perhaps of how effectively the defense had neutralized the bulk of the evidence. Two jurors said unsurprisingly that they did not think it was reliable; the not guilty verdict followed. Nothing would change as a result. There would be no concerted efforts to improve crime lab standards; no seismic shock in the DNA-typing world. In fact, the FBI lab was about to secure a further dilution of standards. As early as April 1993, seeking to dispense with the National Research Council (NRC) report's annoying recommendations, in particular the interim ceiling principle for statistical probability calculations, FBI director William Sessions had written to Dr. Frank Press, president of the National Academy of Sciences. Just one year after the NRC report had been published, Sessions requested a new study.

The logic was amazing. Since the release of the NRC's first report, appellate courts had ruled DNA evidence inadmissible in eleven out of thirty cases; the ceiling principle had "created a climate of confusion for the courts."[67] It was a "crisis," Sessions argued, urging the NRC to "act quickly to resolve the controversy." Once again the bureau would help fund an NRC study; once again the FBI sought to define the parameters. In May 1993, John Hicks threatened to withhold money if the study was not limited to the statistical issue.[68] The advent of PCR testing by now had made the FBI's DNA-typing techniques even more controversial; further scrutiny would be far too risky.

As critics feared, NRC II, as it became known on publication in May 1996, gave the FBI everything it wanted.[69] Citing no evidence or systematic review, the report declared that the technical quality of DNA testing had improved since 1992. On this assumption, NRC II abandoned NRC I's recommendation for external scrutiny. TWGDAM's self-regulatory, FBI-sponsored guidelines, which NRC I had said did not go far enough, were now to be the standard. The report simply called for forensic labs doing DNA typing to "adhere to high quality standards" and "make every effort to be accredited for DNA work."[70] Blind proficiency testing was ruled out. It would impose "formidable" logistical demands on the system, the report concluded.

On subjective interpretation of results and bias, NRC II was even vaguer. The report offered a protocol that it said "should greatly reduce such bias, if it exists." Analysts were told that they should document potential ambiguities, despite the fact that the main problem was getting DNA-typing staff to recognize such ambiguities in the first place. However, NRC II's protocol did insist that visual overrides of the computer-assisted imaging software used for comparisons and measurements of DNA-typing autoradiograms "be noted and explained."

The report's main proposal for dealing with potential error, contamination, or subjective matches was to set aside a portion of samples to allow a defendant to retest. It was an important new principle that might yet have set a precedent for all forensic samples. The problem was that it was probably least practicable in DNA typing. Samples, particularly for the most controversial PCR tests, were often too small for more than one test and very few defendants can afford the price of an independent DNA test anyway.[71] For all but the likes of O. J. Simpson, DNA typing really was the prosecution tool the FBI and their supporters wanted it to be.

What the NRC II report proved is that if you ask the questions you want, you get the answers you want, an old scientific given that both the peer-review process and the validation principle are designed to guard against. Like Roger Martz in the O. J. Simpson case not looking for EDTA, or the FBI lab generally, not looking for bias or errors in its work product, the NRC panel's starting point was that of the FBI: how to insure the admissibility of DNA evidence. The question was, How do we solve this problem, not How do we improve and rebuild confidence in forensic DNA testing. The resulting report was based on weak analysis, unsubstantiated conclusions, and vague assumptions. It would, ironically, have failed the most basic scientific peer review.

The DNA units were the single most important omission of the IG's investigation into the FBI lab. Records of interviews done by the IG released under the Freedom of Information Act make it clear that the concerns raised externally by FBI critics were echoed by several FBI employees as well. One was DNA examiner Greg Parsons, who has a Ph.D. in organic chemistry and said he was transferred out of the FBI's DNA unit primarily because "he could not resolve questions he had regarding DNA analysis," in particular the issue of band-shifting on auto-radiograms.[72] Parsons stated that, according to the scientific literature recognized by the FBI, band-shifted results could not be interpreted as a match. Yet the FBI did just that.

Parsons also reported on a possible incident of suppressed evidence and related how in April–May 1989 all DNA/serology examiners at the FBI lab, bar one, had failed an open proficiency test.[73] He said that the test results had been destroyed, in his presence, because it was feared they were discoverable. The test was readministered and all the examiners passed.[74] In a separate interview with the IG, Al Robillard, the unit chief at the time, admitted ordering the destruction of the tests but argued that it "was set up wrong or had some sort of flaw," although he could not recall what the fault was.[75] Robillard admitted that there had been a debate in the lab, saying that someone (name redacted, presumably Parsons) had said that "he could not go out and testify about the DNA testing and results obtained by the lab" and that he "bought into" many of the issues being raised by defense attorneys.[76]

With the release of NRC II in May 1996, it became clear that the FBI had triumphed on DNA, despite the questions raised even by FBI staff such as Parsons. The DNA-typing revolt—a concerted push for scientific standards and some form of accountability—had been crushed. In the process, the FBI lab had reinforced its grip on crime labs in the United States. But those who had fought the FBI lab through the courts had not done so completely in vain. They had exposed it, although that went almost unnoticed outside their own limited legal or scientific circles. The lab meanwhile had been forced to make some changes in practices and procedures, if only to avoid further embarrassments in the courts.

There were two ironies in this, however. First, the FBI lab remained so closed, so closeted, so unexposed to external scrutiny that no one could be sure what had changed and what had not. The next case, the next challenge, the next batch of discovery documents was the only way of finding out what impact the last case, the last challenge, might have had. Second, it was clear that the FBI lab only made the changes it absolutely had to, invariably the result of legal rather than scientific advice. The preferred policy has always been to deal with the symptoms rather than the causes. In the FBI's strange, incestuous world, the critic, not the criticism, remained the issue, whether it was Whitehurst, Parsons, or the lawyers and scientists who took the lab and its management on over DNA typing.

8

HAIRS AND FIBERS: HANGING BY A THREAD

At the very end of the inspector general's report on the FBI lab is a curious twenty-nine-page section entitled "Tobin Allegations." Even a cursory look belies the contention that Fred Whitehurst was the only employee to make persistent, serious complaints about the FBI lab. William Tobin, the FBI's only qualified metallurgist, is of the same professional mold as Whitehurst, a scientist and a fellow of the American Association of Forensic Sciences. For some time Tobin had been complaining to superiors about practices and personnel, particularly in the Explosives Unit (EU). Their spurious science and behavior amounted to "forensic prostitution," he told the IG's investigators.[1]

One of Tobin's most serious allegations was against Michael Malone, an imposing six-foot-three-inch examiner in the Hairs and Fibers Unit who served twenty years as a microscopy analyst before leaving the lab in 1994 as part of Louis Freeh's efforts to get more agents back onto the streets. In July 1989, Bill Tobin had reviewed a transcript of Michael Malone's sworn testimony to an investigating committee of five judges from the Eleventh Judicial Circuit in Atlanta. The judges were looking

271

into an allegation of bribery against U.S. District judge Alcee Hastings, a federal judge for the Southern District of Florida.

The inquiry dated back to the trial of Frank and Thomas Romano, who were convicted in Miami in December 1980 of racketeering at a trial presided over by Judge Hastings. In May 1981, Judge Hastings ordered the forfeiture of $1.2 million of the Romanos' property, and in July 1981 he sentenced each of the brothers to a three-year prison term. However, that same month William Dredge told federal prosecutors that he had been directed by William Borders, a former president of the National Bar Association and a longtime friend of Hastings, to solicit a one-hundred-and-fifty-thousand-dollar bribe from the Romanos in exchange for reducing their sentences to probation.

An elaborate sting operation followed, with Paul Rico, a retired FBI agent posing as Frank Romano, receiving twenty-five thousand dollars in up-front money from Borders in September and Judge Hastings issuing an order partly reversing his original $1.2-million forfeiture order in October. Borders was arrested when he picked up the outstanding one hundred and twenty-five thousand dollars from Rico at a Washington, D.C., hotel three weeks later. He was convicted of bribery, conspiracy, and obstruction of justice in March 1982. Hastings was tried in Miami in January 1983 and was acquitted the following month, having claimed that he did not participate in the bribery scheme and had been taken advantage of by Borders.

But with two district judges filing a complaint against Hastings for his conduct in the case, an investigating committee of five judges was established. A three-year inquiry began with the judges hearing testimony from over one hundred witnesses and studying twenty-eight hundred exhibits. On October 2, 1985, Michael Malone testified that he had done a tensile test on the strap of a leather purse that Hastings claimed he was having repaired at the time he was supposed to be collecting the bribe. Despite being cleared by the Miami jury, Congress would eventually impeach Hastings and remove him from the bench. It was in preparation for these congressional hearings that Tobin came to review Malone's testimony in July 1989.

In a six-page memo to then Scientific Analysis Section chief Ken Nimmich, Bill Tobin analyzed Malone's testimony line-by-line and made twenty-seven specific complaints. Malone was guilty of numerous "false statements," "contrived, fabricated responses," and views that Tobin variously described as "not true," "inaccurate and deceptive," "completely fabricated," and "unfounded and not supported by data."[2] The most glaring alleged lie was that Malone had stated that he had actually done the tensile test on the strap himself; testifying about the highly specialized field of what is known as material strain or deformation—stress applications and failure assessment—as a result.

In a two-page assessment entitled "Effect of Testimony," Tobin wrote that overall what Malone had said to the judges' investigating committee represented "a glaring pattern of conversion of what should have been presented as neutral data into incriminating circumstances by complete reversal of established laboratory test data with scientifically unfounded, unqualified and biased testimony." He continued: "The transcript reveals a pattern of complete omission of crucial conditions, caveats, premises and/or assumptions which may be viewed as tending towards exculpatory in nature."[3]

The similarity of this mid-1989 memo to the line-by-line analyses that Fred Whitehurst would soon start writing is striking. The response of the FBI lab's management was also remarkably similar. Nimmich did nothing; indeed, the FBI lost Tobin's memo and was unable to provide a copy to the IG's investigators.[4] No one beyond Nimmich and Tobin's boss, Materials Analysis Unit chief Roger Aaron, heard of the allegations, not even Alan Robillard, Malone's section chief. Aaron agreed with Tobin, writing in hand on the copy of the memo he received, "Sad to say, you are right on every point. This has to be done."[5] The inaction mystified the IG. "We cannot understand the Laboratory's failure to further investigate the allegations that Tobin made regarding Malone's testimony," the report notes plaintively.[6]

One obvious explanation was the sheer seriousness of the perjury allegations and the importance of the Hastings case. Nimmich himself was clearly aware of the potential ramifications. In November 1990, as Whitehurst was about to be suspended for contacting the defense in the *Psinakis* case (see Chapter 1), Nimmich held a meeting with both Whitehurst and John Hicks, the laboratory's chief. Knowing Whitehurst was facing disciplinary proceedings, Tobin had told him of his complaints about Malone. Whitehurst mentioned them in the meeting on November 2. In his calendar for November 2, 1990, provided to the IG's investigators, Nimmich had noted: "Tobin story re Malone perjury."[7]

The FBI, on seeing the draft version of the IG report, denied that Malone's testimony could even be classified as false, arguing that it was not intentionally deceptive. The IG disagreed, replying that it used the word "false" as it was employed in other legal contexts, "to describe something that is untrue or not in accord with the facts."[8] Intent was once again something the IG never really dealt with, although the effect, as Tobin made clear, was to make "the evidence" many times more incriminating. Even though lab chief John Hicks knew of the charges by November 1990, if not before, Bill Tobin did not show Whitehurst's persistence, and the whole matter died until the IG's inquiry presented the opportunity to reopen the complaint.

Most of those the IG interviewed about the matter had never even heard of Tobin's complaints. They included Daniel Dzwilewski, who coordinated the appearance of FBI witnesses in the congressional impeachment proceedings; Representative John Conyers, who headed the subcommittee that recommended Judge Hastings's removal; and Alcee Hastings himself, now elected to Congress, whose first inkling of Bill Tobin's complaints came from the press in January 1997. Everyone involved in the Hastings incident was distinctly nervous about the IG's findings. The facts demonstrated that clearly exculpatory evidence was available before Congress voted for impeachment. This evidence—Tobin's memo—had been suppressed and "lost."

This was not an ordinary criminal, "a terrorist or a mad bomber," as Senator Charles Grassley put it speaking from the Senate floor in mid-1997. This was a "sitting federal judge." Moreover, this was the first time the Senate had ever voted to impeach someone acquitted by a jury on the same charge, an impeachment that to many seemed to overturn the sanctity of a jury decision. And to cap it all there were heavy racial overtones. Alcee Hastings is African American, Florida's first black federal judge. Throughout the 1980s, the bureau had been accused of all kinds of racial discrimination, not least by its own employees. In sum, this case was different. It might embarrass Congress as well as the bureau.

Hastings had always protested his innocence, contending that he had been targeted by overzealous prosecutors. The case certainly had all the hallmarks of a grudge match on the part of the FBI. It was the bureau, led by case agent William Murphy, that had managed to get a conviction against Alcee Hastings's alleged coconspirator, William Borders, but had failed to get one against the federal judge. Some thought that Hastings, defending himself, had embarrassed the bureau at his trial in Miami in 1983. Cross-examining Murphy with all the passion and persuasion of the oratory he had honed as a civil rights leader, Hastings posed thirty-two unanswered questions about the holes in the FBI's circumstantial case, while presenting a detailed alibi. "He had an axe to grind because I literally kicked his ass," Hastings insisted of Murphy. "He [Malone] was told to do it."[9]

Representative John Conyers announced in June 1997 that he was considering reopening the case in the light of the new evidence. He had an "unsettling feeling" about possible evidence-tampering and misman-agement at the FBI lab, he told FBI director Louis Freeh, who appeared before Conyers's subcommittee that month. Freeh agreed. "If I, as a judge or FBI director, found any evidence of those matters, then absolutely I would," he replied.[10]

Inspector General Michael Bromwich, while insisting that Malone had not committed perjury, told another congressional subcommittee that he considered it "very substantial misconduct." He added that the Justice Department was investigating whether criminal charges should be pressed against Malone. But if it was not classified as perjury, there seemed little chance of charges even being filed. Hastings himself was incredulous: "He raised his hand and swore he would tell the truth and he told a lie. I don't know how the Inspector General can fail to get perjury out of that."[11]

But, if that was true, what was Malone's intent in testifying falsely? According to the IG there was no perjury if there was no intent. According to Senator Chuck Grassley, one obvious way of determining intent is to investigate other cases worked on by individual examiners to establish whether there is a pattern. And with Michael Malone, there certainly was. In case after case, from Florida to Alaska, Michael Malone was, in Senator Grassley's words, prepared to "provide testimony on hair and fiber that no one else would."[12]

As such, Michael Malone was in great demand among prosecutors and was regarded with deep skepticism by many of his forensic colleagues. "He tended to overstate evidence," said Professor Peter DeForest, a New

York–based hairs-and-fibers expert who has appeared in court with Malone.[13] "You just cannot draw these conclusions from hair and fiber comparisons," says Professor James Starrs, leafing through a ream of cases littered with Malone's references to perfect matches and positive identifications.[14] "Fraudulent," stated Ed Blake of Forensic Science Associates of Richmond, California, of Malone's claims of certainty.[15]

The key to Malone's prosecutorial success was projecting a degree of near certainty in a highly subjective field, the comparison of two hairs or fibers, and it often happened in difficult cases where there was little else to go on. In such cases, he could tip the scales of justice, for these were cases in which Michael Malone and hair and fiber analysis seemed made for each other. The variation, the subjectivity, the absence of standards or rules in the field and the relative paucity of challenges in court, all meant that hair and fiber analysis was ripe for abuse.

Hairs and fibers identification is the main activity of what used to be called the Microscopic Analysis Unit, which then became the Hairs and Fibers Unit and has now been renamed the Trace Evidence Unit. Its last name is the best description of what it does as a catch-all unit for the examination of trace evidence. As Malone himself put it: "If you have to use a microscope to look at something, we're probably going to get it."[16] The principle on which the unit works is what is known as Locard's Exchange Principle, after Frenchman Edmond Locard, one of the founding fathers of forensic science and the author of its most basic principle: every contact leaves a trace. The theory states that when a person comes into contact with another person or place, a cross-transfer of potential evidence takes place: soil, hair, fiber, dust, dirt, debris, whatever, will be left or carried away. Often invisible to the naked eye, this is trace evidence. Such trace evidence is shed easily, so the trace evidence found on an individual will reflect his or her most recent contact or surrounding.

The search for hairs and fibers begins when articles such as clothing are sent to a scraping room, where a technician hangs it on an adjustable rack over a white sheet of paper before scraping it down, inside and out, with a metal spatula. Hairs and fibers found are mounted on slides for alignment with a variety of control samples taken from a victim or the carpet, clothing, or textile in question. Only pubic or head hairs are suitable for comparison, and even the latter can vary on the same person's head. As a result, examiners like to take up to twenty samples from four or five different locations on the scalp, if only to assess the degree of variation in an individual and thus the possibility of a positive comparison.

An unknown hair or fiber is examined first under a low-power stereoscope, magnifying it up to eighty times. By looking at the three major regions of a hair—the root if it was forcibly removed or unnaturally shed, the shaft, and the tip—an examiner can quickly determine if it is human and draw some conclusions as to the race of the individual. With fibers, characteristics such as color, diameter, and texture allows an examiner to determine whether it is natural or manufactured, before identification may be narrowed down further when it is compared to known samples or sample databases. Cotton samples, particularly white, are almost useless since they are so common; the rarer synthetic fibers are the most helpful.

Placing the hair under a high-powered light scope allows an examiner to look inside the hair shaft itself and examine its three layers—the cuticle, the cortex, and the medulla—for the individual characteristics that form the basis of hair identification in a crime lab. Finally, the known and unknown hairs or fibers are placed side by side under a comparison microscope—two compound microscopes magnifying up to four hundred times and bridged together with an eyepiece that allows an examiner to look at both samples simultaneously. The only other instrument used in hair and fiber examination is a microspectrophotometer, a color register for the dyes used in fibers. Beyond that it is all done by eye.

There are no minimum rules in making a match, no guidelines laid down by any national association, and certainly no standards laid down by the courts. No one disputes that hair comparisons can exclude suspects, and few would dispute that they can link suspects with a crime or crime scene. Some people's hair shows real distinguishing features under a microscope; however, most people's does not. Some people's hair varies widely at different locations on their scalp; other people's hair does not. It can be useful corroborating evidence, the value of the use depending on the individual's hair characteristics and the other evidence in the case. But, in essence, the field does not lend itself to science or even semantics.

The terms "match," "identical," "indistinguishable" are personal definitions and interpretations of these words vary from examiner to examiner for the simple reason that the starting point has never been agreed upon. Some examiners insist on an exact match at every point on the hair, from root to tip, while others, citing the variation in a head of hair, seem content with matches in much broader terms, color, structure, cuticle. Some examiners, such as Michael Malone, claim coincidental matches are so rare that they can be discounted; others insist that whatever your definition of a match, two hairs from different sources are often indistinguishable. Some hair-and-fiber examiners cite random match-probability figures as in DNA tests; most insist that such statistical estimates are impossible.

Ask two examiners, even two FBI examiners, what defines a match and you will get radically different answers. "When I am asked on the witness stand how many characteristics matched, my answer has to be, 'All of them,' " FBI hair-and-fiber examiner Wayne Oakes has explained. "People have tried to quantitate this for a long time, but no one has been able to figure out how to do it."[17] Michael Malone does quantify it—to his own satisfaction at least: "If you can't find at least fifteen identifiable characteristics then it's not unique enough to be of value for comparisons. For me, I always looked for twenty characteristics to match."[18]

But what are these characteristics? Even on this there is no agreement. In the mid-1980s, as part of an effort to get some consensus on the whole issue and deflect growing criticism, a Committee on Forensic Hair Comparison met periodically for discussions at the Forensic Science Research and Training Center at the FBI Academy in Quantico. Although no specific protocol proved possible, some interesting guidelines and observations emerged. The deliberations culminated in a huge symposium cohosted by the FBI lab in June 1985.

One paper presented at the symposium defined four classes of characteristics—color, structure, cuticular traits, and acquired characteristics —that examiners could look for, each of these broad definitions having four to six individual characteristics for comparison. "A feeling for whether two hairs are similar," was not enough, the author stressed.[19] The committee itself recommended that the variation factor could best be neutralized by taking one hundred hair samples for comparison from a suspect, twenty from each of five distinct areas of the scalp.

Above all the symposium seemed to reiterate to those attending the limitations of hair comparison and how those limitations and the resulting criticism of them could be mitigated. It was a real problem. As

Harold Deadman, an FBI examiner, acknowledged in a paper presented to those attending: "Microscopical hair comparison, as generally conducted in crime laboratories, is considered by some critics to be too subjective to be a valid method of comparison."[20] It is experience, not standards, that are the key, examiners insist. The only way to become a hairs-and-fibers examiner is experience, Michael Malone would repeatedly tell juries. Having examined about ten thousand different individual known hair samples and "hundreds of thousands" of unknown hairs, Malone portrayed himself as among the most experienced there was.

A *Wall Street Journal* survey of more than a dozen cases in which Malone testified showed that he frequently assured juries that in all his years of staring through the twin eyepieces of the comparison microscope, there had been only two, later three, occasions that the hair of two different individuals had been so similar that it could not be distinguished.[21] What he meant by this was completely unclear and is seen as highly misleading by a number of defense experts. However, the pattern of reassurance was similar in every case.

Malone usually told juries he had found twenty matching characteristics—if a number was ever mentioned—the bare minimum even by his own standards. In later years, perhaps the result of caution induced by growing criticism, Malone sometimes told juries in his introduction to hair and fiber comparison that it was not a fingerprint, an apparent contradiction in that his subsequent testimony often seemed to strain every semantic sinew to prove that hair and fiber comparison was the evidentiary equivalent. For the certainty that had made Michael Malone the star of the FBI Hairs and Fibers Unit also exposed him in the appellate courts, and nowhere more so than in Florida, a state where prosecutors had taken to bypassing local hair-and-fiber examiners in favor of Malone.

In August 1987, Florida's Second District Court of Appeals overturned the conviction of John William Jackson for the rape and murder of Marie Felver Porter in December 1983. The forensic evidence in the circumstantial case had been based on two of the most controversial fields of forensic science: odontology and hair comparison. Bite marks on the victims' wrist had been found to be consistent with Jackson's teeth impressions, but the prosecution expert, Dr. Richard Souviron, had been cautious, saying it was not a positive identification. He emphasized that it had been a tough bite mark to identify, inflicted, as it was, through clothing.

Malone seemed to have no such doubts about the two strands of hair on the victim's pajamas, which he said matched Jackson's. Given the paucity of other evidence the appeals court concluded that the conviction effectively hinged on these two hairs. With fingerprints that exculpated the defendant, along with two more hairs that did not match Jackson's found on the body, the appeals court decided that it was a "reasonable hypothesis that someone else committed the crime."[22]

A 1988 case, the sexual assault and murder of Sandra Peterson in Polk County, Florida, in May 1985, was a similar example. There was little more than hair evidence to go on. Malone testified that the strands of forcibly removed head hair in Peterson's mouth, on her jeans, shirt, knee, blouse, brassiere, and panties were indistinguishable from samples taken from Rodney Horstman, a man she had been seen talking to in three separate bars hours before her nude body was found. A pubic hair indistinguishable from Horstman's, according to Malone, was also found on Peterson's ankle sock. The chances of any of these hairs originating from anyone other than Rodney Horstman were "almost non-existent," Malone had told the jury. Horstman was found guilty of second-degree murder and sentenced to seventeen years in jail.

Malone's certainty was all the more essential to the prosecution given other exculpatory evidence, in particular the fact that Peterson's pubic hair had been singed and that a lighter with a fingerprint matching no one involved in the case had been found nearby. At the appeal, Horstman contended that the hairs simply demonstrated close or intimate contact, not murder. The appeals court agreed, ordering his immediate release and acquittal. "Although hair comparison analysis may be persuasive, it is not 100% reliable. Unlike fingerprints, certainty is not possible," the court ruled. "We do not share Mr. Malone's conviction in the infallibility of hair comparison evidence. Thus, we cannot uphold a conviction dependent on such evidence."[23]

Another Florida case in 1988 where hair evidence was almost as important demonstrated the use aggressive prosecutors could make of someone like Malone. James Duckett, a police officer in the city of Mascotte was charged with the sexual battery and murder of an eleven-year-old child, Teresa McAbee, while on duty in May 1987. Although other experts, including Deborah Lightfoot, a hair-and-fiber expert at the Florida Department of Law Enforcement, could not reach a conclusion in their efforts to match a pubic hair found in the victim's underpants with a sample from Duckett, Malone had no such problems.

The hair, he said, did not match any of the three Mexicans that Teresa had been seen talking to at a Laundromat the evening of her rape and murder. This he could assert as a result of examining dozens of hair samples from "Hispanic type individuals" in other cases, Malone argued. The pubic hair "microscopically matched the pubic hairs of Mr. Duckett," Malone insisted, adding for emphasis, "In other words, it had exactly the same characteristics and the same arrangement. It was completely indistinguishable from his pubic hairs." [24]

Duckett's defense lawyer, Jack Edmund, enjoyed some success in challenging Malone's credibility during the trial in 1988. He started with Malone's usual assertion that he had examined "literally hundreds of thousands of unknown hairs" yet took three hours over each detailed, three-stage examination. How had Malone spent a minimum of six hundred thousand hours examining hairs when he had been a qualified FBI hair-and-fiber examiner for only seventeen years? The math just did not add up. Edmund continued by calling Deborah Lightfoot, the state examiner who had been unable to draw Malone's matching conclusions. It was the first time the state hair-and-fiber examiner had ever testified for a defendant. Lightfoot refused to speak in any detail about the case, but did tell the authors: "I hate it when something like this happens. I think it sort of reflects on everyone in the field." [25]

Lightfoot was not the only expert to disagree with Malone. Having examined the evidence, Peter DeForest, a professor of criminalistics at John Jay College, City University of New York, and a hair-and-fiber examiner for thirty years, says he is suspicious: "There was no match with the original samples taken from Duckett, as Malone claimed. However, there was a good match with a sample they said had been taken six months later. That led me to wonder if something had happened. It suggested to me that somebody had switched something. Certainly something did not smell right." [26] In September 1990, Duckett's appeal was turned down, and he remains on Death Row in Florida. As of this writing, Peter DeForest is waiting to testify about his findings at another hearing that has been delayed repeatedly.

But it was a case in Warren County, Pennsylvania, in which Malone testified in May 1991, that would throw all his other emphatic testimony into sharp relief. The case of William Buckley, accused of kidnapping, raping, and murdering Kathy Wilson, a thirty-three-year-old mother who had disappeared in Falconer, New York, in May 1988 and whose skeletal remains were discovered near Lander, Pennsylvania, sixteen months later, demonstrated clearly how Malone was not just overstating hair and fiber matches but in one case at least was inventing a match that did not exist.

William Buckley was accused by his alleged accomplice, nineteen-year-old Michael Brown, who was offered a reduced sentence in exchange for testifying. With no fingerprints, blood, or convincing eyewitness testimony, the case came to revolve around trace evidence. Hairs found in Kathy Wilson's van—in which Buckley was alleged to have kidnapped her—and hairs found in Brown's van—the vehicle in which the victim was alleged to have been transported to Pennsylvania—seemed the best chance of reinforcing Brown's tainted and somewhat inconsistent testimony.

Hair samples were sent to the New York state police crime lab in Albany. Cathryn Oakes, a hair-and-fiber examiner at the lab, detailed in a written report why she was unable to match any of the samples taken from Wilson's van to William Buckley or from Brown's van to Kathy Wilson. In particular, Oakes noted "unaccountable differences in respect to the microscopic characteristics" between a key hair removed from a blanket in Brown's van and Kathy Wilson's hair samples, which had been recovered from two of her hairbrushes. With his case apparently going nowhere, District Attorney Joseph Massa dispatched the evidence to Michael Malone at the FBI lab.

By the time Malone got to the witness stand, it was clear the prosecution case was in trouble. Buckley's lawyer, Barry Lee Smith, had hammered away at Brown, pointing to numerous inconsistencies in his testimony and listing on a courtroom chalkboard almost eight hundred previously admitted lies to investigators. In two days of testimony, Malone appeared to turn the tables. The FBI agent recounted how he had extracted a brown head hair from vacuum sweepings from the passenger seat side of Kathy Wilson's van that "microscopically matched and was absolutely indistinguishable from the head hairs of Mr. Buckley."[27] But Malone went further, in precisely the way the prosecution needed him to.

He claimed he had "microscopically matched" a number of light brown Caucasian head hairs found in Brown's van with the twenty or so Kathy Wilson samples.

Several of these hairs were found on a piece of carpeted board from the floor of the van; another single hair was discovered among vacuum sweepings from the wheel well of the van; and yet another, a longer hair, measuring five-and-three-quarters inches, was found on a white blanket reportedly found in Brown's van. These hairs exhibited "exactly the same microscopic characteristics of the head hair of Kathy Wilson. In other words they were absolutely indistinguishable from the head hairs," Malone told the court.[28]

But the vital physical evidence corroborating Brown's story and incriminating Buckley did not last long. Under cross-examination, Buckley's defense attorney dropped a bombshell on Malone. The evidence about which he was testifying so definitively had been mislabeled. Malone had examined a hair from the wrong blanket, a white one that had been recovered from a campsite in the woods where Buckley had been living in July 1988. No hair recovered from the blanket found in Brown's van, a patterned one with flowers on a white background, had even been sent to the FBI lab.

The hair had simply been labeled as having come from Buckley's blanket. Malone had been told the blanket was in the van and had made the identification in what seemed a classic case of self-induced pro-prosecution testimony. Yet on the witness stand, he refused to admit any possibility that he had got it all wrong. "I matched a hair on the blanket to Kathy Wilson. I don't know how it got there," he told the court petulantly.[29] The fact was that Malone had coordinated closely with the prosecutors, getting a full briefing from them during a visit to the local police, as he admitted in cross-examination.

On the stand he failed to explain why his trial testimony, riddled with terms such as "perfect match," was much less equivocal than his preliminary hearing testimony, in which he spoke of "possibilities." He failed to explain why his results varied so radically from Cathryn Oakes's conclusions, including disagreeing on the most basic of comparisons such as whether particular hairs had roots or not. Malone further failed to explain how he could speak in such emphatic terms about a field of forensics that eventually he reluctantly admitted to Smith was based on association and exclusion rather than on positive identification. "He was clearly intent on securing a conviction and doing phoney stuff to secure it," complains Smith.[30] "The guy's a total liar. My client could have been electrocuted based on his testimony."[31]

Equally concerned about Malone's testimony was Peter DeForest, the defense team's expert in the *Buckley* case. DeForest was told by Malone and his FBI unit chief, Allyson Simmons, that he could not see the crucial lab notes on which Malone had based his testimony without a court order. As a result, Professor DeForest told the court that he, like Cathryn Oakes, was unable to match the hairs Malone had matched. He explained the complexity of hair comparisons, not least the fact that the hairs on an individual's head could in themselves be very varied: he detailed how subjective such comparisons are and told the court that similar characteristics in two hairs never prove that they came from the same source. Coincidental matches, are, in fact, inevitable, Professor DeForest stated.

He rejected Malone's quantification of a random probability-match of 1 in 4,500 that a particular hair came from William Buckley, saying the theory of quantification in the discipline was based on a "very, very heavily criticized" study—a study that had never been replicated.[32] He expressed concern that Malone's control sample from Buckley was insufficient. Malone had admitted taking only twelve hairs from Buckley, a long way short of the one hundred samples from five different areas of the scalp recommended by the FBI's own hair comparison committee of which Professor DeForest had been a leading member.

After testifying in the *Buckley* case, DeForest was so concerned about the damage Michael Malone's testimony could do to the whole field of hair-and-fiber analysis that he rang the FBI lab to speak to Malone's supervisor. She seemed disinclined to censure her prosecution star. "She didn't seem to be very concerned. She just told me that Malone was a serious guy who really believed in what he was doing," DeForest recalls. "I guess you could say there was no recognition that what Malone had done was a problem."[33] Faith, and pro-prosecution bias, was, it seemed, enough.

———

Inmate number 00131–177 sitting in a federal jail cell in Sheridan, Oregon, knew what Alcee Hastings, William Buckley, and Rodney Horstman felt like. He had not only lost his promising career as an emergency trauma unit surgeon to the machinations of successive FBI lab examiners but his liberty as well. Jeffrey Robert MacDonald, fifty-three, was jailed in 1979 for the brutal murder of his wife, Colette, and his two young daughters, Kimberley, five, and Kristen, two, as they slept in their beds at the military base in Fort Bragg, North Carolina, where he was a Green Beret captain and an army group surgeon.

MacDonald had always protested his innocence, and the exculpatory evidence, in particular hair and fiber evidence, was by 1997 overwhelming. The trouble was that machinations by his prosecutors, in conjunction with the FBI lab, had prevented any jury hearing that evidence at his trial. Indeed, it was beginning to look as though no jury ever would. By 1997, Dr. MacDonald's defense team had had three appeals turned down.

From his townhouse office overlooking Boston Harbor on the other side of the country, MacDonald's lawyer, Harvey Silverglate, argues convincingly that one of these appeal denials in 1992 was directly attributable to another Michael Malone lie. In two affidavits, filed in February and May 1991, Malone had testified that two synthetic fibers found in a clear-handled hairbrush in the MacDonald apartment had to be dolls' hair because they were made of saran. Standard texts in the FBI lab library and personal research showed that saran was not used in wigs, Malone swore. Since then, years of research by Silverglate and his team, along with a release of photocopied pages under the Freedom of Information Act, have proved that standard texts on hairs and fibers in the FBI lab did not say that.

In fact, saran was listed specifically in the FBI lab's texts as being used in wigs. Moreover, it was in fact highly likely that the two hairs, one twenty-four inches in length and too long to have come from the head of any doll on the market at the time, had come from a wig. "Malone perjured himself, and I hope he sues me for saying so," Harvey Silverglate says.[34] What Malone said had been absolutely crucial. In rejecting the 1992 appeal, three judges had ruled: "Without evidence that saran is used in the production of human wig hair the presence of blond saran fibers in the MacDonald home would have done little to corroborate MacDonald's account of an intruder with a blond wig."[35]

MacDonald's consistent version of the night in February 1970 was that while sleeping on the sofa after Kristen had wet his side of the family's double bed, he had been awakened by a band of intruders, apparently drug-crazed hippies. One, a woman, had worn a blonde wig and a floppy hat and carried a candle. MacDonald recalled her chanting: "Acid is groovy, kill the pigs!" He remembered a black man in an army field jacket with sergeant's stripes and two white men, all of whom had set about him with various weapons. An ice pick, a Geneva Forge knife, a wooden club, and an Old Hickory knife were all found at the scene and matched the injuries inflicted.

Extraordinary as MacDonald's story sounded, there was a lot of evidence to support it. He himself was injured badly with as many as seventeen ice-pick wounds, four knife stabs, including one so deep it exposed his stomach muscle. Having passed out he was later treated for a collapsed lung and multiple head contusions. There was a band of drug-using hippies living nearby; several people on the base, including Jeffrey MacDonald, were reported to have given them a hard time. A woman in a blonde wig and floppy hat had been sighted by five different witnesses near the scene, in some cases with male companions, shortly after the incident. And that woman, Helena Stoeckley, who died in 1983, had confessed and passed a polygraph test in doing so. The testimony of those she had confessed to had been ruled inadmissible at the original trial by Judge Franklin Dupree as "not sufficiently reliable" in the absence of any forensic evidence linking her or other intruders to the scene of the crimes.

The blonde saran fibers were just such evidence. And such evidence was the key to opening up the whole case, as both the original judge and the three appeals court judges had stated in their separate rulings. Indeed, that was why, the defense alleged, the blonde saran fibers had been hidden from MacDonald's attorneys at the original trial, their existence revealed only as a result of a separate release of lab notes under the Freedom of Information Act in 1990. Indeed, largely as a result of the detailed analysis of boxes of lab notes and reports, part of three successive releases, there was by 1998 a veritable mountain of other exculpatory evidence in the MacDonald case.

All this had served to make the blonde saran fibers something like the proverbial hanging thread. Tug one of these long blonde fibers and the whole case would unravel. "What the FBI lab did in my case was to effectively reverse the burden of proof," Jeffrey MacDonald says from jail.

"At my trial they kept saying: 'Where is your evidence of intruders?' I kept saying: 'I don't know. You tell me. You're the forensic guys.' Now we know that the evidence that supported my story was suppressed by a succession of lab examiners over more than twenty years." [36]

The MacDonald case exposed almost every shortcoming of the FBI lab. It demonstrates how the effects of the culture of the place could be magnified by the inadequacy of discovery provisions for exculpatory evidence and new restrictions on the right to appeal. The case also illustrates how what has been going on at the FBI lab could result in innocent people being locked up, despite the Justice Department's bland assertion to the contrary. Consequently, the case also reveals the real importance of Fred Whitehurst's dogged criticisms of the FBI lab.

The MacDonald case is a cover-up of a cover-up. It illustrates perfectly why the IG's report needed to be the beginning rather than the end of an investigation of the FBI lab. Although a gross injustice had been done in the Jeffrey MacDonald case, it had not even been mentioned by the IG. With no personal knowledge of the case, Fred Whitehurst had made no complaint. As such, the MacDonald case raises the million-dollar question: How many other cases like this are out there?

"We've known for a long time that the forensic testimony in this case was utter nonsense. For years, people have been telling us 'You don't accuse the FBI lab of perjury. This is the foremost forensic lab in the world!'" said Silverglate. "Maybe now someone will believe us." [37] Jeffrey MacDonald, a man with more scientific training than many FBI lab examiners, was equally adamant. "I've known since the trial in 1979 that something was drastically wrong with the FBI lab. . . . [T]hey are no longer going to a crime scene and saying, 'What does this evidence tell us? Rather, they are going to a crime scene and they're talking to the prosecutor or the chief agent on the case, and they're saying, 'What do you want us to find?'" he told NBC. "I am not saying I am owed a day in court because a government agent perjured himself. . . . I am saying that the evidence he perjured himself about proves that I am innocent. There's a big difference there." [38]

By the time the IG's report had been published, MacDonald and his defense team had already been investigating Malone for five years. They had discovered an amazing pattern of selective reporting, partial inquiry, falsifications, and determination to turn himself into an expert in specialized fields about which he knows little or nothing. It all added up to an investigation designed to have only one outcome: to keep Jeffrey Mac-Donald in jail. "If you go back over what Malone and the others did it could not be clearer," complains Lucia Bartoli, a coordinator of the Jeffrey MacDonald defense campaign.[39]

In his sworn affidavit filed on May 21, 1991, Michael Malone was quite categoric. Saran fibers could not be made in a form suitable for use in human wigs. It could not, he stated, be manufactured as "tow" fiber, in continuous filament form, without the definite twist "essential to the cosmetic wig manufacturing process." Saran, he observed, does not "lay or drape like human hair" and is too shiny to resemble it. Malone claimed that he had consulted "numerous standard references routinely used in the textile industry and as source material in the FBI laboratory. . . . [N]one of these standard references reflect the use of saran fibers in cosmetic wigs; however, they do reflect the use of saran fibers for wigs for dolls."[40]

Harvey Silverglate and colleague Philip Cormier checked their own texts, which they knew contradicted Malone, then filed under the Freedom of Information Act to see what the FBI lab and the Department of Justice had in the way of standard textile reference texts. In April 1993 a photocopied cover and relevant pages from two standard texts arrived at their offices in Boston: Adeline A. Dembeck's *Guidebook to Man-Made Textile Fibers and Textured Yarns of the World (Third Edition)* and Evelyn E. Stout's textbook, *Introduction to Textiles (Third Edition)*.

Both texts were items of evidence that the MacDonald defense team had tried to present to the Fourth Circuit Court in a postargument letter in 1990. The reason was clear: both texts stated without qualification that saran fibers were used in wigs; the Dembeck text stated that saran was made in "tow" form. And it was the Dembeck text that was most incriminating. A slanting stamped impression on the cover page indicated that there were at least two copies in the FBI laboratory. It read:

F.B.I. LABORATORY
M.A. UNI.—3931
COPY No:2

A handwritten notation on the cover page indicated that the text had not only been in the FBI lab library when Malone was examining the evidence, but it had been in the library since at least May 1979, a month before Jeffrey MacDonald's trial began. The notation read: "There will never be another edition—per publisher 5/31/79."

Malone's own research was equally nefarious. Inquiries by Lucia Bartoli into the use of saran revealed that Malone, Assistant U.S. Attorney Eric Evenson, and FBI agent Raymond "Butch" Madden had visited A. Edward Oberhaus, Jr., senior vice president of Kaneka America Corporation in his office in New York on December 4, 1990. Kaneka made modacrylic, or nonsaran, fibers under the trade name Kanekalon for use in wigs and doll hair. According to Oberhaus, in a story he repeated separately to Bartoli, Silverglate and Cormier, the group told him that they were interested in obtaining an affidavit from him stating that saran was not used to make cosmetic wigs.[41]

Despite the fact that Oberhaus told them he could not make such a statement, within five weeks, the U.S. attorney's office for the Eastern District of North Carolina, the prosecuting authority, faxed Oberhaus a draft affidavit for him to sign. It included the statements the government wanted: saran could not be produced as a tow fiber and thus could not be used in the "hairgoods industry." Oberhaus refused to sign. Instead he provided the U.S. attorney's office with his own affidavit, which stated that from 1960 to date, wigs and hairpieces had been manufactured with "human hair, modacrylic fibers, other fibers or a combination of these filaments."[42]

The government's draft memo was never released as part of Freedom of Information Act requests. But it did release a "302" form, the FBI document for recording summaries of interviews, that was equally telling. In the 302 record of the conversation, only released more than three years after the actual Freedom of Information Act request, Oberhaus was reported to have said everything he says he refused to say and certainly refused to swear to in the government's draft affidavit. The Malone group's 302 is so emphatic in its urgency to make the point that it is worth quoting in full: "He [Oberhaus] advised that saran is a synthetic fiber that cannot be used in the hairgoods industry. He advised that saran can only be made as a continuous filament fiber, which is not suitable for the manufacture of wigs."[43]

In going to Oberhaus, someone who knew about the manufacture and use of nonsaran fiber for wigs and doll hair but not about saran's uses, the FBI had tried to set the parameters of their inquiry before it even really started. They did not ask him about dolls. Defense attorney Harvey Silverglate did. He got the response you might expect: twenty-two or twenty-four-inch lengths made it unlikely that the fibers in the hairbrush came from a doll. Even "looping" inside the doll's head, one explanation the prosecution had offered, would not produce a two-foot-long hair, Oberhaus said. Oberhaus mentioned that he had referred the government agents to a real expert in saran fibers, Mr. Yamada of the Asahi Chemical Company of Japan. It was not a reference the FBI seemed to follow up. It would be easier and much more convenient, having failed to get an expert to say what they wanted, to turn Malone himself into an expert on saran.

A search for real expertise by Lucia Bartoli and the defense team quickly demonstrated that saran could be manufactured as a tow fiber and was indeed used in cosmetic wigs. The team quickly located Sue Greco, a chemist specializing in polymers from Annapolis, Maryland. For twenty-eight years through 1994, Greco had worked for National Plastics, a group of companies that made various polymers, including saran fibers. In a devastating rebuttal of Malone's affidavit, Greco said that saran could be manufactured in both monofilament and continuous multifilament or tow form and that these fibers were sold to manufacturers who made wigs for human use. To prove it, Greco even presented the defense team with an actual "tow" or clump of blonde, curled, saran fibers manufactured by National Plastics.

But Greco went further. Being close to Washington, National Plastics had been a focus of attention for the FBI lab on various occasions in the 1980s and 1990s. FBI agents regularly took tours of the manufacturing plant in Odenton, Maryland, and the bureau was routinely given samples of a variety of fibers, including saran. On one tour in which she had participated, Greco recalled the agents being interested in the types of fibers that might be used in disguises. Indeed, Greco had sent samples of saran fibers to the FBI lab every couple of years until 1991 or 1992. Despite all this, no one at the FBI lab had contacted Greco in relation to the MacDonald case.

Since leaving National Plastics in 1994, Greco had established her own company, Pengra Spectro-Analytics, a material analysis group specializing in instrumental analyses of polymers and their components. When retained by the defense, Greco did some analysis of the two, twenty-two- and twenty-four-inch, hairs. A slight difference in chemical composition, a difference noted even by Malone as one of color, suggested to Greco that the fibers were from a wig. "Human wigs often contain a blend of different colored fibers for the purposes of making the wig appear more realistic and natural, since the natural hairs on a head are not uniform in color," she stated.[44]

Many other witnesses from the saran fiber and wig-making industry supported Greco's assertions. Norman Reich, a former president and director of A & B Wig Company, told defense investigators that during the 1960s and early 1970s his company manufactured wigs with saran fibers for use by humans. The company made wigs in a variety of colors, including blonde, some of them using saran fibers of twenty-two inches or more. Jerry Pollack, who worked in a family business called Artistic Wig and Novelty Company until 1970, told the defense team the same thing. Robert Oumano, who ran Franco-American Novelty Company in Glendale, New York, a wholesale firm, confirmed that throughout the 1960s and into the 1970s his company purchased saran wigs for human wear, some of them from Reich's company.

Jaume Ribas, former chief executive of Fibras Omni S.A., a Mexican firm, confirmed a listing in the Dembeck text: his company had indeed made saran for use in human wigs. He even sent Harvey Silverglate an example, a dark-haired wig made with fibers of up to twenty-five inches in length. Two employees of National Plastics, Samuel Walter Umansky and Frank Applebaum, told the defense team that they had sold saran fibers in multifilament form to a number of different wig manufacturers and had worked with a number of them to improve the product for that very use. Every single witness the defense located—Greco, Reich, Pollack, Oumano, Umansky, Applebaum—signed sworn affidavits disputing and denouncing the key contentions in Malone's affidavit.

Equally curious, however, was a December 1990 visit that Malone, Evenson, and another agent made to Judith Schizas and Mellie Phillips, employees of a California firm, Mattel Toys, to "complete" the other side of their research—doll hair. Schizas was a doll specialist at one of the world's largest manufacturers, with a private collection of more than four thousand specimens put together over thirty years. Phillips had spent nearly twenty years as the manager of the firm's doll hair department and was an acknowledged expert in rooting and grooming.

Here the pattern of the FBI interviews was similar to that of Edward Oberhaus, as the 302 records of the two interviews show. These records were once again only released in 1996 under a Freedom of Information Act request, having never been made available to the defense despite containing exculpatory information. Mellie Phillips told the MacDonald defense investigators that she had told Malone's group that saran was manufactured in tow form. This was just one example of a statement that did not appear in the FBI's 302 version of the interview.

Both Schizas and Phillips thought it improbable that any doll had hair fiber of up to twenty-four inches in length—certainly they knew of no such Mattel doll. But the FBI party seemed to know what they were looking for, asking for a blonde-haired ballerina doll, about twenty-four inches in height that they believed played music and stood on a pedestal, and would have been on the market at Christmas in 1969. Schizas retrieved two dolls from her collection. Pollyanna and Dancerina were both manufactured by Mattel and, at Malone's request, Schizas extracted several full-length hair fibers from the head of each doll, using tweezers. According to her affidavit, Schizas measured the length of the strands of hair on both dolls at a maximum of eighteen inches. No dolls in her collection turned out to have synthetic hair composed of fibers up to twenty-four inches in length.[45]

Although Malone's testimony about the blonde saran fibers was the defense team's most probable means of reopening the case to secure a new trial for Jeffrey MacDonald, it was actually part of a much bigger picture of deception by both himself and the FBI lab. By 1996, the defense team's analysis of several sets of notes and lab reports had made it clear that the army's Criminal Investigation Division examiners had found numerous hairs and fibers in critical locations that could not be matched to known sources. All such evidence was found on or near the victims' bodies or where MacDonald said a struggle had occurred.

All of these had been excluded from the FBI's typewritten reports, even when found in association with evidence that the prosecution viewed as crucial to its case. Asked to review all the hair and fiber evidence, Malone ignored much of it in a narrowly focused lab report and his subsequent affidavits. Malone was actually doing what his forensic predecessors on the case had done before, denying that any of the omitted evidence could provide a forensic basis for MacDonald's innocence. Indeed, Malone ignored only the most exculpatory evidence.

Malone acknowledged the presence of an unidentified "brown body hair of Caucasian origin" on the blue sheet found on the floor of the MacDonald residence master bedroom. The hair had been "forcibly removed" and "appears to have a piece of skin tissue attached to the basal area of the hair." Malone seems to have believed it was what he termed a "fringe hair" from the area where groin meets abdomen. He asserted in his affidavit that "body hairs, with the exception of pubic hairs, are not normally deemed to be of value for comparison purposes."[46]

There was no mention of the fact that the forcible removal indicated that Colette had struggled with her assailant and, comparison or not, the fact that it was a brown hair seemed to exclude her husband, who was blond. Malone was even vaguer about four brown limb hairs found in debris removed from Colette MacDonald's left hand, a further indication of a struggle with intruders. These simply did not "possess sufficient characteristics to be of value for significant comparison purposes," Malone concluded.[47]

However, similar hairs littered the scene. A "brown hair of Caucasian origin" found in the bedspread taken from Kristen MacDonald's bedroom and a "brown limb hair of Caucasian origin" taken from the quilt in Kimberley MacDonald's bedroom were both reexamined by Malone but were similarly ruled out for "comparison purposes." And Malone did not even mention the bloody fingernail scrapings from both hands of both the MacDonald children that had revealed fine brown hairs with their roots intact. That suggested that both children had fought with their assailant long enough to gouge hairs from him or her. With the hairs exhibiting dissimilar characteristics, according to one lab note, they may also have suggested more than one brown-haired attacker. Helena Stoeckley and two of her associates who had made at least passing reference to involvement in the murders, Greg Mitchell and Cathy Perry, were all brown-haired.[48]

In not reexamining or mentioning the most exculpatory evidence, Michael Malone was simply upholding a by now long tradition. It had started with the army lab back in 1970 and been upheld by the FBI ever since they had become involved in the case in 1974. The means was simple: abuse of the old standby, the lab report. Examinations, findings, even conclusions reached in handwritten lab notes would not be recorded in the formal typed lab reports handed over to the defense or even to the prosecution.

Apparently believing that the fingernail scraping hairs from the two girls had indeed come from the girls' killer, Janice Glisson, the army lab chemist who did much of the initial examination, had tried in 1970 to match them one by one with samples of Jeffrey MacDonald's head, arm, chest, and pubic hairs. All attempts had failed, and although this was recorded in the lab notes, the formal lab reports ignored all reference to the attempts and even to the hairs themselves. Instead there was a rather cryptic handwritten message in the lab bench notes following the details of the attempts at comparison. It reads: "They are not going to be reported by me."[49]

But just as crucial were a number of unidentified black or blue-black wool fibers found on Colette MacDonald's body and on the wooden club, one of the murder weapons. The fibers were found in the victim's right biceps area and near her mouth and were written off by Malone due to "the absence, at this time, of known standards for comparison."[50] MacDonald's defense team is now disputing that, claiming that Freedom of Information Act materials released to them in May 1996 indicate that Malone had available to him a number of black or navy blue items that had been taken from the MacDonald home "which apparently turned out not to be the source of these bluish-black and dark purple fibers."[51] In other words, more evidence of intruders.

Certainly the fibers did not come from the purple cotton pajamas that no one disputed MacDonald had been wearing at the time of the murders. It was fibers from these pajamas on the wooden club that prosecutor James Blackburn had described as the most important evidence in the case at the trial in 1979. In fact, it now seems clear that there were no cotton fibers among the debris taken from the club, although the unmatched wool fibers were all there, as James Frier, Malone's predecessor as a fiber analyst in the FBI lab, had confirmed in his lab notes in the 1970s.

At the time of the trial, prosecutors James Blackburn and Brian Murtagh got around this little difficulty by not calling Frier as an expert witness. Malone followed suit by simply not referring to any cotton fibers.

Given that Malone had been asked to retest all fibers found on the club, the defense concluded that there were indeed no cotton fibers. This assumption seemed to be correct when in an interview with Rhonda Rigsby, a postgraduate research student studying forensic science, Malone said he had not found any pajama-top fibers.[52]

Over the years, such distortions, omissions, and downright lies were revealed to have affected almost every single piece of evidence against MacDonald. Five bloodstained gloves in the kitchen, a bloody syringe in a closet, an unidentified bloody palm print on the footboard of the double bed, more than three dozen unmatched finger or palm prints, wax drippings that did not match the colors of any of the candles found in the apartment, a burned match, a small unmatched piece of skin found near Colette MacDonald's body—all this seemed to be evidence of intruders, some of it compatible with the group MacDonald had described. Yet all this evidence and more was excluded from the 1979 trial.

Other evidence that counted heavily with the jury was equally explicable. Bloody footprints in the doorway to Kimberley's bedroom, evidence that the prosecution said proved that MacDonald paused as he carried his wife's body into the master bedroom, could have been impressed when MacDonald was helped up after falling off a gurney when being carried out of the house by medical staff, according to eyewitnesses. The lack of evidence to support MacDonald's story that he struggled with the intruders in the hallway was simple: a report that described a "pile" of cotton blue-purple fibers, compatible with his pajama top, as well as blood, probably type B like MacDonald's, went no further than the initial crime scene investigation.

Moreover, the crime scene that army investigators believed was too tidy may have been tidied up by some of their own. An overturned plant pot in the living room was just one item an eyewitness saw someone place upright, part of a now well-documented catalog of errors in evidence collection and failure to secure the crime scene that involved the wiping of fingerprints and unfettered access by mysterious military personnel who had nothing to do with the investigation.[53]

It was this sort of thing that by November 1970 had persuaded J. Edgar Hoover to order his agents, in particular local FBI chief Robert Murphy of Charlotte, North Carolina, to have nothing to do with the case.[54] Hoover had not remained the undisputed Boss for nearly half a century without being able to recognize a lemon when he saw one. The FBI had initially been involved in interviewing witnesses, but the army's Criminal Investigative Division (CID) had always had the lead role. It was their decision in April 1970, a mere seven weeks after the murders, to investigate Jeffrey MacDonald as the sole suspect. It was also the army's decision after a two-month preliminary hearing in the summer of 1970 to drop court-martial charges, prompting Jeffrey MacDonald to accept an army discharge.

Despite this, there were ominous signs for MacDonald. In the end the charges were dismissed for reasons of "insufficient evidence," not because they were considered unfounded. Prosecutors and CID agents presented their case at the military hearings as if they had encountered no physical evidence at the crime scene to support MacDonald's story. In particular, they ignored eyewitness evidence about the woman in the floppy hat and their own suspicions and information about Helena Stoeckley.

By 1971, Jeffrey MacDonald, although now a civilian, was back under illegal surveillance by the army's CID. By December 1971, Brian Murtagh, a small, bespectacled graduate of the Georgetown University School of Law, had joined CID headquarters in Washington as an army lawyer and the legal adviser on the case. By May 1972, J. Edgar Hoover had died at his post. All three of these events would help produce a grand jury investigation, an indictment, and then a trial in which the FBI lab, along with the prosecutors, would plummet to new depths.

In October 1974, with Hoover out of the way, Paul Stombaugh, the head of what was then known as the FBI lab's Chemistry Unit, was dispatched to Fort Bragg to examine the crime scene and study the evidence the CID had collected. In an interview with the authors, Stombaugh claimed that he simply conducted the examinations the army examiners "were not qualified to do."[55] However, a government memo shows that Stombaugh reexamined about 120 items of evidence already examined by the army's CID and then recommended the FBI accept the case.[56] It was a strange decision, ignoring the FBI lab's own policy of not doing "second opinions"; i.e., not accepting evidence for evaluation that had already been examined in the same manner by another government crime lab.

For the next quarter century, the FBI would struggle vainly with the consequences of contravening its own basic rule. Government experts would contradict each other and the bureau would end up embarrassing itself trying to cover up evidence that had been suppressed, poorly collected, or inadequately stored. All the evidence of intruders, including the blonde saran fibers, would not just be overlooked but would be suppressed even more ruthlessly than before. New evidence would be necessary to secure a prosecution. Mysteriously, it would appear. Somehow, evidence that had not existed in the army lab—evidence the examiners there would hardly have ignored—materialized at the FBI lab. It included the appearance of some of the most incriminating items at the trial, in particular a cotton thread from Jeffrey MacDonald's pajamas intertwined with a bloody head hair from Colette, his wife, an indication of a struggle between the two, the prosecution alleged.

Fabrication of evidence aside, the means used to secure a conviction were methods that would become all too familiar in later years. First, key examiners, hair-and-fiber experts Dillard Browning of the CID and James Frier of the FBI for instance, would not take the stand. Stombaugh would, like Tom Thurman in the VANPAC case (see Chapter 3), become the prosecution's professional witness on virtually everything. He would help smooth over the contradictions, inadequacies, and omissions of the forensic investigations, much of which was obvious in the lab notes but not in the lab reports.

Second, almost nothing of any use, nothing detailing anything like the full picture, would be handed over to the defense. Discovery obligations would be abused shamelessly. Formal lab reports that had to be handed over to the defense would reach only one conclusion. Bench notes or anything else that included exculpatory data would be buried. The defense, in sum, would not see the evidence or the FBI lab's real view of the evidence until successive Freedom of Information Act requests forced the bureau's hand years later.

Third, affidavits or 302 form reports of interviews of forensic experts or witnesses who contradicted the government's version of events would be inaccurate, selective, or simply false. By 1990, when Malone and his fellow investigators worked wonders with the saran expert testimony, this particular path had been well worn. For instance, when in 1984, Dr. Ronald Wright, medical examiner of Broward County, Florida, concluded from a study of the government's recently released autopsy photos and crime scene report that the blow that fractured Colette MacDonald's skull had been delivered by a left-handed person, FBI special agent James Reed filed an affidavit in July of that year saying Wright had retracted his statement. Dr. Wright had, in fact, done nothing of the sort.[57] The risk the government was prepared to take was a reflection of the importance of the issue—Jeffrey MacDonald is righthanded.

Such devices became ever more important as the FBI lab sorted, cataloged, and tested the evidence and quickly turned up some rather awkward facts. Murtagh was particularly worried about a blue acrylic fiber that had been found in Colette MacDonald's right hand. Splinters from the attack club had been found within her hand's grasp, suggesting that the source of the fiber had been her attacker. If it could not be related to something in the home this would suggest, once again, one or more intruders. Morris Clark, the assistant section chief of the FBI lab's Scientific Analysis Section, assigned James Frier of Microscopic Analysis and his assistant, Kathy Bond, to the task. The pair were unable to link the fiber to anything recovered from the home.

In trying to do so, however, Bond and Frier made some other rather startling discoveries about the work done by Dillard Browning of the army's CID back in 1970. Browning had matched one of the three fibers found near Colette MacDonald's mouth to Jeffrey MacDonald's pajama top, wording his report ambiguously so that all three might seem to have been matched. Frier found no such match, identifying just two black wool fibers of unknown source. Browning had labeled the three fibers taken from Colette's right bicep area as nylon; Frier identified them as a rayon fiber, a white wool fiber, and a black wool fiber. Again, none of these could be matched with any known source—i.e., everything in the house at the time of the murders. The evidence suggested they were from an external source and hence supported MacDonald's version of events, in particular indicating that Colette was set upon by more than one attacker.

By 1979 all this "new" evidence must have left Brian Murtagh with a real problem. The *Brady* ruling required that the details of clearly exculpatory evidence be released to the defense. Yet in a case being built exclusively on interpretations of physical evidence, his prosecution could easily fall apart if disclosure went ahead. Bernard Segal, MacDonald's then defense lawyer, and his forensic expert, Dr. John Thornton, had been pestering the prosecution for access to the evidence and the release of lab notes and reports since just after the grand jury indictment in January 1975. The prosecution had refused persistently, arguing that the lab reports submitted to the defense included all the pertinent information. By January 1979 Segal had resorted to a Freedom of Information Act request for everything the FBI had in its case files, including all laboratory notes, bench notes and technicians' notes.

Murtagh's main protection during the four years leading up to the trial had been Franklin Dupree, the North Carolina district court judge handling the case. He had consistently refused to order the release of the lab documentation or order defense access to the evidence, accepting the government's case that everything was in the formal lab reports. But the discrepancies between the lab work of the CID and the FBI continued to alarm Brian Murtagh, who took every precaution to minimize the risks of information leaking out. On March 15, 1979, he picked up the formal FBI lab report and the items he had had reexamined personally, loading them into his station wagon. When the defense team's first Freedom of Information Act request reached him, having been fobbed off onto the army's CID by the FBI, Murtagh ordered them not to release anything, saying the defense had been denied access by the court and Judge Dupree.

On June 7, 1979, Murtagh spent the day searching the murder apartment, now sealed for more than nine years. Years later he would explain in court that he had been looking for the source of the blue acrylic fiber found in Colette MacDonald's hand and that he had forwarded a sleeveless blue sweater to the FBI lab as a result of his search. He telephoned his request and given that the report would be released to the defense, got a suitably evasive response. There was no match. The sweater was composed of wool, the FBI lab report concluded helpfully.

But Murtagh was still worried. Sometime during the summer of 1979 he assigned Jeffrey Puretz, one of the young law students in his office, to research a prosecutor's discovery obligations. Need the detailed data of a lab report, as opposed to just the conclusions, be disclosed? At what point in a criminal proceeding must exculpatory material be disclosed to the defense? Entering into the spirit of his boss's aims, Puretz went one step further and made a suggestion. Give the defense the "opportunity" to examine the evidence and they would automatically lose the right to charge the prosecution with suppressing exculpatory evidence. Thus on July 6, ten days before the trial started, Brian Murtagh did a complete volte-face and personally petitioned the court to allow the defense to "microscopically examine fibers" connected with the physical evidence in the case.

The terms and conditions under which Murtagh and Judge Dupree would allow such examination to take place would soon make it clear that the issue was the law, not justice. And even within the scope of the law, the letter and the spirit would be two very different things. Defense expert John Thornton was to be allowed a one-time, supervised visit to the jail cell where the evidence was being held. He would then list the items he wanted to examine, not in his own lab in California, but in the lab of the North Carolina State Bureau of Investigation. Brian Murtagh would still have the right to challenge the defense team's right to test any specific item, with a final decision to be made by Judge Dupree.

Incredibly, the visit, the examinations, the challenges, and any rulings all had to be completed by July 12, just days away. The army lab had taken six months, the FBI lab had been at the evidence for nearly five years. Without the lab notes for guidance and comparison, Thornton and Segal had no way of even knowing whether the evidence in the hundreds of boxes stacked in the jail cell was that from the scene of the crime. There was no catalog or list of the hundreds of fibers, hairs, blood samples, and fabric remnants stored.

Although Thornton was convinced that the prosecution's behavior demonstrated that there was something to hide, being asked to look for the proverbial needle in a haystack with no map and no time seemed designed to ensure that the defense would not find it. "Murtagh held evidence of intruders in his closed hand, brought it near my face, then opened his hand in a flash and cleverly closed it again," laments Segal. "I had an innocent client, and we lost to a malicious prosecution."[58]

The trial began in Raleigh, North Carolina, on July 19, 1979, four and a half years after the grand jury indictment. With Judge Dupree, whose openly pro-prosecution sympathies would soon be the subject of good copy for the scores of journalists, on the bench, piles of physical evidence were paraded into the courtroom. There were vials containing the all-important hairs and fibers, pieces of rug, Jeffrey MacDonald's pajama top, bedsheets, blankets, photographs, bits of bloodstained wall—175 items of evidence in all. "Things do not lie," Assistant U.S. Attorney

James Blackburn, the lead prosecutor told the jury in his opening remarks. "But people can and do." [59] The refrain became his signature tune throughout the trial, a sad irony given the lies and liars on which the whole prosecution case was founded. Blackburn would eventually prove to be one of them, being sentenced to three years in jail in 1993 after pleading guilty to twelve counts of forgery, fraud, and embezzlement as a practicing lawyer.

As the trial began, Segal made one final plea for full disclosure of the handwritten lab notes. Once again, Judge Dupree refused to force the prosecution to hand them over, nonsensically promising the defense that they would "get reversal" if any of the lab notes were later shown to contain exculpatory *Brady* material. How such documents could be shown to contain such data without a court order forcing their release was not explained. The fact that the lab notes have since been released under Freedom of Information Act, that they have been shown to contain a mass of exculpatory data, and that Jeffrey MacDonald remains in jail, only serves to confirm the hollowness of Judge Dupree's promise.

Without their lab test results and with no lab notes, Bernard Segal and John Thornton were reduced to cross-examination of the forensic witnesses to try to ascertain what tests really had been done in both the CID and FBI labs. But here too they faced problems. They could cross-examine only on what had been raised in direct testimony, and then only those the prosecution called. And all this would still have to be done blind—without the lab notes. But the prosecution would still take no risks. James Frier, Kathy Bond, and a number of others who had done basic lab examinations in both the FBI and CID labs would not testify. Paul Stombaugh, now retired, and his technician, Shirley Green, would be the sole FBI lab personnel to take the stand. Those who had done the tests that constituted exculpatory evidence, who might through cross-examination reveal something of the full picture, were left off the witness rosters.

When Stombaugh's credentials as a textile-impression expert, a speciality in which he himself admitted he had never been qualified, were challenged in court, Judge Dupree became visibly angry and overruled Segal. In fact, defense research showed unsurprisingly that the white-haired, authoritative-sounding former head of the FBI's Chemistry Unit was not even a chemist, let alone a fabric-impression expert. He had a bachelor of science degree from Furman University in Greenville, South Carolina, having majored in biology.

As such, it was hardly surprising that Stombaugh's fabric testimony was frequently embarrassing. He could not demonstrate in court how he had concluded that MacDonald's pajama top had been torn after being bloodied, failing to find a single stain visible across the tear in the fabric despite being supplied with a lightbox while on the stand. Stombaugh later admitted that his emphatic assertions that stains on a sheet found in the master bedroom were the murderer's hand and shoulder prints had no scientific basis. He went on to admit that no comparisons were even attempted let alone matched. He had also failed to use a microscope to search for hair follicle patterns within the bloodstains, a normal means of identifying such prints.

But two elements of Stombaugh's evidence testimony at trial were even more suspicious. In a vial containing debris collected from the bedspread in the master bedroom, Paul Stombaugh claimed to have found a hair of Colette's twisted around a blood-soaked thread of purple cotton, a thread from Jeffrey MacDonald's pajamas. This was, in one defense team researcher's words, almost "too cute" to be true—silent testimony of a life and death struggle between husband and wife. If Stombaugh had indeed found the intertwined hair and thread, no one else who had examined the evidence had seen it.

Lab notes released under the Freedom of Information Act well after the trial show that CID lab technician Dillard Browning had inventoried the same vial's contents on March 5, 1970, separating and identifying all the debris within a week. He concluded that the only hair in the vial was daughter Kimberley's, not Colette's, and he found no hair entwined with a pajama yarn or fiber. It seemed unlikely Browning had made a mistake. In fact, CID technicians eventually inventoried all the exhibits on which hairs were found and all the exhibits on which pajama fibers were found. Moreover, Browning himself had reexamined the hair and fiber evidence under a microscope six months after making his initial inventory.

Had there been any such evidence, there would be little doubt that the army would have used this golden nugget. Indeed, such was its significance that it may have tipped the scales in the decision on whether to press charges against Jeffrey MacDonald; it certainly would have been at the center of any prosecutor's case. Equally dubious was the handling of this crucial evidence, which seemed to make its fabrication all too possible. The evidence had not only apparently not existed when the vial left the CID evidence depository on September 24, 1974, it had been transmitted not by the usual registered mail but carried personally by Brian Murtagh in his station wagon. Moreover, according to dispatch and receipt records, Murtagh had taken nine days to transport the evidence from Fort Gordon, Georgia, to the FBI lab in Washington, D.C.

In court, Paul Stombaugh admitted receiving the vial personally from Murtagh at FBI headquarters. When asked about its dubious origin, he categorically denied any possibility of foul play: "It's just a bunch of crap. That defense attorney has suggested everything. He's about as ethical as a one-legged dog."[60] Stombaugh insists that the hair and pajama thread—he recalled it as a yarn or clump of fibers—were listed among the evidence and intertwined when they were delivered to him at the FBI lab. "I know of no evidence—nothing that would indicate to me that something came from another source. Everything I looked at in that case had a reason to be there," he says.[61]

But the intertwined hair and yarn or thread were not the only crucial evidence that mysteriously changed in transit from the army CID depository to Stombaugh at the FBI lab. A short brown hair had been found in Colette MacDonald's left hand. Browning had described it as an "arm or body hair." His colleague Janice Glisson even drew a picture of the hair in her notes and made dozens of attempts at comparison with sample hairs from nine known people, starting rather optimistically with the blond Jeffrey MacDonald. A glass slide with the mounted mystery hair was handed over to Stombaugh along with the other evidence Murtagh delivered personally in October 1974.

Although it had already been used for multiple comparisons, Stombaugh deemed it worthless for others. "This hair fragment does not exhibit enough individual characteristics to be of value for comparison and identification purposes," he concluded in a lab report.[62] Had the hair been swapped, damaged, or tampered with in some way? Who was Stombaugh to make such a judgment? Janice Glisson did, in fact, testify at Jeffrey MacDonald's trial, but Murtagh was careful to qualify her only as a blood expert. As a result the jury not only heard nothing of the mystery hair but also nothing of the comparison tests, evidence that in itself "could have destroyed the government's circumstantial case," according to Segal.[63]

But of all Stombaugh's inadequate forensics, it was perhaps his bizarre folding experiment with Jeffrey MacDonald's pajama top, the key government exhibit, that proved the most ridiculous. The prosecution alleged that MacDonald had stabbed his wife repeatedly with an ice pick through the folded pajama top. Even without the lab notes needed for proper cross-examination, Segal and Thornton managed to expose the efforts to match the forty-eight holes in the fabric with the twenty-one stab wounds in Colette's chest as improbable, unscientific, and incompetent. "I was just stunned by it all," recalls Jeffrey MacDonald. "Anyone with an IQ of more than ten could see that this guy was incompetent— it was beyond belief."[64]

Stombaugh's proof amounted to efforts to match the holes and wounds using skewers inserted into a dummy representing Colette. Yet it demonstrated nothing more than the fact that all the holes could be used by folding the garment in various ways. It did not prove that it had happened, and as defense expert John Thornton pointed out on the stand, it made the huge assumption that the pajama top had not shifted position after each forceful blow. On the stand, a comparison of photos of the crime scene and his own experiment forced Stombaugh to admit that he had not in any case managed to replicate the scene precisely. Segal then made him appear totally at Murtagh's bidding when he asked him why he had not considered the thirty punctures and eighteen cuts that had been made in Colette's own pajama top that had, according to the prosecution, lain between the body and the folded pajama top. "They did not ask that we do that," explained Stombaugh.[65]

The former FBI lab unit chief was also forced to admit that he had ignored the fact that the ice-pick blade was tapered: i.e., the width of the garment hole over a given wound would have to match, as would the actual depth of the wound. No measurements had been taken at the FBI lab, Stombaugh confessed. That fact quickly became obvious in court. Stombaugh had insisted that some of the holes in the pajama top proved that the ice pick had penetrated "up the hilt"—four and a half inches. In fact, the pathologist's report said the deepest wounds in Colette's chest were about one and a half inches. Stombaugh admitted he had not actually read the autopsy report.

The false, flawed science of the pajama experiment should have been enough to warn off the jury, even without all the other evidence that they, like Segal and Thornton, had been denied. The full scale of that suppression was only to become obvious nearly a decade after the jury had taken less than six hours in August 1979 to find Jeffrey MacDonald guilty of triple murder. Working through the boxes of finally released documents in the late 1980s, Raymond Shedlick, Jr., a retired New York homicide detective, and his daughter, Ellen Dannelly, collated and studied more than 250 of the sets of handwritten lab notes that Brian Murtagh had denied MacDonald's defense lawyer. The notes dealt with sixty-four exhibits used in the trial as evidence; thirty-seven of these contained findings that challenged prosecution claims. Only three, less than a tenth of these thirty-seven findings, were transcribed into the typed formal lab reports that had been turned over to the defense.[66]

With her father dying of terminal lung cancer in an adjoining room, Dannelly, a private investigator in her own right, continued her research through January 1989, occasionally reporting what she was finding back to Shedlick. Dannelly finally concluded that the FBI and CID laboratories had disagreed over twenty-two hair exhibits and nineteen fiber exhibits.[67] The disagreements were often incredibly basic, including the numbers and types of hairs or fibers recovered from a particular place at the crime scene. If examiners could not even agree on how many or what type of hairs or fibers they had under the microscopes, Dannelly asked herself, how could they possibly match anything?

Jeffrey MacDonald remains in jail. During a series of appeals, the first made in 1984–85, he has been as much a victim of the judicial system as he was during the investigation and trial. In March 1985, Judge Dupree, by now revealed as the father-in-law of the first Justice Department lawyer to handle the MacDonald case, denied a defense team habeas corpus petition for a new trial. He ignored Helena Stoeckley's confession and, despite the evidence of the bloody syringe, the bloody palm print, the missing piece of skin, and the wiped fingerprints, ruled that: "No direct evidence of the alleged intruders was found to support MacDonald's version . . . of the murders."[68]

If the judge was ruling the appeal out because no laboratory evidence indicated intruders—a result of his own refusal to force Brian Murtagh to hand over the lab notes back in 1979—Harvey Silverglate, by then MacDonald's defense lawyer, aimed to give Dupree the opportunity to keep his promise about getting "reversal." As a result of the release of the lab notes in the 1980s, Silverglate was able for the first time in 1990 to file a motion highlighting the existence of the unmatched black wool and blonde saran fibers. After an oral hearing in Raleigh in June 1991, Dupree again ruled in favor of Brian Murtagh. The prosecutor had by now changed his tune—admitting the existence of such fibers but managing at the same time to dismiss them as insignificant.

In July 1991, Dupree ruled that the lab notes did indeed hold exculpatory information and that information had been withheld. But somewhat more predictably, Dupree went on to rule that the defense had been given the opportunity to examine the physical evidence itself in the jail cell, even though it was now known just how impossible that task had actually been.[69] The released lab notes had, for instance, revealed some apparently willful mislabeling. The blonde saran fibers had been stored in a container labeled "Black and Grey Synthetic Hairs."

The access to the evidence negated the fact that the defense had not seen the lab notes, Dupree ruled. In an ominous note, the judge also ruled that the black wool and blonde saran fibers, now known to have been described openly as wig hair by army CID examiner Janice Glisson in her lab notes, must be ruled out as "new" evidence. They could and should have been presented in the 1984–85 petition, Dupree ruled, since the ten thousand pages of documentation from which they were drawn had been released in 1983.[70] MacDonald's lawyer at the time, Brian O'Neill, who had chosen to concentrate on Helena Stoeckley's confession in the 1983–84 appeal, had lacked due diligence and thus the wig and black wool fibers were effectively "old" evidence, even though no jury had heard about them.

The problem was that by 1991 the goalposts had been moved during the twelve years MacDonald had been in jail. In an effort to cut down on frivolous appeals, a more rightward-leaning Supreme Court had, in April 1991, made it much more difficult for defendants to receive a second appeal hearing, even if they had discovered new evidence or had found proof that the government had withheld evidence. Evidence that in the past would have been sufficient to secure a new trial now had to be sufficient in the view of the appeals court judges to prove actual innocence. It was a much higher threshold. Yet if ever there was a case with such evidence, this was it. Harvey Silverglate and his defense team, Philip Cormier and Alan Dershowitz, framed their February 1992 appeal to three judges at the Fourth Circuit Court of Appeals in Richmond, Virginia, accordingly.

The ruling in June 1992 was another bitter disappointment. The judges denied the petition on the basis of "procedural fault." Jeffrey MacDonald, they decided, should have presented his claims in the 1984–85 appeal, as Dupree had ruled. The judges did not even go beyond this technicality to consider the real issues, which by now included the extraordinary claim by the prosecution lawyers that the unmatched hairs and fibers the defense team were focusing on were "household rubbish." As Alan Dershowitz pointed out to the judges, this was effectively a denial of the Locard theory, allowing the prosecution to include evidence that inculpated Jeffrey MacDonald but exclude at will that which exculpated him. It was the ultimate articulation of the imperative that had driven the investigation from the start: only find, only examine, only present what you are looking for.

On the Richmond sidewalk outside the appeals court, Alan Dershowitz pushed a copy of one of the two texts that listed saran as a polymer used in wigs under the nose of a television reporter. "Can you get your camera on that? Can you see that? Well, so could the prosecutor. He lied to the judge moments ago. He lied to me. He lied to you," he fumed.[71] The prosecutor's alleged lie was of course based on Michael Malone's lie in the infamous affidavit, a document in which he had also reinterpreted Locard's theory to suit the case. "It should be noted that the presence of unknown or unmatched fibers on an individual or his clothing is so common that normally, it is not considered forensically significant," Malone swore.[72] The statement begged a simple question: what then was the purpose of Michael Malone's job as a hair-and-fiber examiner?

Lying was certainly part of the job, as the release of the pages of the FBI lab texts covering saran in 1993 was to prove and the IG's report covering Malone's testimony in the Alcee Hastings matter was to confirm. Such evidence now has become part of another appeal filed in April 1997, an appeal to examine the evidence in an independent lab, an appeal for justice in the apparently endless case of Jeffrey MacDonald. With Judge Dupree now dead and the FBI lab exposed by the IG's report, a new judge, James Fox, is at the time of this writing looking at the evidence. In Harvey Silverglate's words: "The poor guy is going to need a little time." [73]

EPILOGUE

THE END OF THE BEGINNING

On November 5, 1997, Fred Whitehurst could be seen threading his way through dozens of dining tables at a formal luncheon at the Waldorf Astoria Hotel in Manhattan. To loud applause, he shook hands with William Worthy, a professor emeritus at Howard University in Washington, D.C., and accepted a Hugh M. Hefner First Amendment Award. The citation accompanying the plaque was unequivocal. Whitehurst had "with great courage, jeopardized his life's work and despite retaliation for his efforts, made public his assertions of fraud and scientific misconduct within the FBI crime lab." Still suspended from his post yet not fired, Whitehurst was unable to make a speech. He and his attorneys considered the Bureau's demand that he have anything he said cleared beforehand a violation of his First Amendment rights. To those present, the FBI's attitude seemed the perfect endorsement of Whitehurst's receipt of a freedom of speech award.

Until a settlement was reached in March 1998, Fred Whitehurst was in suspended animation, subject to the FBI's gag on speaking out yet forbidden to work, set foot on FBI property, or even talk to colleagues about the issues he has raised. Even the Bureau seemed unclear about why they suspended him when, one Friday afternoon in January 1997, his gun and badge were confiscated and he was marched out of the J. Edgar Hoover Building by armed guards. On March 5, 1997, FBI director Louis Freeh told a congressional committee that the action against Whitehurst was taken "solely and directly" on the basis of a recommendation in the inspector general's report, as then unpublished.[1] The FBI director told the representatives that the IG's office "did not object" to the action.

Freeh's testimony drew a furious response from the IG himself, Mike Bromwich. The following day Bromwich sent Freeh a letter stating that his office had been consistently informed that the FBI had not taken action against Whitehurst solely on the basis of the IG's recommendations. He added that he had in fact consistently opposed any suspension, a position he had held for "more than a year when FBI representatives had repeatedly proposed firing Whitehurst or placing him on some sort of administrative leave."[2] Bromwich added that Freeh's testimony implied that the action had been based on the draft report. "The draft report contains no such recommendation, nor can it be fairly construed to imply that such action should be taken."[3]

Freeh quickly admitted that his testimony to Congress was incomplete and submitted an amendment to the record. However, letters to both Congressman William Rogers and Inspector General Michael Bromwich raised as many questions as they answered. If Freeh had recused himself from Whitehurst-related disciplinary or administrative matters in the face of the accusations about his conduct in the VANPAC case, as he maintained, what was he doing testifying about it to Congress or writing letters on the subject?[4] "What kind of recusal is this? Is this part of a Kafka novel?" asked Senator Grassley from the Senate floor on March 17.

What was clear is that the FBI wanted to get rid of Fred Whitehurst but to deflect the blame for doing so onto someone else. The fact remains that the three people most heavily criticized in the IG's report, Tom Thurman, Roger Martz, and David Williams, are still working for the FBI, but Fred Whitehurst is not. The FBI has suggested that it would be impossible for Fred Whitehurst to return to work given the accusations he made against colleagues. Yet many of those actually doing the work at the FBI lab seem to have no problem with Fred Whitehurst returning to work. "The only problem would be those that have in the past been in the habit of unethical or unprofessional behavior," metallurgist Bill Tobin told congressional hearings in September 1997.[5] It is the FBI as an institution—not the individuals who make it up—that has a problem with Fred Whitehurst. For many lab staff, Whitehurst's return would act as a kind of guarantee that they could feel safe in coming forward with complaints in the future.

In dealing with Fred Whitehurst, the FBI has always aimed to shoot the messenger, to personalize the issue, to hide the failings of its science and management behind a smokescreen of disinformation, diversion, and disengagement. Louis Freeh's testimony to Congress in March 1997 was just one example. In the course of ten years of complaining, Fred Whitehurst has repeatedly found himself investigated while the issues he raised were ignored; he has been referred for psychiatric assessment to determine if he was "fit for work" and has been blackened by leaks to the press then investigated on the same charge—talking to the media. The FBI has released derogatory information about him to prosecutors in both the World Trade Center bombing and O. J. Simpson cases, set up a Whitehurst committee within the FBI to assess the impact of his allegations, and twice transferred him out of his own field of scientific expertise.

The IG determined that none of this was retaliatory, although this may only have meant that the FBI had covered its tracks well. As the IG's report admitted: "Our analysis is limited to determining whether a factual basis exists to conclude that the FBI made certain decisions with a retaliatory purpose. . . . [W]e did not attempt a full legal analysis of Whitehurst's retaliation claims under the technical requirements of the Whistleblower Protection Act (WPA) or any other legal theory of employer liability."[6] In fact the FBI was able to treat Whitehurst as it did only because the president and the attorney general had failed to extend the protections of the 1989 WPA to FBI staff, in defiance of congressional legislation.

These safeguards, which include an independent authority to review whistleblower claims, privacy provisions, and a ban on the distribution of information, were specifically designed to prevent an accused organization from retaliating. Only after Fred Whitehurst and his lawyers had filed an injunction in court requiring the White House to extend these protections to FBI employees—a move both the federal government and the FBI opposed in court—did President Clinton do just that. On April 14, one day before the IG report was finally published, the president issued a memo ordering Attorney General Janet Reno to extend WPA rights to FBI employees.[7]

But the protection of the provisions of the WPA was only one way in which Fred Whitehurst has changed the whole landscape for FBI employees. In the last three years, Louis Freeh has prioritized instruction in ethics during FBI training partially, it seems, in response to the issues raised by Fred Whitehurst. The FBI's new recruits now receive eighteen rather than two hours of instruction in every form of abuse, from inflating overtime, or "banging the books" as it is known in the FBI, an issue Whitehurst first raised more than a decade ago, to "juicing the testimony" —stretching the truth or even lying on the witness stand, the core of Whitehurst's charges. Some reports say that the instruction involves role play and situational training based on the sort of dilemmas Fred Whitehurst faced when the FBI's internal investigation proved inadequate. "They use him as a role model yet throw him out. It's amazing hypocrisy," observes Kris Kolesnik, a senior aide to Senator Chuck Grassley.[8]

Using Fred Whitehurst as a model employee in training yet punishing him for what he did in practice is only one way in which appearance and reality continue to collide in the FBI. Whatever their director's declared beliefs about ethical standards and admitting mistakes, many FBI agents do not subscribe to them. In fact, many are convinced that such ethics are dangerous and impede their ability to do their job—securing prosecutions. Even the director himself seems to have been noticeably more reluctant to admit the shortcomings of the lab than the inadequacies of other areas of the FBI.

Faced with criticism of the lab, Louis Freeh and his press office have engaged in constant damage limitation by stressing that the IG's report criticized just thirteen of more than six hundred lab employees, just three of twenty-seven lab units. They go on to stress the changes made in the lab since Freeh was made FBI director and how fully the bureau is complying with the IG's recommendations for change. In all the public relations spin-doctoring, there is of course no recognition of the limited scope of the IG's investigation or even the merest hint of a willingness to embark on a genuine overhaul by addressing the really key issue: how and why the FBI lab got into the state that necessitated the IG's investigation. The truth is that with thousands of cases at stake, the potential impact of any real recognition of the extent of the shortcomings in the lab is just too awful to contemplate. Moreover, many of these shortcomings have occurred or have continued on Louis Freeh's watch.

The FBI has always sought to make out that the problems at the FBI lab were isolated incidents, the result of explicable shortcomings or scientific disagreements, exaggerated by one obsessive employee whose credibility and even mental stability is suspect. The reality of course is that the problems in the FBI lab are systemic, deeply ingrained, and irresolvable within the current setup. An agency dedicated to securing prosecutions and controlled by law enforcement personnel cannot run a laboratory designed to report objective analytical results obtained by scientists. Many other western nations have come to realize this as a result of major miscarriages of justice; a number have reacted by removing crime labs from police control.

Louis Freeh is fully aware of this inherent conflict of interest yet rather than resolve it he has simply sharpened it. FBI agents are still employed in the lab and continue to dominate management ranks. Indeed, after the initial clean-out in favor of civilian scientists in 1994, the number of FBI agents in the lab has begun to increase again. Senior FBI officials have made it clear that there is no question of the FBI lab being put under independent government control or management. The problem of internal investigation has a simple solution: submit to more external oversight. Yet while saying he welcomes it, Freeh's actions make clear that such statements are primarily for public relations purposes only. The resistance shown to Senator Grassley's hearings is but one example.

Louis Freeh's response to demands for more external oversight has been to reinforce a completely failed internal structure, the Office of Professional Responsibility (OPR). In March, Freeh announced a new director and new resources for an office that has consistently whitewashed investigations. A press release from the FBI just weeks before the IG's report was published stated that the new OPR would be independent yet would report directly back to Louis Freeh and his deputy.[9] It was the sort of conflict of interest that had created a consistent record of failure in the first place. To many in the FBI the lesson of the IG's investigation is not

314 | TAINTING EVIDENCE

what it reported, but the very fact that it was allowed to report in the first place. Had OPR been more effective at keeping investigations in-house, had Whitehurst and his allegations not been allowed to get out of hand, there would have been no embarrassing scrutiny of the FBI lab by the IG.

There are many other indications that whatever the rhetoric, the reality remains unchanged, that the claim that everything is now rosy is as much a part of the image building as the original insistence that the FBI lab was the best forensic laboratory in the world. Lab officials are meeting with IG staff every six months to monitor implementation of the latter's forty recommendations for change. Both sides report the process is going well, with the FBI claiming that it is implementing all the recommendations. We only have their word for it. And on the one issue of significance that has come to light since the IG's report was published, the FBI lab has singularly failed to follow even its own recommendation.

In responding to the draft of the IG's report, the FBI announced that it was looking for a new lab chief. "Among the principal qualifications for the position will be an outstanding academic and practical background in forensic science and reputation for excellence in the forensic community," the FBI claimed.[10] In October, in a decision that seemed to thumb its nose at the IG and its critics, the FBI announced the appointment of Donald Kerr, a physicist-engineer and former director of the government's nuclear laboratory at Los Alamos in New Mexico. He was a man with no forensic science experience at all.

Many were deeply shocked by the appointment. Senator Grassley immediately denounced the choice as that of a "government and industry insider, whose instincts are to co-operate with management."[11] The appointment, he said, showed that the FBI had fallen miserably short of even its own standards, that its stated goals were mere "happy talk." On Donald Kerr himself, he added: "Lacking the requisite experience, how can the new lab director keep from getting snowed, forensically, by examiners who cut corners and who have gotten away with it before?"[12] William Moffitt, vice president of the National Association of Criminal Defense Lawyers, was equally irate: "Once again, the FBI has dealt with Congress and the public with incredible arrogance. . . . [B]ut why should we be surprised. The FBI has been shown to have lied time and time again in the past."[13]

The fact remains that seven years after the FBI established their

ASCLD Study Committee to prepare for accreditation, and five years after Louis Freeh took over as FBI director, the FBI lab remains both uninspected and unaccountable. The longer the delay, the more the suspicion has grown that the FBI lab or parts of it are not only unwilling to submit themselves to inspection but are unable to meet ASCLD/LAB accreditation criteria. That suspicion was only reinforced by the news in September 1997 that the FBI was intending to move the Latent Fingerprint Section out of the lab to the Bureau's Criminal Justice Information Systems Division in West Virginia, thereby removing the FBI's latent fingerprint examiners from ASCLD/LAB inspection.

In a tersely worded letter to Director Freeh, Frank Fitzpatrick, president of ASCLD, warned that the move would be a step backward given efforts "to embrace the principles of the scientific method of analysis." [14] Fitzpatrick added: "By moving Latent Fingerprints from the Laboratory Division, the public perception might be that there is something deficient in the quality assurance program in latent prints. . . . The relationship of the Latent Fingerprints Section with your other scientific sections is deep and strong. It should be allowed to remain under one management team —a team of forensic scientists." [15]

But whatever the future of the Latent Fingerprint Section and the rest of the FBI lab, the past will continue to cast a long shadow. It is now clear that thousands of old cases need to be reexamined; it is equally clear that the means of doing so, the task force within the Criminal Division of the Department of Justice that prosecuted these cases in the first place, involves as profound a conflict of interest as any in this whole story. At the congressional hearings in September 1997, Fred Whitehurst, accepting that he may never get his job back, appealed to senators to be allowed to spend the four and a half years of federal service he had left examining the case files the IG did not look at, rectifying the mistakes that as yet no one else even suspects.

There has been no formal response, but informally Whitehurst has already begun work, securing the release of the files of 150 cases under the Freedom of Information Act. Already he has exposed a raft of problems never touched on by the IG, including, he claims, the alteration of reports by five more examiners beyond those named in the report. It is yet more evidence of the systemic nature of the abuses in the FBI lab, yet more evidence that unless a full inquiry is begun now the issue will simmer on for years, maybe decades, in case after case. On past performance, the FBI will almost certainly be happy to let that happen, relying on its image machine to cover the trail and limit the damage. The question is, are the American public and Congress prepared to do the same? And beyond that, can forensic science in America ever be run by scientists?

NOTES

INTRODUCTION

1. U.S. Department of Justice, FBI Laboratory Division, *Annual Report, Fiscal Year 1996*, p. 15.
2. Beach, Bennett, "Mr. Wizard Comes to Court," *Time*, March 1, 1982.
3. Frank, Laura, and John Hanchette, "Convicted on False Evidence?: False Science Often Sways Juries, Judges," *USA Today*, July 19, 1994, and Gannett News Service, July 1994.
4. Ibid.
5. Hansen, Mark, "Out of the Blue," *American Bar Association Journal* 82 (February 1996), 50.
6. *Doepel v. United States*, 434 A. 2d 449 (D.C. App. 1981).
7. Memorandum from Special Agent Jay Cochran to Dr. Briggs White, dated February 5, 1975.
8. Starrs, James E., "The Ethical Obligations of the Forensic Scientist in the Criminal Justice System," *Journal of the Association of Official Analytical Chemists*, vol. 54, no. 4 (1971), pp. 1–12.
9. Interview with John Kelly, August 1997.
10. Interview with Phillip Wearne, March 1997.
11. Fisher, David, *Hard Evidence* (New York: Simon & Schuster, 1995), p. 23.
12. Interview with Phillip Wearne, March 1997.
13. Hodge, Evan, "Guarding Against Error," *Journal of the Association of Firearms and Toolmark Examiners*, 20 (July 1988), 290–293.
14. Interview with Phillip Wearne, March 1997.

15. National Academy of Science, Committee on Evaluation of Speech Spectrograms, "On the Theory and Practice of Voice Identification" (NAS, 1979).

16. *State v. Kline*, 909 P. 2d 1171 (1996).

17. Barnett, Peter, Edward Blake, and Rogert Ogle, Jr., "The Role of the Independent Expert: Several Case Examples," paper presented at the annual meeting of the American Academy of Forensic Sciences, Los Angeles, California, February 19, 1981.

18. Interview with John Kelly, August 1997.

19. Interview with John Kelly, September 1997.

20. Barnett, Peter, Edward Blake, and Robert Ogle, Jr., "FBI Laboratory Problems," letter appearing in *Scientific Sleuthing Review*, vol. 21, no. 1 (Spring 1997), 19.

21. Letter from Professor Brian Caddy to Robert Nigh, Jr., of Jones, Wyatt & Roberts, dated August 6, 1996.

22. Interview with John Kelly, August 1997.

23. Interview with Phillip Wearne, March 1997.

24. Starrs, James E., "Mountebanks among Forensic Scientists," *Forensic Science Handbook, Vol. II*, New York: Prentice Hall, 1988, pp. 2–37.

25. Peterson, Joseph L., "Ethical Issues in the Collection, Examination and Use of Physical Evidence in Forensic Science," American Chemical Society, Washington, D.C. (1986) Geoffrey Davies, ed., p. 43.

26. Stoney, David, "A Medical Model for Criminalistics Education," 33 *Journal of Forensic Science* (1988), 1088.

27. Interviews of Duayne Dillon and others by John Kelly, September 1997.

28. Interview with John Kelly, September 1997.

29. Interview with Phillip Wearne, March 1997.

30. Starrs, James E., "The Ethical Obligations."

31. Frank and Hanchette.

32. Interview with Phillip Wearne, April 1997.

33. Frank and Hanchette.

34. Interview with John Kelly, August 1997.

35. Lander, Eric, "DNA Fingerprinting on Trial," 339 *Nature* (1989), 501, 505.

36. Peterson, J. L., E. L. Fabricant, K. S. Field, and J. I. Thornton, *Crime Laboratory Proficiency Testing Research Program* (Washington, D.C.: U.S. Government Printing Office, 1978).

37. Letter from James Dempsey to John Kelly, dated October 24, 1997.

38. Interview with John Kelly, October 1997.

39. ASCLD/LAB listing, dated December 8, 1996.

40. Interview with John Kelly, May 1997.
41. Interview with John Kelly, September 1997.
42. Peterson, Joseph L. and Penelope N. Markham, "Crime Laboratory Proficiency Testing Results, 1978–1991, I: Identification and Classification of Physical Evidence and Resolving Problems of Common Origin," *Journal of Forensic Sciences*, vol. 40, no. 6 (November 1995), 994–1008, 1009–1029.
43. Interview with John Kelly, August 1997.
44. Latent Prints Examination, Report No. 9508, Collaborative Testing Services.
45. Grieve, David L., "Possession of Truth," *Journal of Forensic Identity*, vol. 46 no. 5 (1996), 521–528.
46. House of Representatives Subcommittee on Civil and Constitutional Rights, Committee on the Judiciary, *Hearings on FBI Authorization— Forensic Science Laboratories and Jurisdiction on Indian Reservations*, April 2, 1981.
47. Ibid.
48. Interview with John Kelly, September 1997.

1. THE WHISTLEBLOWER VERSUS THE FRIENDS OF LOUIE

1. Undated memo from Fred Whitehurst.
2. U.S. Department of Justice, Office of the Inspector General, *The FBI Laboratory: An Investigation into Laboratory Practices and Alleged Misconduct in Explosives-Related and Other Cases*, April 1997, p. 26.
3. Ibid., p. 26.
4. Ibid., p. 28.
5. Ibid., p. 28.
6. Ibid., pp. 30–31.
7. Interview with John Kelly and Phillip Wearne, July 1996.
8. Ibid.
9. Interview with Phillip Wearne, March 1997.
10. Letter to John Hicks from Joseph Russoniello and Charles Burch, United States Attorney's Office, Northern District of California, dated July 8, 1989.
11. Ibid.
12. Ibid.
13. Memorandum from Administrative Services Division dated July 7, 1990.
14. Interview with John Kelly, August 1997.

15. Theoharis, Athan G. and John Stuart Cox, *The Boss, J. Edgar Hoover and the Great American Inquisition*, Philadelphia: Temple University Press, p. 95.
16. Summers, Anthony, *The Secret Life of J. Edgar Hoover*, Pocket (New York: Pocket Books, 1994), p. 419.
17. Letter from John Hicks to Charles Burch, dated July 28, 1989.
18. Memorandum from the American Society of Crime Laboratory Directors (ASCLD) Study Committee to John Hicks dated March 27, 1991.
19. Ibid.
20. Ibid.
21. Ibid., Technical Procedures Section.
22. Ibid., Proposed Policy, Technical Procedures Section.
23. Memorandum from ASCLD Study Committee to John Hicks dated September 9, 1991.
24. Ibid.
25. Memorandum from ASCLD Study Committee to John Hicks dated September 6, 1991.
26. Ibid.
27. Ibid.
28. Memorandum from ASCLD Study Committee to John Hicks dated September 10, 1991; see also Office of the Inspector General, *The FBI Laboratory*, pp. 5, 6.
29. Memorandum from ASCLD Study Committee to John Hicks, September 6, 1991.
30. Office of the Inspector General, *The FBI Laboratory*, p. 6.
31. Ibid., p. 8.
32. Order Compelling Production, *State of Arizona v. Alvie Copeland Kiles*, CR 15444/15577, June 26, 1989.
33. Letters from James Kearney to Simon Ford, dated September 15 and 21, 1989.
34. Letter from James Kearney to Simon Ford, dated September 21, 1989.
35. *State of Iowa v. Bobby Lee Smith*, No. 41733, December 18, 1989.
36. FBI memorandum from Legal Counsel to Assistant Director, Laboratory Division, April 20, 1990.
37. Ibid.
38. Letter from Jeff Brown to the Honorable Don Edwards, dated November 29, 1989.
39. Editorial, *Journal of Forensic Sciences*, vol 34. no. 5 (September 1989), 1051.

40. Jeff Brown to the Honorable Don Edwards, November 29, 1989.

41. Office of the Inspector General, *The FBI Laboratory*, p. 7.

42. Klaidman, Daniel, "Pushing the FBI into the 21st Century," *American Lawyer*, October 1994.

43. Ibid.

44. Interview with John Kelly, August 1997.

45. Interview with John Kelly, October 1997.

46. Interview with John Kelly, August 1997.

47. Kessler, Ronald, *The FBI* (New York: Pocket Books, 1994), p. 529.

48. Interview with Phillip Wearne, February 1997.

49. Fisher, David, *Hard Evidence* (New York: Simon & Schuster, 1995), p. 62.

50. Ibid., p. 65.

51. Egan, Timothy, "Terrorism Now Going Homespun as Bombings in the U.S. Spread," *New York Times*, August 25, 1995.

52. Interview with John Kelly, October 1997.

53. Memorandum to Howard Shapiro from Steven Robinson and John Sylvester, May 1994.

54. Ibid., p. 5.

55. U.S. Department of Justice, Office of the Inspector General, Audit Division, *Audit Report, Federal Bureau of Investigation, Forensic Services* (June 1994), 94–27.

56. Ibid., p. 14.

57. Ibid., pp. 14–15.

58. For the details of how this happened see Chapter 5.

59. Interview with John Kelly, October 1997.

60. This information comes from FBI briefing documents supplied to congressional representatives.

61. Suro, Roberto and Pierre Thomas, "FBI Lab Woes Put 50 Cases in Jeopardy—Experts Questioned FBI Lab Practices Years Before Inspector General Report," *Washington Post*, February 14, 1997.

62. Executive Summary and Background section of an FBI document announcing the relocation of the FBI laboratory.

63. FBI briefing document including answers to a series of questions arising during lab briefing of appropriations staff, May 26, 1995.

64. Ibid.

65. Office of the Inspector General, *Audit Report*, pp. 16–18.

66. FBI briefing document including answers.

67. Ibid.

68. See for instance, McGee, Jim, "The Rise of the FBI," *Washington Post Magazine*, July 20, 1997.

2. THE UNABOMBER: CLUELESS

1. Letter addressed to *The New York Times*, dated April 24, 1995, mailed Oakland, California.
2. Reuters (Sacramento), "Kaczynski Kin Dispute FBI," *Washington Post*, March 5, 1997.
3. Gibbs, Nancy, et al., *Mad Genius: The Odyessy, Pursuit, and Capture of the Unabomber Suspect* (New York: Warner Books, 1996), p. 141.
4. Douglas, John and Mark Olshaker, *Unabomber—On the Trail of America's Most-Wanted Serial Killer* (New York: Pocket Books, 1996), p. 80.
5. Johnson, Kevin, "Kaczynski cabin like a lab," *USA Today*, November 13, 1996.
6. Despite every effort, the authors have been unable to see a copy of this undated memorandum entitled "UNABOM review by SSA Burmeister" and written sometime in the spring of 1994. However, a copy was obtained by the Inspector General's team investigating the FBI lab (see Office of the Inspector General, *The FBI Laboratory*, page 303) and by journalist Jeff Stein, who detailed its conclusions in an article entitled "Much Unabomber evidence is blown; Internal FBI audit can't track down data," *Baltimore Sun*, April 7, 1996.
7. U.S. Department of Justice, Office of Inspector General, *The FBI Laboratory: An Investigation into Laboratory Practices and Alleged Misconduct in Explosives Related and Other Cases*, April 1997, p. 309.
8. Interview of Terry Rudolph by Special Agent Robert Mellado and others, Office of the Inspector General, Special Investigative Team/ Whitehurst Review, Case No. 9403575, June 4, 1996.
9. Gibbs, et al, Mad Genius, p. 76.
10. Office of the Inspector General, *The FBI Laboratory*, p. 310.
11. Interview of Terry Rudolph, June 4, 1996.
12. Office of Inspector General, *The FBI Laboratory*, p. 310.
13. Interview of Terry Rudolph, June 4, 1996.
14. Rudolph, Terry L., and Edward C. Bender, "A Scheme for the Analysis of Explosives and Explosive Residues," paper delivered at FBI Symposium, Quantico, Virginia, 1983.
15. Interview of Terry Rudolph, June 4, 1996.
16. Ibid.

17. Office of the Inspector General, *The FBI Laboratory*, p. 314.

18. Ibid.

19. Ibid., p. 315.

20. Interview of Special Agent Steven Burmeister by Special Agent Joseph Lestrange and others, Office of the Inspector General, Special Investigative Team/Whitehurst Review, Case No. 9403575, April 22, 1996.

21. Gibbs, et al. *Mad Genius*, p. 89.

22. Ibid., pp. 86, 96.

23. Interview with John Kelly, October 1997.

24. Ibid.

25. Ibid.

26. Interview with John Kelly, September 1997.

27. Howard, John, Associated Press, (Sacramento), April 16, 1997.

28. Ibid.

29. "FBI Crime Lab: Cleanup or Coverup?" *The Champion*, National Association of Criminal Defense Lawyers, June 1997.

30. Office of the Inspector General, *The FBI Laboratory*, p. 32.

31. Ibid., p. 32.

32. Ibid., p. 33.

33. Ibid., pp. 35–36.

34. Ibid., p. 39.

35. Interview of Supervisory Special Agent John Dietz by Special Agent Nicole Cubbage, Office of the Inspector General, Special Investigative Team/Whitehurst Review Case No.9403575, August 29, 1996.

36. Ibid.

37. Office of the Inspector General, *The FBI Laboratory*, p. 43.

38. Ibid., p. 44.

39. Memorandum from Terry Rudolph to John Hicks, dated August 18, 1992.

40. Office of the Inspector General, *The FBI Laboratory*, p. 48.

41. Ibid.

42. Ibid., pp. 48–49.

43. Ibid., p. 49.

44. Interview of Terry Rudolph by Special Agent Joseph Lestrange and others, Office of Inspector General, Special Investigative Team/Whitehurst Review, Case No. 9403575, February 28, 1996.

45. Interview of Ken Nimmich by Special Agent Kim Thomas and others, Office of Inspector General, Special Investigative Team/Whitehurst Review, Case No. 9403575, April 26, 1996.

46. Ibid.

47. Office of the Inspector General, *The FBI Laboratory*, p. 352.

48. Ibid., p. 44.

49. Interview of Steve Robinson by Special Agent Robert Mellado, Memorandum of Investigation, Special Investigative Team/Whitehurst Review, Case No. 9403575, April 5, 1996.

50. Ibid.

51. Interview with John Kelly, September 1997.

52. Interview of Terry Rudolph, February 28, 1996.

53. Ibid.

54. Interview with John Kelly, October 1997.

55. Ibid.

56. Interview with John Kelly, September 1997.

57. Cohen, Laurie P. "FBI Transferred, or Even Promoted Problem Agents," *Wall Street Journal*, September 26, 1997.

58. Interview with John Kelly, October 1997.

3. VANPAC: EXPRESS MAIL JUSTICE

1. Memorandum from John Hicks to James Greenleaf dated October 23, 1990.

2. Fisher, David, *Hard Evidence* (New York: Simon & Schuster, 1995), p. 14.

3. Affidavit of John Phillips, United States District Court, Middle District of Alabama, Southern Division, *Robert Wayne O'Ferrell, et al. v. USA et al.*, Case No. CV-92-A-1450-S, September 23, 1996.

4. Winne, Mark, *Priority Mail* (New York: Scribner 1995), p. 46, and interviews of Frank Lee and Lloyd Erwin with John Kelly, June 1997.

5. Winne, *Priority Mail*, pp. 46–49.

6. Ibid., p. 48.

7. Interview with John Kelly, July 1997.

8. Fisher, *Hard Evidence*, p. 15.

9. Interview with John Kelly, October 1997.

10. Ibid.

11. Fisher, *Hard Evidence*, p. 15.

12. Memorandum from Supervisory Special Agent Frederic Whitehurst to Supervisory Special Agent David Glendinning, dated September 5, 1994.

13. Fisher, *Hard Evidence*, p. 15.

14. Winne, *Priority Mail*, p. 122.

15. Interview with John Kelly, June 1997.

16. Kessler, Ronald, *The FBI* (New York: Pocket Books 1994), p. 287.

17. Ibid., p. 290.

18. FBI teletype, O 182315Z Jan 90, received in Washington January 19, 1990.

19. FBI teletype, P 150132Z May 90, received in Washington May 15, 1990.

20. Government exhibit 1078T in *USA* v. *Walter Leroy Moody, Jr.* Crim. No.1-90-383, June 1991, recorded April 19, 1990.

21. Kessler, *The FBI*, p. 291.

22. McConnell, Malcolm, "Hunt for a Mad Bomber," *Readers Digest*, August 1993.

23. Memorandum from Supervisory Special Agent Frederic Whitehurst to Scientific Analysis Section chief James Kearney, no date, believed to be May or June 1995, p. 26.

24. U.S. Department of Justice, Office of the Inspector General, *The FBI Laboratory: An Investigation into Laboratory Practices and Alleged Misconduct in Explosives-Related and Other Cases*, April 1997, p. 81.

25. Kessler, *The FBI*, p. 287.

26. Ibid., p. 294.

27. Ibid.

28. Interview with John Kelly, February 1997.

29. FBI lab report, FBI file No. 89B-BH-37993, Lab. No. 50518046 S QF, dated August 14, 1995.

30. Affidavit of Edward Tolley, United States District Court, Northern District of Georgia, Atlanta Division, *USA* v. *Walter Leroy Moody, Jr.* Criminal Indictment No. 1:90-CR-383, April 16, 1996.

31. Affidavit of James Thurman, United States District Court, Northern District of Georgia, Atlanta Division, *USA* v. *Walter Leroy Moody, Jr.* Criminal Indictment No. 1:90-CR-383, April 8, 1996.

32. Office of the Inspector General, Interview of Louis J. Freeh by Special Agent Kimberly Thomas, Memorandum of Investigation, Special Investigative Team/Whitehurst Review, Case No. 9403575, April 24, 1996.

33. Interview with John Kelly, December 1996.

34. Ibid.

35. *USA* v. *Walter Leroy Moody, Jr.* Crim. No.1-90-383, June 4, 1991.

36. Ibid.

37. Ibid.

38. Ibid., June 14, 1991.

39. Ibid.

40. Ibid.

41. Letter from Louis Freeh to the Hon. G. Kendall Sharp, United States District Judge, dated July 15, 1991.
42. *USA v. Walter Leroy Moody, Jr.* Crim. No. 1-90-383, June 14, 1991.
43. Office of the Inspector General, *The FBI Laboratory*, p. 62.
44. Interview with Phillip Wearne, March 1997.
45. Office of the Inspector General, *The FBI Laboratory*, p. 77.
46. Memorandum from Supervisory Special Agent Frederic Whitehurst to Scientific Analysis Section Chief James Kearney; Ibid.
47. Ibid.
48. Ibid.
49. *USA v. Walter Leroy Moody, Jr.* Crim. No. 1-90-383, June 17, 1991.
50. Ibid.
51. Ibid.
52. Ibid.
53. Ibid.
54. Ibid.
55. Office of the Inspector General, *The FBI Laboratory*, p. 68.
56. Ibid., p. 69.
57. *USA v. Walter Leroy Moody, Jr.* Crim No. 1-90-383, June 14, 1991.
58. Rush, Robert, Jr., *Comparative Analysis, Improvised Explosive Devices re USA v. Walter Leroy Moody, Jr.* 1:90-CR-383.
59. Hansen, Donald, *Examination of Bomb Related Evidence in Criminal Indictment No. 1:90-CR-383.*
60. Rush, Jr., *Comparative Analysis.*
61. Hansen, *Examination of Bomb Related Evidence.*
62. Rush, Jr., *Comparative Analysis.*
63. Interview with John Kelly, January 1997.
64. Interview with John Kelly, February 1997.
65. *USA v. Walter Leroy Moody, Jr.* Crim. No. 1-90-383, June 26, 1991.
66. Interview with John Kelly, February 1997.
67. FBI teletype from FBI Atlanta to Director FBI, O 060107Z, date received redacted, sometime March 1990.
68. Rush, Jr., *Comparative Analysis.*
69. Interview with John Kelly, February 1997.
70. Winne, *Priority Mail*, p. 290.
71. Interview of Louis J. Freeh.
72. *USA v. Walter Leroy Moody, Jr.* Crim. No. 1-90-383, June 26, 1991.
73. Winne, *Priority Mail*, p. 99.

4. RUBY RIDGE: SCREW-UP, COVER-UP, CONSPIRACY

1. Interview with Phillip Wearne, June 1997.
2. Department of Justice Task Force, *Report Regarding Internal Investigation of Shootings at Ruby Ridge,* June 1994.
3. Kerr, Christophir, "Ruby Ridge Investigation Astray," *Washington Times,* September 15, 1995.
4. *Report Regarding.*
5. Kevin Keating, "Bullet that Killed Sammy Weaver Found Sheriff Says," *Spokesman Review,* May 15, 1996.
6. Interview with John Kelly, August 1997.
7. *Report Regarding.*
8. Ibid.
9. Interview with John Kelly, August 1997.
10. This information comes from a memorandum to Barbara Berman, assistant counsel, Office of Professional Responsibility, Department of Justice, and coordinator of the Department of Justice Task Force on Ruby Ridge, from prosecutors Ronald Howen and Kim Lindquist, dated August 11, 1993.
11. Hearings before the Subcommittee on Terrorism, Technology and Government Information, *The Federal Raid on Ruby Ridge, ID,* September/October 1995, U.S. Government Printing Office, 1997, p. 1131.
12. *Report Regarding.*
13. Ibid.
14. George Lardner, "FBI Aide Admits Obstruction," *Washington Post,* October 31, 1996.
15. Memorandum to Barbara Berman.
16. *The Federal Raid on Ruby Ridge, ID,* p. 856.
17. Memorandum to Barbara Berman.
18. *Report Regarding.*
19. Memorandum to Barbara Berman.
20. FSSI Case #95/61CV Report Re: Investigation into the Fatal Shooting of Samuel Weaver by Lucien C. Haag to Senate Subcommittee on Terrorism, Technology and Government Information.
21. Ibid., table 2, p. 8.
22. *The Federal Raid on Ruby Ridge, ID,* p. 1128.
23. *Report Regarding.*
24. Ibid.
25. Memorandum to Barbara Berman.

26. Spence, Gerry, *From Freedon to Slavery*, (New York: St. Martin's Griffin, 1996), p. 42.
27. Interview with John Kelly, October 1997.
28. Ibid.
29. Walter, Jess, *Every Knee Shall Bow—The Truth and Tragedy of Ruby Ridge and the Randy Weaver Family* (New York: Regan Books, HarperCollins, 1995), p. 330.
30. Spence, *From Freedom to Slavery*, p. 40.
31. Bock, Alan, *Ambush at Ruby Ridge* (Irvine, California: Dickens Press, 1995), p. 151.
32. Spence, *From Freedom to Slavery*, p. 45.
33. Ostow, Ronald, "Freeh Reign," Los Angeles Times Sunday Magazine, February 5, 1995, p. 20.
34. Memo from Louis Freeh to Jamie Gorelick, dated March 7, 1995.
35. Ibid.
36. Letter from Special Agent in Charge Eugene Glenn to Michael Shaheen, dated May 3, 1995.
37. Klaidman, Daniel, "Ruby Ridge Cover-Up Probe Widens," *Legal Times*, November 6, 1995, and interview of the writer by John Kelly, August 1997.
38. Press release from the Department of Justice, August 15, 1997.
39. Letter from Maurice Ellsworth to Janet Reno, dated August 6, 1993.
40. Interview with John Kelly, October 1997.
41. Interview with John Kelly, August 1997.
42. *The Federal Raid on Ruby Ridge ID*, p. 1129.
43. Klaidman, Daniel, "Five Years after Ruby Ridge, the Fighting Rages On," *Newsweek*, September 1, 1997.
44. "Government Ins and Outs," *Washington Post*, October 22, 1997.
45. Klaidman, Daniel, "Five Years after Ruby Ridge."
46. Egan, Timothy, "Idaho Prosecutor Charges 2 in Killings at Ruby Ridge," *New York Times*, August 22, 1997.
47. *The Federal Raid on Ruby Ridge, ID*, p. 1097.
48. Ibid., p. 1131.
49. Ibid., p. 1132.
50. Kerr, "Ruby Ridge Investigation Astray."
51. Ibid.
52. House of Representatives Committee on the Judiciary, Subcommittee on Crime, *Oversight Hearing on the Activities of the FBI*, May 13, 1997.

5. WORLD TRADE CENTER: THE EXPLOSIVE TRUTH

1. *PrimeTime Live*, ABC Television, September 13, 1995.
2. Ibid.
3. Ibid.
4. FBI Press Office, September 13, 1995.
5. House of Representatives Committee on the Judiciary, Subcommittee on Crime, *Oversight Hearing on the Activities of the Federal Bureau of Investigation*, May 13, 1997.
6. Department of Justice, Office of the Inspector General, *The FBI Laboratory, An Investigation into Laboratory Practices and Alleged Misconduct in Explosives-Related and Other Cases*, April 1997.
7. Letter from David Ries to Thomas Bondurant dated June 15, 1995.
8. Ibid.
9. See Chapter 4.
10. Office of the Inspector General, *The FBI Laboratory*, p. 83.
11. Interview with John Kelly, June 1997.
12. Fisher, David, *Hard Evidence* (New York: Simon & Schuster, 1995), p. 77.
13. Ibid., p. 78.
14. Ibid., p. 80.
15. Memorandum from Frederic Whitehurst to John Hicks, undated.
16. *USA v. Omar Ahmad Ali Abdel Rahman, et al.*, S593 Cr. 181, August 14, 1995.
17. Office of the Inspector General, *The FBI Laboratory*, p. 140.
18. Ibid., p. 135.
19. *USA v. Omar Ahmad Ali Abdel Rahman, et al.*, August 14, 1995.
20. Office of the Inspector General, *The FBI Laboratory*, p. 135.
21. Memo from Jim Corby to James Kearney, undated.
22. Memo from Frederic Whitehurst to John Hicks, July 19, 1993.
23. Memo from Frederic Whitehurst to John Hicks, undated.
24. Interview with John Kelly and Phillip Wearne, July 1996.
25. Memo from James Kearney to Milton Ahlerich, Laboratory Director, November 4, 1994.
26. Office of the Inspector General, *The FBI Laboratory*, p. 319.
27. Interview with John Kelly, June 1997.
28. Memo from Jim Corby to James Kearney, undated.
29. Office of the Inspector General, *The FBI Laboratory*, pp. 323–329.

30. Ibid., p. 323.

31. Ibid.

32. Ibid., p. 324.

33. Ibid., p. 333.

34. Ibid., p. 340.

35. Ibid., p. 352.

36. Ibid., p. 332.

37. Ibid., p. 479.

38. Executive Order 12731, signed into law October 17, 1990, clarified by a formal rule and explanatory notes from the Office of Government Ethics and the FBI's *Manual of Administrative Operations and Procedures*.

39. Interview with John Kelly and Phillip Wearne, July 1996.

40. House of Representatives Committee on the Judiciary, Subcommittee on Crime, *Oversight Hearing*, May 13, 1997.

41. Office of the Inspector General, *The FBI Laboratory*, p. 329.

42. U.S. Senate Committee on the Judiciary, Subcommittee on Administrative Oversight and the Courts, *Oversight Hearing*, September 29, 1997.

43. Bernstein, Richard, "Trade Center Witness Tells of Manuals on Bombs," *New York Times*, November 10, 1993.

44. Office of Inspector General, *The FBI Laboratory*, p. 88.

45. Bernstein, Richard, "Gap in the Prosecution's Chain of Evidence," *New York Times*, January 21, 1994.

46. *USA v. Mohammad A. Salameh, et al.*, S593CR.180 (KTD), January 25, 1994.

47. Ibid., February 7, 1997.

48. Office of the Inspector General, *The FBI Laboratory*, p. 134.

49. Bernstein, Richard, "Bombing Trial Witness Sums up Evidence," *New York Times*, February 8, 1994.

50. Office of the Inspector General, *The FBI Laboratory*, p. 104.

51. *USA v. Mohammad Salameh, et al.*, S593CR.180 (KTD), February 7, 1994.

52. Ibid.

53. Ibid.

54. Office of the Inspector General, *The FBI Laboratory*, p. 107.

55. U.S. Armament Research and Development Commands, *Encyclopedia of Explosives and Related Items* (1983), p. U103.

56. Office of the Inspector General, *The FBI Laboratory*, p. 108.

57. Ibid.

58. *USA* v. *Mohammad Salameh, et al.*, S593CR.180 (KTD), February 8, 1994.

59. Ibid.

60. Office of the Inspector General, *The FBI Laboratory*, pp. 127, 128.

61. Interview with John Kelly, June 1997.

62. Office of the Inspector General, *The FBI Laboratory*, pp. 145–146.

63. Letter to Phillip Wearne dated August 19, 1997.

64. Interview with John Kelly, June 1997.

6. OKLAHOMA CITY: CONTAMINATING,
COMMINGLING, CONSPIRING?

1. Carlson, Peter, "With Others Unknown," *Washington Post Magazine*, March 23, 1997.

2. Ibid.

3. Ibid.

4. As described by Ryan Ross, *National Law Journal*, vol. 19, No. 30 (March 24, 1997) and *ABA Journal*, March 1997.

5. Interview of Ed Kelso by Special Agent Kimberly Thomas, Memorandum of Investigation, Special Investigative Team/Whitehurst Review, Case No. 9403575, November 27, 1995.

6. Interview of James Powell by Special Agent Robert Mellado, Memorandum of Investigation, Special Investigative Team/Whitehust Review, Case No. 9403575, February 29, 1996.

7. Interview of Ed Kelso.

8. Ibid.

9. Interview of LaTonya Gadson by Special Agent Kimberly Thomas, Memorandum of Investigation, Special Investigative Team/Whitehurst Review, Case No. 9403575, November 29, 1995.

10. Interview with John Kelly, July 1997.

11. U.S. Department of Justice, Office of the Inspector General, *The FBI Laboratory Practices and Alleged Misconduct in Explosives Related and Other Cases*, April 1997, p. 218.

12. Citations in the following paragraph are taken from the inspector general's report, *The FBI Laboratory*, pp. 223–225.

13. Letter to Phillip Wearne, August 1997.

14. Office of the Inspector General, *The FBI Laboratory*, p. 226.

15. Ibid., p. 227.

16. Ibid., p. 235.

17. Ibid., p. 238.
18. Ibid., p. 237.
19. Interview of James Kearney by Special Agent Kimberly Thomas, Memorandum of Investigation, Special Investigative Team/Whitehurst Review, Case No. 9403575, January 22, 1996.
20. FBI lab's Protocol for Explosives Residue Analysis, sections covering "Visual and optical microscopic analysis" and "Mechanical removal of residue," part of court records obtained by the authors.
21. Office of the Inspector General, *The FBI Laboratory*, p. 240.
22. Ibid.
23. Ibid.
24. Ibid.
25. Interview with John Kelly, August 1997.
26. Interview with John Kelly, January 1997.
27. Hedges, Michael, "FBI Lab's Cleanliness Questioned; McVeigh Alleges Area Contaminated," *Arizona Republic*, September 22, 1996.
28. Interview of Mary Tungol by Special Agent Kimberly Thomas, Memorandum of Investigation, Special Investigative Team/Whitehurst Review, Case No. 9403575, November 30, 1995.
29. Ibid.
30. Letter from Professor Brian Caddy to Robert Nigh, Jr., dated August 6, 1996.
31. Affidavit of John Brian Ford Lloyd dated August 24, 1996.
32. Interview with John Kelly, July 1997.
33. Letter from Steven Burmeister to Donald Thompson dated December 19, 1996.
34. Letter from John Lloyd to Phillip Wearne dated August 19, 1997.
35. Interview with Phillip Wearne, August 1997.
36. *USA v. Timothy James McVeigh and Terry Lynn Nichols*, Criminal Action No. 96-CR-68-M 1997 U.S. Dist. Lexis 2274, February 26, 1997.
37. Ibid.
38. Abbot, Karen, *Rocky Mountain News*, September 18, 1996.
39. UPI, Denver, September 12, 1996.
40. Interview with John Kelly, July 1997.
41. Sniffen, Michael J., Associated Press, Washington, D.C., January 31, 1997.
42. Letter from Stephen Kohn to Janet Reno, Attorney General, dated January 26, 1997.
43. Sniffen, Michael J.

44. Interview with Phillip Wearne, August 1997.
45. Letter to John Kelly, August 1997.
46. *USA* v. *Timothy James McVeigh*, CA No. 96-CR-68, May 27, 1997.
47. Ibid., May 20, 1997.
48. Interview with Phillip Wearne, March 1997.
49. *USA* v. *Timothy James McVeigh*, CA No. 96-CR-68, May 27, 1997.
50. Ibid., May 20, 1997.
51. Ibid., May 27, 1997.
52. Ibid., May 20, 1997.
53. Ibid., May 28, 1997.
54. Ibid., May 27, 1997.
55. Ibid., May 28, 1997.
56. Ibid., May 27, 1997.

7. O. J. SIMPSON: DIRTY HANDS, BAD BLOOD

1. *Rivera Live*, November 22, 1995.
2. Schiller, Lawrence, and James Willwerth, *American Tragedy: The Uncensored Story of the Simpson Defense* (New York: Avon Books, 1997), p. 288.
3. Wecht, Cyril, M.D., J.D, *Grave Secrets* (New York: Dutton, 1996), p. 64.
4. Ibid., pp. 63–64.
5. The authors are indebted to Judge Gerald Sheindlin and his book, *Blood Trail*, written with Catherine Whitney (New York: Ballantine Books, 1996) for observations here.
6. *People's Motion to Dismiss without Prejudice*, No. 1102265, Superior Court, State of California, County of Sacramento, September 15, 1993.
7. Ibid.
8. Schiller and Willwerth, p. 236.
9. Taylor, Charles, "Survey of Population Geneticists Concerning Methods for Calculating Matches in Forensic Applications of VNTR," *Loci*, July 9, 1991.
10. *People* v. *Halik*, No. VA00843, Los Angeles County Superior Court, September 26, 1991.
11. Schiller and Willwerth, p. 548.
12. *People of the State of California* v. *Orenthal James Simpson*, No. BA097211, Los Angeles Superior Court, April 11, 1995.
13. Budowle, B., H. A. Deadman, R. Murch, and F. S. Baechtel, "An Introduction to the Methods of DNA Analysis Under Investigation in the FBI Laboratory," *Crime Laboratory Digest*, vol. 15 no. 1 (January 1988).

14. Adams, D. E., "Validation of the FBI Procedure for DNA Analysis," *Crime Laboratory Digest*, vol. 15 no. 4 (December 1988).
15. *Biotechnology Newswatch*, vol. 9 no. 18 (September 18, 1989).
16. *Crime Laboratory Digest*, vol. 18 no. 1 (January 1991).
17. Grunbaum, Benjamin W., "A Foundational Objection to DNA Evidence: A Critique of the FBI's Process for Self-Validation of Methods for Protein and DNA Genetic Marker Typing of Biological Evidence," *California Attorneys for Criminal Justice/Forum*, vol. 21 no. 3 (June 1994).
18. D'Eustachio, Peter G., *Expert's Report in the United States v. Yee et al. An Evaluation of the FBI's Environmental Insult Validation Study and the FBI's Quantitative Matching Criteria*, 134 FRD 161, Northern District Ohio, 1991.
19. Ibid.
20. Memorandum from FBI Legal Counsel to John Hicks, Assistant Director, FBI Laboratory Division, dated April 20, 1990.
21. Hagerman, Paul, *Expert's Report United States v. Yee et al. Loading Variability and the Use of Ethidium Bromide: Implications for the Reliability of the FBI's Methodology for Forensic DNA Typing*, 129, FRD, 629, Northern District Ohio, 1991.
22. Hartl, Professor Daniel L., *Expert's Report in the Case of United States v. Yee et al.*, p. 5.
23. Ibid. Addendum to above, "False Positives in the FBI Test and Retest data."
24. *United States v. Yee et al.*, 134 FRD, 207, Northern District Ohio, 1991.
25. Ibid.
26. Frank, Laura, and John Hanchette, "DNA on Capitol Hill," *Gannett News Service*, July 1, 1994.
27. *State v. Despain*, No. 15589, Yuma County, Arizona, Superior Court, February 1991.
28. Ibid. Testimony of Dr. Simon Ford on October 10, 1991.
29. Interview with John Kelly, August 1997.
30. Lewontin, R. C., and Daniel L. Hartl, "Population Genetics in Forensic DNA Typing," *Science*, vol. 254 (December 20, 1991) 1745.
31. Chakraborty, Ranajit, and Kenneth K. Kidd, "The Utility of DNA Typing in Forensic Work," *Science*, vol. 254 (December 20, 1991) 1735.
32. Roberts, Leslie, "Was Science Fair to its Authors?" *Science*, vol. 254 (December 20, 1991).
33. Neufeld, Peter, "Have You No Sense of Decency?" *Journal of Criminal Law and Criminology*, vol. 84, no. 1 (1993) 189.

34. Quoted in Roberts, Leslie, "Science in Court: A Culture Clash," *Science*, vol. 257 (August 7, 1992) 736.
35. Quoted in Anderson, Christopher, "Academy Approves, Critics Still Cry Foul," *Nature* vol. 356 (April 16, 1992) 552.
36. Ibid.
37. Ibid.
38. Quoted in Anderson, Christopher, "FBI Gives In On Genetics," *Nature*, vol. 355 (February 20, 1992) 663.
39. National Research Council, *DNA Technology in Forensic Science*, April 1992.
40. Interview with John Kelly, August 1997.
41. *United States* v. *Porter*, No. 3F-6277-89, 1994.
42. Interview with John Kelly, August 1997.
43. Ibid.
44. *The Testifying Expert*, vol. 1, issue 11 (November 1993).
45. Thompson, William C. "Accepting Lower Standards: The National Research Council's Second Report on Forensic DNA Evidence," *Jurimetrics*, vol. 37, no. 4 (1997) 405–424.
46. Interview with John Kelly, June 1997.
47. Levy, Harlan, *And the Blood Cried Out* (New York: Basic Books, 1996), p. 122.
48. Lander, Eric S., and Bruce Budowle, "DNA Fingerprinting Dispute Laid to Rest," *Nature*, vol. 371 (October 27, 1994) 735–738.
49. Ibid.
50. Ibid.
51. Correspondence, *Nature*, vol. 372 (December 1, 1994), 398, 399.
52. Ibid.
53. Lander and Budowle, "DNA Fingerprinting Dispute Laid to Rest."
54. Office of the Inspector General, *"The FBI Laboratory: An Investigation into Laboratory Practices and Alleged Misconduct in Explosives-Related and Other Cases,"* April 1997, p. 211.
55. *People of the State of California* v. *Orenthal James Simpson*, Los Angeles County Superior Court, BA097211, July 25, 1995.
56. Ibid.
57. Office of the Inspector General, *The FBI Laboratory*, p. 216.
58. Ibid.
59. Interview with Phillip Wearne, October 1997.
60. *People* v. *Simpson*.
61. Schiller and Willwerth, *American Tragedy*, p. 690.

62. Levy, *And the Blood Cried Out*, p. 170.

63. Memorandum from K. Nimmich to M. Ahlerich, dated August 30, 1995.

64. Ibid.

65. See Office of the Inspector General, *The FBI Laboratory*, pp. 206–207.

66. Unofficial transcript of a hearing on a defense motion to recall Roger Martz and admit Frederic Whitehurst as witnesses in the O. J. Simpson trial, September 19, 1995.

67. Letter from William Sessions to Dr. Frank Press, dated April 16, 1993.

68. Letter from John Hicks to Richard Rau, National Institute of Justice, dated May 27, 1993.

69. National Research Council, Committee on DNA Forensic Science, *An Update: The Evaluation of Forensic DNA Evidence*, 1996.

70. Ibid.

71. For an excellent comparison of the two NRC reports, see Thompson, William C., "Accepting Lower Standards."

72. Interview of Special Agent Greg Parsons by Special Agent Robert Mellado, Memorandum of Investigation, Special Investigative Team/Whitehurst Review, Case No. 9403575, January 23, 1996.

73. Ibid.

74. Ibid.

75. Interview of Special Supervisory Agent Alan Robillard by Special Agent Kimberly Thomas, Memorandum of Investigation, Special Investigative Team/Whitehurst Review, Case No. 9403575, February 28, 1996.

76. Ibid.

8. HAIRS AND FIBERS: HANGING BY A THREAD

1. Interview of William Tobin by Special Agent Joseph LeStrange, Memorandum of Investigation, Special Investigative Team/Whitehurst Review, Case No. 9403575, December 6, 1995.

2. Undated memo from Special Agent William Tobin to FBI Lab Scientific Analysis Section Chief Ken Nimmich. "Exceptions to the Testimony of Special Agent Michael Malone in the Matter of U.S. District Judge Alcee S. Hastings."

3. Ibid.

4. Office of the Inspector General, *The FBI Laboratory: An Investigation into Laboratory Practices and Alleged Misconduct in Explosives-Related and Other Cases*, April 1997, p. 388.

5. Ibid., p. 383.

6. Ibid., p. 388.

7. Ibid., p. 384.

8. Ibid., p. 385.

9. Connolly, Ceci, "Alcee Hastings: Rejection and Redemption," *St. Petersburg Times*, April 20, 1997.

10. House of Representatives Judiciary Committee, *Hearing of the Crime Subcommittee*, June 5, 1997.

11. Connolly, Ceci, "Impeachment of Judge May Be Flawed, Internal Memo Shows FBI Agent May have Lied," *St. Petersburg Times*, May 18, 1997.

12. Seper, Jerry, "MacDonald Case Probe Sought: Lawmaker Asks FBI to Review Lab Experts' Inconsistencies," *Washington Times*, June 12, 1997.

13. Cohen, Laurie P., "Strand of Evidence, FBI Crime-Lab Work Emerges as New Issue in Famed Murder Case," *Wall Street Journal*, April 16, 1997.

14. Interview with Phillip Wearne, March 1997.

15. Cohen, "Strand of Evidence."

16. Fisher, David, *Hard Evidence* (New York: Simon & Schuster, 1995), p. 122.

17. Ibid., p. 105.

18. Ibid.

19. Bisbing, Richard E., "Human Hair in a Forensic Perspective," *Proceedings of the International Symposium on Forensic Hair Comparisons, June 25–27, 1985*, The Laboratory Division, FBI.

20. Deadman, Harold A., "Human Hair Comparison Based on Microscopic Characteristics," *Proceedings of the International Symposium on Forensic Hair Analysis*.

21. Cohen, "Strand of Evidence."

22. *John William Jackson, Appellant v. State of Florida, Appellee*, No. 85–1727, Court of Appeals of Florida, Second District, 511 So 2d 1047.

23. *Rodney Charles Horstman, Appellant, v. State of Florida, Appellee*, Case No. 86–2925, Court of Appeals of Florida, Second District, 530 So 2d 368.

24. *State of Florida v. James Aren Duckett*, Fifth Judicial Circuit, Lake County, Florida. Case No. 87-1147-CF-A-01.

25. Interview with John Kelly, June 1997.

26. Interview with John Kelly, October 1997.

27. *Commonwealth of Pennsylvania v. Jay William Buckley*, 37th Judicial District of Pennsylvania, Warren County Branch, Case No. 309, May 28, 1991.

28. Ibid.

29. Ibid.

30. Interview with John Kelly, June 1997.

31. Cohen, "Strand of Evidence."

32. See Gaudette, B. D., and Keeping, E. S., "An Attempt at Determining Probabilities in Human Scalp Hair Comparison," *Journal of Forensic Sciences*, vol. 19 no. 3 (July 1974) 599–606; Gaudette, B. D., "Probabilities and Human Pubic Hair Comparisons," *Journal of Forensic Sciences*, vol. 21 no. 3 (July 1976), 514–517; and Gaudette, B. D., "Some Further Thoughts on Probabilities and Human Hair Comparisons," *Journal of Forensic Sciences*, vol. 23 No. 4 (Oct. 1978), 758–763.

33. Interview with John Kelly, July 1997.

34. Interview with John Kelly, August 1997.

35. *USA v. Jeffrey R. MacDonald*, 966 F.2d 854 (4th Cir. 1992).

36. Interview with Phillip Wearne, October 1997.

37. Shalit, Ruth, "Fatal Revision," *The New Republic*, (May 26, 1997).

38. *Today*, NBC, April 24, 1997.

39. Interview with Phillip Wearne, October 1997.

40. Supplemental Affidavit of Michael P. Malone, *USA v. Jeffrey R. MacDonald*, Crim. No. 75-26, CR-3, May 21, 1991, paragraph 6, p. 3.

41. Memorandum of Law in Support of Jeffrey R. MacDonald's Motion to Reopen 28 U.S.C. & 2255 Proceedings and for Discovery, April 22, 1997, Attorneys for Jeffrey MacDonald.

42. Affidavit of A. Edward Oberhaus, sworn New York City, New York, January 24, 1991, attached to afffidavit of Harvey A. Silverglate, April 17, 1997, submitted in support of Jeffrey R. MacDonald's Motion to Reopen 28 U.S.C. 2255 Proceedings and for Discovery, *USA v. Jeffrey R. MacDonald* No. 75-26-CR-3, 90-104-CIV-3.

43. FD-302 record of interview with A. Edward Oberhaus in New York on December 4, 1990, dictated, December 7, 1990, transcribed January 7, 1990, File No. 70A-3668 received May 1996 as part of FOIA request by Bisceglie & Walsh on January 14, 1993.

44. Affidavit of Sue P. Greco, *USA v. Jeffrey R. MacDonald*, No. 75-26-CR-3, sworn Annapolis, MD, 11, April 1997.

45. Affidavit of Judith Schizas, U.S. District Court, Eastern District of North Carolina, Fayetteville Division, *USA v. Jeffrey R. MacDonald*, April 15, 1997, El Segundo, California.

46. Affidavit of Michael Malone, February 14, 1991. para. 23, p. 14.

47. Ibid., para. 22, p. 13.

48. See Potter, Jerry Allen, and Fred Bost, *Fatal Justice* (New York: W.W. Norton, 1997), pp. 248–271 for full details. This book is by far the most comprehensive analysis of the MacDonald case.

49. The handwritten lab notes are designated only as R-11 and record various examinations carried out by Army CID chemist Janice Glisson sometime between July 20 and 29. The two cursory formal lab reports that resulted from these examinations, two pages and one page in length respectively, are numbered P-FA-D-C-FP-82-70-R-11 and are dated July 29, 1970, and September 2, 1970.

50. Affidavit of Michael Malone, February 14, 1991, paras. 16, 18, pp. 10, 12.

51. Affidavit of Philip Cormier, No. 2 "Request for Access to Evidence to Conduct Laboratory Examinations," *USA* v. *Jeffrey MacDonald*, Eastern District of North Carolina, Fayetteville Division, Nos. 75-26-CR-3 sworn April 19, 1997, Commonwealth of Massachusetts.

52. Potter and Bost, *Fatal Justice*, p. 401; and interview with John Kelly, October 1997.

53. See Potter and Bost, pp. 46–61.

54. FBI teletype from J. Edgar Hoover to Robert Murphy, October 28, 1970.

55. Interview with John Kelly, October 1997.

56. Department of Justice memorandum from M. Williams to Mr. White dated November 6, 1974.

57. Potter and Bost, *Fatal Justice*, p. 283.

58. Ibid., pp. 127, 295.

59. *USA* v. *Jeffrey R. MacDonald*, No. 75-26-CR-3, July 19, 1979.

60. Interview with John Kelly, October 1997.

61. Ibid.

62. Report of the FBI Laboratory to Special Agent in Charge Charlotte, FBI File No. 70-51728, November 5, 1974.

63. Potter and Bost, *Fatal Justice*, p. 186.

64. Interview with Phillip Wearne, October 1997.

65. *USA* v. *Jeffrey R. MacDonald*, No. 75-26-CR-3, August 7, 1979.

66. Potter and Bost, *Fatal Justice*, p. 147.

67. Ibid., p. 147 and e-mail from Fred Bost to Phillip Wearne, October 1997.

68. *USA* v. *Jeffrey R. MacDonald*, 640 F. Supplement 286 (1985).

69. *USA* v. *Jeffrey R. MacDonald*, 778 F. Supplement 1342 (1991).

70. Ibid.

71. Potter and Bost, *Fatal Justice*, p. 382.

72. Affidavit by Michael Malone, dated February 14, 1991.
73. Interview with John Kelly, August 1997.

EPILOGUE: THE END OF THE BEGINNING

1. Subcommittee on Commerce, Justice, State and Judiciary of the House of Representatives Committee on Appropriations, March 5, 1997.
2. Letter from Michael Bromwich, Inspector General to Louis Freeh, Director FBI, dated March 6, 1997.
3. Ibid.
4. This information emerged in a memo to Waldon Kennedy, FBI deputy director, from Louis Freeh, Director FBI, dated January 23, 1997.
5. Subcommittee on Administrative Oversight and the Courts of the Senate Committee on the Judiciary, September 29, 1997.
6. Office of the Inspector General, *The FBI Laboratory: An Investigation into Laboratory Practices and Alleged Misconduct in Explosives-Related and Other Cases,* April 1997, p. 401.
7. Memorandum for the Attorney General signed by William J. Clinton entitled "Delegations of Responsibilities Concerning FBI Employees Under the Civil Service Reform Act of 1978" dated April 14, 1997.
8. Interview with Phillip Wearne, September 1997.
9. Press Release, FBI National Press Office, March 5, 1997.
10. Comments on the January 21, 1997 Draft Report of the Department of Justice Office of the Inspector General, February 12, 1997, Federal Bureau of Investigation, p. 69.
11. Seper, Jerry, "Senator attacks new FBI lab director," *Washington Times,* October 22, 1997.
12. Statement of Senator Charles Grassley, responding to appointment of FBI's crime lab head October 21, 1997.
13. Seper, "Senator Attacks"; speech statement at press conference, October 17, 1997.
14. Letter from Frank Fitzpatrick to Louis Freeh, September 22, 1997.
15. Ibid.

INDEX